SHOULD DIFFERENCES IN INCOME AND WEALTH MATTER?

SHOULD DIFFERENCES IN INCOME AND WEALTH MATTER?

Edited by

Ellen Frankel Paul, Fred D. Miller, Jr., and Jeffrey Paul

CAMBRIDGE UNIVERSITY PRESS
Cambridge, New York, Melbourne, Madrid, Cape Town,
Singapore, São Paulo, Delhi, Mexico City

Cambridge University Press
The Edinburgh Building, Cambridge CB2 8RU, UK

Published in the United States of America by Cambridge University Press, New York

www.cambridge.org
Information on this title: www.cambridge.org/9780521005357

First published 2002

A catalogue record for this publication is available from the British Library

Library of Congress Cataloguing in Publication Data

Should differences in income and wealth matter? / edited by Ellen Frankel Paul,
Fred D. Miller, Jr., and Jeffrey Paul. p. cm.
Includes bibliographical references and index.
ISBN 0-521-00535-3
1. Income distribution—Moral and ethical aspects. 2. Equality. 3. Social justice.
I. Paul, Ellen Frankel. II. Miller, Jr., Fred D. III. Paul, Jeffrey.
HB523 .S535 2002
339.2–dc21 2001043944
CIP

ISBN 978-0-521-00535-7 Paperback

CONTENTS

INTRODUCTION

Is there a moral obligation to reduce differences in income and wealth? There is an egalitarian tradition that condemns these differences, particularly as they arise in free-market capitalist society, as unfair or unjust. The opponents of this view argue that the material disparities of capitalist society have been brought about by voluntary mechanisms and thus accord with the freely exercised liberties of its citizens. Hence, they conclude that capitalist inequality is not vulnerable to the ethical complaints of its critics. Furthermore, they maintain that the standard of living achieved as a by-product of the marketplace and its inequalities could not be adequately reproduced under egalitarian institutions.

The thirteen essays in this volume, written by prominent economists, philosophers, and academic lawyers, assess the empirical and theoretical questions raised by inequalities of income and wealth. Some of the essays consider empirical claims about the amount of equality in modern market economies, assessing the allegation that income and wealth have become more unequally distributed in the past quarter-century. Other essays consider the extent to which various government initiatives can ameliorate the problems inequality putatively poses. Some of the essays consider which standards of equality meet the requirements of distributive justice. Still others ask if inequality is intrinsically immoral regardless of its consequences.

The first two essays in this collection examine theoretical and practical considerations that arise from the welfare state's attempts to help the poor. In "Egalitarianism and Welfare-State Redistribution," Daniel Shapiro begins by noting that private charity is a serious rival to the welfare state. Contemporary egalitarians generally assume, however, that aiding those who are poor through no fault of their own requires government provision of aid. As welfare-state redistribution relies on coercive transfers, while private charity relies on voluntary transfers, Shapiro examines both sorts of aid provision by assessing the justness of each type of transfer. A system of coercive transfers takes some income and wealth that was accumulated through individuals' choices and voluntarily assumed risks, and this is unjust on egalitarian grounds. While a system of voluntary transfers will also involve injustice, since some who would be obligated to transfer income and wealth will not do so, egalitarians lack theoretical grounds for arguing that this injustice is worse than that associated with coercive transfers. Furthermore, Shapiro argues, private charities are more effective than state programs in helping those disadvantaged through no fault of their own. Unlike bureaucratic state agencies, private organizations have more flexibility in designing policies and are better able to monitor their policies' effects. After laying out these arguments, Shapiro presents a pair of ways in which proponents of the welfare state might respond. Nongovernmental forms of aid, they could argue, cannot by themselves provide enough resources to alleviate the problems of poverty; alternatively, they might contend that welfare-state policies express a shared social commitment to justice that private charity fails to convey. In analyzing both of these claims, Shapiro argues that they suffer from serious flaws. As a result, he concludes, egalitarians should view a system of private charity in a much more favorable light.

In "Does the Welfare State Help the Poor?" Tyler Cowen considers how the American welfare state affects the poor. He first discusses the amount of money transferred to lower-income individuals, finding that it is small relative to the total stock of U.S. wealth. Those favoring the contemporary welfare state are, therefore, supporting an outcome that is not extremely egalitarian, nor does the system provide substantial aid to its recipients. While some conservatives and libertarians, led by the work of Charles Murray and others, claim that the welfare state has significant negative effects on aid recipients, Cowen contends that this argument suffers from poor empirical justification and relies on questionable theoretical assumptions. The prima facie belief that monetary transfers make recipients better off is, he says, a correct one, and the most plausible claim concerning the U.S. welfare state's effects on those it serves is that these effects are limited, but positive. But this, Cowen states, is not the end of the story, for the welfare state damages the interests of the poor—the poor more generally, not just current aid recipients—in two significant respects. First, economic growth is far better than the welfare state at lifting people out of poverty. As a result, to the extent that the welfare state lowers future levels of economic growth—and the evidence suggests that it does—people in the future will be worse off than they might have been. Second, the American welfare state operates without regard for much poorer individuals abroad. If the United States were truly egalitarian, it would reject its current welfare policies and instead send money to other nations, allow for significantly more immigration, or both. From these arguments concerning the future poor and the foreign poor, Cowen concludes that if the U.S. welfare state is to be defended, it must be done on non-egalitarian grounds.

The next three essays each use empirical data to reach different conclusions about the extent, direction, and desirability of inequality in the United States in the previous few decades. In "The Stagnating Fortunes of the Middle Class," Edward N. Wolff details a number of disturbing economic changes that the United States underwent in the last quarter of the twentieth century. Between 1973 and 1998, real wages declined by 9 percent. After doubling between 1947 and 1973, real median family income grew by only 12 percent in the next twenty-five years. Inequality of family income, which stood virtually unchanged between the end of World War

II and the late 1960s, has been increasing sharply ever since. Though current policy discussions emphasize that we could increase income and reduce inequality by educating the labor force better, Wolff raises doubts about the efficacy of this potential solution. The problematic statistics just cited, Wolff points out, emerged as the United States underwent a significant rise in educational attainment. Even though average levels of education rose—and educational opportunities improved for societal groups that had historically lagged behind—these gains did not lead to a more equitable society. Wolff goes on to consider the claim that the stock market boom of the late 1990s led to wealth gains for the lower classes. Examining historical statistics on stock ownership, Wolff contends that the middle class and the poor by and large did not share in the benefits of that bull market. Faced with the increasing inequality of American society, and the fact that programs aimed at fostering educational advancement do not seem to effectively address this problem, Wolff closes his essay by advocating a different set of remedies: direct subsidies for the poorest Americans; tax relief for the middle class; and legal reforms to strengthen the labor movement.

Like Wolff, Donald R. Deere and Finis Welch begin their essay, "Inequality, Incentives, and Opportunity," by noting recent increases in U.S. wage inequality. Nevertheless, they point out, people seem satisfied with the status quo. Why? Distinguishing opportunity from actual achievement, Deere and Welch suggest that what people truly care about is equality of opportunity. Surveying the empirical evidence on inequality of achievement, Deere and Welch argue that over the last thirty years, an increase in the wage differential between college graduates and high school graduates led to increased investment in education. This was good: unequal wages provided people with an incentive to act in ways that were more productive from a societal standpoint. Yet the authors point out that circumstances can create incentives that are more problematic. For example, because a social safety net lowers the relative value of work in comparison to unemployment, one should expect that the expansion of the U.S. welfare state in the 1960s would have reduced people's incentive to work. In support of this expectation, Deere and Welch show that after the 1960s, employment among men with the lowest wage potential dropped. After making these points about inequality of achievement, the authors present empirical evidence on inequality of opportunity. The recent shrinking of the wage gaps between blacks and whites and between women and men implies, they contend, that wage differences emerge more from differences in individual actions than from uncontrollable individual characteristics. Economic opportunity, in other words, has become more equal. Given that inequality of achievement is not necessarily a bad thing, and that equality of opportunity has increased, Deere and Welch conclude that the economic changes in the United States over the past thirty years have been largely for the good.

In "Misunderstanding Distribution," Young Back Choi notes that social critics in the United States are much more concerned than the general public is about unequal distribution of income and wealth. For these critics, Choi claims, inequality is wrong and undesirable, and collective action is needed to reduce it. Choi attributes these critics' concerns to three perceptions: that the United States has excessive inequality, that the competition displayed in the marketplace is rigged to favor the rich, and that inequality is unjust. Drawing on empirical evidence, Choi contests each of these claims. First, he argues that the critics' estimates of the extent of income and wealth inequality are exaggerated. Once biases built into the data are properly accounted for—that is, once we adjust for factors such as household size, income fluctuations, and so on—we find that estimates of income inequality drop. Likewise, differences in wealth look smaller once we account for things like the value of entitlement programs and of human capital. Turning to the second claim, Choi points out that the critics' assertions that the marketplace is unfair revolve around certain empirical beliefs—namely, that income and wealth are becoming increasingly polarized over time, and that income mobility is relatively low. Yet Choi suggests that inequality, after rising in the 1980s and early 1990s, has remained relatively stable; furthermore, income mobility is quite high. Lastly, he addresses the claim that inequality is unjust. Here, Choi argues that social critics find inequality of income and wealth to be a sign of injustice because they fail to appreciate how profit comes about and how the quest for profits benefits society. Choi concludes his essay by briefly noting that critics' misunderstandings on all of these matters are paired with another important misunderstanding: the critics fail to adequately consider the dire economic consequences that a nation would suffer were it to attempt to engage in thoroughgoing equalization of income and wealth.

One tool governments use in trying to reduce inequality is progressive taxation. In "Can Anyone Beat the Flat Tax?" Richard A. Epstein explores the pros and cons of the flat tax, progressive taxation's most prominent rival in recent years, and determines that it fares well as a matter of both equity and efficiency. Ordinary private firms use flat systems of assessment to support their own collective expenditures. They do this because flat systems offer overall administrative simplicity: while it might be "fairer" to try to make each individual's payment into a venture correspond to the subjective value he derives from it, this goal is difficult to accomplish in practice. Dividing a venture's costs in a flat fashion, though perhaps less fair, is vastly easier, and such a system's increased ease may well compensate for its lower degree of fairness. The flax tax would serve the same goal in the public arena, where it would be superior to the more complex taxation arrangements presently in place. The flat tax represents a rough effort to tax citizens in proportion to the benefits that they receive from government. Yet at the same time, the flat tax also allows for limited amounts of redistribution based on need. Proponents of progressive taxation argue that a flat tax does not generate an optimal level of redistribution. However, even if we put aside important questions about a state's right to coercively redistribute its citizens' assets, Epstein claims, progressive taxation's proponents will have a difficult time showing that the costs of their system, in terms of harmful incentives and administrative expenses, will outweigh its redistributive benefits. The flat tax's overall simplicity makes it a suitable replacement: though it might not be the ideal system in theory, our real-world circumstances make it extremely attractive.

Even if we could agree on which method of redistributing resources was the most practical, this would still leave open to question who ought to be helped and the extent to which they should be aided. In "Why Justice Requires Transfers to Offset Income and Wealth Inequalities," Richard J. Arneson examines two candidate principles of justice, exploring their plausibility in light of their implications. According to "sufficientarianism," justice requires that as many people as possible, of all those who will ever live, experience a "good enough" quality of life. In contrast, "prioritarianism" asserts that justice requires us to maximize a function of human well-being that gives more weight to securing gains in well-being for those who are worse off. Arneson argues that the prioritarian view is the superior of the two. Intuitively, it seems plausible to deny, as sufficientarians do, that how one's condition compares to that of others is in itself morally important. Yet sufficientarianism runs into trouble on a number of levels. First, it is difficult to specify a nonarbitrary definition of the good-enough quality of life. Examining the efforts of prominent sufficientarians such as Michael Walzer and Martha Nussbaum, Arneson argues that their accounts, the most plausible in the literature, fail. Second, even if it were possible to devise a satisfactory definition of the good-enough quality of life, the sufficientarian doctrine generates counterintuitive conclusions. A committed sufficientarian gives lexical priority to ensuring that people have good-enough lives, and it is easy to construct hypothetical cases that make this lexical priority look unappealing. Though one can construct modified versions of sufficientarianism that deal with this latter problem, Arneson argues that these versions themselves face serious problems of their own. After rejecting sufficientarianism, Arneson briefly discusses his preferred version of prioritarianism, which gives special attention to helping not simply those who are worse off, but those who are worse off through no fault of their own.

In "The Importance of Being Sufficiently Equal," James K. Galbraith analyzes the reasons why inequalities of income and wealth are bad. Looking first at income inequality, Galbraith argues that because income inequality is associated with high rates of poverty, it is aesthetically ugly. Furthermore, more equal societies have less unemployment, less crime, and better public services. Why, given this, do we accept inequality?

Galbraith suggests that we do so because of the influence of the textbook view of economics, according to which attempts by government to reduce inequality create market inefficiencies and unemployment. But this textbook view is based on unrealistic assumptions, and we should be wary about drawing policy conclusions based on them. If there is no general reason in economic theory to favor large amounts of income inequality, the question becomes whether reducing such inequality would really have harmful effects. Canvassing studies of the United States, Europe, and developing nations, Galbraith argues that high levels of income inequality in fact retard economic growth. Fortunately, the means to ensuring that incomes remain relatively equal are straightforward—a minimum wage, progressive taxation, social security programs, and publicly funded education and health care. Turning to differences in wealth, Galbraith suggests that the problems that arise from this sort of inequality are political in nature. Societies with highly unequal wealth, he argues, are always dominated by the rich, and cannot function as coherent social units or govern themselves on legitimate terms. Political decisions reached in such systems will generally favor the wealthy and organized, at the expense of the common good. As a result, Galbraith maintains, for a collection of people to be considered a society, and to function together as a democracy, they must exhibit a sufficient degree of wealth equality. To accomplish this, a society must provide forms of capital wealth that everyone in the society can hold. Expanding access to social security wealth, home ownership, and education are key to a more egalitarian distribution of wealth.

The effect of inequality on society is also the focal point of the next essay. In "Does Inequality Matter—For Its Own Sake?" Alan Ryan starts from the presumption that the answer to that question is no. Several reasons support this presumption; each is connected to the idea that it seems absurd to secure literal equality of treatment where this is obviously wasteful—doing so does no good to any of the parties whose welfare is being compared. Once we tentatively reject the claim that inequality is inherently bad, a further assessment of why inequality matters requires an examination of inequality's impacts. Ryan proceeds by surveying several effects of inequality. According to Rousseau, Ryan notes, inequality has serious psychological effects on people: because of the way human nature combines elements of animal instinct with higher-order rational thought, inequality creates in us a psychological war of all against all. Furthermore, inequality has effects on political life as well. Numerous theorists have discussed how inequalities of income and wealth lead to inequalities in individuals' political power. Lastly, Ryan considers certain economic effects of inequality. Principally, he argues, it can lead to markets ignoring the desires of the poor because the purchasing power of the wealthy makes it uneconomic to attend to those desires. These effects and others suggest that inequality is problematic, but none demonstrates that inequality is inherently bad. Inequality, then, does not seem to matter for its own sake. Ryan ends his essay, however, by suggesting one way in which inequality might be intrinsically harmful. In a social context marked by a strong sense of fraternity and a mutual commitment by people to one another's well-being, equality could have an intrinsic value as the expression of that commitment. The possibility of creating and sustaining this sort of society is, however, another matter entirely.

The collection's final four essays each assess other theoretical aspects of egalitarian thought. Rawls contended that even under extreme egalitarian assumptions, unequal shares can be justified. David Schmidtz's essay, "Equal Respect and Equal Shares," provides the complementary argument that even within an otherwise nonegalitarian theory of justice, there is room for distributing some things according to an "equal shares" principle. He begins by briefly noting the virtues of allocating certain goods into equal shares. Schmidtz refers here to a story used by political theorist Bruce Ackerman: if you and I happen upon an apple tree with two apples, and you take both of them, it seems intuitively compelling that you've done something wrong—I should have received one of the apples. Though intuitively compelling, this equal-shares aspect of egalitarianism is not egalitarianism's most important component, Schmidtz maintains. Though the equal-shares principle's usefulness in certain sorts of cases ensures that the principle will play at least some role in any adequate theory of justice, the key commitment of contemporary egalitarianism is not to an equal-shares principle, but to a principle of equal respect. Important as each of these aspects of egalitarian thought is, Schmidtz argues, a proper account of justice ultimately will also make room for a rule of first possession; it will have to, not because that rule is necessarily a principle of justice in its own right, but because society would not be viable without it. The upshot of Schmidtz's pluralistic account of justice is a conception that makes room for egalitarian principles, but also acknowledges that they have limits.

In "Too Much Inequality," Richard W. Miller begins by noting that typical arguments egalitarians used in the 1970s and 1980s have fallen on tough times. Key premises common to these arguments no longer appear reasonable. Rather than give up on egalitarianism, Miller suggests that we adopt a "fragmented" view of its foundations. On this view, reasons to reduce economically based inequalities of various kinds emerge not from a single overarching argument, but from aspects of various specific relationships among parties who are unequal. Miller examines three such relationships. First, when citizens impose rules of self-advancement that give rise to lesser life prospects for some, the disadvantaged have reason to complain. Second, when government policies fail to show equal concern for all citizens in providing economic benefits, those whose relevant needs are neglected have reason to object. Finally, people sharing a social environment can find that economic inequalities conflict with the aspiration to milieus that facilitate mutual appreciation and acceptance, both in political life and in personal interactions. In each of these three situations, terms of interaction provide certain people with morally serious reasons to object that a particular kind of inequality is too great; however, in all of these situations, the terms of interaction also give others—namely, those who benefit from the inequalities—morally serious reasons to object to remedies as going too far in pursuit of greater equality. In each case, the inequality that is ultimately at issue is not one of income or wealth. Nevertheless, the reduction of income and wealth inequalities is an important part of the pursuit of economic justice—above all, because it is appropriate to use monetary indices to monitor progress in reducing the primary inequalities. Miller concludes his essay by claiming that justice currently demands the reduction of inequalities in the United States on all the dimensions he explores, and that income and wealth inequalities are a sign of the need for such political measures and an appropriate gauge of their success.

Eric Mack's contribution, "Equality, Benevolence, and Responsiveness to Agent-Relative Value," begins with Mack's contention that differences in income and wealth matter morally only if they generate differences in well-being that themselves matter morally. On Mack's understanding, these differences matter morally only if they are inherently morally problematic, a condition that is met only if morality includes a strong presumption on behalf of an equal distribution among individuals of what really matters in life. It is difficult, however, to find any plausible argument for the inclusion within morality of such a presumption. Mack's essay explores two arguments for the presumption, both of which assert that it is an essential part of the best explanation for the goodness and reasonableness of benevolence. The "impersonalist argument" maintains that benevolence's goodness and reasonableness is best explained if one invokes the impersonal value of every individual's well-being. The easiest way to do this, the argument suggests, is to accept egalitarianism. The "pretheoretical argument" removes the impersonalist argument's intermediate step: it asserts that egalitarianism itself is the best explanation of our positive view of benevolence, and that this makes egalitarianism inherently plausible. Both arguments, Mack notes, depend on an impersonalist conception of benevolence, and thus would be undercut by an alternative conception of benevolence under which benevolence consists of a personally valuable responsiveness to the personal good of others. To the extent that this personalist account of benevolence is better than the impersonalist account—and Mack thinks that it is clearly superior—both of the major arguments supporting the egalitarian presumption fail.

In this collection's final essay, "How Equality Matters," Hillel Steiner considers how much egalitarian redistribution is justifiable if one respects a libertarian commitment to self-ownership. He begins by noting the common view that some moral value attaches to the "sibling parity" of wealth. This notion of parity refers to the intuition that a set of parents with several children should act to ensure that, all other things being equal, their children enjoy equal well-being. Using sibling parity as our backdrop, we can consider various ideas about which disparities of wealth are permissible. Steiner states that the crucial issue for those interested in our moral responsibilities is how we ought to deal with differences in well-being created by bad luck that individuals suffer through no fault of their own. Assessing this "brute bad luck," Steiner argues that we must see it as caused by the doings of nature—no one is liable for them. If an individual is not compensated for the losses suffered due to brute bad luck, he is effectively being held liable for something for which he is not really responsible. As a result, if we are to ensure that liability for adversities will adequately track personal responsibility, we must pool the costs of those adversities that occur as a result of brute bad luck. This idea, Steiner suggests, is perfectly compatible with libertarianism, and motivates the egalitarian provisions of Locke's famous "enough and as good" proviso on the ownership of natural resources. Though Steiner's discussion of these points emerges in an overall framework of sibling parity, Steiner ends his essay by observing that there is no obvious reason why parity of wealth among nonsiblings should not also be subject to the considerations that emerge in the sibling context.

How we should measure and evaluate differences of income and wealth, and what, if anything, we should do about them, rank among the most contentious questions in contemporary political philosophy. The thirteen essays in this volume, written from diverse viewpoints, provide valuable contributions to these ongoing debates.

ACKNOWLEDGMENTS

The editors wish to acknowledge several individuals at the Social Philosophy and Policy Center, Bowling Green State University, who provided invaluable assistance in the preparation of this volume. They include Mary Dilsaver, Terrie Weaver, and Carrie-Ann Khan.

The editors would like to extend special thanks to Publication Specialist Tamara Sharp, for attending to the innumerable day-to-day details of the book's preparation; and to Managing Editor Matthew Buckley, for providing dedicated assistance throughout the editorial and production process.

CONTRIBUTORS

Daniel Shapiro is Associate Professor of Philosophy at West Virginia University. He has published articles in social and political philosophy on such topics as rights theory, liberalism, communitarianism, free speech, drug policy, Social Security, and national health insurance. He is currently at work on a book, *Justice, Community, and Efficiency: Can the Welfare State Be Justified?* in which he compares welfare-state institutions and free-market alternatives with respect to the central values of contemporary political philosophy.

Tyler Cowen is Professor of Economics at George Mason University, where he holds the Holbert C. Harris Chair in Economics. He is also General Director of the Mercatus Center and General Director of the James M. Buchanan Center for Political Economy. He has published in such economics and philosophy journals as the *American Economic Review*, the *Journal of Political Philosophy*, *Ethics*, and *Philosophy and Public Affairs*. He is the author of two books on the economics of culture, *In Praise of Commercial Culture* (1998) and *What Price Fame?* (2000); his next book, *Minerva's Owl: The Sources of Creative Global Culture*, is forthcoming from Princeton University Press.

Edward N. Wolff is Professor of Economics at New York University, where he has taught since 1974. He is also a Senior Scholar at the Jerome Levy Economics Institute at Bard College, Managing Editor of the *Review of Income and Wealth*, and Vice President of the Eastern Economics Association. His principal research interests are productivity growth and income and wealth distribution. He is the author of *Growth, Accumulation, and Unproductive Activity* (1987) and *Top Heavy: A Study of Increasing Inequality of Wealth in America* (1996), and is a coauthor of *Productivity and American Leadership* (with William J. Baumol and Sue Anne Batey Blackman, 1989) and *Competitiveness, Convergence, and International Specialization* (with David Dollar, 1993).

Donald R. Deere is Associate Professor of Economics at Texas A&M University, and also teaches in the George Bush School of Government and Public Service at Texas A&M University. His research interests are in labor economics, with particular emphasis on government labor-market policies and their impact on wages and employment, education-system incentives, and wage inequality. His research has been published in various economics journals, including the *American Economic Review*, the *Journal of Political Economy*, the *Quarterly Journal of Economics*, and the *Journal of Labor Economics*.

Finis Welch is Distinguished Professor of Economics and George T. and Gladys H. Abell Professor of Liberal Arts at Texas A&M University. His early studies of income changes among blacks and whites over time have played a role in advancing understanding of how the incomes of minorities are affected by education, affirmative action, and business conditions. More recently, he has published work on the growth, in the U.S. economy, of both wage inequality and the value of skill.

Young Back Choi is Professor of Economics and Finance at St. John's University. He is the author of *Paradigms and Conventions: Uncertainty, Decision Making, and Entrepreneurship* (1993), and a coeditor of *Economic and Political Reforms in Asia* (with Thomas Chen and Sung Lee, 1992), *Financial and Economic Integration in Asia* (with Thomas Chen and K. Thomas Liaw, 1993), and *Borderlands of Economics* (with Nahid Aslanbeigui, 1997). He has also published articles in such journals as *Kyklos, Constitutional Political Economy,* and *History of Political Economy.*

Richard A. Epstein is James Parker Hall Distinguished Service Professor of Law at the University of Chicago. He is the author of *Forbidden Grounds: The Case against Employment Discrimination* (1992), *Simple Rules for a Complex World* (1995), *Mortal Peril: Our Inalienable Right to Health Care?* (1997), and *Principles for a Free Society: Reconciling Individual Liberty with the Common Good* (1998). He is an editor of the *Journal of Law and Economics* and a member of the American Academy of Arts and Sciences.

Richard J. Arneson is Professor of Philosophy at the University of California, San Diego, where he was department chair from 1992 to 1996. His teaching and research interests are in the areas of political and moral philosophy. He has published essays recently in *Ethics*, the *Proceedings of the Aristotelian Society, Philosophical Issues, Social Theory and Practice,* the *Canadian Journal of Philosophy,* and *Social Philosophy and Policy.*

James K. Galbraith is Professor of Public Affairs and Government at the Lyndon B. Johnson School of Public Affairs and the Department of Government at the University of Texas at Austin. He is also Director of the University of Texas Inequality Project and a Senior Scholar at the Jerome Levy Economics Institute at Bard College; he previously served as Executive Director of the Joint Economic Committee of the U.S. Congress. The author of *Created Unequal: The Crisis in American Pay* (2000), he is also a coeditor of *Inequality and Industrial Change: A Global View* (2001).

Alan Ryan is Warden of New College, Oxford University. He is the author of *Property* (1987), *Russell: A Political Life* (1993), *John Dewey and the High Tide of American Liberalism* (1995), and *Liberal Anxieties and Liberal Education* (1998); he is also the editor of *Mill: A Critical Edition* (1997).

David Schmidtz is Professor of Philosophy and Joint Professor of Economics at the University of Arizona. He is the author of *Rational Choice and Moral Agency* (1995) and a coauthor of *Social Welfare and Individual Responsibility* (with Robert Goodin, 1998). He is also the editor of *Robert Nozick* (2001) and a coeditor of *Environmental Ethics: What Really Works* (with Elizabeth Willott, 2001).

Richard W. Miller is Professor of Philosophy at Cornell University. His writings in social and political philosophy, ethics, epistemology, the philosophy of science, and aesthetics include numerous articles as well as three books: *Analyzing Marx* (1984), *Fact and Method* (1987), and *Moral Differences* (1992).

Eric Mack is Professor of Philosophy at Tulane University, where he is also a faculty member at the Murphy Institute of Political Economy. He has published numerous articles in moral, political, and legal philosophy in various scholarly anthologies as well as in *Ethics*, the *Journal of Ethics*, the *Monist*, *Nous*, *Philosophical Studies*, *Philosophy and Phenomenological Research*, and *Philosophy and Public Affairs*. He has compiled new editions of Auberon Herbert's *The Right and Wrong of Compulsion by the State, and Other Essays* (1978) and Herbert Spencer's *Man versus the State, with Six Essays on Government, Society, and Freedom* (1981).

Hillel Steiner is Professor of Political Philosophy in the Department of Government at the University of Manchester, and a Fellow of the British Academy. He is the author of *An Essay on Rights* (1994) and a coauthor of *A Debate over Rights: Philosophical Enquiries* (with Matthew Kramer and Nigel Simmonds, 1998). He is also a coeditor of *Freedom and Trade* (with Geraint Parry, 1998), *The Origins of Left-Libertarianism: An Anthology of Historical Writings* (with Peter Vallentyne, 2000), and *Left-Libertarianism and Its Critics: The Contemporary Debate* (with Peter Vallentyne, 2000). His current research interests include the application of libertarian principles to global, and to genetic, inequalities.

EGALITARIANISM AND WELFARE-STATE REDISTRIBUTION*

BY DANIEL SHAPIRO

I. INTRODUCTION

A central idea of contemporary philosophical egalitarianism's theory of justice is that involuntary inequalities or disadvantages—those that arise through no choice or fault of one's own—should be minimized or rectified in some way. Egalitarians believe that the preferred institutional vehicle for fulfilling these obligations of justice is some form of a welfare state. Of course, contemporary egalitarians disagree about the best way to interpret or understand their theory of justice and institutions: Which inequalities are chosen and which are unchosen? What form of a welfare state will best serve justice? However, no contemporary egalitarian denies that egalitarian justice requires a welfare state that will redistribute income and wealth to aid the involuntarily disadvantaged.

My aim here is to argue that egalitarians are wrong about the institutional implications of their theory. Egalitarianism does not mandate state redistribution of income and wealth. Indeed, from an egalitarian perspective, voluntary methods of aiding the involuntarily disadvantaged are at least as good as, and possibly superior to, state redistribution. If my argument is successful, then egalitarian institutional implications are not that far removed from libertarian views that voluntary methods of aiding the disadvantaged are superior to state redistribution. This is a significant result. In general, if a certain institution is supported by all or virtually all plausible normative principles, then that institution has a firmer justification than it would have if it were supported by only one principle or viewpoint, and perhaps more important, rational agreement on what kind of institutions we should have can be achieved. While I cannot show that all plausible perspectives in contemporary political philosophy should converge in preferring voluntary alternatives to welfare-state redistribution—or at least in not finding voluntary methods to be worse—I suspect that if this convergence holds for libertarianism and egalitarianism, two political perspectives usually thought to have quite different institutional implications, then it will hold for other perspectives as well.

* I wish to thank N. Scott Arnold and David Schmidtz for their comments on an earlier draft of this essay, and Ellen Frankel Paul for her comments on a later draft.

In the next section I discuss in more detail the institutional background that frames my later arguments. In Section III I explain how contemporary philosophical egalitarians (henceforth, simply labeled as "egalitarians") argue for welfare-state redistribution. Any redistribution involves a "donor" and a recipient, and in Section IV I argue that egalitarians have no basis for preferring coerced over voluntary donors. In the subsequent section I look at the recipients, and argue that egalitarians also have no basis for preferring coerced over voluntary transfers as a way of reducing involuntary disadvantage. Section VI addresses a very common worry about private alternatives to welfare-state redistribution: will they be enough? In Section VII I refute the claim that coercive redistribution is required because state welfare is better than voluntary charity in expressing a social commitment to aiding the disadvantaged.

II. The Institutional Alternatives

A. State welfare

The welfare state consists, at least in large part, of two kinds of programs. First, there are social insurance programs—for example, government-administered retirement pensions, health insurance, and unemployment insurance—that are awarded regardless of the recipients' income or wealth, but instead are based on some kind of contribution test (payment of certain kinds of taxes) and on the basis of some specified contingency (e.g., old age, incurring medical expenses, or unemployment). Second, there are social assistance or pure welfare programs that are awarded on the basis of some kind of income or wealth test—again, usually on the basis of some contingency. Examples are cash benefits for heads of households who have children, housing subsidies, and medical care for the poor or for immigrants, even those who have paid no taxes.[1]

Social insurance makes up the bulk of the welfare state.[2] Yet my focus here will be on income-tested programs, for two reasons. First, I have

[1] I rely here on Nicholas Barr's cataloguing in Nicholas Barr, "Economic Theory and the Welfare State: A Survey and Interpretation," *Journal of Economic Literature* 30, no. 2 (1992): 742–45, 755. It is worth noting that the terminology of "social insurance" is somewhat misleading, since these programs are not based on actuarial insurance principles of charging people according to expected risk.

[2] For example, a World Bank policy research report, *Averting the Old-Age Crisis: Policies to Protect the Old and Promote Growth* (New York: Oxford University Press, 1994), states that around 25 percent of the budget and 9 percent of the gross domestic product (GDP) of the countries comprising the Organization for Economic Cooperation and Development (OECD) was devoted to social security systems. See ibid., 358–60. Those figures covered the years 1986 to 1991. Recent (1999) information from the OECD shows that the latter figure has risen to 13.5 percent. See Organization for Economic Cooperation and Development, "Government Sector, 1999," available on-line at http://www.oecd.org/publications/figures/2001/anglais/036_037_government.pdf. By contrast, income-tested benefits play a major role in only four welfare states: the United States, the United Kingdom, Australia, and New Zealand. See Barr, "Economic Theory and the Welfare State," 744, 755. Brian Barry points out that the small role for income-tested benefits in many welfare states is not surprising. They

argued elsewhere that egalitarians should oppose social insurance.[3] Second, in a sense, pure welfare programs should be the easiest case for egalitarianism. If an egalitarian should be able to justify any government redistribution, one would think he could justify government redistribution from the affluent to (at least some of) the less affluent.

B. Nongovernmental aid

The usual description of the alternative to state welfare is charitable institutions. This is correct, but it is an incomplete description because it does not tell us how these charities would function. Today's charities are not necessarily a model. Charities that exist today in the shadow of state welfare are not the same as the charities that would exist if it were absent. Numerous charities today receive government subsidies and view themselves as adjuncts to the welfare state.[4]

Charities that would exist absent state welfare would tend to have two central features. First, at least for able-bodied adults, aid would be conditional. Since conditional aid is usually premised on the idea that some recipients are deserving of aid and others are not, another way to put this point is that charities would generally make a serious attempt to distinguish deserving from undeserving recipients. Second, there would tend to be more emphasis on personal involvement by the donors. For many donors today, charity involves writing a check and perhaps reading a

are unnecessary if social insurance programs cover a wide enough range of "contingencies"—including the contingency of earning insufficient income from employment—and provide a high enough level of benefits. See Brian Barry, "The Welfare State versus the Relief of Poverty," *Ethics* 100, no. 3 (1990): 503–5, 526–27. However, in the last few years, almost all welfare states have increased their income-testing. See Organization for Economic Cooperation and Development, *Benefit Systems and Work Incentives* (Paris: Organization for Economic Cooperation and Development, 1998), chap. 5.

[3] Daniel Shapiro, "Can Old-Age Social Insurance Be Justified?" *Social Philosophy and Policy* 14, no. 2 (1997): 116–44, esp. 128–32; and Daniel Shapiro, "Why Even Egalitarians Should Support Market Health Insurance," *Social Philosophy and Policy* 15, no. 2 (1998): 84–132.

[4] In the United States in 1992, around 31 percent of nonprofit organizations' revenue was from tax revenues. This is roughly equivalent to the figure in Britain today. For the former figure, see Virginia Hodgkinson and Murray S. Weitzman, *Nonprofit Almanac 1996–1997* (San Francisco: Jossey-Bass, 1997), 4–5; for the latter, see Robert Whelan, *Involuntary Action* (London: Institute for Economic Affairs, 1999), 3, 23. (Admittedly, these studies include cultural and educational organizations as part of the voluntary or nonprofit sector, and if donations to these organizations were excluded, the degree of government support for nonprofit organizations would be somewhat lower.) In other European countries the percentage of government support is even higher, and in some countries, such as Italy and Sweden, there is barely an independent or voluntary, nonmarket sector. See David Harrington Watt, "United States: Cultural Challenge to the Voluntary Sector," in Robert Wuthnow, ed., *Between States and Markets: The Voluntary Sector in Comparative Perspective* (Princeton, NJ: Princeton University Press, 1991), 273. For the common view among charities that they are merely a supplement to the welfare state, see Laurie Goodstein, "Churches May Not Be Able to Patch Welfare Cuts," *Washington Post*, February 22, 1995, A1; Karen Arenson, "Gingrich's Welfare Vision Ignores Reality, Charities Say," *New York Times*, June 4, 1995, sec. 1, p. 1; and "Weak Foundations," *Economist*, September 18, 1993, 64–65.

report from the recipient institution. In the absence of state welfare, charities would place a greater emphasis on giving time rather than money.

Why think that charities will have these features in the absence of state welfare? One reason is that a significant percentage of donors are unlikely to give aid with no strings attached. While some donors may be indifferent to how their money is spent, or view conditional aid as objectionable, as the size of one's donation rises, the incentive to give to a charity that engages in monitoring increases. Another reason is that since the state will not be forcing people to provide welfare for the disadvantaged, the assumption that others will take care of this problem is gone. Once it is gone, the incentive to get personally involved increases. Of course, not everyone, and not even most people, want to get involved with others' problems. But it seems reasonable to assume that this increased incentive will make some kind of difference.[5]

It is also worth noting that when state welfare, particularly by the federal or national government, was at a very low level, namely, in nineteenth- and early-twentieth-century Britain and the United States, charities made a deserving/undeserving distinction and personal involvement by donors was stressed.[6] Deserving recipients were considered those who were poor due to no fault of their own and who were unlikely to change their situation quickly without assistance, while the undeserving were considered those who were poor because of their own faults and who were unlikely to change their lives even with assistance. (As we shall see, this distinction is very close to contemporary egalitarians' distinction between those who are disadvantaged because of their choices or faults and those who are disadvantaged through no choice or fault of their own.) Charities generally used two kinds of tests to divide potential recipients: investigation of a person's situation or circumstances and, for able-bodied adults, a work test. If the potential aid recipients were orphans, elderly, incurably ill, children who could not be supported by their one-parent families, disabled, or suffering from an accident, no investigation was needed: these people were clearly deserving. Investigation generally occurred for able-bodied adults. It was generally done by affluent or middle-class volunteers (usually from a church or synagogue, for many charities were faith-based), who attempted to determine if fraud was present, or if the person's problems stemmed from what were viewed

[5] A counterargument is that people will not contribute because they believe their contributions will be ineffective. I discuss this in Section VI.

[6] For some helpful accounts, see Kathleen Woodroofe, *From Charity to Social Work in England and the United States* (London: Routledge and Paul, 1962); Gertrude Himmelfarb, *The De-Moralization of Society* (New York: Alfred Knopf, 1994), chaps. 4 and 5; Marvin Olasky, *The Tragedy of American Compassion* (Washington, DC: Regnery Gateway, 1992); and Michael B. Katz, *In the Shadow of the Poorhouse: A Social History of Welfare in America*, rev. ed. (New York: Basic Books, 1996). Himmelfarb and Olasky favor private charity, Katz opposes it, and Woodroofe is relatively neutral, but they all agree that prior to the welfare state, charities made the deserving/undeserving distinction and stressed personal involvement.

as faults—too much drink, laziness, or thriftlessness.[7] Even if the person's problems were considered his own doing, the work test was considered a good indicator of whether or not the person was willing to help himself, and thus be deserving of aid. Men were generally asked to chop wood, women to sew, and the chopped wood and clothing were given to other needy persons. Besides helping to reveal whether the recipient had good work habits, the provision of goods that other needy people needed was meant to instill some sense of reciprocity—a sense that the recipients were contributing, not just taking.

As for personal involvement by donors, this was considered essential, particularly for those aid recipients whose problems were not temporary and who needed more than just material aid (e.g., food, clothing, shelter, and help finding employment). For those whose problems ran deeper, aid meant restoring family ties if possible; in those cases in which it was not, volunteers tried to bond with the recipient. Volunteers had a narrow but deep responsibility: to become, in effect, part of the family (or a newly created family). Sometimes the recipient's problem was the neighborhood itself, and so some volunteers literally lived with the disadvantaged, as occurred with the mission movement in the United States and the settlement houses in the United States and England.[8] This intense personal involvement was an attempt to break down the barrier between donor and recipient, a problem inherent in any charitable enterprise in which donors are from a different class or milieu than the recipients.

One final point before I conclude this section. So far I have focused only on charities as the alternative to the welfare state, and have not discussed mutual aid or fraternal societies, or, as they were known in England, friendly societies.[9] Fraternal societies were voluntary associations, formed along ethnic, occupational, and sometimes ideological or religious lines, that provided low-cost medical care, life and accident insurance, death

[7] Sometimes charities worked with government authorities, even visiting homes of potential recipients with them, which meant that the latter did not clearly perceive a difference between private charity and government welfare. To the extent that this occurred, charities took on a coercive character. See Stephen T. Ziliak, "The End of Welfare and the Contradiction of Compassion," *Independent Review* 1, no. 1 (1996): 63–64.

[8] Missions, begun by Jerry McAuely, an ex-convict and alcoholic, were meeting halls in the worst parts of cities, where locals were invited for cheap, hot food and stories of depravity, with follow-up stories of how others had changed their lives through God's help and acceptance of personal responsibility. The settlement houses were houses, built in poor areas, populated by both local residents and middle-class volunteers; the latter viewed themselves as "settlers" who would both teach and learn from the locals. The homes fulfilled the role of a residential and civic club with the aim of social and moral improvement of the neighborhood. The "settlers" taught classes in a variety of areas, such as literature, languages (including teaching immigrants English), and science; they also helped the local residents with child care and assisted them in handling many of the daily problems of life. See the references cited in note 6 above.

[9] See David T. Beito, *From Mutual Aid to the Welfare State: Fraternal Societies and Social Services, 1890–1967* (Chapel Hill: University of North Carolina Press, 2000); and David G. Green, *Reinventing Civil Society: The Rediscovery of Welfare without Politics* (London: Institute for Economic Affairs, 1993).

and burial benefits, and assistance during periods of unemployment. They were guided by the principle of reciprocity, not charity, and were funded by their members' dues. Those who were aided were then expected, when they were able, to provide help to fellow members in need, to pay dues, and to attend meetings. These meetings often took place at lodges, which were the centers of social life as well as places where one could get medical care from the lodge doctor, find out about job opportunities, and so forth. Fraternal societies did provide help for those who could not pay them back—for example, like charities, many mutual aid societies ran orphanages—but even though the mutual aid societies did offer a safety net, their main concern was not charity.

Fraternal or friendly societies were at least as important, if not more important, than charities in the voluntary provision of welfare services. In the United States, they were particularly vital in the lives of certain groups, such as blacks and immigrants from eastern and southern Europe.[10] Up until 1920 they dominated the market for life and health insurance, to the dismay of commercial life insurance and organized medicine. In England, historian David Green estimates that by 1910 three-fourths of the working male population belonged to one friendly society or another (women often had their own society, but as time went on spouses and children received benefits from their husband's society).[11] Furthermore, fraternal societies overcame a problem endemic to charities—the distance between donors and recipients when they come from different backgrounds, classes, or milieus. Since mutual aid societies were founded on dues, and since the sense of identification between members in ethnically or occupationally based societies was quite strong, there was little of the sometimes alienating sense of *noblesse oblige* and paternalistic meddling that can haunt even the best charities. Yet despite their importance and their moral attractiveness, it is not clear that mutual aid societies can be considered a viable alternative to today's welfare state. This is because they were primarily combinations of an insurance society, a social club, and a community. Thus, the benefits provided by the welfare state that correspond to (some of) what mutual aid societies offered is (for the most part) social insurance, not state welfare. And, in any event, with the rise of widespread commercial insurance, it is hard to see how these societies could play an important role today were the welfare state to disappear.[12]

It is also worth noting that despite their differences, fraternal societies and charities had much in common. Both made the deserving/undeserving

[10] Beito, *From Mutual Aid to the Welfare State*, 2.

[11] Green, *Reinventing Civil Society*, 66.

[12] Perhaps, though, immigrant groups who are not comfortable with commercial insurance might offer insurance benefits tied to a social network. In any event, since I wish to stick with real institutional alternatives that exist today, I will focus on charities and not fraternal societies as the alternative to state welfare, since the former are today far more important than the latter.

distinction. Mutual aid societies were less likely to offer medical treatment, for example, to those whose medical problems were due to venereal disease or excess drinking.[13] Like charities, they did not give aid automatically—fear of malingerers was widespread, and aid to able-bodied adults was considered a right only for those who paid dues. Both offered personal, not impersonal, aid. And both stressed reciprocity, that is, that aid was based on some ability to pay back or contribute in some way—although this was much easier for fraternal societies, since they were founded on dues, whereas charities had to rely on less formal modes of reciprocity. These similarities will play a role in my arguments to come.

III. How Egalitarians Argue for Welfare-State Redistribution

Contemporary philosophical egalitarianism's theory of justice contains two parts: one part having to do with choice and responsibility, the other with luck.[14] Respect for persons requires that individuals have the right to act in accordance with their genuine or uncoerced choices. Furthermore, respect for persons requires that individuals be held responsible for their choices and the costs of their choices. It would be unfair to require others not to interfere with a right-holder's freedom to act on his choices, and then also require these others to subsidize the cost of the right-holder's choices. The other side of the coin of holding individuals responsible for the costs of their choices is that they are entitled to the advantages they gain through their choices. Inequalities or advantages resulting from choice are just. On the other hand, when luck rather than choice rules, fairness dictates that the unlucky be compensated for their disadvantages. Justice requires that those whose disadvantages are a

[13] Beito, *From Mutual Aid to the Welfare State*, 10–11, 44–45, 49–62.

[14] Good guides to the literature of contemporary philosophical egalitarianism can be found in Elizabeth Anderson, "What Is the Point of Equality?" *Ethics* 109, no. 2 (1999): 289–95; Richard J. Arneson, "Equality," in Robert E. Goodin and Philip Pettit, eds., *A Companion to Contemporary Political Philosophy* (Cambridge, MA: Blackwell, 1995), 489–507; G. A. Cohen, "On the Currency of Egalitarian Justice," *Ethics* 99, no. 4 (1989): 906–44; and Peter Vallentyne, "Self-Ownership and Equality: Brute Luck, Gifts, Universal Dominance, and Leximin," *Ethics* 107, no. 2 (1997): 321–43. Prominent exponents of egalitarianism are Richard Arneson, G. A. Cohen, Ronald Dworkin, Thomas Nagel, Eric Rakowski, John Roemer, and Philippe Van Parijs. (Arneson, however, has recently changed his mind. See Richard J. Arneson, "Equality of Opportunity for Welfare Defended and Recanted," *Journal of Political Philosophy* 7, no. 4 [1999]: 488–97. For my purposes here, it is Arneson's egalitarian writings that are of interest.)

Anderson advocates a different form of egalitarianism than the one discussed in this essay. She attacks what she calls "luck egalitarianism"—the idea that justice requires that the victims of bad brute luck be compensated—and instead defends a view she calls "democratic equality." (For a discussion of "brute luck," see note 15 below.) Democratic equality is the idea that all competent adults should be treated as moral equals, and that all hierarchies based on birth or social identity should be abolished. I will not discuss Anderson's views, or other alternatives to luck egalitarianism, in this essay, since luck egalitarianism is the dominant egalitarian view in contemporary analytic political philosophy.

matter of bad luck are owed compensation; those whose disadvantages are due to their choice or fault are owed nothing—or at least nothing as a matter of justice.

This description of the two parts of egalitarianism is only a first approximation, because egalitarians distinguish between "option luck" and "brute luck." Option luck is the kind of luck or risks one reasonably could have taken into account when making choices, and brute luck is the kind of luck or risks one could not reasonably have avoided having or undertaking.[15] Since option luck is the kind of luck one can choose to take into account, egalitarians view advantages derived from option luck as justly acquired, and thus option luck is placed, in effect, in the part of the theory having to do with choice and responsibility. Thus, a more precise description of egalitarianism is that its primary concern or aim is to extinguish or at least minimize the effects of bad brute luck. I insert the modifier "bad" because egalitarians generally do not see extinguishing or minimizing the effects of good brute luck as an essential aim of justice.[16] However, the beneficiaries of good brute luck are the ones who are supposed to compensate the victims of bad brute luck; those whose advantages are achieved by choice or option luck are entitled to their advantages, so they cannot justly be compelled to aid the unlucky. Since the point of the transfer from the beneficiaries of good brute luck to the victims of bad brute luck is not to harm the former, but to aid the latter, some egalitarians insist that the transfers are justified only if the benefits to the latter significantly outweigh the costs to the former, or only if the transfers are efficient.[17]

[15] The distinction between brute and option luck originated with Dworkin, who played the crucial role in contemporary egalitarianism's incorporation of a responsibility or choice condition. See Ronald Dworkin, "What Is Equality? Part 2: Equality of Resources," *Philosophy and Public Affairs* 10, no. 4 (1981): 293. There is, unfortunately, no canonical definition of the brute/option luck distinction. Dworkin originally defined option luck as resulting from a deliberate or calculated gamble, but later egalitarians have modified this, probably because Dworkin's definition seems too restrictive—the key intuition behind the distinction is whether choices significantly influence one's outcomes, and choices can exert a significant influence even when one does not deliberate or calculate. My use of the distinction comes from Vallentyne's gloss on Dworkin's use of it; see Vallentyne, "Self-Ownership and Equality," 329.

[16] There are at least two reasons for this. First, as Vallentyne notes, to the extent that egalitarians endorse some kind of principle of self-ownership, certain ways of attempting to limit persons' good brute luck, such as preventing them from exercising their native talents, are unjust. Vallentyne, "Self-Ownership and Equality," 329–32. Second, as Cohen notes, egalitarians are generally not interested in reducing inequalities among those who are very well off (e.g., between someone very, very rich and someone who is just rich), in part because egalitarianism becomes a very unappealing doctrine if it focuses on leveling down or worsening the position of the better off when this produces no benefit for those who are significantly disadvantaged. See G. A. Cohen, "Incentives, Inequality, and Community," in Stephen Darwall, ed., *Equal Freedom: Selected Tanner Lectures on Human Values* (Ann Arbor: University of Michigan Press, 1995), 335.

[17] Eric Rakowski, *Equal Justice* (Oxford: Oxford University Press, 1991), 2, 74. Arneson endorses what he calls a "weak Pareto norm," according to which principles of distributive justice should not recommend outcomes from which it is feasible to effect a Pareto-improvement. See Arneson, "Equality," 25.

To apply egalitarianism, we need to know what sorts of advantages or disadvantages are due to brute luck, as opposed to option luck and choice. While egalitarians do not all speak with one voice on this, there is broad agreement. Paradigm examples of brute luck are advantages and disadvantages stemming from one's genetic or native physical and mental abilities and traits, one's race or sex, or unproduced natural resources (e.g., an accidental discovery of a mineral deposit). Paradigm examples of option luck or choice are advantages and disadvantages stemming from one's ambitions or conceptions of the good life, or from one's voluntarily acquired preferences and tastes. We can understand the point of these distinctions by using a thought experiment: if we all began with roughly equal or similar circumstances—similar natural endowments, similar unproduced resources—then any inequalities that resulted would be a matter of choice and, therefore, just. In this sense, contemporary egalitarianism is a theory that advocates equal opportunity or equal access, not equal outcomes. Given a fair or suitable starting point, egalitarians say, justice would not require any redistribution.[18]

Of course, we do not begin at such a starting point. In the real world, people find themselves in unchosen circumstances of varying degrees of advantage and disadvantage. Egalitarians see the welfare state as, in effect, an equivalent of insurance for bad brute luck. The idea, roughly, is that the state compensates individuals for whatever bad brute luck they could have insured themselves against were there a market for such insurance.[19] Of course, sometimes there is such a market, and where there is—and when private insurance is available at fair terms—we are in the realm of option luck, not brute luck, and egalitarians maintain that the state has no legitimate role to play (except, perhaps, to make insurance compulsory). The qualifier "at fair terms" is important, since egalitarians typically argue that when victims of bad brute luck are charged higher premiums because they are greater-than-average risks, insurance is not available at fair terms. This is why, for example, egalitarians favor government-administered health insurance and oppose private health insurance.[20] In any event, for the problems dealt with by pure welfare programs, the sort of programs I am concerned with here, private insurance is not generally available: I cannot insure against the risk of defective genes or a bad family.

Egalitarians have argued amongst themselves about what kind of welfare state best approximates this compensation for bad brute luck. Is it a

[18] Richard J. Arneson, "Equality and Equal Opportunity for Welfare," in Louis P. Pojman and Robert Westmoreland, eds., *Equality: Selected Readings* (New York: Oxford University Press, 1997), 235.

[19] This is developed in most detail by Dworkin, "Equality of Resources," 293–335; and Rakowski, *Equal Justice*, 97–106, 120–48.

[20] For an examination and critique of egalitarian arguments for national health insurance, see Shapiro, "Why Even Egalitarians Should Favor Market Health Insurance."

standard tax-and-transfer scheme that redistributes income? Or is something more radical required, such as a redistribution of assets and wealth that borders on, or perhaps spills over into, a form of socialism? Perhaps the issue that has garnered the most attention has been the "Equality of what?" question: for what kind of unchosen inequalities or disadvantages do egalitarians wish to compensate? Bad brute luck can produce inequalities in resources—for example, income and wealth—but also in welfare, that is, happiness or other psychologically desirable states. The main dispute here is whether, in addition to compensating for unchosen inequalities in income and wealth, compensation for unchosen inequalities in welfare is also appropriate.

My arguments that egalitarianism does not mandate welfare-state redistribution will be independent of these intramural disputes. I first turn to the "donor" side of the redistributive relationship.

IV. Coercive versus Voluntary Transfers: The "Donors"

A necessary condition for a justly imposed government redistribution is that the taxable income and wealth of the "donor" must be due (mainly) to brute luck. How do egalitarians tell whether someone's income or wealth is or is not mainly a product of choice rather than circumstance? A two-part procedure seems necessary. First, one must categorize the voluntariness of different factors involved in obtaining income and wealth. Second, since no one's income and wealth is due solely to one factor, a causal account of individuals' income and wealth is necessary. This account would seek to explain the various factors that interacted with each other, and to explain which factors did and did not play a primary role in producing someone's or a group's income and wealth over a certain time period.

A. Categorizing sources of income and wealth

As I mentioned in the previous section, egalitarians believe that inequalities resulting from different conceptions of the good life, different ambitions, or voluntarily or deliberately acquired preferences and tastes are chosen. Thus, differences in income and wealth resulting from effort, different trade-offs between leisure and work, and different trade-offs between income and consumption are viewed by egalitarians as voluntary,[21] since they are manifestations of different ambitions and different life goals. The same is true for differences in income and wealth resulting from different occupational choices. Business losses and profits are, according to at least some egalitarians, to a considerable extent due to

[21] Dworkin, "Equality of Resources," 303–6; Rakowski, *Equal Justice*, 107–12; Thomas Nagel, *Equality and Partiality* (New York: Oxford University Press, 1991), 108.

option luck—gambles and risks knowingly taken or assumed, opportunities seized or ignored, and so forth—and thus fall on the side of voluntary inequalities.[22] In general, the results of deliberate gambles—for example, lotteries (assuming they are run fairly)—are also treated as voluntary inequalities, for the same reason.

Egalitarians believe that genetic or native endowments are unchosen,[23] and thus that inequalities in income and wealth resulting from such differences are unchosen. The same holds for inequalities or disadvantages that are due to race, sex, or national origin, as these are unchosen or altered only with great difficulty. Losses of income and wealth due to illness, disease, injury, and accident are nonvoluntary, provided one was not negligent and did not voluntarily or deliberately choose a lifestyle that was known to have the risks of such losses. Those business losses and gains that one cannot insure against, and which it would be unreasonable to take into one's calculations—for example, a completely accidental or freakish loss or gain—are matters of brute luck as well. Since one does not choose one's parents or family, egalitarians argue, inequalities due to one's initial start in life are also unjust—for example, inequalities resulting from inherited wealth.

One's psychological characteristics, such as one's cheerfulness or grumpiness,[24] one's ability to cope with adversity, one's sense of self-efficacy, and one's character traits (for example, diligence and persistence), also affect one's ability to succeed. Egalitarians find these rather difficult to classify, and they are probably best viewed as mixed cases. On the one hand, they are obviously influenced by one's unchosen genetic and family background. On the other hand, to some extent some of these are alterable by late teenage and adult choices.

What about education and schooling? Here again, this would seem to be a mixed case. On the one hand, for much of one's childhood, the type of schooling one receives is due to legal and political structures and parental decisions, which are brute luck. On the other hand, at some point children become old enough to be able to make some kinds of choices independently of parental influence and to exercise whatever options exist within their political and legal structures.

B. The problem of causal interaction

The existence of hard cases—here, mixed cases—by itself presents no special problem for egalitarians. All theories have hard cases (although the number of hard cases for egalitarians might give one pause). The problem is that most if not all of the uncontroversial cases of choice or

[22] Rakowski, *Equal Justice*, 83.
[23] And of course, so do nonegalitarians, unless they believe in reincarnation!
[24] Cohen, "On the Currency of Egalitarian Justice," 930–31.

brute luck reciprocally influence each other, so that almost *everything* becomes a mixed case. While genetically based or native abilities and traits differ, people choose to develop (or not develop) these abilities and traits, and so differences in these things are partly a matter of choice and partly a matter of brute luck. One's ambitions and preferences in part depend on one's talents and background, so different conceptions of the good life and different ambitions are partly chosen and partly unchosen. Egalitarians are aware of this[25]—how could they not be? Yet the main way they have dealt with this problem is through intramural disputes about whether or not *certain* factors are correctly classified as belonging on the voluntary or the nonvoluntary side of the spectrum. So, for example, there is a lot of discussion of the problem of expensive tastes: to what extent is the costliness of a person's preferences his responsibility if they were formed in a social or economic background for which he is not responsible?[26] Some egalitarians have also discussed the issue of responsibility for health care risks: is it fair, for example, to charge smokers higher insurance premiums if their decision to smoke was formed before they were fully responsible adults?[27] But the problem is global, not local. Without a causal theory that shows how much of an individual's or group's situation is due to choice and how much of it is due to brute luck, egalitarians are in the dark about whether or not or to what extent the income and wealth that is used to fund redistribution is justly acquired. But egalitarians have no such theory. Instead, they offer a theory about a different subject—about how much one would insure against the risk of being disadvantaged if one were in a hypothetical insurance market in which one did not know one's social and natural disadvantages and all had equal purchasing power.[28] However, even if we knew how much and what kind of insurance persons ignorant of their own vulnerabilities would purchase in a hypothetical insurance market, this would be irrelevant to the point at hand: how much of one's income and wealth, in the real world, is due to one's own choice, and how much is due to brute luck? While some egalitarians make *claims* about this matter, I have been unable to locate anything that amounts to a sustained argument about this important question.[29]

[25] See, for example, Dworkin, "Equality of Resources," 313–14; and Nagel, *Equality and Partiality*, 110–21.

[26] See, for example, Cohen, "On the Currency of Egalitarian Justice," 921–27; and Arneson, "Equality and Equal Opportunity for Welfare," 230–31.

[27] Ronald Dworkin, "Will Clinton's Plan Be Fair?" *New York Review of Books*, January 13, 1994, 4 n. 10; Rakowski, *Equal Justice*, 89.

[28] See the references cited in note 19 above.

[29] Nagel says that egalitarianism would require more redistribution and less inequality of income and wealth than exists at present in contemporary welfare states (although he worries that such redistribution will undermine the incentives necessary for the talented to produce wealth). See Nagel, *Equality and Partiality*, 74–75, 93, 123–25. Dworkin makes a similar claim about the United States; see Ronald Dworkin, "Why Liberals Should Care about Equality," in Dworkin, *A Matter of Principle* (Cambridge, MA: Harvard University

Egalitarians may object that they need no argument or causal theory to justify redistribution. They may point out that some portion of virtually everyone's income and wealth is due to brute luck (e.g., one's family background and genetic inheritance) and that whatever is infected with brute luck is due to brute luck, period.[30] On this account, we are justified in redistributing from the affluent to the less affluent because it is a redistribution from the lucky to the unlucky.

However, this attempt to avoid determining how much of one's income and wealth is caused by brute luck is a dead end, for two reasons. First, the claim that whatever is infected with brute luck is due to brute luck, period, needs defense, and it does not seem obviously true. In fact, it seems clearly false: normally, when X is partially due to Y we do not infer that it is completely due to Y. Second, were egalitarians to accept that whatever is infected with brute luck is due to brute luck, period, the point or motivation for their theory of justice would be mysterious. It is odd to spend time explaining that justice requires compensation only for inequalities due to bad brute luck, not simply inequalities per se, when it turns out that one's theory is practically equivalent to those that claim that inequalities per se require correction or compensation.

So egalitarians cannot avoid the need for a theory or argument that gives us at least a rough idea how much of one's income and wealth is due to choice and how much is due to bad brute luck. That they apparently lack such a theory or argument does not mean, however, that one does not exist. Perhaps social scientists who specialize in these matters can help them out.

Under certain circumstances, social science information could indeed help. If longitudinal studies showed that there is very limited income and wealth mobility, it might be reasonable to conclude that one's income and wealth is largely a matter of brute luck. After all, since most people want to improve their situation, if they are blocked in their attempts to do so, then circumstances, not choice, rules. Indeed, some egalitarians hold something like this view, seeing family background, particularly the economic holdings of one's family, as virtually determining one's lot in life in contemporary America.[31] However, that view is false. While there are a range

Press, 1983), 208. However, since egalitarians do not object to inequalities per se, but only to unchosen ones, Nagel's and Dworkin's confidence that more redistribution is required would need to be based on an argument that bad brute luck produces a significant amount of present-day inequality of income and wealth. They provide no such argument.

[30] Nagel may be suggesting something like this in Nagel, *Equality and Partiality*, 112–13, although I am not sure.

[31] At ibid., 93, Nagel says that capitalism gives rise to "large and inheritable inequalities in the conditions of life." Cohen thinks that the condition of the proletariat in capitalism can be understood using the following thought experiment: A group of people are locked in a room. A key exists, but it works only for the first person who uses it. Although each is free to seize the key and leave, one's freedom depends on others not getting the key. G. A. Cohen, "The Structure of Proletarian Unfreedom," *Philosophy and Public Affairs* 12, no. 1 (1983): 11. Thus, both Nagel and Cohen see capitalism as very close to a kind of caste system.

of views among economists about how much income and wealth mobility there has been in recent decades in the United States, the consensus seems to be that it is alive and well—in general.[32] There are some specific groups for whom mobility does seem to be a problem and/or for whom it may have lessened in recent decades: poor single parents find it difficult to escape from poverty, and the growth of earnings of men with a high school education or less has been sluggish or perhaps has diminished in absolute terms.[33] However, that certain population groups may be experiencing mobility problems is irrelevant to the issue at hand, which is whether the vast majority of the income and wealth that will be the source of the funds for transfers is due to good brute luck. Admittedly, the existence of mobility problems for some groups would be relevant, as far as the vast majority of the population is concerned, if that majority was causing the group's problems. But that does not seem to be the case in the United States right now—those with a college or professional degree are not causing the decline in mobility among men with a high school degree

[32] In Stephen Rose, "Is Mobility in the United States Still Alive? Tracking Career Opportunities and Income Growth," *International Review of Applied Economics* 13, no. 3 (1999): 417–37, Rose surveys the views of economists on income mobility in the United States and finds their differences to be largely due to methodological differences concerning how to measure such mobility; he also finds that the extreme view that income mobility has largely vanished for most of the population is erroneous. For an optimistic account of income mobility, see W. Michael Cox and Richard Alm, *Myths of Rich and Poor: Why We're Better Off Than We Think* (New York: Basic Books, 1999), 72–87. For somewhat less sanguine accounts, see Richard Freeman, *When Earnings Diverge: Causes, Consequences, and Cures for the New Inequality in the U.S.* (Washington, DC: National Policy Association, 1997), 28–30; and Isabel V. Sawhill, "Still the Land of Opportunity?" *Public Interest*, Spring 1999, 3–18. Studies of wealth mobility are scarcer than studies of income mobility, but see Erik Hurst, Ming Ching Luoh, and Frank P. Stafford, "The Wealth Dynamics of American Families, 1984–1994," in William C. Brainard and George L. Perry, eds., *Brookings Papers on Economic Activity—1998* (Washington, DC: Brookings Institution, 1998), 1:267–337, which argues at 285 that there is rising wealth mobility in the United States. In Nancy A. Jianakoplos and Paul L. Menchik, "Wealth Mobility," *Review of Economics and Statistics* 79, no. 1 (1997): 18–32, Jianakoplos and Menchik studied mature American men from 1966 to 1981 and found somewhat less wealth mobility than did Hurst, Luoh, and Stafford. However, one would expect Jianakoplos and Menchik's study to find more limited mobility, since the men in their survey (who were between 45 and 59 years old) may have already achieved a significant amount of mobility as they went from being young adults to being middle-aged.

[33] On single parents and poverty, see Peter Gottschalk and Sheldon Danziger, "Income Mobility and Exits from Poverty of American Children, 1970–1992," in Bruce Bradbury, Stephen P. Jenkins, and John Micklewright, eds., *The Dynamics of Child Poverty in Industrialized Countries* (Cambridge: Cambridge University Press, 2001). On men with a high school diploma or less, see Freeman, *When Earnings Diverge*, 10–11; and Sawhill, "Still the Land of Opportunity?" 11–12.

Gottschalk and Danziger's study was misinterpreted in Michael Weinstein, "America's Rags-to-Riches Myth," *New York Times*, February 18, 2000, A28; Weinstein interpreted the study as showing that it is difficult to escape from poverty in today's America. In fact, as David Schmidtz points out in David Schmidtz, "Equal Respect and Equal Shares," in this volume, the study shows a great difference between poor two-parent households and poor one-parent households: children in the former sort of household had a substantial ability to exit from poverty during the 1970s and 1980s.

or less, and two-parent families are not the ones that bring it about that single parenthood makes it harder to get out of poverty.[34]

Of course, even if there is on the whole income and wealth mobility, it does not follow, strictly speaking, that the mobility that does exist is due to choices or a mixture of choices and unchosen circumstances. Thus, another way social science studies could help the egalitarian case is by showing that most of the income and wealth of the middle class and the rich, or those groups' rise into the middle class or affluence, is due largely to good brute luck. However, if we look at the usual explanations for income and wealth inequalities, we find that the usual causes listed either fall clearly on the chosen side of the chosen/unchosen spectrum, or are one of the mixed cases. Consider the following four points:

(1) Inheritance does not play a large role in the fortunes of the very rich.
(2) Entrepreneurship does play a large role in the fortunes of the very rich.[35]
(3) Forming a family, working full-time all year round, sticking with a job long enough to get skills and training, completing college, and moving to areas with high-paying jobs all help, maintain, or propel one into the middle class.[36]
(4) Character traits such as diligence, reliability, and persistence are valued by employers; people with those traits are more likely to be hired, stay hired, and be promoted, thus increasing their chances of improving their situations.[37]

[34] While I presume it is relatively obvious that the existence of two-parent families is not among the reasons that single parenthood makes it harder to get out of poverty, my analogous claim about the situation of men with a high school diploma or less may not be so obvious. It might seem that when an economy increasingly rewards jobs that require greater skills and education, those with average or below-average education and skills will *therefore* suffer diminished income and wealth mobility. However, this is a fallacious inference. Setting aside the fact that the sluggishness and perhaps real loss of earnings of those with high school diplomas or less has occurred mainly among men, not among all who earned a high school diploma or less, an increasing economic return to the well educated does not mean that the mobility of the less educated must decrease. Both groups could experience significant mobility, although of course the increasing return to the college-educated group means that its income will rise faster than that of the less educated group.

[35] On these first two points, see Young Back Choi, "On the Rich Getting Richer and the Poor Getting Poorer," *Kyklos* 52, no. 2 (1999): 239–58; Rudolph C. Blitz and John J. Siegfried, "How Did the Wealthiest Americans Get So Rich?" *Quarterly Review of Business and Economics* 32, no. 1 (1992): 5–26; and James P. Smith, "Inheritances and Bequests," in James P. Smith and Robert J. Willis, eds., *Wealth, Work, and Health: Innovations in Measurement in the Social Sciences* (Ann Arbor: University of Michigan Press, 1999), 137.

[36] Cox and Alm, *Myths of Rich and Poor*, 85–87.

[37] In Susan Mayer, *What Money Can't Buy* (Cambridge, MA: Harvard University Press, 1997), Mayer examines to what extent parental income affects children's outcomes. She finds that once basic minimal material needs have been met, parental income per se does not make that much difference. Rather, when parents have the characteristics that employers value and are willing to pay for—skills, diligence, honesty, reliability, and so on—this

As we have seen, (1) is an example of good brute luck, (2) is an example of option luck, and (3) and (4) are mixed cases. Thus, these four points falsify any claim that the middle class and the rich got where they are purely or largely by brute luck.

So the real problem for egalitarians is not that they lack—and have not done—the social science research they need in order to demonstrate that government transfers are justified. Their real problem is that such research does nothing to remove the problem we began with—the situation of the donors is due to some indeterminate mix of choice and brute luck.

C. *Comparing injustices*

Since we have no basis for determining the extent to which people's advantages are or are not the product of brute luck, any coercive transfer[38] will involve injustice, because it will take some income and wealth from some (or perhaps many) of those who earned it through their choices or option luck, and who thus have a right to it. It is unclear how unjust these transfers will be, but there is no doubt, given egalitarianism's theory of justice, that such coercive transfers will deprive some (or perhaps many) people of income and wealth to which they have a right. On the other hand, some injustice will also occur if there is no coercive redistribution and transfers to the unfortunate or the poor are purely voluntary. While it is not unjust to voluntarily transfer some of one's income or wealth to the unfortunate or poor, it is unjust to refrain from transferring income or wealth derived from good brute luck, since one is not entitled to that income or wealth. While we cannot predict to what extent this would occur if transfers to the poor and unfortunate were purely voluntary, it is quite safe to predict that some of this would occur, and thus that a system based on voluntary transfers, like one based on coercive transfers, will involve some injustice.[39]

---

improves their children's life chances, independently of the effects of parents' income. In fact, children of parents with these attributes do well even when their parents do not have much income.

[38] A coercive transfer (or redistribution) is a transfer that is not voluntary. A voluntary transfer (or redistribution) is a transfer that occurs with the donor's consent, and which is not an ordinary market exchange (e.g., the recipient receives something without necessarily providing some good or service in return).

[39] Perhaps it might be thought that there is a causal difference between the two kinds of injustice. Coercive transfers, one might argue, will definitely *cause* or *produce* some acts of injustice, as some individuals' rights to their justly acquired income and wealth are violated, while if voluntary transfers are relied upon, injustice will be *allowed*, as some individuals refrain from transferring the income and wealth to which they are not entitled. If this was a correct way of characterizing the egalitarian choice between coercive and voluntary transfers, then we could settle the question of which choice is worse by settling the question of whether it is worse to do injustice or refrain from doing justice. However, this way of characterizing the egalitarian choice is probably mistaken. When one has a positive obligation—in the voluntary-transfer scenario, the positive obligation of those whose income and wealth is derived from good brute luck to transfer it to those with bad brute

Thus, for egalitarians the choice between coercive and voluntary transfers is a choice between different kinds of injustice. Which choice is worse: to coerce persons who have a right to their income and wealth, or to fail to coerce those who unjustly fail to transfer income and wealth to which they are not entitled? I see no way to answer this question within egalitarian theory. Either option involves some indeterminate amount of injustice, and we are in the dark about which injustice is worse. Thus, using voluntary transfers—that is, abolishing state welfare and relying on private alternatives—is no worse than using coercive welfare-state transfers, if we focus just on the side of the donors.

To summarize the arguments in this section: Egalitarians believe that some kinds of income and wealth are a result of choice and option luck, that others are a result of brute luck, and that some are mixed cases. However, since one's total income and wealth is a result of an interaction among these factors, all egalitarians can say is that as a result of this interaction, individuals' income and wealth results from some indeterminate mix of choice and brute luck. Were there social science evidence that showed that mobility was quite limited in market societies, or that most of the wealthy or middle class achieved most of their income and wealth through good brute luck, then egalitarians could say that most people's income and wealth is due to brute luck, but there is no such evidence. Given that individuals' income and wealth emerge from some indeterminate mix of choice and brute luck, the choice between coercive transfers and voluntary charity as a way of helping those suffering from bad brute luck is a choice between one kind of injustice—forcibly taking income and wealth from those entitled to it—versus another kind—allowing some of those who are obligated to transfer their income and wealth to avoid doing so. There is nothing in egalitarian theory that dictates a choice either way here, so egalitarians should not think that coercive transfers are any better than voluntary charity.

V. Coercive versus Voluntary Transfers: The Recipients

A. *Holding someone responsible versus taking responsibility*

At first glance, it appears as if the argument made in the previous section applies to the recipients of transfers as well. If we cannot tell to what extent a person's advantages are due to choice as opposed to brute luck, then we cannot tell to what extent a person's disadvantages are due to choice as opposed to brute luck. However, things are different when we look at the recipients of transfers, because a new matter arises here that

luck—failing to do what one is obligated to do is not a mere refraining. It is an act of injustice. Thus, both sorts of transfers involve acts of injustice. I thank Eric Mack for setting me straight on this point.

does not arise with the donors—namely, *changing* the recipient's situation so that his lot in life is more influenced by genuine choices than by bad brute luck. Even if a person's disadvantages up to the present were due primarily to bad brute luck, he might *now* be in a position to do something about it, or he could be placed in a situation where his future lot in life could be due more to his choices than to brute luck. Notice, however, that this distinction between the cause of a person's present situation and what he might now be able to do was irrelevant for the egalitarian rationale for taking some of the donor's income and wealth. That rationale did not center on the idea that we should change the donor's situation so that in the future he could make genuine choices.[40] The rationale there, the reader will recall, was that justice requires compensating the involuntarily disadvantaged and that those with good brute luck cannot claim that it is unjust for them to be forced to redistribute some of their income or wealth. Furthermore, except perhaps in extraordinary cases, no one doubts that those blessed with good brute luck will, after redistribution, be able to lead a life in which their lot in life is to a significant extent determined by their choices. However, this is in doubt with the victims of bad brute luck, since merely giving them monetary compensation for their bad luck may not thereby make them able to change their situation if their problems are *internal* ones having to do with their character traits, abilities, skills, or uncorrectable severe disabilities. (I return to this point below.)

Given that the point of taking the donor's money was not to change his situation so that in the future his lot in life could be to a considerable extent determined by his choices, why should egalitarians be interested in changing the recipient's situation in this way? To explain why, let us introduce a distinction between holding someone responsible versus taking responsibility.[41] Holding someone responsible for his actions is a matter of assessing his past behavior and making judgments of blame and praise. Taking responsibility, by contrast, is forward-looking: it means that one will regard one's welfare, one's future, and the consequences of one's actions as one's own responsibility, not that of others. The two notions are logically distinct. I may not be to blame for my past problems—that is, it may be wrong to hold me responsible for my bad situation—but it may nevertheless be appropriate or justified to regard me as responsible for cleaning up the mess I am in—that is, for taking responsibility for my

[40] Which is not to say that egalitarians would not view it as *desirable* if redistribution resulted in the situations of the beneficiaries of good brute luck being altered so that they were closer to what life would have been like if those beneficiaries had not been so lucky. However, as I noted earlier, egalitarians generally do not view the existence of good brute luck as an *injustice* (see note 16 above for the reasons why). It is *bad* brute luck that is an injustice.

[41] On this distinction, see David Schmidtz, "Taking Responsibility," in David Schmidtz and Robert E. Goodin, *Social Welfare and Individual Responsibility* (Cambridge: Cambridge University Press, 1998), 8–10.

life, starting now. Though it is wrong to hold those harmed by bad brute luck as being responsible for their situation, there are two reasons why egalitarians want, or should want, recipients to take responsibility for their future. First, the egalitarian vision involves, in part, a world where individuals are able to make their choices and have their fate determined, to a significant extent, by their choices. This means that justice requires changing the situation of those dominated by bad brute luck so that their lives are more under the control of their choices, and this will not occur unless they can take responsibility. One's life is not under one's control if one is unwilling or unable to regard one's future as one's responsibility. Second, as I noted above, monetary compensation is not always sufficient to fundamentally change the situation of those whose lives have been harmed by bad brute luck. It may not significantly raise their welfare or their resources if their problems are internal ones having to do with their character traits, skills, abilities, or disabilities.

B. Conditional versus unconditional aid

Since there is an asymmetry in egalitarianism between the donors and the recipients with respect to the point or aim of redistribution, the next question to consider is whether or not discovering whether recipients will take responsibility for their future is any easier than discovering whether or not the donors' advantages were chosen. It is easier, because there are some commonsense tests that can be used: Is the person willing to work if work is made available? Does the person try to change his life by grasping or taking advantage of opportunities to learn new skills, develop his talents, or change his behavior and thus alter his character traits?[42] If a disadvantaged person refuses offers of work when options are made available, or refuses offers that would help improve his situation by helping him develop skills or talents or change his behavior, this shows that the person is not taking responsibility for his future and his welfare.

None of these tests is available if aid is unconditional. However, before we can conclude that egalitarians should favor conditional aid, let us consider two important objections to the argument I made in the previous paragraph: the first is an epistemic objection, the second, a moral one.

Richard Arneson argues that a healthy, nondisabled person's refusal to work may not reveal sufficient information to allow one to pass a negative judgment upon that person. For his refusal may be due to such terrible or discouraging circumstances that his refusal is excusable in the sense that it would have been exceedingly difficult for the person to

[42] These are the kinds of tests charities used prior to the rise of the welfare state, and, as I discuss later in this subsection, to some extent recent welfare reform incorporates these tests as well. See also note 51.

accept the offer.[43] Or to put matters in a slightly different way, the person's character traits may have been severely warped by bad brute luck, and as a result, he is simply so discouraged that it is not reasonable for him to accept the offer. In this case, it is not simply that the person is unwilling to take responsibility; the deeper problem is that taking such responsibility is too difficult for him.

In one sense, Arneson's epistemic objection is sound. The tests I described do not necessarily reveal *why* someone fails to take responsibility, and so a person who fails the tests may well not be culpable. My point, though, was that conditional aid at least provides a way of determining *whether* a person is willing to take responsibility, which is what egalitarians should want the disadvantaged to do, while unconditional aid provides no way of determining this.[44] My response, however, raises a moral objection to a system of conditional aid: since some of those who refuse to take responsibility will be nonculpable, any system of conditional aid will inflict significant injustice on those who nonculpably fail to take responsibility. After all, those who decline job offers or other forms of help in a system of conditional aid will get either no aid or less aid than those who accept the offer.[45] But if the refuser is not at fault for refusing, then a denial of aid is unjust, and giving a lesser amount of aid for the refusal may also be unjust. A system of unconditional aid avoids this injustice, even if it does create injustice by giving unconditional aid to those who are simply unwilling to take responsibility and by failing to even attempt to determine whether someone is willing to take responsibility. Given this, one could argue, a system of unconditional aid is at least as just, on egalitarian principles, as a system of conditional aid.

I suspect that this moral objection to a system of conditional aid fails. Most adults are willing to respond to offers of conditional aid.[46] Further-

[43] Richard J. Arneson, "Egalitarianism and the Deserving Poor," *Journal of Political Philosophy* 5, no. 4 (1997): 331–32.

[44] True, a person who receives unconditional aid may later take responsibility by earning a living and removing himself from state welfare. But the point is that the acceptance of unconditional aid by itself does not tell us that the person is willing to take responsibility.

[45] Conditional aid might be viewed not as a pure offer, but as a mixture of an offer and a threat—a "throffer." The offer is that aid will be given if the person is willing to work, learn new skills, and so on; the threat is that aid will be lessened or cut off if the offer is not accepted. Threats and offers are typically defined in terms of whether they improve or worsen the situation, relative to some status quo, of the person to whom they are given. Depending on how one defines the status quo, the lessening or cutting off of aid might make the person's situation worse than it was prior to the existence of conditional aid. If the status quo is unconditional aid, then conditional aid is a throffer; if the status quo is no aid at all, then conditional aid is a pure offer. See Robert Goodin, "Social Welfare as a Collective Social Responsibility," in Schmidtz and Goodin, *Social Welfare and Individual Responsibility*, 180.

[46] I presume that this claim reflects common sense. It is also supported by some (admittedly incomplete) evidence from surveys conducted by organized charities in the nineteenth century; see Olasky, *The Tragedy of American Compassion*, 105–7. It is also supported by the evidence from welfare reform; see Douglas J. Besharov and Peter Germanis, "Welfare Reform—4 Years Later," *Public Interest*, Summer 2000, 17–36. In addition, surveys of welfare recipients show a high degree of approval for linking welfare benefits with a work require-

more, egalitarians should presume that an unwillingness by an able-bodied adult to take responsibility is culpable. After all, we are talking here about making an effort—about a willingness to respond to a challenge, incur an obligation, and contribute rather than just take. Since egalitarians find a person's effort to be among the least suspect sources of income and wealth, it seems that they should presume that a failure to take responsibility is culpable. Even if this presumption can be overcome, the only way the moral objection could succeed is if the injustice done in a system of conditional aid to the people who nonculpably fail to take responsibility outweighs the injustice done in a system of unconditional aid by giving aid to people who are not entitled to it. If both of these injustices are of the same type, then the issue becomes a purely quantitative one. Since most adults are culpable if they fail to take responsibility, it seems clear that fewer people are unjustly harmed by a system of conditional aid than are unjustly benefited by a system of unconditional aid. As there is no basis in egalitarian writing for assuming that failing to give aid to nonculpable refusers is worse than giving aid to those who are not entitled to it, the fact that the system of unconditional aid unjustly affects more lives means that it creates more injustice. Therefore, the moral objection fails, and egalitarians should favor conditional aid.

Conditional aid does not entail private aid. State welfare can be conditional as well. For example, in the United States in 1996, the federal entitlement to Aid to Families with Dependent Children (AFDC, which provided cash benefits mainly to unmarried mothers) ended and was replaced by capped block grants to the states. Under this system, the federal government gives the states a fixed amount of money for welfare, but the states get to keep any money they do not use. In addition, states are penalized if they do not institute work requirements for welfare recipients.[47] Since AFDC was abolished, many states have responded by instituting such requirements, placing time limits on benefits, eliminating extra payments given for having more children, and turning welfare offices into job-placement centers. Do egalitarians have some basis for preferring this kind of conditional aid to the conditional aid provided by charities? I now turn to this question.

C. *Conditional aid: comparing the alternatives*

A system of conditional aid should be a flexible system, because while commonsense tests can help reveal whether someone is willing to take responsibility, there are a variety of ways of implementing or instantiat-

ment; see Robert Solow, "Who Likes Workfare?" in Amy Guttman, ed., *Work and Welfare* (Princeton, NJ: Princeton University Press, 1998), 11–13.

[47] Details about the Personal Responsibility and Work Opportunity Act of 1996, which ended AFDC and set up the system of capped block grants, can be found in Mary Ellen Hombs, *Welfare Reform: A Reference Handbook* (Santa Barbara, CA: ABC-CLIO, 1996), 98–103.

ing these tests, and given the diversity of human nature, different methods will be needed for different kinds of people. In order to change their lives or fates, some people just need to work; others need skills; others need to alter their attitudes, habits, and character; and some need some combination of these. For each of these types of people, there are numerous particulars that need to be answered: Does this person need to learn how to budget his income or write a resume? Does that person need transportation to work? Does that other person need to learn how to be a good parent, remain in a marriage, or stay sober? One size most certainly does not fit all. Thus, decentralized solutions are better than centralized ones.

While state welfare can be decentralized,[48] it is unlikely that a decentralized state welfare system can be as flexible as a private one. Part of the reason for this is sheer numbers. Unless the political system is extremely decentralized, it is unlikely that the number of different types of programs or approaches in a political system can rival the pluralism of a competitive system of private charities. Private institutions have more freedom to treat those receiving aid as individuals and to target their aid to specific groups with very specific problems. More importantly, flexibility also involves the ability to quickly change policies if need be, and private institutions need to jump through fewer hoops or go through fewer intermediaries than a political system does in order to get approval or permission to try a new approach or alter their policies.

Of course, the reasonableness of an institution changing its policies or approaches depends on its ability to obtain and evaluate information about whether or not it is reaching or making progress toward reaching its goals, and here also private institutions have a comparative advantage. It is easier to determine how a policy is working when it is for a small, specific group rather than a larger, heterogeneous group. Furthermore, private institutions tend to be more effective monitors because those doing the monitoring have a greater incentive to do a better job. The ultimate monitors of state welfare are the voters, and this means that state welfare runs headlong into the problem of rational ignorance. In modern democracies, particularly when governments take on an enormous range of functions, it is perfectly rational for voters to be ignorant of, and not take a terribly strong interest in, the workings or effectiveness of the government. The time and energy needed to become knowledgeable about the wide range of areas that governments regulate and control is enormous, and the extent to which one can actually make a serious difference is fairly limited—these points, combined with the obvious fact that time

[48] In recent years, welfare programs in the United States, the United Kingdom, Canada, Australia, and the Netherlands have become more decentralized. See Organization for Economic Cooperation and Development, *The Local Dimension of Welfare-to-Work: An International Survey* (Paris: Organization for Economic Cooperation and Development, 1999).

and energy are scarce resources in the first place, mean that it is unsurprising and perfectly appropriate that most voters rely on a kind of impressionistic approach when making political decisions. The political process is thus not an impressive mechanism for generating interest in ascertaining the best way to relieve involuntary disadvantage or in evaluating whether programs have been effective in achieving their purported aims. Private charities have an advantage here, since they are more likely to be supported by people who have an incentive to closely monitor and evaluate whether the charities' approaches are succeeding—namely, those who voluntarily supply the funds. This is not to say that private donors cannot be as uninterested as voters generally are in figuring out how well their money is spent. The point, though, is that when one's own money is being used, one's incentive to evaluate the relevant programs increases, particularly when one selects the charity and is personally involved with it.

It may be objected that the problem of rational ignorance means that state bureaucracies administering aid have a great deal of autonomy, and that given the right kind of professional ethos, bureaucrats will carefully monitor the progress of their programs, or perhaps hire consultants to do the evaluating. Political scientist Lawrence Mead argues, in fact, that something like this occurred in the U.S. state of Wisconsin.[49] Even if Mead is right, however, this does not overcome the rational ignorance problem. Wisconsin may be a special case. Mead himself cites the unusually high quality of the Wisconsin welfare bureaucracy, and if overcoming rational ignorance requires unusual circumstances, then it will as a general rule not be overcome.

Another way to see if state or private conditional aid is better at reducing involuntary disadvantage is to see which is better at reducing moral hazard. In the context of welfare policy, moral hazard refers to the observation that paying those who are disadvantaged tends to bring about more disadvantaged people. Since egalitarians oppose subsidizing people's choices, they must view the reduction of moral hazard as an important criterion for evaluating welfare policies. Moral hazard is a far worse problem for unconditional aid than it is for conditional aid, since the attachment of conditions to aid reduces the incentives for people to be eligible for welfare. Still, it is a problem for both kinds of aid, since conditional aid with rather loose conditions and weak enforcement of those conditions increases moral hazard. In order to combat moral hazard, one needs a credible threat to cut off aid for those not meeting the requirements for aid. However, it seems that for two reasons, government agencies are in a worse position than private institutions are to

[49] Lawrence Mead, "The Twilight of Liberal Welfare Reform," *Public Interest*, Spring 2000, 35.

make this kind of credible threat.[50] First, making a credible threat involves a willingness to tolerate the misery that will occur if the threat is carried out. If governments (national or state) are providing most of the aid to the disadvantaged, then they will be virtually the only agencies held accountable for any misery that results from a cutoff of aid. But if any particular private agency cuts off aid, it is not solely accountable in the same way because there are other agencies; hence, any particular charitable society can credibly threaten to cut off aid.[51] Second, the arguments I gave earlier that those who donate to charities have a greater incentive than voters to see how well their money is spent applies here as well: bureaucrats are likely to face fewer negative consequences, if conditions for receiving aid are not strictly enforced, than employees of private institutions would face. Furthermore, government officials are rarely subject to the bottom line: they are typically paid regardless of how well they do their job.

It may be objected that there are institutional mechanisms for reducing these various problems. Government officials' pay could be tied to performance, and performance could be defined in terms of reducing clientele. So, for example, bonuses could be paid in accordance with how many people government welfare officials removed from the welfare rolls for an extended period of time. Or the incentive could operate at a higher level. Welfare reform in the United States has succeeded remarkably well in driving down the number of people on welfare, partly because, as noted above, it turned welfare into a system of capped block grants to the states. Because the states get to keep any unexpended funds, they have an incentive to cut caseloads. Indeed, in a few short years there has been a remarkable turnaround in the ethos of welfare departments in the United States: whereas they used to focus on enrolling people to get them benefits, their concern now is getting people jobs and diverting away from welfare those who will not seek work.[52]

[50] I have been influenced here by Richard Wagner, *To Promote the General Welfare: Market Processes versus Political Transfers* (San Francisco: Pacific Research Institute for Public Policy, 1989), 164–76.

[51] Of course, in the absence of state welfare, private charities will differ in their willingness to cut off aid as a way of enforcing their policies. Indeed, if some donors favor unconditional aid, then some charities may give aid unconditionally. Thus, there will be a tendency in a system of private charities toward a kind of match between donors and recipients: the donors who are more willing to put up with some moral hazard will in effect pay for that by tending to donate to those charities that give unconditional aid or aid with rather loose conditions, while those who are not willing, or less willing, to put up with moral hazard will tend to donate to charities that give conditional aid with stricter conditions. But the system of private charities as a whole will tend to have less moral hazard than will government welfare because, for reasons noted in the text, branches of government tend not to be able to make credible threats of cutting off aid, while at least some charities, and perhaps many of them, do tend to be able to do this.

[52] For a good summary of the progress of welfare reform in the United States, see Besharov and Germanis, "Welfare Reform—4 Years Later."

These are legitimate points, and the fact that welfare reform in the United States has drastically reduced the welfare rolls may seem to show that state conditional aid can be reasonably effective in reducing moral hazard. However, the jury is still out, because the reforms have had the good fortune to coexist with a booming economy, which probably accounts for some of their success; we do not know whether the reforms can continue if times turn bad. Furthermore, the usual *modus operandi* of government is not to tie pay to performance or to reward bureaucracies for shrinking their clientele. Thus, for state conditional aid to be as effective as private charities are in reducing moral hazard, it must push against the grain, so to speak; this does not seem to be true of private charities. So it still seems like the latter has an edge with respect to the problem of moral hazard.

Thus, overall, private charities seem more effective in reducing involuntary disadvantage: they will be more flexible in designing policies, in monitoring their effects, and in reducing moral hazard. Since I argued in the previous section that egalitarians have no basis for preferring coerced donation over voluntary donation, and since private charities seem more effective in achieving the egalitarian goal of reducing involuntary disadvantage among aid recipients, should we conclude that egalitarians should favor private charities over state welfare? This may be too strong, because I have not argued that egalitarians must view state conditional aid as unjust. The arguments in this section have been about effectiveness, and it is not obvious that egalitarians are required by their theory to favor the most effective system of aid. So while there are some reasons for egalitarians to favor private charities over state welfare, they are not decisive ones, and we are left with the somewhat weaker, although still quite significant, conclusion that egalitarians should view private charities as no worse than state welfare. However, even this weaker conclusion will look suspect unless we address two arguments against private charities: that they will not provide sufficient aid, and that voluntary methods of reducing involuntary disadvantage do not express a social commitment to justice. I discuss these arguments in the next two sections.

VI. Will Private Charity Be Enough?

One of the most common reactions to any proposal to replace state welfare with private charity is that voluntary provision of aid will be insufficient. How should we understand this claim? One way to do so would be to interpret it as saying that private charities will not spend as much as the state does on aid. One could support this claim by arguing that people are more likely to vote for welfare than to give aid voluntarily, since they will perceive the former as being cheaper.[53] However, even if it is true that the quantity of aid produced by political means outweighs the amount that would be produced by voluntary means, this is irrelevant, because private aid does not have to match exactly the expenditure level of state welfare policies. As I argued in the previous section, private charity will likely be more efficient and discriminating in its choice of recipients than state welfare is, and thus, if state welfare were abolished, the need to have a sufficient amount of private charity would not entail that the amount of aid provided be equal to that provided under state welfare.[54] In the context of egalitarianism and the arguments in this essay, it seems more reasonable to understand the claim of insufficiency as meaning that the quantity of voluntary aid provided, were state welfare abolished, would be so small that it would cancel out the virtues of private aid—that it avoids doing injustice by not forcing those entitled to their income and wealth to surrender part of it, that it is more effective than state welfare in reducing involuntary disadvantage, and so forth. At the extreme, the claim would also mean that a system of voluntary aid would be stingy to the point that enormous suffering would be tolerated—widespread malnutrition, large numbers of people without shelter, and so forth. If these things really would occur, then regardless of whether or not one is an egalitarian, support for state welfare would be quite plausible.

Is there any empirical evidence supporting the claim of insufficiency when it is considered in the more reasonable way? At first glance, it is hard to see how there could be, since there has never been a period, even in the United States or England, when state welfare was completely absent or abolished at all levels of government. However, the situation of the United States in the late nineteenth century provides us with something

[53] I thank Tyler Cowen for this point. His argument rests on two ideas: that voting involves expressive preferences, and that it is cheaper to express a preference that an outcome occur than to bring the outcome about oneself. These ideas are elaborated in Geoffrey Brennan and Loren E. Lomasky, *Democracy and Decision: The Pure Theory of Electoral Preference* (Cambridge: Cambridge University Press, 1993).

[54] I will not discuss here two other factors that affect how much private charity would be needed were state welfare abolished. First, it is arguable that certain government regulatory programs increase the need for state welfare. If these programs were abolished along with state welfare, this would provide an additional reason why private charity need not equal state welfare expenditures to be sufficient. For example, rent control and zoning increase the cost of housing, and minimum wage and licensing laws worsen the employment situation for those with minimal skills. Thus, these regulatory programs increase the need for state welfare because they reduce the disposable income of those with below-average income. I thank Richard Epstein for reminding me of these points. Second, a consideration pointing in the opposite direction is that recessions tend to decrease donations to private charity. If this pattern would continue or worsen if state welfare were abolished, this might, all other things being equal, make it somewhat more difficult for private charity to be sufficient. I thank Edward Wolff for reminding me of this. Indeed, to the extent that one thinks that certain government policies and programs, such as government control of the money supply, cause business cycles, one might argue that it is wrong to eliminate state welfare until the policies and programs that cause business cycles are abolished. I cannot consider this argument, proposed by Jeffrey Paul, in this essay.

very close to a natural experiment for testing the claim that private charity would be insufficient absent state welfare, because from the mid-1870s until around the turn of the century, unconditional aid to able-bodied needy people—"outdoor relief," as it was called—was either abolished or curtailed drastically in large, and some medium-sized, cities.[55] Since organized charities kept fairly detailed records of their activities, we can see whether the claim that private charity alone would be insufficient is historically accurate. It does not appear to be. In almost all of the relevant cities, private giving rose to the occasion, and the amount contributed was roughly comparable to the amount given by outdoor relief.[56]

[55] I say that this is *very close* to a natural experiment because although unconditional government aid was abolished in these cities, not all forms of government welfare were abolished. Prior to the rise of an extensive welfare state at the national level, government aid in England and the United States was of two types: the outdoor relief mentioned in the text, which involved cash and in-kind aid such as food or fuel for the winter, and "indoor relief," which involved poorhouses. Poorhouses were workhouses that had rather harsh conditions: long hours were mandatory, and whipping and other punishments for infractions of a house's rules were common. This harshness was designed to deter people who were thought capable of working from applying for government aid. See Michael Tanner, *The End of Welfare: Fighting Poverty in the Civil Society* (Washington, DC: Cato Institute, 1996), 34–35. Poorhouses were not abolished in the U.S. cities that abolished outdoor relief in the late nineteenth century. Still, examining whether or not private giving made up for the absence of outdoor relief in those cities is relevant for the issue at hand: a major form of government welfare was abolished or drastically reduced for a quarter-century, and thus these cities relied on private aid for a substantial portion of the provision of aid to the needy and unfortunate.

[56] In Ziliak, "The End of Welfare and the Contradiction of Compassion," 56–58, 61–62, Ziliak shows that this occurred in Indianapolis. In 1899, Frederic Almy, secretary of the Buffalo Charity Organization, gathered data on outdoor relief and private charity in forty cities, ten of which had completely abolished outdoor relief, and found that the cities with the lowest level of such aid had the highest level of private charity, and vice versa. See Frederic Almy, "The Relation between Private and Public Outdoor Relief—I," *Charities Review* 9, no. 1 (1899): 22–33; and Frederic Almy, "The Relation between Private and Public Outdoor Relief—II," *Charities Review* 9, no. 1 (1899): 65–71. Almy's study does have some drawbacks. The relationship he found did not hold very well for cities with intermediate levels of outdoor relief; for these cities, the main observable relationship was that northern cities provided more total aid (public and private) than southern cities did. (Almy thought that the explanation for the regional difference was the harsher winters in the north.) Also, Almy's study only measured private giving by regularly organized charitable societies; it omitted charity provided by individual churches, mutual aid societies, and the Salvation Army, so it may be that his study systematically underestimated the amount of private charity. Still, Almy's study seems to refute the claim that when state welfare is abolished or drastically cut back, enormous harm must result since private charity will not pick up the slack.

As with any correlation, of course, Almy's study by itself cannot prove causation. In Katz, *In the Shadow of the Poorhouse*, 44–45, Katz speculates that other factors—in particular, the proportion of women that worked outside the home—may explain why those cities that abolished outdoor relief had large amounts of private charity. In cities with high percentages of working women, Katz argues, local officials could safely vote to abolish outdoor relief, knowing that this would not bring about great hardship even if male breadwinners became unemployed. I find Katz's argument unconvincing because he only mentions two cities of the ten Almy listed as having abolished outdoor relief; furthermore, Katz's explanation would seem to show less need for aid, period, not just less need for government aid—yet the total amount of aid in the cities where public relief was abolished remained high.

Of course, that individuals seem to have risen to the occasion a century ago does not prove that this would occur today. However, there is a more general argument that explains why the results of the late-nineteenth-century United States should not be too surprising. Economists frequently discuss the "crowding-out" effect of government welfare, by which they mean that when government provides aid, individuals react by giving less than they otherwise would. However, if crowding-*out* occurs when there is government welfare, then we should expect crowding-*in* when there is not.[57] If people react to government welfare by decreasing their donations to charity, then it is plausible that they will react to its absence by increasing their donations.[58]

A natural response to this argument is that we cannot rely on crowding-in. Even if it is plausible that the abolition of state welfare would increase donations, this response goes, the increase may not be sufficient in today's circumstances. This is correct: it may not be. The question, though, is that if history does not support a claim of insufficiency, and if the crowding-out that occurs because of state welfare suggests that some crowding-in will occur when such welfare is absent, why think that private charity will be insufficient? Since so far no decisive reason has been found for egalitarians to favor state welfare over private charity, some kind of argument for insufficiency is needed if one wishes to tip the balance of reasons in favor of state welfare. The most likely argument at this point is that voluntary provision of charity is a public good, and as such will tend to be underproduced.

A standard argument that public goods will be underproduced if supplied voluntarily goes roughly as follows. A public good is non-excludable—it is impossible or exceedingly costly to exclude nonpayers or nonusers from using it—and is jointly consumed—one person's consumption or enjoyment of the good does not diminish others' consumption or enjoyment. Faced with the decision to contribute to a public good,

[57] Ziliak, "The End of Welfare and the Contradiction of Compassion," 60–62. It is worth noting that Ziliak believes that along with crowding-in comes what he calls "futility," by which he means that private charity will produce roughly the same negative effects as government welfare does as far as promoting moral hazard is concerned. He argues that if private charity's funding matches what government welfare expenditures would have been, then private charity will be no more effective in getting people into the workforce (ibid., 62–64). He thinks that the empirical evidence supports this claim, since the average duration of a spell on private charity in Indianapolis in the late nineteenth century was not significantly different from the average duration of a spell on government welfare in recent (pre–welfare reform) times. Ziliak's argument for futility, however, seems flawed: comparing the Indianapolis of 1870 to 1900 with recent times proves little, since other factors could obviously account for the lack of a significant difference. To support Ziliak's point, one would need to use, at the very least, a study of the same city (or cities) before and after a drastic reduction in state welfare, which is what Ziliak and Almy (see the previous note) each used to support the crowding-in thesis.

[58] Notice also that the abolition of state welfare means, all other things being equal, that the tax burden on individuals is lessened, which means that more money is available for donations to charity.

a rational person will reason in this manner: If I believe that some amount of the good will be provided by others' contributions, then since I can get the benefits of the good without paying for it, I will "free ride" and not contribute. If I think that some amount of the good will not be provided by others' contributions, then I still will not contribute, because my contribution will be wasted if it is insufficient to bring about the good, or to bring about enough of it so that the benefit I receive will outweigh the cost of my contribution. Thus, noncontribution is a "dominant strategy"—I will not contribute regardless of what others do.

But is provision of charity a public good? At first glance, it appears not to be, because it is excludable. Those who do not contribute to charity are excluded from the good, if what they value or what is a good for them is their own contribution to charity. By not contributing, people with these values or views are, by definition, excluded from the benefits of contributing, since the good for them is simply their contributing or something that accompanies it (e.g., psychic benefits, the sense that one has done the right thing, etc.).[59]

One can get out of this problem by assuming that what potential contributors value is simply that charity be provided, and that they are indifferent as to whether it is themselves or others who provide the

[59] Allen Buchanan, in Allen Buchanan, "The Right to a Decent Minimum of Health Care," *Philosophy and Public Affairs* 13, no. 1 (1984): 70–72, provides an argument that noncontribution will be a dominant strategy even if one values one's own contribution to charity. Imagine that potential contributors to charity realize that some of the most important forms of aid, such as the provision of sophisticated medical technology, require coordinated collective giving, and that they realize that these projects requiring coordinated giving may very well be more effective than any uncoordinated giving that people might perform. When deciding whether to give aid to such a coordinated collective effort, potential donors must consider two possibilities. If other people contribute enough to make the project that requires coordinated aid a success, a donor's contribution will provide little benefit, for it is others' aid, not his, that is decisive to the project's success. Furthermore, the donor also incurs a cost by giving to the project, since by giving he loses opportunities to channel the donated resources into alternative individual charitable acts whose success does not depend upon the actions of others. Thus, it is more rational for a donor to "free ride" (in scare quotes here because this is not free-riding in the literal sense) and provide aid instead to a project whose success does not depend upon others. Alternatively, if a donor thinks that too few people will give to the project needing coordinated aid, then he will lack assurance that his contribution would not be wasted; as a result, he will perform an individual act of charity whose success does not depend upon others. If enough potential contributors think along these lines, then an insufficient amount of aid will be given to those important large-scale projects that require coordinated giving.

Buchanan's argument fails because it depends on the assumption that after a certain threshold has been reached, and a project's success assured, one's contribution to it does not add any significant benefit. This assumption is clearly crucial to the argument: if it is false, a potential contributor's contribution need not be decisive to produce nontrivial benefits, and therefore the temptation not to contribute will sharply diminish. And while it is possible that there are projects for which the assumption is applicable, Buchanan provides no evidence that the most important elements of assistance for the needy are in fact such projects. Indeed, his own example of medical technology belies his argument. Even after sufficient funds have been provided to acquire, say, some piece of complicated medical equipment, more funding hardly produces nontrivial benefits: the equipment can be made more widely available, more people can be trained to use it, and so on.

contributions. Let us assume, for the sake of the argument, that a significant number of people think this way. For them, provision of charity seems to be a public good: noncontributors cannot be easily excluded from enjoying the benefits generated when others provide charity, and one's enjoying those benefits does not seem to diminish others' enjoyment. Some economists argue that for people like this, noncontribution will be a dominant strategy. If a potential contributor thinks that an adequate amount of charity will be provided, then he will free-ride, because he does not value contributing when others have provided an adequate amount. On the other hand, if he thinks that others will not provide an adequate amount of charity, then he lacks assurance that his contribution will be able to produce an adequate amount without others' contributions; hence, here again he will refrain from donating. Thus, no matter what a donor thinks others will do, he will withhold his contribution.[60]

This argument has two problems, however. First, the claim that there is an assurance problem is flawed. There is an assurance problem only if a potential donor does not value his contribution (or values it less than its cost) if it fails to produce, in conjunction with others, a *sufficient* amount of charity—in this context, a *sufficient* reduction in the problem of involuntary disadvantage.[61] It is this assumption that supports the claim that a potential donor will prefer withholding his contribution if he thinks enough others will not contribute; if he thought that there was some net value in helping reduce poverty or disadvantage even if a sufficient reduction was not achieved, he would contribute even if others did not. It is hard to see, however, why a potential donor of this type would place no or almost no value on the partial reduction of involuntary disadvantage. Even if someone thinks that one should address the whole problem, this implies not that addressing the parts has virtually *no* value, but only that doing so has less value than addressing the problem in its entirety.[62]

Thus, it seems that there are good grounds for contributing to charity even if one thinks that others will not adequately contribute. If this is so,

[60] An argument of this sort seems to have originated with Milton Friedman, *Capitalism and Freedom* (Chicago: University of Chicago Press, 1962), 190–91. Since then the argument has been employed by a variety of economists. See Robert Sugden, *Who Cares? An Economic and Ethical Analysis of Private Charity and the Welfare State* (London: Institute of Economic Affairs, 1983), 11–22; and the references cited therein. Friedman's argument only refers to a potential donor's lack of assurance that others will contribute sufficiently. This by itself will not show that noncontribution is a dominant strategy; one also needs to mention that free-riding will occur when others do contribute sufficiently. Hence I mention both of these elements in the text.

[61] This seems implicit in Friedman's presentation of the argument: "we might all of us be willing to contribute to the relief of poverty, *provided* everyone else did." Friedman, *Capitalism and Freedom*, 191. One explanation of why I need assurance that everyone else contributes is that I only value relieving the problem of poverty if a certain threshold of relief is produced.

[62] As pointed out in Robert Nozick, *Anarchy, State, and Utopia* (New York: Basic Books, 1974), 267.

then there is no dominant strategy here: I will not contribute (that is, I will free-ride) if others give a sufficient amount, but I will give if others do not. In game-theory parlance, we have a game of "chicken" here. There is no settled view about what strategy is rational in a game of chicken, but noncontribution is clearly not a dominant strategy.

A second problem with the public-goods argument is that a plausible case can be made that just as there really is no assurance problem, there really is no free-rider problem, either. This is because it is not obvious what amount of charity is "sufficient," and therefore one should probably reason as if providing some sufficient amount of charity is not a real option. In these circumstances, contribution becomes a dominant strategy—one gives because one is never sure that others have given a sufficient amount, and one values the bringing about of a partial reduction of poverty or disadvantage.

Since neither the historical evidence nor the public-goods argument supports the claim that private charity would be insufficient were state welfare abolished, and since the sensitivity of private aid to the amount of state welfare provided suggests that private aid would rise if state welfare were ended, it is hard to see what basis there is for claiming that private aid would be insufficient in the absence of state welfare. I have not, it is worth emphasizing, *proved* that private aid will be sufficient. This is probably impossible to prove. We need to keep in mind, however, where the burden of proof lies here. So far I have argued that egalitarians should view private charity as no worse (and possibly better) than state welfare. To raise the question "But will private charity be enough?" as a way of showing that state welfare is better, one needs a positive argument that private aid will be insufficient. If such an argument is lacking—and the common ways of providing such an argument do seem to fail—then the case I made in the previous sections still stands.

VII. Sending a Message

One of the functions of law or particular laws is that it or they can be used to express a community's—or a significant part of a community's—values.[63] Law can send a message, indicate that we—or at least some of us—stand for something, or show that we find certain actions or ways of life valuable. Egalitarians may want the law to express the value of aiding the involuntarily disadvantaged, and it may seem as if state welfare has a significant advantage over private charity in this regard. Since state welfare is provided by taxes from most citizens, while voluntary contributions to charity are provided only by some, state welfare may seem to

[63] This has been a central theme of some modern legal theorists—in particular, Cass Sunstein. See Cass Sunstein, "Social Norms and Social Roles," in Sunstein, *Free Markets and Social Justice* (New York: Oxford University Press, 1997), 32–69; and Cass Sunstein, "Incommensurability and Valuation in Law," in Sunstein, *Free Markets and Social Justice*, 70–107.

send a stronger message about the importance of aiding the involuntarily disadvantaged. Furthermore, in a democracy, elected representatives vote for welfare programs, which provides a message of a kind of social approval; this message is not matched when some members of the community voluntarily provide aid to the unfortunate.

An argument for the expressive function of particular laws works best when there is widespread consensus favoring those laws, the message of those laws is quite clear to those who vote for them, and this message remains clear during the existence of those laws and is understood and affirmed by the citizens. When any of these conditions are absent, the argument becomes weaker. When there is no obvious consensus favoring particular laws, there is no overriding social commitment. When laws have multiple and conflicting messages, talk about "the" message of these laws is exaggeration if not fiction. And when the original program changes in ways that were not anticipated, then even if there was a consensus among the voters and citizens about the message of particular laws at the time the program began, that meaning can disappear or change as the program evolves and as citizen sentiment alters.

In the context of state welfare, it is unclear whether any of the three conditions are met. There is no consensus (anymore) about state welfare: unlike social insurance, it is politically contentious. Someone might argue that there is a consensus that there should be state welfare, and that the disagreements are just about what form (e.g., conditional versus unconditional) it should take. But if this is so, then these disagreements are likely to involve disagreements about what values the law does or should express, which suggests that there is no obvious single message sent by state welfare. Does state welfare express our solidarity with the unfortunate, or let us off the hook so that we don't have to choose to expend our time and resources helping them? Does it show that we care for the unfortunate, or that we are buying them off so that they don't revolt? Does a work requirement or a time limit on benefits get people to take responsibility for themselves, or are these things vindictive attempts to blame the victim? All of these ways of interpreting "the" message of state welfare have some plausibility; the interpretation one accepts will depend on one's values and beliefs. As for the matter of changed or altered meanings, state welfare, like almost all major government programs, evolved slowly over time, and grew into something that was not anticipated. In the United States, for example, AFDC originated as part of the Social Security Act of 1935, and was originally intended to provide federal aid to widows with children.[64] No one at the time thought of it as creating a new federal entitlement for never-married women with chil-

[64] AFDC was a federal program giving matching grants to the states, many of which had already set up "mother's pensions" designed chiefly for widows with children. In effect, AFDC federalized mothers' pensions. See Tanner, *The End of Welfare*, 49; and the references cited therein.

dren. One could argue here that after it became apparent that the program had created this new entitlement, Congress nevertheless reappropriated funds for AFDC, thus demonstrating a social commitment to it. However, the link between reappropriating funds for an established program and expressing a social commitment to that program is rather weak. Established government programs are hard to alter or abolish. Indeed, AFDC was unpopular long before it was abolished in 1996.[65]

Suppose, however, that I am wrong, and the fact that state welfare creates larger numbers of "contributors" and generates a political endorsement allows it to send a stronger message than voluntary contributions do about aiding the unfortunate. On the other side of the ledger, there are three reasons why private charities are better vehicles than state welfare for expressing the value of aiding the unfortunate.[66]

First, private charities provide more flexibility in the way that one can express the value of, or participate in, aiding the unfortunate. One can donate money, time, or advice—or any combination thereof—to a charity, in accordance with one's own preferences. Indeed, as I mentioned in Section II, there will be a tendency for personal involvement in charities to increase if state welfare is abolished. Right now, unless one works for a welfare department, one's only participation in state welfare programs is simply as a taxpayer or as a recipient (or both).

Second, the fact that private charities are likely to be more decentralized than state welfare means that they provide the opportunity for people to express their commitments in ways that are more individualized and focused. One may, for example, wish to aid a specific group in a specific area with a specific problem through a specific kind of program. State welfare provides little or no opportunity for these kinds of very particularized ways of expressing one's values.

Third, suppose one believes that private charities or state welfare programs are not really expressing, or not expressing in an appropriate way, the value of helping the unfortunate. In these circumstances, the main strategy for rectifying this mismatch between an institution and one's values is to change the institution or leave it. Neither private charities nor government agencies have a comparative advantage with respect to ease of change: such ease depends on the size of the relevant institution, be it private or public, and on the degree of bureaucracy found in it. (It is easier to change the policies of a local government than it is to change those of the United Way; it is easier to change the policies of a small charity than it is to change those of a state or federal government.) However, while one can exit from a private charity when one believes it is not

[65] For a discussion of popular disenchantment with AFDC, see Theodore R. Marmor, Jerry L. Mashaw, and Philip L. Harvey, *America's Misunderstood Welfare State: Persistent Myths, Enduring Realities* (New York: Basic Books, 1990), 82–83.

[66] I am indebted here to N. Scott Arnold, "Postmodern Liberalism and the Expressive Function of Law," *Social Philosophy and Policy* 17, no. 1 (2000): 98–101.

really expressing one's deepest values, there is no exit, short of migration, from contributing to or participating in state welfare.

It may be replied that these three advantages of private charity can be maintained when there is state welfare, since state welfare only crowds out private charity to some degree. This is correct. The choice here, though, is between state welfare with some provision of charity and no state welfare with a greater provision of charity. Clearly, the latter provides more scope for the three advantages I mentioned above.

Thus, we are left with two possible ways to weigh the expressive advantages of state welfare versus private charities. If its larger numbers of "contributors" and its generation of a political endorsement of welfare gives state welfare some expressive advantages over private charity, then this is counterbalanced by private charity providing a more flexible and individualized way of expressing one's values as well as the ability to exit if one disapproves of a charity's activities. If, as I suspect, state welfare's alleged expressive advantages do not really let it send a stronger message than voluntary charity does, then the latter's three advantages catalogued above show that it is a better expressive vehicle than state welfare for sending a message about aiding the unfortunate. Either way, though, an egalitarian cannot use the expressive function of the law to tip the balance of reasons in favor of state welfare.

VIII. Conclusion

Egalitarians should view private charity as being no worse than state welfare. This has some rather important implications. First, egalitarians should not argue that attempts to reduce or get rid of state welfare are unjust. They can, of course, argue that such proposals will make matters worse, but their principles do not support the claim that state welfare is essential for justice. Second, egalitarians should endorse (some version of) welfare reform, that is, making state provision of aid contingent upon recipients agreeing to work, learn new skills, and so forth. I argued in Section V that egalitarians should favor conditional over unconditional aid, because only the former helps to reveal whether a recipient is willing to take responsibility for his future, and egalitarians should view taking responsibility as essential for enabling victims of bad brute luck to get their lives under their control.[67] While egalitarians need not favor private conditional aid over state conditional aid, a change from state unconditional aid to state conditional aid is an improvement from an egalitarian point of view.

[67] Patrick Boleyn-Fitzgerald comes to the same conclusion, using somewhat different arguments; see Patrick Boleyn-Fitzgerald, "Misfortune, Welfare Reform, and Right-Wing Egalitarianism," *Critical Review* 13, nos. 1–2 (1999): 141–63.

It is perhaps worth asking how egalitarianism ended up with institutional implications not that far removed from libertarianism. The answer can be found in a compliment G. A. Cohen paid Ronald Dworkin, who, Cohen said, "performed for egalitarianism the considerable service of incorporating within it the most powerful idea in the arsenal of the anti-egalitarian right: the idea of choice and responsibility."[68] This idea does indeed help to make egalitarianism an attractive doctrine: it links egalitarianism with most people's firm intuition that inequalities obtained through choice or voluntary assumption of risk are acceptable, and it provides a way to refute claims that egalitarianism is a doctrine that favors leveling down the productive, hard working, and deserving. However, the powerful idea of choice and responsibility also turns out to undermine support for forcing the affluent to surrender part of their income and wealth to the (involuntarily) disadvantaged. Since choice and brute luck are so interwoven, a coercive redistribution will unjustly take away voluntarily produced income and wealth, and, as I argued in Section IV, this seems no better than the injustice involved in relying on voluntary transfers to aid the unfortunate. Since egalitarians want people's lives to be governed as much as possible by choice, they should favor the system of aid that induces victims of bad brute luck to take responsibility for their lives—and a private system of charity, I argued in Section V, is at least as good as, and possibly better than, state welfare in performing this task.

Thus, the idea of choice and responsibility turns out to be a double-edged sword for egalitarians: it makes their principles more attractive, but it undermines the institutional implications that they thought followed from those principles. My hunch is that it is not just egalitarianism and libertarianism that place the idea of choice and responsibility at center-stage, but any credible political philosophy. If I am right, then the arguments in this essay suggest that the case for welfare-state redistribution is on shaky intellectual ground.

Philosophy, West Virginia University

[68] Cohen, "On the Currency of Egalitarian Justice," 933.

DOES THE WELFARE STATE HELP THE POOR?*

By Tyler Cowen

I. Introduction

Does the welfare state help the poor? This surprisingly simple question often generates more heat than light. By the welfare state, I mean transfer programs aimed at helping the poor through the direct redistribution of income. (This excludes general economic policy, antitrust, the volunteer military, and many other policies that affect the well-being of the poor.) Defenders of the welfare state often assume that the poor benefit from it, while critics suggest that the losses outweigh the gains. The most notable of such criticisms is Charles Murray's *Losing Ground*, which suggests that the welfare state has failed to achieve its stated ends.[1]

I attempt to revise both positions in this debate. I look first at how much the welfare state transfers to the poor, which turns out to be a surprisingly small sum, relative to the stock of wealth. This, of course, limits both the benefits and the costs of the welfare state. I then consider the empirical evidence for the traditional conservative argument that the welfare state is bad for the poor. In general, the evidence indicates that current recipients of welfare benefit from the transfers, contrary to what Murray and some other critics have suggested. Nonetheless, the welfare state appears to harm the interests of future generations and foreign citizens, and in this regard it does not help the poor more generally.

The debate over the welfare state thus should be recast. Common philosophical opinion suggests that impersonal consequentialism favors the welfare state by creating obligations to support others in need. If good consequences matter, and all persons are to count equally in the social-welfare function, it would seem that our obligations to the poor, through the welfare state, are very large. In contrast, I argue that impersonal consequentialism is more likely to militate *against* a welfare state, once the interests of all individuals are considered. The case for a welfare state

* The author wishes to thank Bryan Caplan, Robin Hanson, Rebecca Menes, Ellen Frankel Paul, David Schmidtz, and the contributors to this volume for useful comments and discussion.

[1] Charles Murray, *Losing Ground: American Social Policy 1950–1980*, 2d ed. (New York: Basic Books, 1994). The moral foundations of the welfare state have been criticized by Robert Nozick in his *Anarchy, State, and Utopia* (New York: Basic Books, 1974), and by David Schmidtz in David Schmidtz and Robert E. Goodin, *Social Welfare and Individual Responsibility* (Cambridge: Cambridge University Press, 1998). Schmidtz also questions whether the welfare state has in fact benefited the poor. On the other side of the philosophical debate, John Rawls, Michael Walzer, Robert E. Goodin, Ronald Dworkin, and Shelly Kagan number among the defenders of the welfare state.

rests upon assigning priority to the claims of one particular set of individuals—namely, currently living domestic citizens—over the claims of future generations and foreign citizens. Throughout the essay I focus on a U.S. context, although the central arguments can be generalized to any modern capitalist economy with a welfare state.

II. How Much Does the Welfare State Redistribute?

In the developed Western democracies, most government expenditures recycle tax dollars rather than create a net movement of tax dollars from rich individuals to poor individuals. These expenditures and their associated programs affect individual behavior at the margin, through taxes and subsidies, but many do not redistribute net wealth to the poor. Direct antipoverty programs account for only 8 percent of federal expenditures, rising to 14 percent if we count the federal contribution to Medicaid. Another estimate is that U.S. antipoverty expenditures comprised roughly 4 percent of gross domestic product (GDP) in 1992.[2]

The net effects of the U.S. Social Security system are complex, and I do not count them as part of the welfare state in this essay.[3] In any case, most of this redistribution is across generations rather than to the poor per se. Earlier generations (the current elderly) get the best deal, and subsequent generations receive increasingly inferior deals, given the pay-as-you-go feature of the system (i.e., the very first generation received benefits but did not pay a comparable tax burden). More generally, returns are tied to what individuals put into the system. Many aspects of Social Security are regressive, given that (1) the payroll tax stops at $76,200, and (2) the poor start working earlier (thus increasing their contribution) and tend to die sooner, thus lowering their payout.

Many of the largest and most expensive government programs benefit the rich or the middle class rather than the poor. Sociologist Christopher Jencks estimates that in 1980 only one-fifth of all social-welfare spending was explicitly aimed at the poor.[4] Subsidies to higher and lower education do most for the upper middle class. The real value of public goods is greater in wealthy communities, even relative to local tax expenditures. Many health care subsidies benefit the elderly, who tend to be wealthier

[2] For the 8 percent figure, see Rebecca Blank, *It Takes a Nation: A New Agenda for Fighting Poverty* (Princeton, NJ: Princeton University Press, 1997), 83. The 4 percent figure is from Sar A. Levitan, Garth L. Mangum, and Stephen L. Mangum, *Programs in Aid of the Poor* (Baltimore, MD: Johns Hopkins University Press, 1998), 41; this book also provides the best empirical survey of the American welfare state and its scope. These figures are the most widely accepted and best-informed estimates. Since the time of these estimates, there has not been a significant expansion in the size of the welfare state, and in some respects it has been curtailed.

[3] I do not count Medicare either, which subsidizes many well-off elderly people.

[4] Christopher Jencks, *Rethinking Social Policy: Race, Poverty, and the Underclass* (Cambridge, MA: Harvard University Press, 1997), 76.

than the national average. Our tax system is only weakly progressive, all things considered, and many kinds of taxes, such as sales taxes, have a regressive impact. Milk price supports, most tariffs, and corporate welfare are but a few of the many regressive policies enacted by the American government.

The American welfare program that comes closest to representing a pure transfer payment is the program that, before the Clinton-era welfare reforms, was called AFDC, or Aid to Families with Dependent Children. AFDC, which originated in 1935, provided welfare supplements to families below a certain income level. AFDC now has become Temporary Assistance for Needy Families (TANF), which provides block grants to the states to help finance their welfare programs. Federal TANF expenditures have been capped yearly at $16.4 billion through 2002, or less than a fifth of 1 percent of 1999 GDP.[5] In-kind assistance adds to this total but does not significantly change the picture. The food stamps program, for instance, costs about $21 billion a year, just slightly more than TANF expenditures.

The point is simple. In any given year, the welfare state engages in net redistribution of only a *very* small portion of total wealth. This is true even in the more extensive European welfare states.

Let us look at some numbers more closely. Consider an economy where government expenditures account for 50 percent of GDP. As a very generous approximation, perhaps one-fifth of those expenditures represent net transfers of wealth to the poor. So 10 percent of GDP is redistributed, in net terms, in a given year. If we are considering the extent of egalitarianism, however, the relevant question is how much of the total stock of wealth is transferred. Given typical growth rates, a national stock of wealth might plausibly be twenty or thirty times greater than the output of a single year. For purposes of a very conservative estimate, let us say twenty times.

Given these numbers, each year only one-half of 1 percent of the national stock of marketable wealth is redistributed to the poor, on net. The real extent of redistribution, however, is arguably much lower, since the true stock of wealth includes more than just the marketable commodities represented in national income statistics. A variety of assets have little or no measurable market value, even though they contribute greatly to individual well-being. This includes human capital, the value of leisure time, the value of one's marriage and friends, and the general intellectual and cultural heritage of mankind, much of which has entered the public domain or is available very cheaply. For the most part, these "goods" are not redistributed by welfare policy. It is difficult to value these goods scientifically, relative to the stock of material wealth. But if we think they are equal in value to the stock of material wealth, the calculations suggest

[5] See Levitan, Mangum, and Mangum, *Programs in Aid of the Poor*, 80.

that in a given year only one-quarter of 1 percent of the stock of total wealth is redistributed. And this is the figure for a relatively generous welfare state, one more generous than the United States is.

Of course, less conservative estimates could drive the figure down considerably. If the capital stock is worth thirty years of output (rather than twenty years), and if net redistribution is only 5 percent of GDP (rather than 10 percent), then only one-twelfth of 1 percent of the stock of total wealth would be redistributed each year.

Egalitarians may regard these numbers with disappointment, but I view the matter in a different light. They show that the welfare state represents a smaller philosophical difference between classical liberals and modern liberals than is usually believed. For better or worse, the welfare state is not a widespread engine for wealth redistribution, relative to the available total. Individuals who call themselves egalitarians usually are only very weakly egalitarian, once the larger picture is examined. In reality, few commentators wish to put all property rights on the table, regardless of their rhetoric. The available alternatives include very moderate redistribution, extremely moderate redistribution, and no redistribution at all. Complete or fully egalitarian redistribution is simply not on the agenda.

III. Costs to the Poor?

Given these numbers, it is plausible that the welfare state yields only small benefits to the poor, in aggregate dollar terms. (Of course, to a single poor individual, a small dollar amount may still make a big difference.) Nonetheless, some critics wish to go further and argue that the welfare state makes the poor worse off. Most notably, Murray portrays in *Losing Ground* a world where rising welfare expenditures have led to increasing poverty and worsening social conditions.

This critique of the welfare state involves an analytic tension. In most matters, conservatives and libertarians argue from neoclassical and Chicago-school economic theories. In these approaches, a gift of cash always makes individuals better off, as evidenced by the classroom demonstration of how such gifts shift individuals onto higher "indifference curves." This is a basic lesson of any intermediate course in microeconomics, regardless of the political persuasion of the instructor. Furthermore, it does not matter whether strings or conditions are attached to the gift. After getting the gift, individuals have more options, and they can always turn down the money if the conditions are too onerous or unpleasant.

When it comes to welfare payments, critics often discard or neglect this argument. The cash payments are portrayed as breaking up families, destroying self-dignity, and creating a destructive culture of welfare dependency. The notion of freely choosing individuals who equate costs and benefits at the margin is suddenly ignored or de-emphasized. Of course, if receiving welfare makes these individuals worse off, they could refuse to cash the check or give the money away. In fact, some programs, such as AFDC/TANF, find that as many as a third of the potential recipients do not apply for the benefits. Some may not apply for benefits out of simple ignorance, but others do not find it worthwhile to work through the welfare bureaucracy, given that they expect their lot to improve through other means. In other words, individuals who do not expect to benefit turn the money down.[6]

The available evidence supports the view that "transfer programs unambiguously make people less poor," to cite a literature survey by economist Rebecca Blank. Controlled experiments in this area are hard to come by, but the few we have suggest that welfare does benefit those who receive the money. In 1981, the Reagan administration changed AFDC rules to take 12 percent of the recipients off the rolls, essentially the least poor of the AFDC families. Several studies in the 1980s tracked these recipients, and found that subsequent private sector employment did not make up for the loss in income. A cross-national comparison of the United States and Canada shows that work behavior of single-parent families is roughly comparable, but that there is much less poverty amongst such families in Canada, primarily because the level of public assistance is higher. All of this evidence suggests that abolishing welfare would make its current recipients worse off, not better off.[7]

Nor do government welfare programs appear to displace an equivalent amount of private charity. Private giving does not vary inversely with the size of government programs, and there is little evidence of a "crowding-out" effect. Many private charities, in fact, rely on government funding to some extent. Private charitable giving to the poor, defined in narrow terms, runs in the range of $10 to $15 billion a year, and few observers believe that this sum is capable of significant augmentation in the short run, regardless of government policy.[8] Total philanthropy is of course much higher, and many of these donations benefit the poor as well.

[6] On nonapplicants, see Blank, *It Takes a Nation*, 155. That many do not apply for the benefits suggests that the gain to the recipients is less than the full value of the cash. This further supports the claim that the egalitarian effects of the welfare state are small.

[7] The quotation summarizing the evidence is from ibid., 135. On AFDC studies, see, for instance, Sheldon Danziger, "Budget Cuts as Welfare Reform," *American Economic Review* 73, no. 2 (1983): 65–70; Robert M. Hutchens, "The Effects of the Omnibus Budget Reconciliation Act of 1981 on AFDC Recipients," *Research in Labor Economics* 8 (1986): 351–87; and Robert A. Moffitt and Douglas A. Wolf, "The Effect of the 1981 Omnibus Budget Reconciliation on Welfare Recipients and Work Incentives," *Social Service Review* 62, no. 2 (1987): 247–60. On Canada, see Rebecca M. Blank and Maria J. Hanratty, "Responding to Need: A Comparison of Social Safety Nets in Canada and the United States," in David Card and Richard B. Freeman, eds., *Small Differences That Matter* (Chicago: University of Chicago Press, 1993), 191–232.

[8] Blank, *It Takes a Nation*, chap. 5.

Cutting welfare benefits nonetheless would reduce the net size of the transfer to current recipients.

I sometimes hear the claim that the welfare state presents a prisoner's dilemma to poor communities. (I have not seen this argument in print in these terms, though I think it is implicit in the arguments one does find.) That is, perhaps each single individual is better off taking the cash, given that other individuals take the cash. But the collective effect is to make the entire community worse off, due to some increase in dependency or some destruction of values. We might imagine, for instance, that welfare dependency turns a formerly vibrant inner city community into a ghetto.

The first question is whether this argument is empirically true. Even if we accept the stated mechanism as analytically coherent, it may not apply to most of the poor. Just slightly more than 10 percent of the poor and 25 percent of all black poor live in urban ghettos. American poverty is more rural than is commonly recognized.[9]

Even as a matter of logic, the prisoner's dilemma argument is unlikely to lead to significant losses. The costs of a prisoner's dilemma are limited whenever individuals have the option of leaving the game, or in this case the option of leaving the community. The United States has many communities that are not wrecked by widespread acceptance of welfare, some of them quite poor and with low residential rents. Furthermore, the poor have proved to be extremely mobile throughout American history. Given the possibility of exit, well-being in a welfare-dependent community cannot fall below the level of well-being available in other communities.

The aggregate evidence provides little support for the view that cash transfers hurt those who receive them. If we examine *Losing Ground*, usually considered the seminal work in this regard, little empirical evidence is presented with direct bearing on this question, despite the ambitious claim embodied in the title of the book.

Murray does provide one central fact, which is presented as follows:

> The unadorned statistic gives pause. In 1968, as Lyndon Johnson left office, 13 percent of Americans were poor, using the official definition. Over the next twelve years, our expenditures on social welfare quadrupled. And in 1980, the percentage of poor Americans was—13 percent. Can it be that nothing has changed?[10]

This fact does not establish that welfare programs have had no impact. In most cases, income-transfer programs bring individuals closer to the poverty line, rather than pushing them over the poverty line. (If welfare pushed people over the poverty line, the incentive effects might be disastrous.) Even if a constant percentage of the population remains below

[9] Ibid., 27.
[10] Murray, *Losing Ground*, 8.

the poverty line, they have higher real incomes because of welfare. Murray's statistic indicates that the welfare state will not "end poverty in our time," but it does not show that the expenditures fail to make people better off.[11]

Furthermore, the poverty line is a misleading measure of well-being, as it does not count in-kind transfers. Jencks attempts to adjust for this factor and estimates that the real "net" poverty rate was 29 percent in 1950, 18 percent in 1965, and 10 percent in 1980. This shows more improvement than Murray's statistic would indicate.[12]

A second set of corrections involves inflation. Many economists believe that the consumer price index (CPI) has been overestimated, typically in the range of 0.8 to 1.2 percentage points per year. If this is the case, real incomes are higher than measured and poverty has been declining at a higher rate than the statistics would indicate. Under one common way of adjusting for this measurement error, the poverty rate fell from 19 percent in 1965 to 13 percent in 1980. This adjustment, unfortunately, does not take in-kind transfers into account, and thus it differs from the numbers stated directly above; I have found no single comprehensive correction for all the potential biases in the poverty rate.[13]

Finally, the poverty rate may have been sluggish for non-welfare-related reasons. It is commonly recognized that relative wages for unskilled labor have been falling. Murray's comparison also starts in a boom year, 1968, and ends in a recession, 1980. Economic cyclicality has always been a significant determinant of the poverty rate. The 1965–80 period also saw slow increases in productivity growth, relative to the historical average (although part of this effect goes away if we adjust for CPI mismeasurements).

An alternative attempt to measure poverty looks at data on *consumption* rather than on formally reported income. For individuals living from savings, or engaged in black-market activity, their consumption level will provide a better measure of how poor they are than will their income. The measurement techniques used to support this approach are by no means uncontroversial, but consumption data provide further support for the view that the poverty rate has been falling. Economist Dale W. Jorgenson, for instance, uses consumption data to find a low and declining rate of

[11] For some exact numbers on how welfare programs lower the "poverty gap," the difference between the incomes of the poor and the poverty line, see Blank, *It Takes a Nation*, 139–40.

[12] See Jencks, *Rethinking Social Policy*, 72–74, on various ways of adjusting the poverty rate.

[13] On inflation, see Richard W. Stevenson, "Economists Readjust Estimate of Overstatement of Inflation," *New York Times*, March 1, 2000, C14. Murray himself admits that the poverty line does not count various benefits, although he correctly notes that even an improved measure of the poverty line does not show continual upward progress for the poor; Murray, *Losing Ground*, 63–64. For a comprehensive discussion of how poverty is measured, see Constance F. Citro and Robert T. Michael, eds., *Measuring Poverty: A New Approach* (Washington, DC: National Academy Press, 1995).

poverty; another economist, Daniel T. Slesnick, finds that the poverty rate in 1989 was only 2.2 percent.[14]

Since the publication of Murray's book, we also have more years of data on poverty. From 1994 to 1997, for instance, the (unadjusted) income-poverty rate declined to 10.3 percent.[15] This is more likely due to economic growth rather than the welfare state, but it does show that the welfare state does not *prevent* the poor from bettering their lot.

Beyond his single statistic—the 1968–80 comparison—Murray offers little or no evidence that the welfare state has made the poor worse off. He effectively catalogues and criticizes a variety of ineffective government programs in the areas of education, housing, and crime, among others, but he does not focus on how the welfare state has affected the overall well-being of the poor.

One commonly cited cost of the welfare state is more properly regarded as a benefit. Especially in the American context, critics frequently charge that the welfare state encourages single, poor women to have more babies than they otherwise would. Murray, for instance, writes that "[i]n 1984, at every college speaking engagement I had to defend the proposition that illegitimate births are a problem for children and for society. Now only the most militant feminists argue otherwise."[16] Yet under most plausible assumptions, illegitimate births should not be counted as a cost. The new life created is certainly a benefit to the individual who lives it. Furthermore, that individual is likely to pay taxes over the course of his or her life, thus making the birth subsidy self-financing. I am not arguing that we face a moral compulsion to increase the number of people to the highest possible level, but certainly such population increases should not be counted as a net cost, especially in an uncrowded country such as the United States.[17]

Illegitimate births prove costly only to the extent that these babies grow up to be violent criminals. But if the expected value of another individual is positive, any birth-inducing effects of welfare are unlikely to involve net social costs. Certainly in the European context, where violent crime rates are relatively low, the new babies are likely to prove to be net benefits. Even in the United States, with a much higher violent crime rate, welfare babies are not typically future drug pushers and murderers. As noted above, poverty is more likely a rural than an urban phenomenon.

Nor should we recoil at the fact that the welfare state might encourage births amongst *unwed* mothers, as those babies otherwise might not have

[14] See Dale W. Jorgenson, "Did We Lose the War on Poverty?" *Journal of Economic Perspectives* 12, no. 1 (1998): 79–96; and Daniel T. Slesnick, "Gaining Ground: Poverty in the Postwar United States," *Journal of Political Economy* 101, no. 1 (1993): 1–38.

[15] See Garth Mangum, Andrew Sum, and Neeta Fogg, "Poverty Ain't What It Used to Be," *Challenge* 43, no. 2 (2000): 97–130.

[16] Murray, *Losing Ground*, xvi.

[17] For a more detailed discussion of normative population theory, see Tyler Cowen, "What Do We Learn from the Repugnant Conclusion?" *Ethics* 106, no. 4 (1996): 754–75.

been conceived or carried to term. If a mother has a child "only because of welfare," then we know the system is producing at least one benefit, whatever other costs it may involve.[18]

For these reasons, I believe that the traditional conservative critique of the welfare state fails. Within the context of this debate, the welfare state does appear to bring net benefits to the poor. I will now consider two additional (and stronger) arguments that welfare may damage the interests of the poor, the "growth argument" and the "international argument."

IV. The Growth Argument against the Welfare State

Although I have argued that the welfare state helps the people who receive the cash, this does not imply that the welfare state benefits the poor more generally. The secondary consequences of having a welfare state may in fact be negative for a wide variety of individuals, including the future poor.

Many of the future poor, of course, will not be so poor by today's standards, due to continued economic growth. Nonetheless, they will still be poor by the standards of their time, and the poorest of them may be poor by the standards of any time. We do not cease worrying about today's poor simply because some of them enjoy comforts that Napoleon never dreamed of. In similar fashion, we should not assume that poverty will disappear as an issue in the future.

If the welfare state damages the prospects for economic growth, it is unclear whether it benefits the poor as a general class. As shown in the early part of this essay, redistribution has only a very limited ability to make the poor better off, given the small amount that is redistributed. As a matter of empirical fact, it is economic growth that lifts most people out of poverty, not transfer payments. If we consider the city-state of Hong Kong, we see that virtually all of its citizens were poor in 1950. By 1990 Hong Kong had per capita income comparable to other developed countries, even given that it absorbed a periodic influx of poor migrants from mainland China. This elimination of poverty was fueled almost completely by economic growth.

The economic growth of the West has been an effective antipoverty mechanism in similar fashion. By modern measures, most of the individuals in the 1920s were poor. Yet the 1920s, in their time, were thought of

[18] The elasticity of response, however, appears to be small. See Robert Moffitt, "Incentive Effects of the U.S. Welfare System: A Review," *Journal of Economic Literature* 30, no. 1 (1992): 1-61; and Blank, *It Takes a Nation*, 148–51 for a survey of the evidence. It also should be noted that a split family is not a cost per se to whatever extent the welfare state causes families to dissolve. The higher income, for instance, gives women who receive welfare the option to leave abusive men. Many of the costs of split families are internalized by family members, which suggests that increased freedom of decision-making in this regard brings net social benefits rather than net costs. See Jencks, *Rethinking Social Policy*, 84–85.

as a highly prosperous decade. Similarly, about one-third of the American population was poor in the 1950s, by current measures, although, again, at the time the 1950s were regarded as wealthy without precedent. The difference, again, comes from continued economic growth.

Casual observers frequently underestimate the effects of compounded economic growth on real income. If the annual growth rate of American GDP had been one percentage point lower between 1870 and 1990, America today would be no richer than Mexico. Similarly, if a country grows at a rate of 5 percent per annum, it takes just over 80 years for it to go from a per capita income of $500 to a per capita income of $25,000. At a growth rate of 1 percent, that same improvement takes 393 years.[19]

It remains an open question how much the welfare state limits growth, but some negative effect appears to be present. First, the empirical literature on economic growth suggests that noninfrastructure government spending lowers the growth rate, although systematic data on welfare-state spending per se have not been available.[20]

Second, a welfare state will cause some people to substitute welfare dependency for private work, thus lowering the number of individuals in the active workforce or causing them to work less hard. Welfare payments are typically withdrawn from individuals as they earn more income, and thus serve as a high marginal tax rate on the economic efforts of the poor. The poor could be engaging in more productive exchange with other individuals in the economy, but to some extent they desist for fear of losing welfare benefits.[21]

Third, the taxes used to support the welfare state discourage taxpayers from working or otherwise creating economic value. Measures of the "excess burden" of taxation vary, but most public-finance economists regard as reasonable a figure of twenty cents on each dollar raised in the United States, and more in countries with higher marginal tax rates, such as several Western European nations and Canada. In other words, for each dollar raised by taxation, the resulting distortions bring twenty cents' worth of cost.

[19] Schmidtz discusses some of these numbers at Schmidtz and Goodin, *Social Welfare and Individual Responsibility*, 61; I have calculated others myself.

[20] Robert J. Barro, "Economic Growth in a Cross Section of Countries," *Quarterly Journal of Economics* 106, no. 2 (1991): 407–43, is the classic study here.

[21] One obvious (but incorrect) measure of welfare's real economic burden is to look at the quantity of money spent on welfare programs. This is the measure most frequently cited by critics of the welfare state (though they do not wish to restrict the costs to this magnitude). We have already seen that the redistributive component here is quite small. More importantly, counting these expenditures as direct costs neglects the difference between monetary transfers and actual consumption of real resources. The transfer of money from one person to another does not itself occasion economic costs, net of the administrative costs of transfer. One individual has more money, and another individual has less money, but no real resources are destroyed. The correct measure of the costs of the welfare state will involve the economic distortions it creates.

The extensive welfare states of Western Europe typically are bundled with labor-market protections and interventions. It is not politically or economically feasible to give the nonworking significantly more risk protection than the working. Western European welfare states therefore tend to create a privileged class of working "insiders" with high real wages, high benefits, and near-guaranteed positions of employment. This practice, of course, lowers the number of new jobs that are created, limits labor-market mobility, and raises unemployment (which also creates a built-in constituency for the welfare programs). Even politicians on the left, such as German prime minister Gerhard Schroeder, are looking for ways to cut welfare-state expenditures given these costs. To these considerations we may also add the administrative costs of the welfare state and the expenditures of real resources on lobbying the state for welfare privileges.

A. Growth rates vs. once-and-for-all changes

Once we postulate the costs of the welfare state, the question still remains whether the economy bears the costs up front in a once-and-for-all fashion, or whether there is a systematic decline in the growth *rate* over time. This somewhat arcane distinction is in fact of great importance for evaluating the welfare state.

Economists sometimes use growth models, such as the model of Robert Solow, to argue that a decrease in wealth lowers the base on which growth occurs, but has no necessary implications for the succeeding rate of growth. To use a biological metaphor, the Solow growth model portrays the economy as akin to a lobster. If an arm is lopped off, another arm grows rapidly to replace it, and in the long run the economy looks virtually the same and is only slightly worse off. In economic terms the mechanism runs as follows: A decline in the capital stock raises the rate of return on capital, which induces more savings, which tends to restore a higher capital stock. In the long run, an increase in the savings rate makes up for "destroyed" resources. The very rapid recovery of some economies after wars or major natural disasters would appear to represent this mechanism in operation.

But the Solow model, properly understood, still allows the welfare state to lower the rate of economic growth. In the Solow model, a distortion lowers the growth rate when it causes the economy to develop new technologies and new ideas at a slower rate. In this case, there is no mechanism of replaceability to restore the initial state of affairs and the initial rate of growth.

A welfare state will plausibly have a negative effect on innovation. If individual labor is withdrawn from the productive sector of the economy, the rate of discovery is likely to fall. Both the poor and the taxpaying nonpoor will work less when a welfare state is in place. If we think of research and development, broadly construed, as one kind of work, we can expect the rate of growth to decline. Even if the poor do not participate in ideas-production directly, they do so indirectly. To provide a simple example, to the extent it is harder or more costly to hire good janitors, and other forms of cheap labor, fewer research laboratories will be opened. Note that these costs are not "replaced" by an increase of labor supply or investment elsewhere in the economy. The welfare state permanently discourages various individuals from contributing to technological development and thus lowers the rate of economic growth in lasting fashion.[22]

In the Solow model, the induced lowering of the growth rate might be small. First, the poor might not create much economic value in any case (they are, after all, poor and thus relatively unproductive, in economic terms). Second, to some extent welfare recipients will move into the underground economy, where they can keep their welfare benefits without reporting their income. Third, a decline in labor supply may lead parents to spend more time caring for their children, which may have some offsetting positive effects on long-run growth.[23]

Even if the induced decline in the growth rate is small, however, the difference in terms of national income will compound over time. Over a long enough temporal horizon, real income in a world with a large welfare state will be *much* lower than it would be in a world with no welfare state or a smaller welfare state.

[22] In Robert E. Goodin et al., *The Real Worlds of Welfare Capitalism* (Cambridge: Cambridge University Press, 1999), the authors argue that a democratic social-welfare state does not lower the rate of economic growth, but they use only two data points, the Netherlands and the United States. Their conclusion is contradicted by the findings of more general studies, such as that of Barro, "Economic Growth in a Cross Section of Countries."

[23] When individuals receive welfare, they cut back their labor supply for two reasons: an "income effect" and a "substitution effect." The income effect arises because the individual has more cash and feels less need to work, just as Hugh Hefner might choose to consume leisure at the expense of more income. This is simply an optimal reallocation of the individual's portfolio and occasions no real economic cost. The substitution effect arises because individuals find that additional work, at the margin, brings in less than otherwise, given that welfare is not awarded to high earners. Unlike the income effect, the substitution effect represents foregone gains from trade and thus involves a real economic loss. Ironically, many critics of the welfare state offer an account under which the income effect is relatively large, implying that the real economic costs of welfare are small. Popular criticisms frequently allege that welfare recipients are lazy or otherwise disinclined to work; sometimes a "culture of dependency" is postulated. To the extent these charges are true, the gains from trade from having the poor work are relatively small. The poor would produce little, but they would hate work intensely, meaning it would be hard to profitably employ them. They would shirk work at the first chance they got, if they could manage to live by any alternative means at all. In other words, this account postulates that the income effect is the primary reason why the poor do not work once they receive welfare. In this case, however, the economic costs of welfare are correspondingly small. It does not save the critics to charge that welfare "makes" these individuals lazy. That is precisely the income effect we are talking about. If individuals stop working once they have a little cash, they prefer not to work given that distribution of wealth. Again, this does not count as a real economic cost of the welfare state. For empirical evidence on the incentive effects of the welfare state, see Moffitt, "Incentive Effects of the U.S. Welfare System."

Under alternative growth scenarios, such as "increasing-returns models," the negative effects of a welfare state can be even more serious. In an increasing-returns model, the welfare state lowers the rate of growth directly by shrinking the private sector. Intuitively, we can think of the increasing-returns concept as suggesting that resources multiply themselves. The larger the economy, the faster it will grow. To continue with the biological metaphor, cutting the arm off in this case does not lead to the regeneration of a new arm (as in the Solow model), but rather causes other parts of the body to decay as well, perhaps through the spread of gangrene. Increasing-returns models imply that policy mistakes, even small ones, have disastrous long-run consequences; in other words, there are no small mistakes.

Whether the Solow model or the increasing-returns model better describes reality has been the subject of ongoing debate.[24] It is impossible to resolve or even survey this debate in an essay of this length. Nonetheless, the welfare state will lower the rate of economic growth to some extent in either model, although the effect is greater if there are increasing returns to scale. The welfare state thus provides benefits for the current poor at the (great) expense of the future poor. Whether the Solow model or increasing-returns model is correct simply determines how far into the future we must look to find big losers.

B. Discounting the future?

There is no commonly accepted framework for evaluating whether a current benefit to the poor, as provided by welfare, outweighs the larger losses to be suffered by the poor in the future. Many economists typically apply a positive rate of discount to make current and future magnitudes commensurable. They make a future benefit worth less than a current benefit by some magnitude roughly comparable to the market rate of interest. This procedure, however, fails to yield clear answers in this context. Economic cost-benefit analysis applies only to the extent that the relevant benefits and costs are small for all relevant individuals, relative to their stock of wealth. More precisely, the benefits and costs should keep the marginal utility of money roughly constant for all individuals involved; otherwise we do not have a constant measuring rod for comparing the two states of affairs. But if a policy imposes very large costs on temporally distant individuals by lowering the growth rate, we are no longer dealing with small changes in wealth for the individuals concerned. Cost-benefit analysis then will not apply in traditional form, and

[24] See the symposium on this topic in the Winter 1994 issue of the *Journal of Economic Perspectives*.

there will be no unambiguously correct rate of discount within an economic framework.[25]

The use of a positive discount rate may be subject to more fundamental objections as well. Many philosophers and some economists are skeptical of placing a positive discount rate on the well-being of future individuals simply because those individuals are more distant in time. If we use a discount rate of zero, the lower growth rate will mean that the future costs outweigh the present benefit. This would incline us to reject a welfare state, given its very large negative impact on future generations.[26]

I find that the zero-discounting argument is frequently accepted by individuals with left-wing political views, and usually dismissed by those on the right. But in reality, the political implications of zero discounting, when consistently pursued, may push us toward conclusions that the right may welcome more than the left. Zero discounting implies a rather ruthless commitment to maximizing the rate of economic growth, more typically a right-wing position than a left-wing position. This does not necessarily imply no welfare state at all, since some amount of welfare spending may create political stability and thus increase the rate of economic growth. Nonetheless, welfare spending would be justified on consequentialist grounds only insofar as it contributed to economic growth in some fashion or another.

This essay will not attempt to survey and resolve the issues surrounding the discount rate controversy, which are beyond the scope of this investigation. We are nonetheless left with the following, regardless of the appropriate rate of discount: If we institute a welfare state today, at some point in the sufficiently distant future many people, including the future poor, will be much, much poorer. It cannot be said that the welfare state makes the poor better off in general terms, once we consider the future.

V. The International Argument

A. The welfare state and immigration

Just as the welfare state hurts future generations, so does it hurt individuals in other countries. Most directly, the higher the level of welfare

[25] For a standard defense of discounting, see John Broome, "Discounting and Welfare," *Philosophy and Public Affairs* 23, no. 2 (1994): 128–56, although Broome too is wary of using discounting for very large policy changes. The point can be put another way as well. The market rate of interest represents the willingness of market participants to trade off the marginal dollar. When a given policy causes significant changes in wealth, it is no longer just the marginal dollar we are evaluating, and to that extent the market interest rate does not express the relevant resource trade-offs.

[26] This conclusion, of course, does not follow *a priori*. It might be the case, for instance, that we think the world will end soon, or stop growing, with or without a welfare state. For a skeptical view on discounting, see Tyler Cowen and Derek Parfit, "Against the Social Discount Rate," in Peter Laslett and James Fishkin, eds., *Justice between Age Groups and Generations* (New Haven, CT: Yale University Press, 1992), 144–61.

payments, the more difficult it is for a country to absorb large numbers of immigrants.

The dilemma is simple. If welfare in a given country promises a certain dollar sum a year, this will stand above the real income in most poor countries. People will immigrate simply to receive the welfare benefits, putting a strain on the system. Continuation of the system therefore requires limits on immigration. Most treatments of the welfare state neglect this cost or ignore it altogether.

One alternative is for a country to take in many migrants, but not offer them full or any welfare privileges. Germany, for instance, has pursued such a policy with its *Gastarbeiter* (guest worker) system, most notably for the immigrant Turks. The United States also has moved to limit certain welfare benefits to citizens rather than permanent residents. Even these nations, however, must limit the number of entrants. If the number of immigrants becomes sufficiently high, it will prove difficult to deny them full political rights. The Israelis have experienced a comparable problem with the Palestinians, to cite one example, which is one reason why they allowed the creation of a separate Palestinian state.

It is difficult to estimate how far differential treatment of foreign residents can extend. We do, however, find some clues from the German context. Currently there is a strong, but not overwhelming, movement to give full legal status to the *Gastarbeiter* Turks in Germany. These individuals currently comprise 2.4 percent of the population in Germany. German critics of freer immigration frequently point out that if many more Turks were let in, it would be hard to deny them the same rights as German citizens. As a very rough estimate, then, we might believe that a doubling or tripling of the number of Turks would lead to an end to differential treatment. In the case of Germany, the relevant threshold is a relatively low one. Differential treatment can be extended to a small percentage of the population, but probably not to 10 or 15 percent. Differential treatment thus has severe political limits, however much economic sense it might make.

If our only goal is to make people less poor, the most effective antipoverty program might be to abolish or shrink the welfare state and allow in more immigrants. We can think of nineteenth-century and early twentieth-century America as providing an example here. During this period, there was essentially free immigration and not much of a welfare state. Many people suffered greatly under their poverty, but many others rose to riches or at least to a middle-class existence. Even if some poor Americans experienced lower wages because of the new workers, the immigrants gained far more in wages and wealth than the poor Americans lost.[27]

[27] Of course, many would-be migrants might not improve their lot by switching countries. They might be suffering from malnutrition, be illiterate, be elderly, and so on, and thus be unable to exploit their new environment. The point remains that looser immigration standards would attract more people who would benefit from the change in venue.

It therefore misses the point to argue that welfare payments benefit those individuals who receive them. The relevant comparison also must include those individuals who, as a result of welfare, have a smaller chance of being able to enter the richer country. And unlike welfare states, most forms of labor immigration raise the rate of economic growth rather than lower it. Lowering welfare payments and raising immigration rates would benefit future generations, at least provided that immigration did not rise to the point of extreme crowding.

We do not know that freer immigration would do more to alleviate poverty than current welfare states do, but the possibility cannot be dismissed. Poor immigrants to richer countries enjoy significantly higher real incomes as a result of their migration, and immigration arguably is the most effective antipoverty program that has been devised. Immigration not only enriches the new arrivee, but also supports remittances back home. Many nations already receive a significant percentage of their national income from remittances; it is common for remittances to account for 20 percent of national income or more in a poor country.[28] Freer immigration would further support this kind of transfer.

There is less evidence on how much a welfare state requires limits on migration, but a Western welfare-state existence provides a higher standard of material living than most of the individuals in the Third World currently enjoy. If migrants had free access to those benefits, we would expect the rate of migration to be very high, probably unsustainably high. The ability of migrants to receive welfare benefits is already a significant political issue throughout Western Europe. In the United States the welfare privileges of noncitizens were restricted in 1996, when health care and food stamp benefits were cut for legal immigrants.

B. Patriotic egalitarianism

The welfare state damages citizens of foreign countries in yet another sense. The money spent on domestic welfare payments could have been sent abroad to people who are much poorer. Economists correctly insist that the appropriate measure of the cost of a policy is its "opportunity cost," or in other words, the options that are forgone when a choice is made.

Economist Gordon Tullock frequently refers to the dilemma of "patriotic egalitarianism." Tullock notes that most advocates of redistribution are inconsistent, favoring redistribution only within national boundaries. If we are to take antipoverty motivations seriously, however, we should also redistribute resources from the United States, or other rich countries,

[28] See various country studies put together by the Library of Congress's Federal Research Division; several can be found at www.loc.gov/harvest/query-lc by searching under "remittances."

to the very poor countries in the world. In fact, almost all of the so-called "poor" in the United States are wealthy by global standards. A significant percentage of today's American poor have automobiles, televisions, and telephones, to name a few items that are uncommon in, say, Haiti.[29]

A consistent welfare policy, if based on egalitarian or antipoverty reasoning, would produce few disbursements within this country, if any. Given that practical considerations limit the size of the U.S. welfare state, domestic recipients will never be the neediest individuals at the margin or even close to it, given the vast scope of global poverty.

Foreign aid, of course, is a relatively small percentage of the budget, well under 1 percent in the United States, and it is also unpopular with voters. But there is no reason why domestic welfare spending could not be reallocated to foreign citizens, especially if foreign aid were made a humanitarian program rather than a tool of American foreign policy. If we wished, we could disburse the funds quite efficiently. Rather than using helicopters to spray for drugs in Latin America, we could fly those same helicopters over Haiti and have them drop packages of dollar bills. In this manner we could be sure that the foreign aid would bypass the corrupt Haitian government.

Under most accounts of human rights, borders are morally arbitrary. If there is an argument for redistribution from X to Y, it is not clear why it should matter whether Y lives on the same side of the border or not. Why, for instance, is the U.S. government obliged to pay welfare to poor Mexicans in San Diego but not to poor Mexicans fifteen minutes away in Tijuana? The primary difference between the groups is their location relative to a line drawn when the Mexican-American War ended, over 150 years ago.

It might be argued that communitarian considerations limit the scope of our welfare obligations to a single country, or that we have stronger duties to individuals with whom we share a common national history. Whether these arguments succeed is irrelevant for the purposes at hand. Even if they did, it would remain the case that the welfare state damages the interests of the truly poor, relative to the available alternatives.

Most individuals do not accept this perspective. They are convinced that the domestic welfare state is a good idea, and they do not waver in their support when they see that it violates some egalitarian principles. They hold the dual intuitions that doing something domestically is better than doing nothing, and that it is uncertain how far foreign commitments should extend. These intuitions, however, do not address why the marginal dollar should be spent at home rather than abroad. Quite simply, current welfare states represent a decision to give resources to the relatively wealthy rather than to the truly poor. The consistent egalitarian

[29] Tullock is well known for making these points in conversation, although by his own account he has not written up a systematic treatment of them.

should always favor the rerouting of this expenditure, and thus the elimination of the domestic welfare state.

One rejoinder formulates a two-step argument in response to the dilemma. This two-step argument first tries to establish that the national state (rather than world government) is the appropriate unit for supplying public goods, and then tries to argue that the welfare state is a public good. If both steps of the argument were to succeed, we would have a case for a domestic welfare state rather than foreign aid. This two-step argument, however, begs the question and still does not explain why the marginal welfare dollar should be spent at home rather than being spent abroad. Even if most public goods are produced on a local or regional basis, cash transfers are relatively easy to effect at an international level. If the helicopter-drop model does not work, the U.S. Treasury could simply wire funds to various small accounts in foreign banks. It would not be difficult to ensure that most of the money ended up in the hands of the poor, especially if the effort concentrated on countries filled almost entirely with poor people.

The two-step argument has another problem, namely, that the boundaries of the nation-state can vary. We can imagine richer countries promising to adopt poorer ones and to support them. Some of the current French colonial arrangements can be interpreted along these lines; French transfers account for almost half of the GDP of some of their island colonies, such as Martinique, for instance. The citizens of Martinique do not seem greatly upset by this arrangement, relative to their alternatives. The United States has adopted an intermediate arrangement with Puerto Rico, which receives food stamps and other forms of welfare, but would cease doing so if it declared its full independence. (Puerto Rican voters have rejected independence in referenda.) If we were true egalitarians, and yet still believed that national boundaries mattered for some reason, presumably we should feel compelled to set up more arrangements of this kind. But in reality, governments are moving in the opposite direction. The relatively poor Faeroe islands have recently stated their intent to secede from Denmark, and the Danes have responded by threatening to cut off all aid and subsidies within a few years of secession.[30]

These global comparisons further support suspicions that the case for the welfare state is not based in egalitarian reasoning. More likely, a citizenry spends welfare money at home, rather than abroad, to make their country the best possible country by some moral standard it holds, and to bring the country to the highest possible peak. This is achieved, to some extent, *at the expense* of starving people abroad. We help the relatively rich—the American lower class—rather than the truly poor, such as the Haitian lower class. The domestic welfare state, in this account, is

[30] On the Faeroes, see "Danes Take Hard Line on Islands' Secession," *New York Times*, March 18, 2000, A6.

based on a philosophy closer to perfectionism rather than egalitarianism or theories of positive rights to material goods. Once again we see that impersonal consequentialism would militate against a domestic welfare state, although not necessarily against foreign aid.[31]

VI. Concluding Remarks

Welfare-state defenders are correct to believe that the traditional conservative and libertarian critiques, as exemplified by Charles Murray, do not succeed. Yet this does not imply that all is well with the welfare state. The welfare state does not benefit the poor and the disadvantaged when we consider those categories broadly, to include future generations and foreign citizens. It is thus difficult to defend the welfare state in impersonal consequentialist terms.

If we are utilitarians, the costs of the welfare state are likely to exceed its benefits, at least if we give substantial weight to future generations. If we are consistent egalitarians, the current poor in North America and Western Europe are not close to being the most deserving recipients of resources. For these reasons, the "macro" normative arguments for welfare, usually based in some account of distributive justice, are peripheral or irrelevant to the actual practices and effects of welfare states. A defense of the U.S. welfare state, beyond the level needed to insure political stability and continued economic growth, thus requires that the current American needy be given a moral priority over future generations and over the needy in other countries.

In the current U.S. political context, a "person who cares" is assumed to identify with the interests of the current domestic poor. I have tried to show that this presumption is unwarranted. A person who cares ought to consider limiting the welfare state in the interests of the greater good of other, less visible poor persons.

Economics, George Mason University

[31] Of course, the empirical point remains that even the poorest countries in the world might be better off, in a suitably long run, if the United States and Western Europe retain their current status as rich, prosperous nations rather than shipping all of their surplus off to the very poor. The resolution of this question might then turn upon the rate of time discount we use when evaluating such decisions.

THE STAGNATING FORTUNES OF THE MIDDLE CLASS

By Edward N. Wolff

I. Introduction

The media is aglow with reports of the booming economy and rising prosperity in the United States since the early 1990s. Indeed, the run-up in stock prices between 1995 and the end of 1999 has created the impression that all families are doing well in terms of income and wealth.[1] This, however, is certainly not the case. As I shall demonstrate, most American families have seen their level of well-being stagnate over the last quarter-century.

Despite the recent boom, the last two and a half decades have brought some disturbing changes in the standard of living and inequality in the United States. Perhaps the grimmest news is that the real wage (the average salary and hourly wage of production and nonsupervisory workers in the total private sector, adjusted for inflation) has been falling since 1973. Between 1973 and 1993, the real wage declined by 14 percent, though it rose by 5 percent between 1993 and 1998, for a net change of –9 percent.[2] Changes in living standards have followed a somewhat different course. Median family income, after increasing by 8 percent in real terms between 1973 and 1989, fell back to its 1973 level in 1993, though it did grow by 12 percent between 1993 and 1998.[3] Despite falling real wages,

[1] Over that time period, the S&P 500 composite index increased by a factor of 2.5.

[2] These figures are based on the Bureau of Labor Statistics' hourly wage series. The sources of this data are U.S. Council of Economic Advisers, *Economic Report of the President, 1999* (Washington, DC: U.S. Government Printing Office, 1999); and U.S. Council of Economic Advisers, *Economic Report of the President, 1981* (Washington, DC: U.S. Government Printing Office, 1981). I use 1998 as the last date for many of the series cited in this essay because this is the last year (as of the time of writing this essay) that comparable household wealth data were available. The wage figures, as well as those for other data series, are converted to constant dollars on the basis of the consumer price index (CPI). The CPI has recently been criticized for overstating the rate of inflation. While this may be true, it is not clear that the degree of bias in the CPI has risen in recent years. As a result, the sharp break in the wage series and the various income series before and after 1973 would likely still remain even if the bias in the CPI were corrected.

[3] The data on median family income used in these calculations is from U.S. Census Bureau, "Historical Income Tables," available on-line at http://www.census.gov/hhes/income/histinc/histinctb.html.

Much of the data referred to in this essay comes from tables located on the U.S. Census Bureau's website. A number of pages on the website that link to large numbers of tables have very similar names but link to different materials. As a result, throughout the remainder of this essay, I use *"supra"* references in shortened citations to previously cited Census Bureau webpages. This will help readers find the best location from which to find the various tables to which I refer.

living standards were maintained for a while by the growing labor-force participation of wives, which increased from 41 percent in 1970 to 57 percent in 1988. However, since 1989, married women have entered the labor force more slowly, and by 1998 their labor-force participation rate had increased to only 61.6 percent; this slower rate of entrance led to a slowdown in the growth of real living standards.[4]

The turnaround in inequality in the United States has also been troubling. Inequality in the distribution of family income, which remained virtually unchanged between the end of World War II and the late 1960s, has increased sharply since then. What makes the rise in inequality particularly worrisome is that not only has the *relative* share of income held by the bottom half of the income distribution fallen, but that group's *absolute* income has declined as well. The poverty rate, which had fallen by half between a postwar peak in 1959 (the first year the poverty rate was computed) and 1973, has since risen.

The main source of the rising inequality of family income stems from changes in the structure of the labor market. Among male workers alone, wage disparities widened between high-pay and low-pay workers. Another indication of the dramatic changes taking place in the labor market is the sharp rise in the financial returns of education, particularly a college degree, that occurred during the 1980s and 1990s.

Current policy discussions in the United States and other advanced industrial countries have emphasized the need for better education of the labor force and the importance of the school-to-work transition. The underlying theme is that more education, more training, more apprenticeship programs, and, in general, more skill creation will lead to a more productive labor force and hence higher wages and faster economic growth. Moreover, a more equal distribution of income will presumably ensue from a more equal distribution of human capital.

Abundant evidence has been accumulated suggesting that individual workers benefit in the job market when they receive additional training and education. But it is much less clear that, in the aggregate, U.S. economic growth will increase and economic inequality decline if the government enhances opportunities for Americans to improve their job skills. Indeed, this essay will explore the reasons for this apparent paradox by investigating two other underlying paradoxes. First, even as educational attainment has increased in recent decades, wages have fallen after inflation is taken into account. Second, as educational opportunities have improved for a broader swathe of the U.S. population, economic inequality has not fallen, but rather has increased.

This essay will attempt to weigh whether government investment in education and training would be more or less effective at alleviating

[4] The source for this data is U.S. Census Bureau, *Statistical Abstract of the United States, 1999* (Washington, DC: U.S. Government Printing Office, 1999), 416.

economic inequality and strengthening the U.S. economy than direct subsidies to workers who are falling behind. Improved educational and training opportunities are essential for society for several reasons: education provides benefits that transcend the job market, particularly by aiding in the development of the sort of more knowledgeable citizenry that is important in a democratic society (this was the original rationale for public education in the United States); greater schooling and skills lead to more satisfying work opportunities; and firms' investments in training lower worker turnover. However, the evidence this essay will explore seems to show that government investments in education and training will not substantially alleviate inequality or bolster economic growth or labor earnings. Confronting the inequality challenge may require direct subsidies to those at the bottom and tax relief for those workers in the middle (who also have been falling behind). Labor law reform aimed at promoting unionization may also prove necessary if we are to improve living standards for most workers.

II. Recent Trends in Income, Poverty, and Inequality

Before discussing trends in schooling and earnings, it will be helpful to review what has happened to income, poverty, and inequality in the United States since the end of World War II. As suggested in the previous section, there have been some disturbing changes in the United States over the last quarter-century in the average standard of living, the poverty rate, and inequality. Let us consider these in turn, starting with the standard of living. As shown in Figure 1, median family income (the income of the family found in the middle of the distribution when families are ranked from lowest to highest in terms of income) grew by 12 percent in real terms between 1973 and 1998.[5] (All of the figures I refer to herein appear following the text of this essay.) In contrast, between 1947 and 1973, median family income more than doubled.[6] Personal disposable income (personal income minus tax payments) per capita, after doubling between 1947 and 1973, increased by only 46 percent in the succeeding twenty-five years.[7] Likewise, average household wealth, after surging by 42 percent over this earlier period, gained only another 10 percent be-

[5] It would actually be preferable to use median household income rather than median family income. Unfortunately, official U.S. Census Bureau series on household income begins only in 1967, whereas family-income data is available from 1947 onward.

[6] See note 3 for the source of the data used in this calculation.

For the reader's convenience, I provide citations to the sources of the various data series used in this essay both in the footnotes in the text and (in shortened form) in source notes accompanying each of the figures.

[7] The data on disposable income is from U.S. Council of Economic Advisors, *Economic Report of the President, 1999* (Washington, DC: U.S. Government Printing Office, 1999).

tween 1973 and 1995, though it did rise an additional 18 percent between 1995 and 1998 because of the stock market boom of the late 1990s.[8]

The main reason for this turnaround is that the real hourly wage has been falling since 1973. As noted above, between 1973 and 1998, real hourly wages fell by 9 percent. This contrasts with the period from 1947 to 1973, when real wages grew by 75 percent. Indeed, in 1998, the hourly wage was $12.77 per hour, about the same level (in real terms) as it was in 1967.[9]

In assessing poverty, we find more reasons for concern about the past quarter century. Between 1959 and 1973, there was great success in reducing poverty in America, with the overall poverty rate declining from 22.4 percent to 11.1 percent (see Figure 2). Since then, the poverty rate has generally trended upward, climbing to 15.1 percent in 1993, though it did fall by 1998 to 12.7 percent, about the same level as was observed in 1968.[10] Another indicator of the well-being of lower-income families is the share of total income received by the bottom quintile (20 percent) of families. From 1947 to 1961, their share fell from 5.0 percent to 4.7 percent, but it then rose rather steadily over time. After reaching 5.7 percent in 1974, however, the bottom quintile's share has fallen off rather sharply, to 4.2 percent in 1998.[11]

A related statistic is the mean income (in 1995 dollars) over time of the poorest 20 percent of families, which shows the absolute level of well-being of this group (the share of income, by contrast, shows the relative level of well-being). Their average income more than doubled between 1947 and 1974, from $6,000 to $12,300, but it then fell by 5 percent by 1998, to $11,700.[12] The difference in post-1974 trends between this series and the series representing the bottom quintile's share of income—the latter series falls much more sharply—occurs because mean income was rising in the general population after 1974.

Yet another indicator of deprivation is the average Aid to Families with Dependent Children (AFDC) benefit received per recipient family per month. AFDC (or welfare, as it is more typically called) covers only a small proportion of the poor—historically about one-third of the poor, or about 5 percent of the population. However, it is a good indicator of the

[8] The data on average household wealth is from the U.S. Federal Reserve's annually published *Flow of Funds Accounts*, available on-line at http://www.federalreserve.gov/releases/z1/Current/data.htm.

[9] See note 2 for the sources of this data on real hourly wages. Other wage series, such as the National Income and Product Accounts measures of wages and salaries per person engaged in production (PEP) and of employee compensation (the sum of wages, salaries, and employee benefits) per PEP, show roughly similar trends.

[10] In 1999, the poverty rate was down to 11.8 percent, still above the 1973 level. The data on the poverty rate is from U.S. Census Bureau, "Historical Poverty Tables, Table 2, Poverty Status of People by Family Relationship, Race, and Hispanic Origin: 1959 to 1999," available on-line at http://www.census.gov/hhes/poverty/histpovhstpov2.html.

[11] The data on the bottom quintile's income share is from tables located at U.S. Census Bureau, "Historical Income and Poverty Tables," available on-line at http://www.census.gov/hhes/poverty/histpov/history.html.

[12] The data on the bottom quintile's mean income is from tables located at ibid.

level of resources available to the most destitute section of American society. Average AFDC benefits have declined by half over time, from $839 (in 1995 dollars) a month in 1970 (the first date available for the series) to $446 in 1996.[13]

Finally, we turn to inequality, where again the United States has seen a disagreeable turnaround over the last quarter-century. Figure 3 shows different indices measuring economic inequality in America. The first series is the Gini coefficient for family income. (The Gini coefficient ranges between zero and one, with a low value indicating less inequality and a high value indicating more.) Between 1947 and 1968, it generally trended downward, reaching its lowest value, .348, in 1968. Since then, it has experienced an upward ascent, gradually at first and then more steeply in the 1980s and 1990s, culminating at its peak value of .430 in 1998.[14]

The second index in Figure 3, the share of total income received by the top 5 percent of American families, has a similar time trend. It fell gradually from 17.5 percent in 1947 to 14.8 percent in 1974, and then rose after this point, especially in the 1990s, reaching a peak value of 20.7 percent in 1997 and 1998. Figure 3's third index is the ratio of the average income of the richest 5 percent of families to the average income of the poorest 20 percent; it measures the spread in income between these two groups. This index generally declined between 1947 and 1974, going from 14.0 to 10.4, and then trended steadily upward, reaching 19.7 in 1998.[15]

The fourth inequality indicator in Figure 3 is wealth inequality, as measured by the share of total personal wealth owned by the richest 1 percent of households. This series shows a somewhat different pattern, generally trending downward—from 31.1 percent in 1947 to 21.8 percent in 1976—and then rising steeply thereafter, reaching 38.1 percent in 1998.[16]

To complete this examination of the American economy after World War II, I use Figure 4 to show trends in marginal tax rates, since these also

[13] The data on average annual AFDC benefits is from U.S. House of Representatives, Committee on Ways and Means, *1996 Green Book* (Washington, DC: U.S. Government Printing Ofice, 1996); and U.S. Census Bureau, *Statistical Abstract of the United States, 1999*. The 1996 figure is the last in this series because the federal AFDC program was replaced in 1997 by the Temporary Assistance to Needy Families (TANF) program. It would have been desirable to include the value of food stamps, Medicaid, and housing subsidies to the poor along with AFDC benefits, but the requisite time-series data is not available.

[14] The data on the Gini coefficient is from U.S. Census Bureau, "Historical Income Tables—Families, Table F-4, Gini Ratios for Families, by Race and Hispanic Origin of Householder: 1947 to 1999," available on-line at http://www.census.gov/hhes/income/histinc/f04.html. These figures are based on unadjusted data.

[15] The data used to compile both series discussed in this paragraph is from tables located at U.S. Census Bureau, "Historical Income Tables" (*supra* note 3). With respect to the average-income ratio, it would have been preferable to compare the average income of the top 5 percent of families with that of the bottom 5 percent, but figures for the latter are not available.

[16] This data on wealth inequality is from Edward N. Wolff, *Top Heavy: The Increasing Inequality of Wealth in America and What Can Be Done about It* (New York: New Press, 1996), 78–79. The series presented in that work is extended to 1998 using data from Federal Reserve Board, *1998 Survey of Consumer Finances*, available on-line at http://www.federalreserve.gov/pubs/oss/oss2/98/scf98home.html.

affect the well-being of families. The first series shows the top marginal tax rate, the marginal tax rate faced by the richest tax-filers. Back in 1944, the top marginal tax rate was 94 percent! After the end of World War II, the top rate was reduced to 86.5 percent (in 1946), but during the Korean War it was raised back to 92 percent (in 1953). Even in 1960, it was still at 91 percent. It then generally declined over time as various packages of tax legislation were implemented by Congress. It was lowered to 70 percent in 1966, raised to 77 percent in 1969 to finance the war in Vietnam, lowered to 70 percent again in 1975, and then lowered to 50 percent in 1983 (Reagan's first major tax act) and to 28 percent in 1986 (through the famous Tax Reform Act of 1986). Since then, it has trended upward, to 31 percent in 1991 (during the first Bush presidency) and then to 39.6 percent in 1993 (under President Clinton).[17]

The second series shows the marginal tax rate faced by filers with an income of $135,000 in 1995 dollars. This income level typically includes families at the 95th percentile (the top 5 percent). This series generally has the same trajectory as the first, declining in 1966, rising in 1975, falling in 1983 and 1986, and then increasing in 1991 and again in 1993.[18]

The last two series in Figure 4 show the marginal tax rates for those earning $67,000 and $33,000, respectively, both in 1995 dollars. The overall trends for these series are quite different from those of the first two. The marginal tax rate at $67,000 (about the 60th percentile) stood at a relatively low 36 percent in 1947, then generally trended upward, reaching 49 percent in 1980. It subsequently declined to 28 percent in 1986, where it has remained ever since. The marginal tax rate at $33,000 (about the 30th percentile) was also relatively low in 1946, at 25 percent, but it actually increased somewhat over time; it reached 28 percent in 1991 and has since remained at this level.[19]

All in all, tax cuts over the postwar period have been much more generous for the rich, particularly the superrich. Since 1947, the top marginal tax rate has fallen by more than half (54 percent), while the marginal rates at $135,000 and $67,000 have dropped 32 percent and 22 percent, respectively. At the same time, the rate at $33,000 has actually increased by 12 percent.

III. Trends in Schooling and Earnings

One of the great success stories of the postwar era is the tremendous growth in educational attainment in the U.S. population. This is documented in Figure 5. Median years of schooling among all people 25 years

[17] The data on top marginal tax rates is from Edward N. Wolff, *Economics of Poverty, Inequality, and Discrimination* (Cincinnati, OH: South-Western College Publishing, 1997), 631–32.

[18] The data on marginal tax rates for those earning $135,000 in 1995 dollars is from ibid.

[19] The data on marginal tax rates that appears in this paragraph is from ibid.

old and over grew from 9.0 years in 1947 to 13.4 in 1998. Most of the gain occurred before 1973. Between 1947 and 1973, median education increased by 3.3 years; from 1973 to 1998 it only rose by another 1.1 years.[20]

Trends in the percentages of adults who completed high school and college are even more dramatic. In 1947, 33 percent of all adults had finished high school; this grew to 83 percent in 1998. Progress in the high school completion rate was just as strong before and after 1973—it went from 33 percent in 1947 to 60 percent in 1973, and from 60 percent in 1973 to 83 percent in 1998. The percentage of college graduates in the adult population soared from 5.4 percent in 1947 to 24.9 percent in 1998. In this statistical series, progress was actually greater after 1973 than it had been before. Between 1947 and 1973, the percentage of adults who had graduated from college rose by 7.2 percentage points, while between 1973 and 1998 it grew by 12.3 percentage points.[21]

Figure 5 also shows the trend in real hourly wages between 1947 and 1998 previously illustrated in Figure 1. As noted above, such wages rose by 75 percent between 1947 and 1973 and then declined by 9 percent in the ensuing twenty-five years. Yet educational attainment continued to rise after 1973 and, indeed, in terms of college graduation rates, even accelerated. This is the first paradox noted above, the growing discordance between wages and skills.

As noted in Section I, the main source of the rising inequality of family income stems from changes in the structure of the labor market. One indication of the dramatic changes taking place in the labor market is the sharp rise in the returns of education, particularly a college degree, that occurred during and after the 1980s. This trend is documented in Figure 6. Among males, the ratio in annual earnings between a college graduate and a high school graduate increased slightly between 1975 and 1980, from 1.50 to 1.56, and then surged to 1.92 in 1998. For females, the ratio actually dipped slightly between 1975 and 1980, from 1.45 to 1.43, before climbing to 1.76 in 1998.[22]

The increase in the return of a college degree relative to a high school degree was due, in part, to the stagnating earnings of high school graduates (see Figure 7). Between 1975 and 1998, there was no net change in this group's annual earnings (in 1995 dollars), while the earnings of those with a bachelor's degree increased by 17 percent. The biggest increase in

[20] The data on median years of schooling is from various tables located at U.S. Census Bureau, "Historical Income Tables—People," available on-line at http://www.census.gov/hhes/income/histinc/incperdet.html. This series, and the others illustrated in Figure 5, refer only to those persons 25 years old and over who are in the noninstitutional population (i.e., they do not include members of the armed forces living in barracks).

[21] The data on high school and college graduation rates is from various tables located at ibid.

[22] The series in Figure 6 consider annual earnings, which are not adjusted for hours worked or the experience level of the workers. The source for the data on annual-earnings ratios is various tables located at ibid.

earnings occurred among workers with an advanced degree (master's or higher), who saw their annual incomes grow by 25 percent. Among those who did not graduate high school, earnings plummeted by 15 percent.[23]

Alongside the aforementioned increase in general educational attainment, another indicator of America's success in education is the dramatic decline in the inequality of schooling in the United States. According to the human capital model of earnings, there is a direct and proportional relationship between earnings inequality and the variance of schooling. In the standard human capital earnings function,

$$\log E_i = b_0 + b_1 S_i,$$

where E_i is the earnings of individual i, S_i is i's level of schooling, and b_0 and b_1 are positive coefficients.[24] This equation states that labor earnings should rise with years of schooling. It then follows that

$$\text{var}(\log E) = b_1{}^2\, \text{var}(S),$$

where var is the variance. The variance (or dispersion) of the logarithm of earnings is a standard inequality index used in the economics literature, and this equation indicates that earnings inequality should rise at the same rate as that of the variance of schooling levels among workers.

Yet as shown in Figure 8, while income inequality has risen since the late 1960s, the variance of schooling has trended sharply downward since 1950. In fact, the variance of schooling fell by 47 percent over this period (from 13.2 to 7.0). The simple correlation between the variance of schooling and income inequality is in fact –.78. This finding leads to the second paradox referred to above—namely, the growing discrepancy between the inequality of income and the inequality of human capital.[25]

A. *Racial differences*

A further major success story of the postwar period is the rising educational attainment among black Americans. As shown in Figure 9, the percentage of black males 25 years old or over with a high school degree increased from only 12.7 percent in 1947 to 74.3 percent in 1996 (the last date of data availability). As a result, the difference in the percentage of white males and black males with a high school degree narrowed from 20 percentage points in 1947 to 8 percentage points in 1996. The fraction of

[23] The data on mean annual earnings for all of the mentioned groups is from various tables located at ibid.

[24] See, for example, Jacob Mincer, *Schooling, Experience, and Earnings* (New York: National Bureau of Economic Research, 1974), chap. 2.

[25] The data on the variance of schooling is from various tables located at U.S. Census Bureau, "Historical Income Tables—People." Computed using the Census Bureau's Current Population Surveys, this data only counts those individuals who are 25 years old or over. These ratios appear low because they do not adjust for the fact that women work, on average, fewer hours per year than men do.

black males 25 years old and over that completed four years of college or more has also risen in the postwar period, from 2.4 percent in 1947 to 12.4 percent in 1996. However, the gap in college completion rates between black and white males actually widened over these years, from 4.2 percentage points in 1947 to 14.5 percentage points in 1996. Patterns are similar for white and black females.[26]

Despite the apparent increase in educational attainment among blacks, there has been little progress in closing the income gap separating blacks and whites. As documented in Figure 10, the ratio of average annual earnings between black and white male high school graduates fell off slightly between 1975 and 1995 (the first and last dates for which data on this was available), from 73 percent to 71 percent, though the corresponding ratio among college graduates increased from 70 percent to 77 percent. Overall, from 1975 to 1995, the average annual earnings among all black male workers rose from 66 percent of the average annual earnings of white males to 70 percent of that level. The racial gap in earnings has historically been much lower among female workers than among male workers, though it did widen between 1975 and 1995, going from a 5 percent difference to an 11 percent difference. All told, the ratio in median family income between black and white families was actually slightly lower in 1995 than it was in 1975—61 percent compared to 62 percent—and even a bit lower in 1998, at 60 percent. Indeed, median family income among black families, after climbing from 51 percent of the corresponding level among white families in 1947 to 61 percent of that level in 1969, has failed to advance any further.[27]

B. Gender differences

One of the most important changes in the postwar labor market has been the increasing participation rate of women. The percent of women in the labor force climbed from 33 percent in 1948 to 60 percent in 1998. The participation rate has increased not only for single women, but also for married women and, in particular, married women with young children.[28]

Another piece of good news is that despite the large increase in female employment, the gender gap in wages has been narrowing since 1975.[29] As documented in Figure 11, the ratio of annual average earnings between female and male workers increased from 46 percent in 1975 to 62 percent in 1998 among those with a high school degree, from 44 percent to 57 percent among college graduates, and from 50 percent to 58 percent

[26] This data on educational attainment is from various tables located at ibid.

[27] The data in this paragraph is from various tables located at U.S. Census Bureau, "Historical Income Tables" (*supra* note 3).

[28] These findings involving women's labor-force participation are from U.S. Census Bureau, *Statistical Abstract of the United States, 1999*, 416.

[29] I use "despite" here because usually, when the supply of a factor of production rises, its relative price declines.

among those with an advanced degree. Among all workers, the gender earnings ratio increased from 45 percent to 60 percent.[30]

What makes these relative gains even more notable is that while real earnings among male workers were relatively stagnant over those two and a half decades, they were rising for women. Among females, real annual earnings grew by 52 percent over this period, while among men they advanced by only 13 percent.[31] However, there is no evidence that these large gains in earnings made by women relative to men are due to significant gains in education. Indeed, in 1998, the percentage of women who had graduated from high school was exactly the same as the percentage of men, and the percentage of women who had attended four or more years of college was actually about 3.8 percentage points lower than the corresponding figure for men.[32]

IV. Wealth and Profitability

As noted in Section I, the media has promoted the idea of "people's capitalism"—the idea that all families are benefiting from the stock market boom of recent years. In this section, I look at recent trends in household wealth.

I use marketable wealth (or net worth), which is defined as the current value of all marketable or fungible assets minus the current value of debts. Net worth is thus the difference in value between total assets and total liabilities or debt. A household's total assets are defined as the sum of (1) the gross value of owner-occupied housing; (2) the gross value of other real estate owned by the household; (3) cash and demand deposits; (4) time and savings deposits, certificates of deposit, and money market accounts; (5) government bonds, corporate bonds, foreign bonds, and other financial securities; (6) the cash surrender value of life insurance plans; (7) the cash surrender value of pension plans, including IRAs, Keogh plans, and 401(k) plans; (8) corporate stock and mutual funds; (9) net equity in unincorporated businesses; and (10) equity in trust funds. Total liabilities are the sum of (1) mortgage debt; (2) consumer debt, including auto loans; and (3) other debt.

The data sources used for this part of this study are the 1983, 1989, 1992, 1995, and 1998 Surveys of Consumer Finances (SCFs) conducted by the U.S. Federal Reserve Board.[33] Each survey consists of a core representative sample covering all U.S. households as well as a supplement focusing

[30] This data on gender earnings ratios is from various tables located at U.S. Census Bureau, "Historical Income Tables" (*supra* note 3).

[31] This data is from various tables located at ibid.

[32] This data is from various tables located at ibid.

[33] Each of these surveys can be accessed through the Federal Reserve Board's website; links to each survey are provided at http://www.federalreserve.gov/pubs/oss/oss2scfindex.html.

TABLE 1. *Mean and median wealth, 1983–98*

	1983	1989	1992	1995	1998	Percent Change, 1983–98
Median[a]	54.6	58.4	49.9	48.8	60.7	11.1
Mean[a]	212.6	243.6	236.8	218.8	270.3	27.1
Percent with net worth						
Zero or negative	15.5	17.9	18.0	18.5	18.0	
Less than $5,000[b]	25.4	27.6	27.2	27.8	27.2	
Less than $10,000[b]	29.7	31.8	31.2	31.9	30.3	

[a] In thousands of 1998 dollars.
[b] Constant 1998 dollars.

on high-income households; this supplemental sample is drawn from the Internal Revenue Service's Statistics of Income data file. The survey questionnaire consists of hundreds of questions on different components of family-wealth holdings. Though there are other data sources available for analyzing household wealth in the United States, the SCFs are the best ones for capturing both the wealth at the top of the distribution and the complete wealth portfolio of households in the middle.[34]

A. Wealth trends

Table 1 presents mean and median wealth figures (in 1998 dollars) for the United States between 1983 and 1998. Perhaps the most striking result from Table 1 is that median wealth (the wealth of the household in the middle of the distribution) was only 11 percent greater in 1998 than it was in 1983. After rising by 7 percent between 1983 and 1989, median wealth fell by 16 percent between 1989 and 1995, and then rose by 24 percent between 1995 and 1998. One reason for the slow growth in median wealth is evident from the third row of Table 1, which shows that the percentage of households with zero or negative net worth increased from 15.5 percent in 1983 to 18.0 percent in 1998. The shares of households with net worths lower than $5,000 and $10,000 (both in 1998 dollars) also rose over the period.

Mean wealth is much higher than the median—$270,000 versus $61,000 in 1998. This implies that the vast bulk of household wealth is concen-

[34] Full technical details on the data sources and methods I use here can be found in Edward N. Wolff, "Recent Trends in Wealth Ownership, 1983–1998," in Thomas M. Shapiro and Edward N. Wolff, eds., *Assets and the Disadvantaged: The Benefits of Spreading Asset Ownership* (New York: Russell Sage Foundation, 2001).

TABLE 2. *Percent of households owning stock directly or indirectly, 1983–98*

Stock Holdings	1983	1989	1992	1995	1998
Any stock holdings	24.4	31.7	37.2	40.4	48.2
Stock worth $5,000 or more[a]	14.5	22.6	27.3	29.5	36.3
Stock worth $10,000 or more[a]	10.8	18.5	21.8	23.9	31.8

Note: Includes direct ownership of stock shares and indirect ownership through mutual funds, trusts, and retirement accounts such as IRAs, Keogh plans, and 401(k) plans.
[a]Constant 1998 dollars.

trated in the richest families. Like median wealth, mean wealth showed a sharp increase from 1983 to 1989, suffered a rather precipitous decline from 1989 to 1995, then surged again in 1998, largely as a result of rising stock prices. Overall, mean wealth was 27 percent higher in 1998 than it was in 1983, and 11 percent higher than it was in 1989.[35]

B. Who has a stake in the stock market?

There have been widespread reports in the media that stock ownership substantially widened in the United States over the last twenty years, particularly during the 1990s. There is some truth to these reports. The proportion of households who own stocks either outright or indirectly through mutual funds, trusts, or various pension accounts increased from 24.4 percent in 1983 to 48.2 percent in 1998 (see Table 2). Much of the increase was fueled by the growth in pension accounts like IRAs, Keogh plans, and 401(k) plans. Indeed, between 1983 and 1989, direct stock ownership declined somewhat, from 13.7 percent to 13.1 percent—likely a result of the 1987 stock market plunge. However, the share of households with pension accounts more than doubled over this period, from 11 percent to 23 percent, accounting for the overall increase in stock ownership. Between 1989 and 1998, the direct ownership of stocks grew by a modest 6 percentage points, while the share of households with a pension account again doubled; again, the increasing use of pension accounts was responsible for the bulk of the overall increase in stock ownership. (I computed these figures separating out direct from indirect stock ownership, though they are not shown in Table 2.)

As Table 2 shows, despite the overall gains in stock ownership, less than half of all households had any stake in the stock market by 1998. More-

[35] The time trend is similar when the value of vehicles is also included in net worth, as some researchers are wont to do. When this value is counted, instead of rising by 11 percent between 1983 and 1998, median net worth increases by 15 percent, and the mean rises by 28 percent instead of 27 percent. (Statistics on the value of households' vehicles are included in the SCFs.)

TABLE 3. *Concentration of stock ownership by wealth class, 1998*

	Percent of Households Owning Stock Worth More Than			Percent of Stock Owned	
Wealth Class	Zero	$4,999	$9,999	Shares	Cumulative
Top 1 percent	93.2	92.9	91.2	42.1	42.1
Next 4 percent	89.0	87.0	86.1	25.0	67.2
Next 5 percent	83.9	80.4	78.9	10.6	77.7
Next 10 percent	78.7	74.0	71.6	11.1	88.8
Second quintile	58.9	49.8	45.4	7.7	96.5
Third quintile	45.8	32.7	25.9	2.6	99.1
Fourth quintile	35.1	15.1	8.6	0.7	99.8
Bottom quintile	18.6	4.6	1.8	0.2	100.0
All	48.2	36.3	31.8	100.0	

Note: Includes direct ownership of stock shares and indirect ownership through mutual funds, trusts, and retirement accounts such as IRAs, Keogh plans, and 401(k) plans. Due to rounding error, the cumulative share at each income level in this table does not always equal the sum of the relevant income level's share and the prior cumulative share.

over, many of these families had only a minor stake. In 1998, while 48 percent of households owned some stock, only 36 percent had total stock holdings worth $5,000 or more, and only 32 percent owned $10,000 or more.

Stock ownership is also highly skewed by wealth and income class. As shown in Table 3, 93 percent of the very rich (the top 1 percent) reported owning stock either directly or indirectly in 1998, compared to 46 percent of the middle quintile and 19 percent of the poorest 20 percent. While over 91 percent of the very rich reported stock holdings worth $10,000 or more, only 26 percent of the middle quintile and less than 2 percent of the bottom quintile did so. Moreover, the top 1 percent of households accounted for 42 percent of the value of all stock owned, and the top 5, 10, and 20 percent accounted for 67, 77, and almost 90 percent, respectively, of the same value.

Stock ownership also tails off by income class (see Table 4). Whereas 93 percent of households in the top 1.6 percent of income recipients (those who earned $250,000 or more) owned stock in 1998, 52 percent of the middle class (incomes between $25,000 and $50,000), 29 percent of the lower middle class (incomes between $15,000 and $25,000), and only 11 percent of poor households (income under $15,000) reported stock ownership. The comparable ownership figures for stock holdings of $10,000 or more are 92 percent for the top 1.6 percent, 27 percent for the middle class, 13 percent for the lower middle class, and 5 percent for the poor. Moreover, about three-quarters of all stocks were owned by households

TABLE 4. *Concentration of stock ownership by income class, 1998*

Income Level	Share of Households	Percent of Households Owning Stock Worth More Than			Percent of Stock Owned	
		Zero	$4,999	$9,999	Shares	Cumulative
$250,000 or more	1.6	93.3	92.7	91.9	36.1	36.1
$100,000–$249,999	6.9	89.0	85.5	82.8	27.7	63.9
$75,000–$99,999	7.7	80.7	70.4	66.5	10.8	74.7
$50,000–$74,999	17.4	70.9	55.6	48.8	13.1	87.8
$25,000–$49,999	29.0	52.0	34.3	27.4	8.5	96.3
$15,000–$24,999	16.1	29.2	16.9	12.9	2.6	98.9
Under $15,000	21.3	10.6	5.2	4.5	1.1	100.0
All	100.0	48.2	36.3	31.8	100.0	

Note: Includes direct ownership of stock shares and indirect ownership through mutual funds, trusts, and retirement accounts such as IRAs, Keogh plans, and 401(k) plans. Due to rounding error, the cumulative share at each income level in this table does not always equal the sum of the relevant income level's share and the prior cumulative share.

earning $75,000 or more (the top 16 percent), and 88 percent was owned by the top third of households in terms of income. Breakdowns of stock ownership by wealth and income class for earlier years show very similar patterns of concentration at the top.

Substantial stock holdings, it seems, have still not penetrated much beyond the reach of the rich and the upper middle class. The big winners from the stock market boom of the last few years have been these groups; the middle class and the poor have not seen sizable benefits from the bull market. It is also apparent which groups benefit from the preferential tax treatment of capital gains.

C. *Trends in profitability*

The final part of this study is an investigation of recent trends in profitability in the United States. The basic data is from the U.S. Bureau of Economic Analysis's National Income and Product Accounts, as well as the Bureau's data on net capital stock.[36]

For the definition of gross profits, I use total gross property-type income, including corporate profits, interest, rent, half of proprietors' income, and the capital consumption allowance (CCA). The gross rate of profit is defined as the ratio of total gross property-type income to total private fixed capital; it indicates the rate of return on capital. The gross rate of profit declined by 4.5 percentage points between 1947 and 1980, the year it reached its postwar nadir of 20.4 percent (see Figure 12). It then rose by 4.0 percentage points from 1980 and 1987, and by another 3.4 percentage points by 1997. By that time it had reached 27.9 percent, close to its previous postwar peak of 29.2 percent in 1965. This trend suggests that recent economic conditions have become more and more favorable for capital-owners—typically, the wealthy.

Figure 12 also shows trends in the gross profit share in national income. The ratio of total gross property-type income to the total national income, gross profit share expresses how the total national income generated over the course of a year is divided between owners of capital, on the one hand, and workers, on the other. As gross profit share rises, it indicates that more income is going to those owning capital, and that less is going to workers. Gross profit share rose by 3.1 percentage points between 1947 and 1965, then fell by 3.9 percentage points between 1965 and 1974, the year it reached its low point of 32.9 percent. Since then, it has generally drifted upward, rising by 4.6 percentage points between 1974 and 1997. Indeed, the gross profit share was at its postwar peak in 1997, at 37.5 percent, indicating again that the recent condition of capital-owners represents a high point for them.

[36] This data can be found at U.S. Bureau of Economic Analysis, "National Accounts Data," available on-line at http://www.bea.doc.gov/bea/dn1.htm.

V. Conclusion

In sum, the last twenty-five years or so have seen stagnating earnings and income, rising poverty, and rising inequality. In contrast, the early postwar period witnessed rapid gains in both wages and family income, a sharp decline in poverty, and a moderate fall in inequality. Personal tax rates have generally fallen over time, but by much more for the rich than for the middle class.

The descriptive statistics presented above suggest a growing disconnect, in at least four dimensions, between earnings and schooling. First, despite the substantial progress in educational attainment made by all races and by both men and women over the last two decades, real earnings have generally been stagnant (or declining in the case of average hourly earnings). Second, despite incredible progress in reducing disparities of schooling within the American population, the inequality of income has not only failed to decline but has actually risen sharply over the last three decades. Third, there has been virtually no closure in the racial gap in both earnings and income over the last two and a half decades, in spite of the great strides made in the black community in increasing blacks' schooling levels, particularly at the high school level. Fourth, women have gained on men in terms of earnings even though they have not gained on men in terms of schooling.

Though stock ownership has spread in the United States, particularly over the last decade, stocks still remain highly concentrated in the hands of the rich. Moreover, many families who do own stock hold only relatively small amounts. As a result, the booming stock market of the late 1990s has failed to make much of a dent in the overall wealth position of the average family, and median wealth grew by only 4 percent between 1989 and 1998.[37]

Finally, there has been a clear shift in national income away from labor and toward capital, particularly since the early 1980s. Between 1989 and 1997, both overall and corporate profitability rose rather substantially, reaching almost postwar highs. The stock market has, in part, been fueled by rising profitability. While the capitalist class has gained from rising profits, workers have not experienced progress in terms of wages. On the surface, at least, there appears to be a trade-off between advances in income and wealth made by the rich and advances in income and wealth among the working class.

What can be done about the stagnating fortunes of the average (working) American? Current policy discussions in Washington have emphasized better education of the labor force and improved training. Education and training are seen to be the key remedies for two major problems that ail the economy. First, it is argued that they will lead to higher levels of skills, thus leading to more high-paying jobs and an increase in the real

[37] See Table 1.

wage. Second, it is argued that they will lead to a more equitable distribution of skills in the labor force and thus reduce wage inequality. The results of this essay seem to cast doubts on both of these arguments.

What else should Washington do? I believe that the most effective way to reverse the decline of the real wage and to reduce income disparities is through policies that influence incomes directly. Among the remedies that I propose are the following:

(1) *Restore the minimum wage to its 1968 level.* The minimum wage in 1998 was down about 32 percent in real terms from its peak level in 1968 (when the unemployment rate was only 3.6 percent!).[38] Raising the minimum wage will help increase the wages of low-wage earners.

(2) *Extend the earned income tax credit (EITC).* The EITC provides supplemental pay to low-wage workers in the form of a tax credit on their federal income tax return. In fiscal year 1999, the EITC provided $29 billion in supplemental aid. An expansion of this credit will further raise the (posttax) income of low-income families.

(3) *Make tax and transfer policy more redistributive.* A more potent way to raise the real wage and reduce inequality is to redesign our tax and income-support systems so that they transfer more income from the rich to the poor. Tax policy over the last two decades, as shown above, has clearly benefited the rich over the poor (and capital over labor). Comparisons between the United States and other advanced industrial countries (including Canada), which face similar labor-market conditions, indicate that tax and transfer policies can be effective in reducing inequality and increasing posttax income.[39]

(4) *Re-empower labor.* The findings presented here and the cross-national evidence compiled elsewhere suggest that one of the principal reasons for the greater level of inequality in the United States—and for this level's relatively rapid rise in recent years in comparison to the levels found in other advanced economies—is the low level of unionization in this country.[40] This is also a principal factor in explaining declining real wages in the United States. Steps should be taken to help promote unionization in the workplace and expand the power of labor generally. This could start with reform of existing labor law. Other work has documented how existing labor law is biased against the establishment of new unions, and how the certification process is notoriously difficult.[41]

Economics, New York University

[38] Wolff, *Economics of Poverty, Inequality, and Discrimination*, 597.

[39] See, for example, Anthony B. Atkinson, Lee Rainwater, and Timothy M. Smeeding, *Income Distribution in OECD Countries: Evidence from the Luxembourg Income Study* (Paris: Organization for Economic Cooperation and Development, 1995).

[40] See, for example, Francine D. Blau and Lawrence M. Kahn, "International Differences in Male Wage Inequality: Institutions versus Market Forces," *Journal of Political Economy* 104, no. 4 (1996): 791–836.

[41] See, for example, David M. Gordon, *Fat and Mean: The Corporate Squeeze of Working Americans and the Myth of Managerial "Downsizing"* (New York: Martin Kessler Books, 1996).

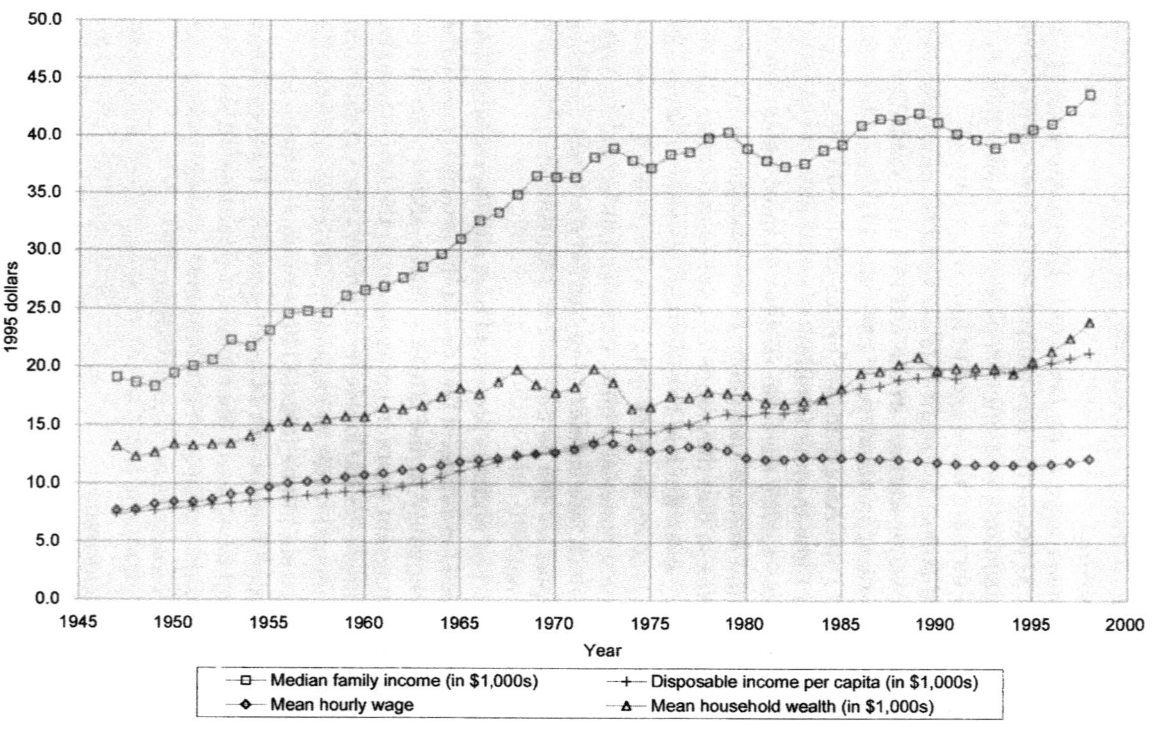

FIGURE 1. Average income, earnings, and wealth, 1947–98.

Data sources: Median family income: U.S. Census Bureau, "Historical Income Tables" (*supra* note 3). Disposable income per capita: U.S. Council of Economic Advisors, *Economic Report of the President, 1999*. Mean household wealth: U.S. Federal Reserve, *Flow of Funds Accounts*. Real hourly wages: U.S. Council of Economic Advisers, *Economic Report of the President, 1999*; U.S. Council of Economic Advisers, *Economic Report of the President, 1981*.

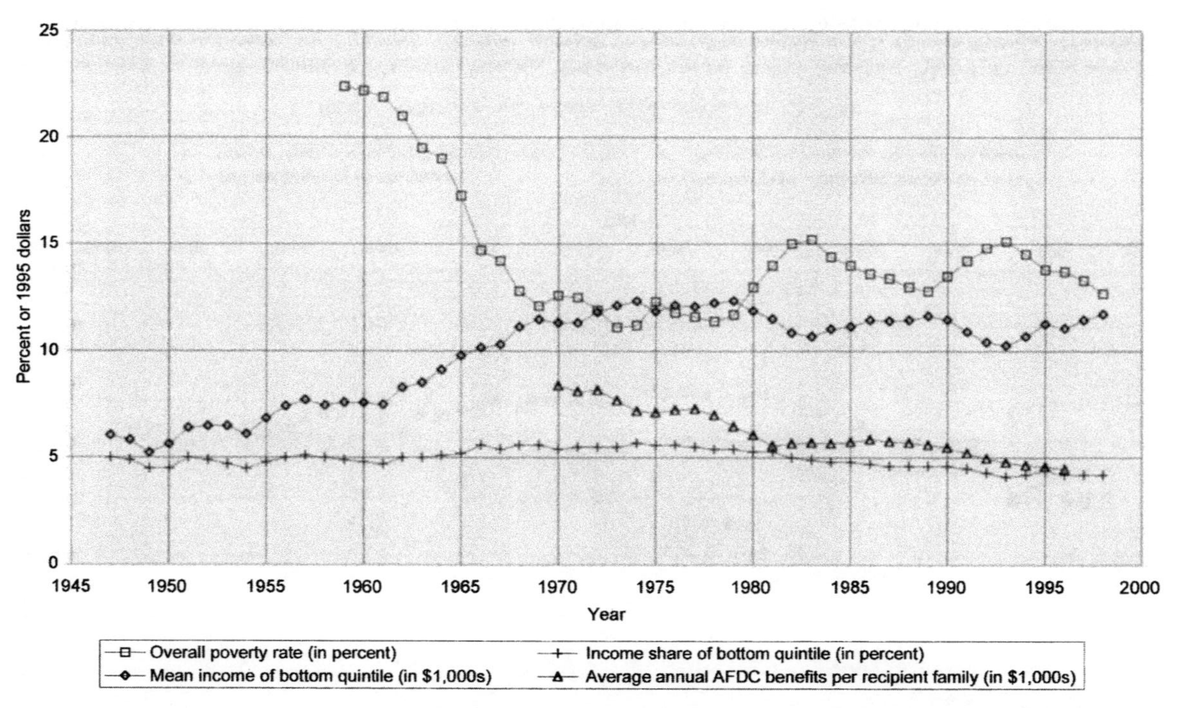

FIGURE 2. Poverty rate, income share and mean income of the lowest income quintile, and average AFDC benefits, 1947–98.

Data sources: Overall poverty rate: U.S. Census Bureau, "Historical Poverty Tables, Table 2" (*supra* note 10). Income share of bottom quintile, mean income of bottom quintile: various tables located at U.S. Census Bureau, "Historical Income and Poverty Tables" (*supra* note 11). Average annual AFDC benefits per recipient family: U.S. House of Representatives, Committee of Ways and Means, *1996 Green Book*; U.S. Census Bureau, *Statistical Abstract of the United States, 1999*. (This series ends in 1996 because AFDC was replaced in 1997 with TANF; see note 13.)

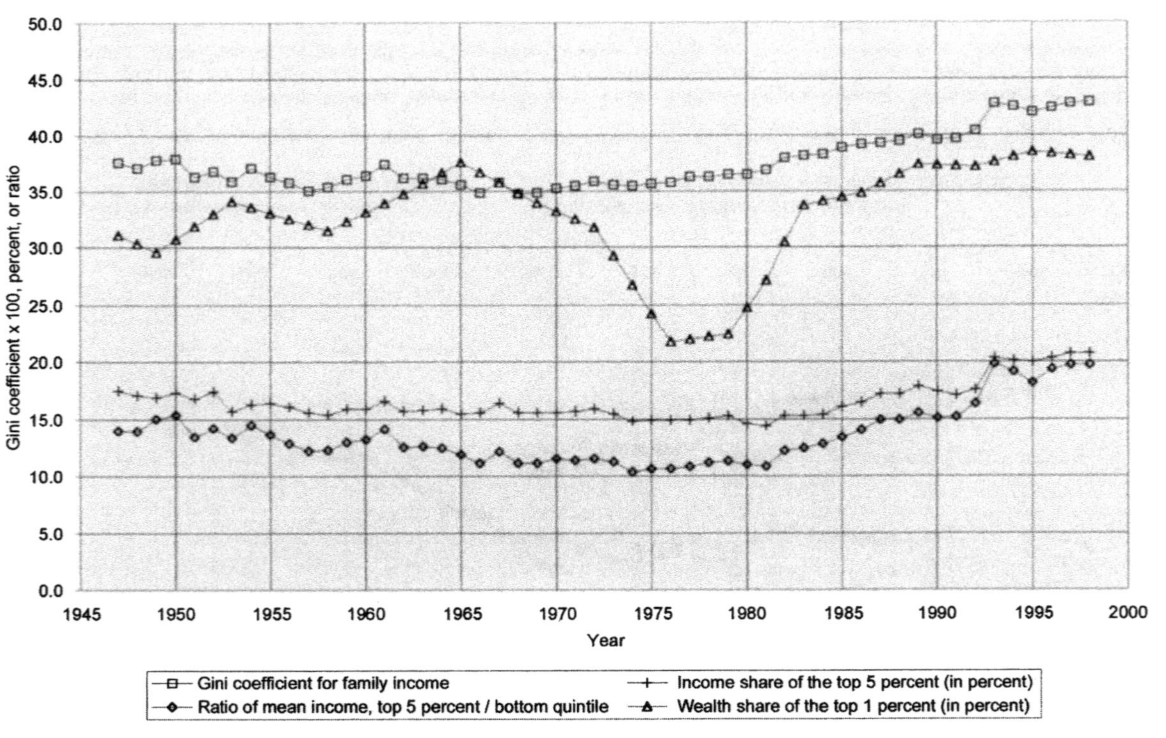

FIGURE 3. Income and wealth inequality trends, 1947–98.

Data sources: Gini coefficient for family income: U.S. Census Bureau, "Historical Income Tables—Families, Table F-4" (*supra* note 14). Income share of the top 5 percent; ratio of mean income, top 5 percent to bottom quintile: various tables located at U.S. Census Bureau, "Historical Income Tables" (*supra* note 3). Wealth share of the top 1 percent: Wolff, *Top Heavy*; Federal Reserve Board, *1998 Survey of Consumer Finances*.

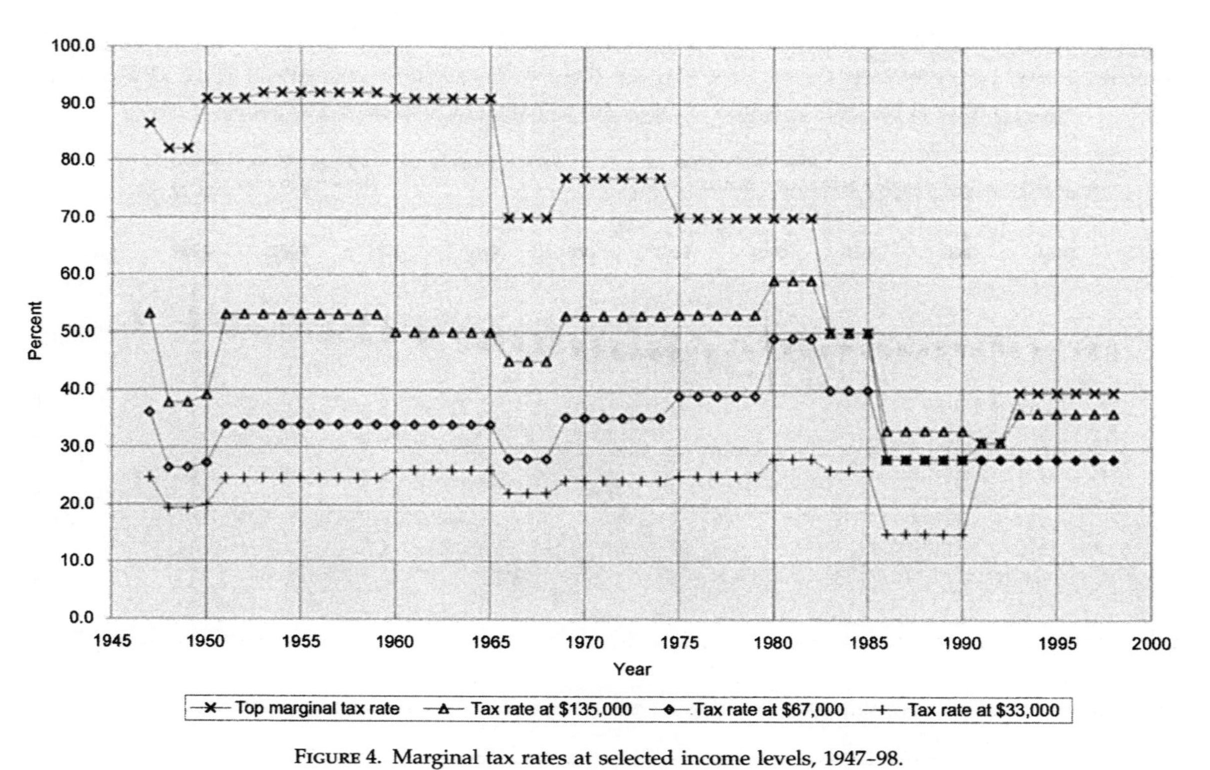

FIGURE 4. Marginal tax rates at selected income levels, 1947–98.

Data source: All series: Wolff, *Economics of Poverty, Inequality, and Discrimination.*

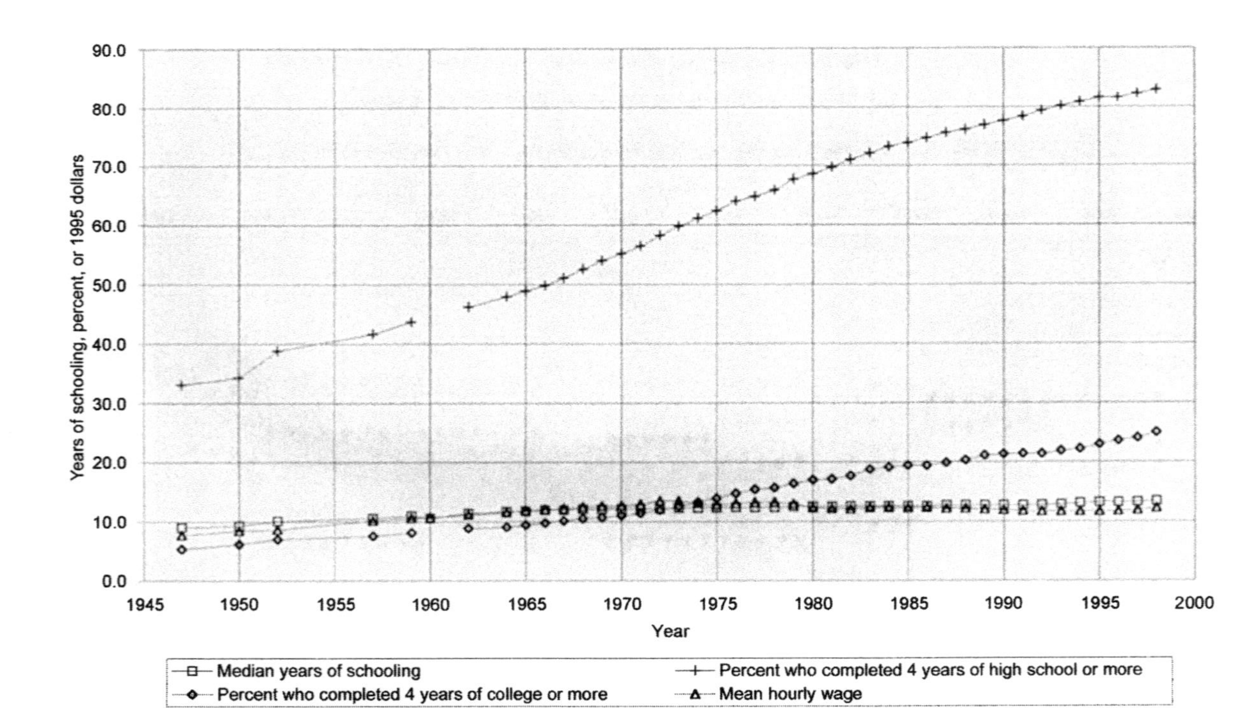

FIGURE 5. Educational attainment and mean hourly wages of people 25 years old or over, 1947–98.

Data sources: Mean years of schooling, percent who completed 4 years of high school or more, percent who completed 4 years of college or more: various tables located at U.S. Census Bureau, "Historical Income Tables—People" (*supra* note 20). (For several of these series, data was unavailable for the period of 1959–62.) Mean hourly wage: U.S. Council of Economic Advisers, *Economic Report of the President, 1999; Economic Report of the President, 1981.*

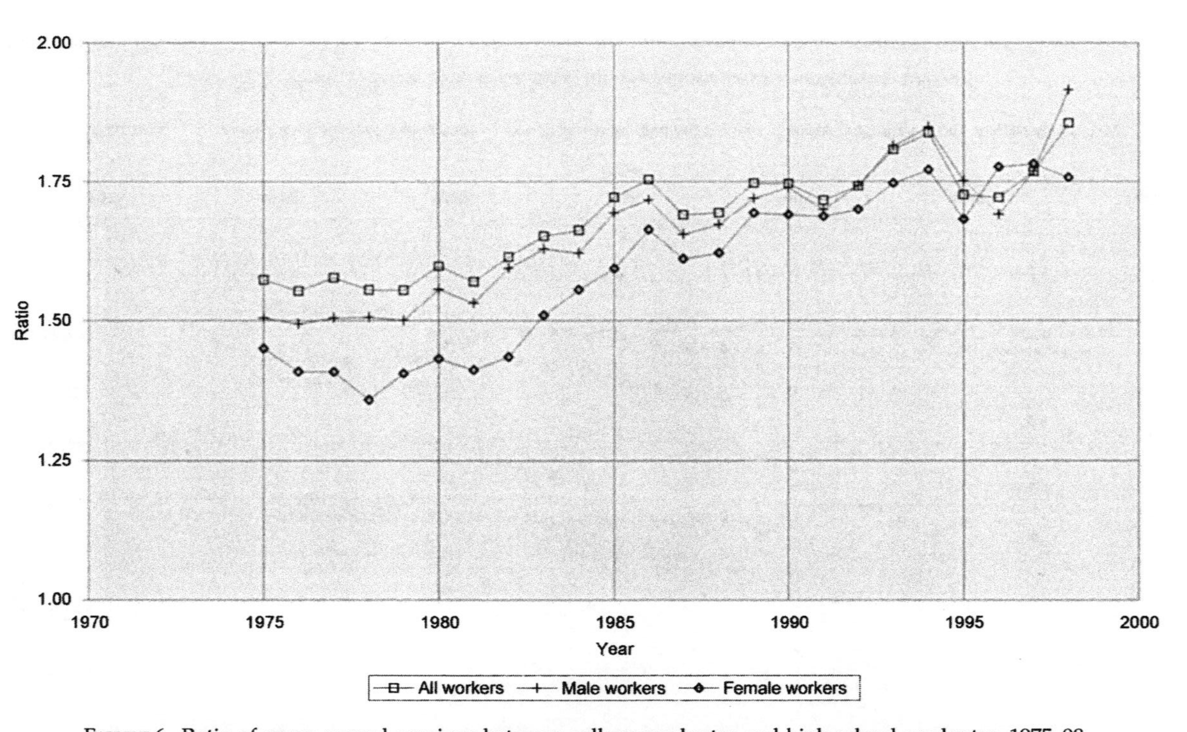

FIGURE 6. Ratio of mean annual earnings between college graduates and high school graduates, 1975–98.

Data sources: All series: various tables located at U.S. Census Bureau, "Historical Income Tables—People" (*supra* note 20).

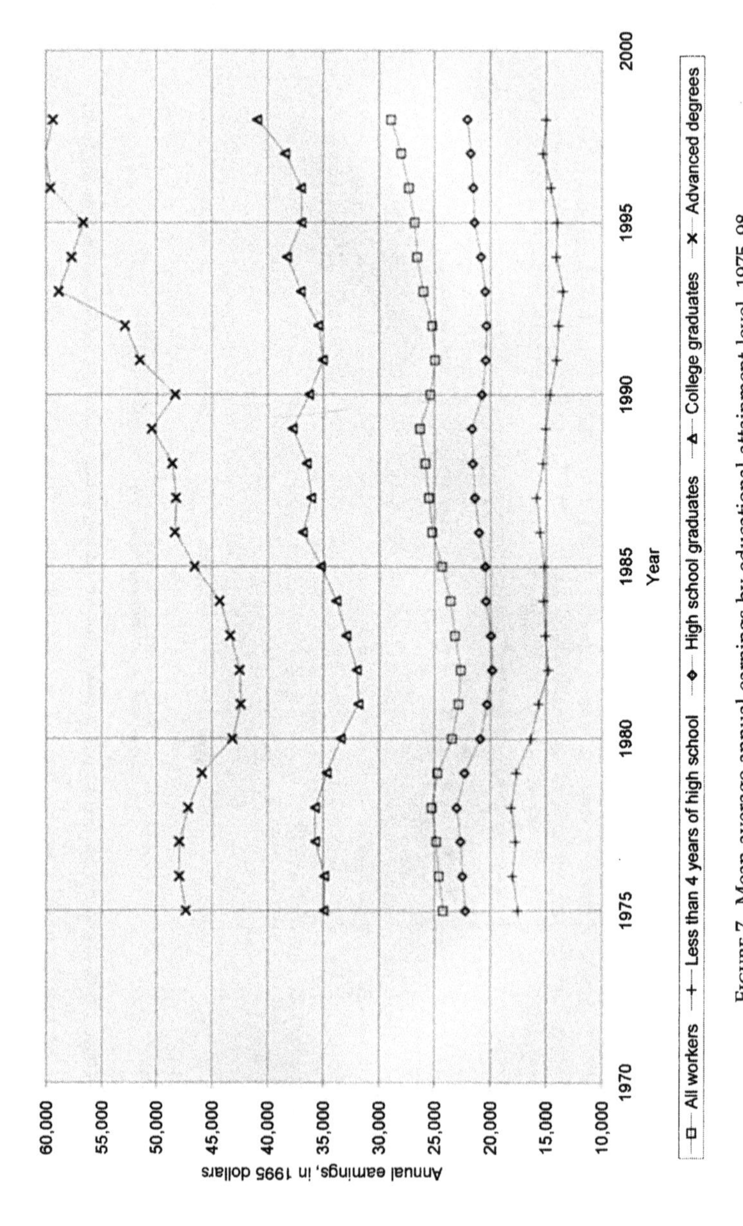

FIGURE 7. Mean average annual earnings by educational attainment level, 1975–98.

Data sources: All series: various tables located at U.S. Census Bureau, "Historical Income Tables—People" (*supra* note 20).

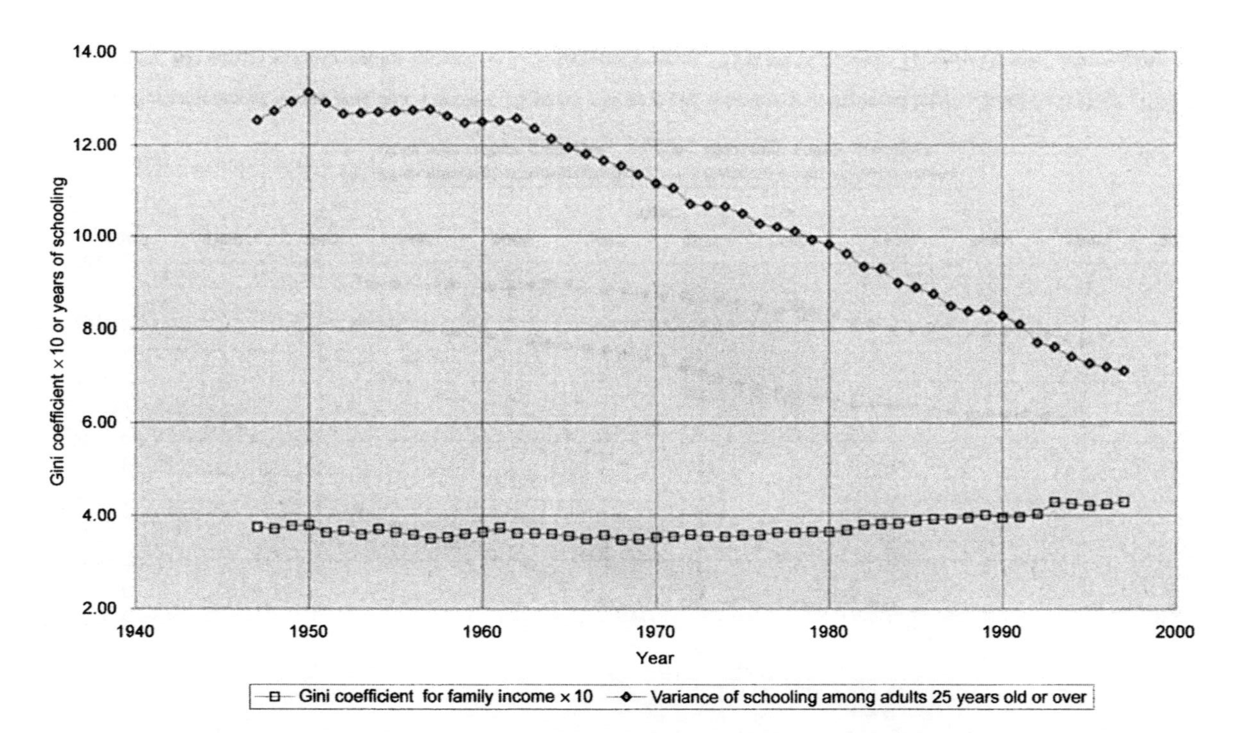

FIGURE 8. Family income inequality and variance of schooling among those 25 years old or over, 1947–97.

Data sources: Gini coefficient for family income (× 10): U.S. Census Bureau, "Historical Income Tables—Families, Table F-4" (*supra* note 14). Variance of schooling among adults 25 years old or over: table located at U.S. Census Bureau, "Historical Income Tables—People" (*supra* note 20).

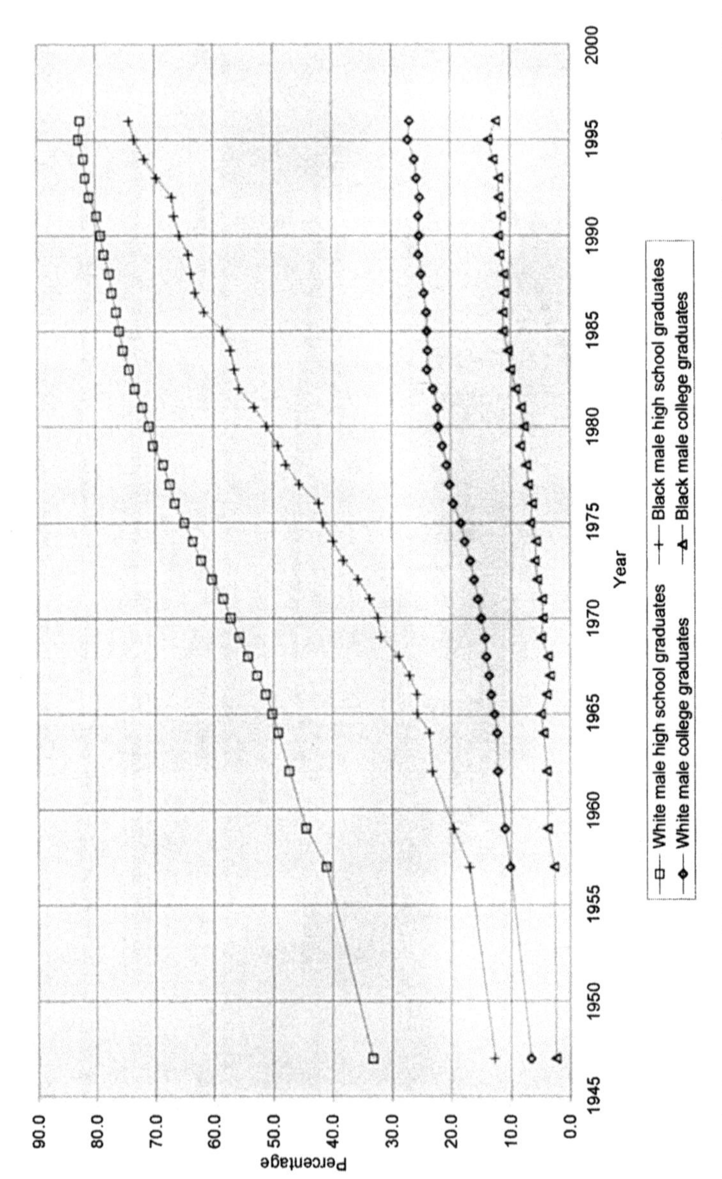

FIGURE 9. Percentages of white and black males, 25 years old or over, who have completed high school or college, 1947–96.

Data sources: All series: various tables located at U.S. Census Bureau, "Historical Income Tables—People" (*supra* note 20).

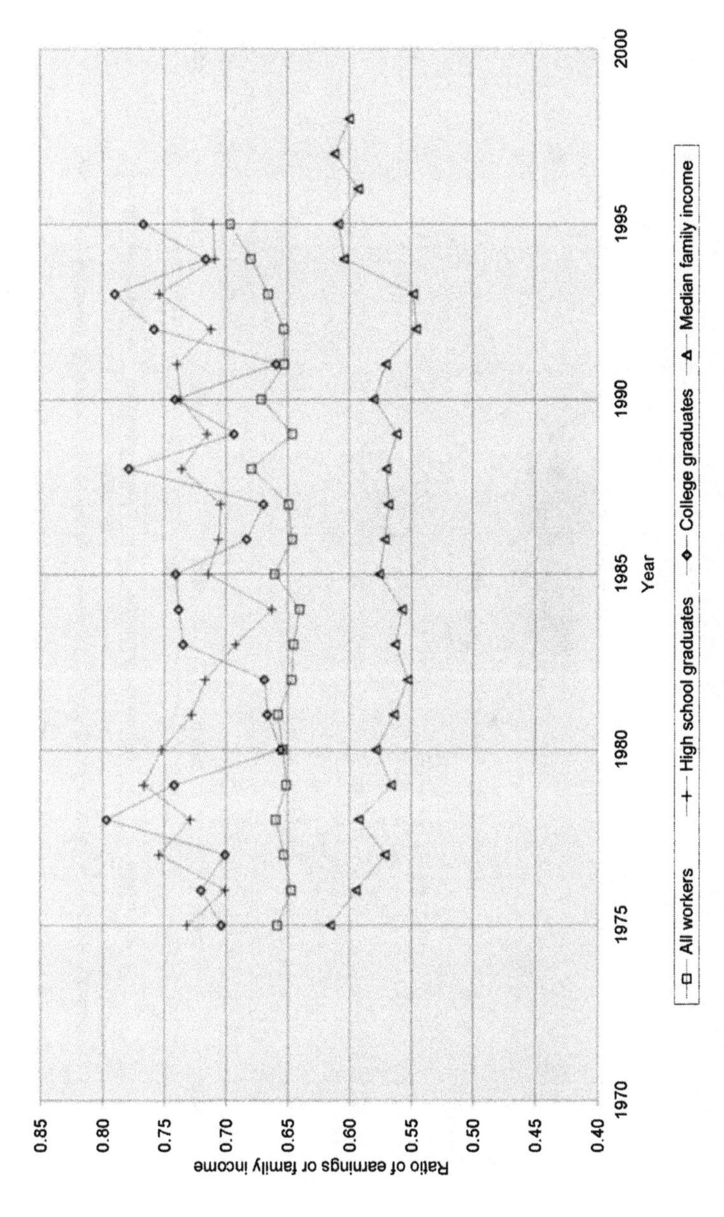

FIGURE 10. Ratios of mean annual earnings between black and white males by education, and ratio of median family income between black and white families, 1975–98.

Data sources: All series: various tables located at U.S. Census Bureau, "Historical Income Tables" (*supra* note 3).

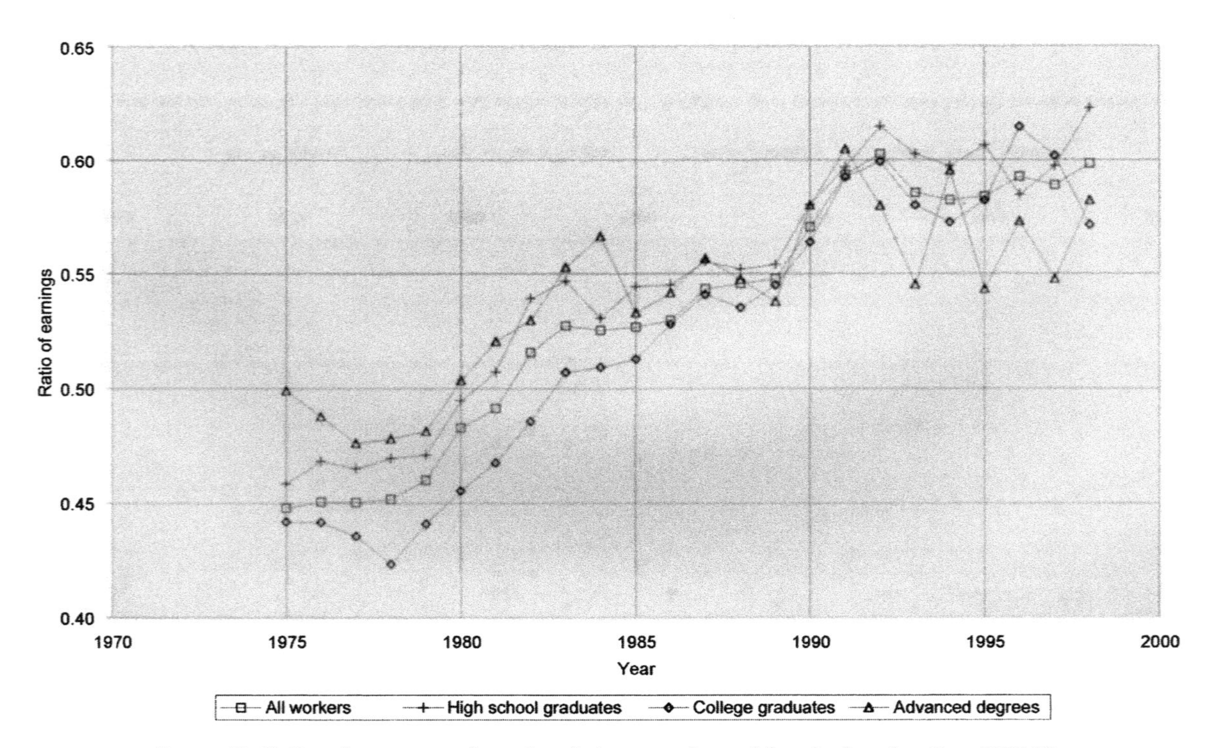

FIGURE 11. Ratios of mean annual earnings between males and females by education, 1975–98.

Data sources: All series: various tables located at U.S. Census Bureau, "Historical Income Tables" (*supra* note 3).

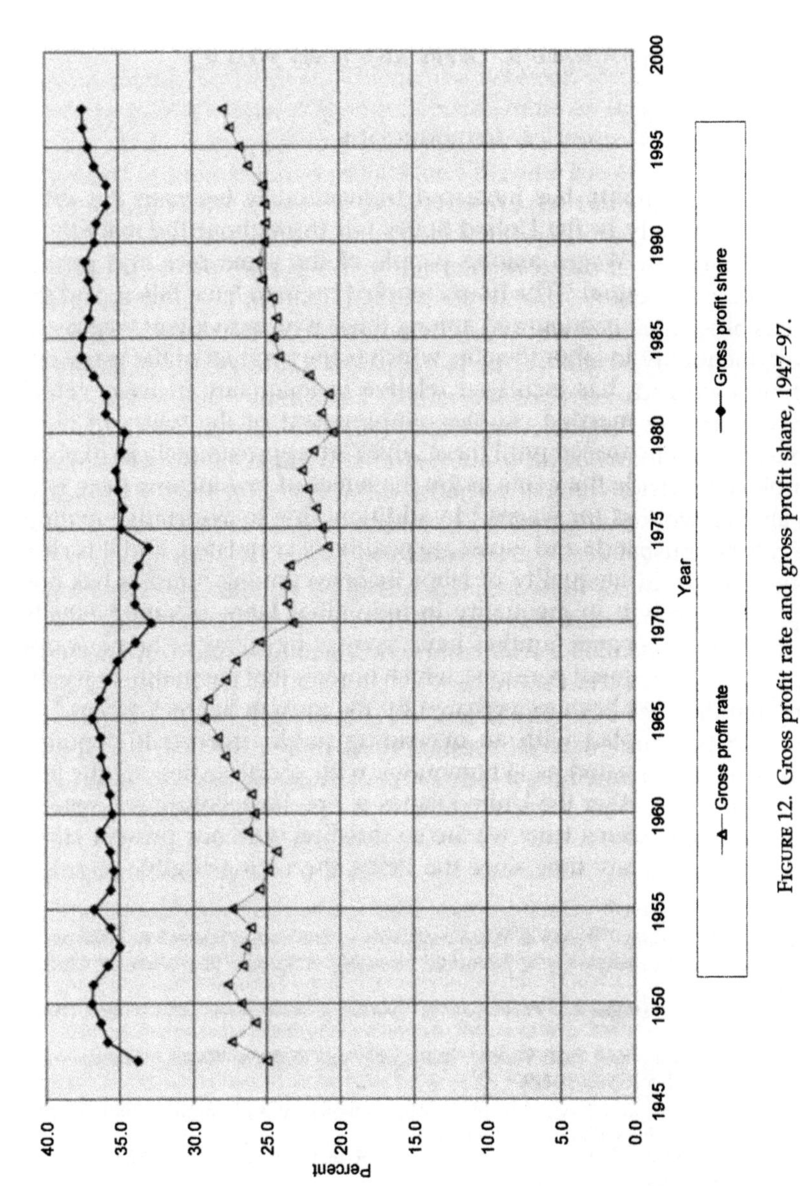

FIGURE 12. Gross profit rate and gross profit share, 1947–97.

Data sources: Both series: various tables located at Bureau of Economic Analysis, "National Accounts Data."

INEQUALITY, INCENTIVES, AND OPPORTUNITY

BY DONALD R. DEERE AND FINIS WELCH

I. INTRODUCTION

Measured inequality has increased tremendously between the 1960s and 1990s, not only in the United States but throughout the majority of industrial nations. Wages among people of the same race and gender have become less equal.[1] The hours worked by men have fallen, and the drop has been more pronounced among those who earn lower wages—as a result, inequality in labor income, which is the product of the wage rate and hours worked, has increased relative to inequality in wage rates.[2] Moreover, among married couples, employment of the wives of high-income men has increased until these wives are approximately as likely to be employed outside the home as are the wives of low-income men, who have always worked for wages.[3] In addition, due to assortative mating, wage rates of husbands and wives are positively correlated, and it is clear that the growth in inequality of labor incomes among families has outstripped the growth in inequality in individual labor income.[4] Finally, only the highest-income families have savings in excess of home equity and company-sponsored pensions, which implies that inequality in wealth among families has been exacerbated by the growth in stock prices.[5]

These facts, coupled with an overriding public interest in "equity," which is usually treated as synonymous with social justice, might lead one to wonder whether the United States is ripe for revolution![6] Instead, just the opposite seems true: we are so satisfied with our present status that, more than at any time since the 1950s, the voting-eligible populace

[1] See Donald R. Deere, "Trends in Wage Inequality in the United States," in Finis Welch, ed., *The Causes and Consequences of Increasing Inequality* (Chicago: University of Chicago Press, 2001).

[2] See Finis Welch, "Wages and Participation," *Journal of Labor Economics* 15, no. 1 (1997): S77–S103.

[3] See Kevin Murphy and Finis Welch, "Inequality and Relative Wages," *American Economic Review* 83, no. 2 (1993): 104–9.

[4] See Chinhui Juhn and Kevin Murphy, "Wage Inequality and Family Labor Supply," *Journal of Labor Economics* 15, no. 1 (1997): 72–97.

[5] See James P. Smith, "Why Is Wealth Inequality Rising?" in Welch, ed., *The Causes and Consequences of Increasing Inequality*.

[6] According to the 1996 General Social Survey (GSS) administered by the National Opinion Research Center (NORC), over two-thirds of those responding indicated that they either agreed or strongly agreed with the statement, "Differences in income in America are too large." See National Opinion Research Center, "Codebook Variable: INCGAP," available on-line at http://www.icpsr.umich.edu/GSS/rnd1998/merged/cdbk/incgap.htm.

appears to be uninterested in its ability to effect change.[7] Evangelical zeal for changing the rules of economic behavior and accumulation is not only at a half-century low, but the predominant mood is at least as favorable to changes that would immediately increase inequality as it is to those that would reduce it.[8]

We believe that the explanation for this apparent contradiction, and the current mood, lies with the distinction between *opportunity* and *achievement*; the public's sense of justice depends more on the former, and a case can be made that opportunities have become more equal even though measured economic achievements have become less equal.[9] With equality of opportunity, differences in achievement arise from differences in individual actions rather than factors over which individuals have no control.

Social scientists distinguish opportunity from achievement as concepts, but when it comes to the numbers, opportunity is hard to measure and too often we opt for achievements instead. We use wage, income, and wealth statistics as proxy measures of equity, although recent evidence suggests that they can mislead. Let us take as given increasing inequality in wage rates and consider the associated changes in individual labor incomes, family incomes, and household wealth that have added to our measures of inequality. In reverse order, we begin with household wealth. As stock prices have soared, instead of a growing sense of disenfranchisement among the low-income populace, there has been enthusiastic "why not me too" speculation.[10] Here, one might want to distinguish between wealth resulting from one's own savings and inherited wealth, but perhaps not. Is it unjust to invest in your children's education or to save for their future? Many of us publicly bemoan inequality and, especially, increasing inequality, but there is not one among us who will not do one's best to see that one's children get ahead! We also strive to succeed, and most of us do; should we try less because we understand that others will not be as successful?

[7] The 1996 GSS also indicates that fewer than one-third of those responding agreed or strongly agreed with the statement, "It is the responsibility of the government to reduce the differences in income between people with high incomes and those with low incomes." See National Opinion Research Center, "Codebook Variable: EQINCOME," available on-line at http://www.icpsr.umich.edu/GSS/rnd1998/merged/cdbk/eqincome.htm.

[8] Witness the popular attempts to eliminate the so-called "marriage" and "death" taxes. Of course, other popular reforms, such as proposed changes to increase accountability for student performance, ought to be equalizing in the long run.

[9] The 1993 GSS (the question was not asked in 1996) indicates that over 86 percent of those responding favored "promoting equal opportunity" over "promoting equal outcomes." See National Opinion Research Center, "Codebook Variable: OPOUTCME," available on-line at http://www.icpsr.umich.edu/GSS/rnd1998/merged/cdbk/opoutcme.htm.

[10] Stock ownership has become more widespread at all income levels. Stock ownership increased by about 50 percent between 1989 and 1998 for all families, and doubled for families with incomes below $25,000 (in 1998 dollars). See Arthur B. Kennickell, Martha Starr-McCluer, and Brian J. Surette, "Recent Changes in U.S. Family Finances: Results from the 1998 Survey of Consumer Finances," *Federal Reserve Bulletin* 86, no. 1 (2000): 1–29.

Regarding family incomes, would we be a better, more just society if the wives of high-wage men did not work? Should high-wage women marry only low-wage men?

Finally, we come to individual labor income. At one time, men with the lowest wages worked longer hours and at least as many days each year as did high-wage men; they had to then, but now they do not. It may be that some of today's low-wage men cannot work, but others can and choose something else. Would they be better off if forced to work? Would our society be more just? Here, the answers seem to be "No" and "Maybe," but as we hope to show, declining employment levels of those with low wage potential are a likely result of the "War on Poverty," an earlier attempt to legislate equity. This brings us to the two points we hope to make: inequality is not necessarily bad and, from a societal perspective, the costs of reducing measured inequality—inequality of achievement—often exceed the benefits.

The empirical part of this essay examines trends in wage rates showing increasing equality between women and men and between blacks and whites; this has coincided with the growing differentials among those of the same race and gender. We also summarize responses in levels of education that have accompanied changes in education wage premiums, which declined in the 1970s and then increased sharply thereafter. And, to further illustrate responses to the incentives implicit in changing wage differentials, we show how the trend of increasing differences in time worked between those with high wages and those with low wages runs parallel to the trend in the high-to-low wage differential. Prior to this empirical analysis, Section II considers some of the basics regarding inequality. In brief, it is the individual's ability to capitalize on opportunities that helps to allocate labor to the highest-valued pursuits. Without inequality, there are no incentives, and without incentives, there is no efficiency.

II. Some of the Basics

We begin with a simple economy whose members have identical preferences. Using identical abilities as the benchmark, we consider inequality in abilities and in acquired skills to illustrate some dimensions of equity and efficiency. We assume each person in this economy has identical preferences; this allows us to set aside concerns about conflicts arising from disagreements regarding values.

To fix terminology, we will say that "abilities" are assumed to be endowed at birth, whereas "skills" may be acquired later; our initial cases do not involve skill-acquisition, however. In Case I, all members of the simple economy are assumed to have equal abilities and to be equally diligent. The economy is assumed to have multiple activities so that, with transaction costs, there will be gains from specialization where different individuals enter different "occupations." As an example, specialization would be efficient if jobs were separated spatially so that once one has begun on one job, it makes sense to continue rather than switch to another. Individuals might switch jobs from day to day, but would stay in the same job during the day. Longer-term specialization would result if job experience increased productivity. In this case, even though there is specialization, if all jobs are equally difficult and have similar amenities, and if all workers are fully informed, then regardless of the job or occupation chosen, all would receive the same wage, earn the same income, and experience the same level of well-being.

It is important that the wage that is received is an equilibrium wage that, within job, tends to increase to attract more workers when there are too few of them, and to fall when there are too many. In this, the simplest case, it is the fact of equal ability and taste, together with the associated freedom to switch jobs in pursuit of higher wages, that results in wage equality. If wages differed across jobs, reflecting differences at the margin in the value of labor in those jobs, workers would move from those paying less to those paying more until wages were equal everywhere. If equality were mandated by a supervisory authority, there would be no incentive to change jobs and, although equality might be able to be maintained, labor would be inefficiently allocated among jobs and society's product would be reduced. The equity/efficiency contrast that occupies much of economics and makes economists so much more reticent than many others to mandate wages or redistribute incomes stems from the dual role of wages in a market economy. Wages translate to income (rather, potential pretax income), but they also signal relative scarcity and abundance.

We believe that Case I, our reference case, is the only one where equal abilities and diligence, along with identical preferences, result in full equality of observable outcomes—wages and incomes. To see just how easily equality of outcomes can be broken, consider cases where the amenities of jobs differ. Those entering the more onerous jobs would have to be compensated with higher wages and would earn greater incomes. All would experience the same level of well-being, but observable outcomes would differ.

In Case II, we assume that abilities vary. In this case, if some are better suited to certain activities than others, then the gains from specialization are supplemented by the added gain from matching jobs and abilities.

Once we move into the realm of differences in abilities, we need to distinguish between type and level. Suppose, for example, that there are only two abilities, and that one group in the population has one and the remainder has the other. The two groups need not be of equal size. Suppose further that all members of each group have the same level of ability. Ignoring differences in job amenities, as in Case I, all members of each group will have the same wage, but the wages of the two groups will most likely differ. How they differ depends on the value consumers place on the products of the occupation where each group prevails, and on the respective sizes of the two groups. In Case I, consumers' valuation of the products did not affect wage inequality because abilities were equal, but product values matter when abilities are unequal. The group with the relatively scarce ability will receive a wage premium. In this case, we know that differences among the individuals permit occupational sorting to increase efficiency in production. In an important sense the economy is better off than it would be if all had the same ability set, say, a simple blend of the two abilities. It is unclear, however, that all within the economy would be better off.

The equity/efficiency contrast is clearer if abilities are one-dimensional, where individuals differ only in the level of ability. Here, if there is scale economy—if one fast runner can provide a service that two slow runners cannot, if two with IQs of 70 cannot solve problems that one with an IQ of 140 can—then inequality of ability enhances gains from specialization in the sense that total product is larger when ability levels differ than it would be if all had the average level of ability. Except for relatively perverse conditions, however, there is a general principle to the effect that, without redistribution, the least able in the heterogenous case will not be as well off as they would be if everyone had the average level of ability.

In comparing different economy-wide outcomes, economists distinguish two forms of change that can be viewed as beneficial. The more stringent is the sort of change where no one loses and at least one gains; such a change is called *Pareto optimal*. The less stringent is the sort of change where there are winners and losers, but the gains to the winners are sufficient to compensate the losers and leave something over. This latter form of change is acceptable under the *compensation principle*, which only asks whether, with redistribution, the more stringent form of optimality could be realized in principle, regardless of whether compensation in fact occurs. The gains from specialization that arise from heterogenous labor are gains under the compensation principle. They fall within the same class of improvements as do the gains from immigration and international trade. (Immigration may reduce the wages of the native workers with abilities most similar to those of the immigrants, but overall national product will increase. Likewise, the import of certain goods may harm those in the domestic industry, but consumers gain more.) In addition, if the redistribution to compensate those with less ability were in fact made, it would be without the cost of lost output, because ability, and thus occupational choice, is endowed at birth under our assumptions here.[11]

We saw in Case I that with differing job amenities, it is not straightforward that one can infer well-being from wages. The problem becomes

[11] This puts to the side labor supply, or quantity of work, considerations.

more severe in a complex economy where skills can be developed through investments. Let us maintain the Case I assumption that everyone is equal—in this case, equal in what they can do with and without a given level of acquired skill as well as equal in the ability to acquire skill. If we also maintain the assumption that individuals are fully informed and free to choose among diverse occupations, then regardless of the individual choices made, all will be equally well off.

Now consider education as an example of skills or occupations that require investments. There are several costs of attending school, including the income that is given up or deferred while in school, and for the investment to be worthwhile the wage of educated workers will have to be sufficient to compensate for these costs. Learning on the job is also an option for those in careers in which one can divert some of today's potential income toward being more productive later.

Continuing with the Case I assumptions, if we have an economy whose members differ in the skills they acquired in school and on the job, and, furthermore, are of differing ages and thus at different points in their careers, then we would expect to observe differences in wages without differences in lifetime well-being. Despite marked differences in observable outcomes (i.e., wages and incomes) at any given point in time as well as over a career, there is no role for redistribution. Any attempt to reduce observed inequality would not only be inequitable, but would also reduce the economy's total product, as taxes on higher earnings would reduce skill investment. All of the observed inequality is, with respect to well-being, equalizing.

There is nothing to add by extending this case to allow for differing abilities. As before, differences in abilities create comparative advantage, where individuals acquire the skills and enter the occupations that best suit them. The efficiency gains are obvious, and the compensation-principle gains will continue as in the earlier case; effects on individual welfare are conjectural.

The simple economies described above have highlighted the basic value of inequality—it allows specialization that increases the total product of an economy. In addition, it is worth noting that the value of heterogenous abilities and activities is, in a real sense, enhanced by differential preferences, since we are not only able to choose between alternatives that accommodate our abilities, but among those that accommodate our interests as well.[12]

In discussing these economies we have isolated two sources of wage inequality—differences in endowed abilities and differences in skill investments (not to mention differences in job amenities). There may be a role for redistribution in offsetting differences in abilities, but not for

[12] We assume that the tendency to rationalize more often than not results in compatible interests and abilities.

altering the returns on skill investments. To the extent that differences in wages, and, in particular, increases in wage inequality, are due to differences in skill investments and their value, fairness suggests a cautious approach. Furthermore, attempts to generate greater equality of economic outcomes may destroy incentives to remain productive and develop skills.

III. Overview: Introduction to the Data and the Conclusions

We hope that we have set the stage for the first of our two main points, that due to the incentive role of wages in signaling relative labor scarcity and surplus and the potential gains in efficiency that result when individuals respond to these signals, inequality is not necessarily bad. The empirical sections that follow (Sections IV and V) begin with a description of the U.S. experience in increasing wage inequality. After providing this description, we illustrate what we consider to be the good and the bad regarding responses to the incentives that result from growth in wage inequality. In Subsection A of Section IV, we trace the college-enrollment responses to increasing education wage premiums. In Section IV's Subsection B, we document the declines in employment and hours worked among those with the lowest wage potential. We conclude the empirical analysis in Section V by showing how race and gender differences in wages have narrowed substantially.

During the past twenty years, the college/high school wage differential has increased by two-thirds, and during this same period, the proportion of young men who have more than a high school education increased by more than a quarter.[13] The growing wage differential between those with more education and those with less, alongside rapid increases in average levels of education, is perhaps the primary reason that this three-decade period of increasing wage inequality has been characterized as, predominantly, one of growing demand for skill. A paper by Kevin Murphy and Finis Welch provides a rough estimate approximating the growth in levels of education required to match the growth in demand that has already occurred.[14] Murphy and Welch then translate the estimated increase in levels of education into the implied increases in average wages in order to derive an order-of-magnitude estimate of the import of the increase in the demand for a more highly educated workforce. If the requisite increase in education levels were realized over two decades, the addi-

[13] At the same time, education levels have increased even more rapidly for women than for men, but part of the increase seems to have resulted from the shift from working inside the home to working elsewhere, and therefore we cannot say whether the incentive response of women to the increased wage premium outstripped that of men.

[14] Kevin Murphy and Finis Welch, "Wage Differentials in the 1990s: Is the Glass Half-Full or Half-Empty?" in Welch, ed., *The Causes and Consequences of Increasing Inequality*.

tional growth in average wages during this period would exceed the economy-wide rates of growth that were realized during the 1980s.[15]

Although we begin here with an underlying change in the structure of the economy that initially increases wage inequality, the response to the incentive for individuals to acquire more education is beneficial. Society is better off because the size of the economic pie has increased. Moreover, as educational levels increase, the education wage premium will be reduced, and the ultimate effect of the response will be to reduce wage inequality.

The first so-called "law" of economics is that of diminishing returns or variable proportions. It is fundamental to all ideas of equilibrium. The calculations just described assume that the response to increasing education wage premiums is an increase in education levels; due to diminishing returns, this reduces the education wage premium. With diminishing returns, the effect of the responses to the incentives implicit in increasing wage inequality is to reduce the inequality. This is not to say that, following the response, wages will be more equal than before the increased demand; the point, instead, is that the change creates an incentive for its partial amelioration. That is the good; next comes the bad.

There probably is no more deeply seated belief among labor economists than the notion that learning by doing enhances individual productivity; the more you work, the higher your wage. The converse is obvious and unfortunate, because the experience of the last three decades is that employment levels have nose-dived among men with the lowest wage potential. Thus, following the illustration regarding education, we examine the association between wages and time worked.

As a matter of principle, economists know that the wage/work gradient can be positive or negative. The argument for the positive interpretation is that if it pays, people will work. The argument for the negative interpretation is that people work to live, and higher wages permit less work. The early labor economists, steeped in the experiences of the Great Depression, took the negative view, but the positive view is clearly relevant now.

During the late 1960s, men in the prime earning ages of 25 to 54 worked an average of 2,190 hours per year, and high school dropouts worked almost as much—2,060 hours. By the late 1990s, the annual average work-time for all men had dropped 160 hours (the equivalent of four 40-hour work weeks), and the drop is due disproportionately to those with the lowest potential wages. In the late 1960s, the average annual work-time reported by prime-aged high school dropouts was 270 hours less than the average reported by college graduates; by the late 1990s, the differential had more than doubled, to 580 hours—more than a quarter of a 40-hour

[15] This calculation ignores effects of investments in skills other than education, and also ignores the value of further increases in the demand for skills.

by 52-week year. Time worked did not drop uniformly; instead, it became more varied between individuals, with increasing proportions not working at all. For example, during the thirty years from 1968 to 1998, the proportion of prime-aged men who did not work increased from 2.4 to 7.1 percent; imagine, one in fourteen men not employed for even one week during a full year. This change toward an increasing fraction of the population not working pervades all levels of schooling, but is more pronounced at the lower levels, where wages are lowest. The proportion of prime-aged college-graduate men who do not work increased from 1.1 to 3.3 percent, while the proportion of high school dropouts who do not work increased from 4.2 to an astonishing 16.0 percent. Among male high school dropouts, nearly one in every six did not work during the late 1990s when, according to the data for unemployment among job-seekers, jobs were more available than at anytime in the last quarter-century.

Often, when we point out the extraordinarily low employment levels among low-wage prime-aged men, we are asked, "What do they do; how can they live?" To illustrate, we follow the data for wages and time worked with an examination of sources of income among men who do not work.

We know that welfare programs have two sides: a "safety net" and a "magnet." It is the "magnet" that concerns us and lends support for the second of our two propositions, that the costs of reducing inequality can exceed the benefits. If any of us had had perfect foresight in forecasting employment trends following the mid-1960s introduction of the Great Society programs, we would have been well advised to keep our predictions to ourselves so as to avoid being dismissed as crackpots! With the luxury of alternative means of support, declining wages for those with the lowest wage potential have induced a response that is doubly negative; the economic pie is smaller than it otherwise would be and, with the link from work to wages, wages are less equal. We note below that declining employment among those with the lowest wage potential seems to be a result of falling wages instead of increasing wage inequality.

The history of increasing wage inequality is that during the mid-to-late 1970s, wage dispersion increased rapidly while real median wages trended slowly downward and real wages below the median dropped much more rapidly. In contrast, wages above the median increased in real terms. Since the mid-1980s, and especially since the late 1980s, real wages have increased throughout the wage distribution, and during this later period there have been marked increases in hours worked among those at all wage levels.

If one were to try to find a simple way of monitoring a society to form an idea as to the trend and the level of social justice, perhaps two of the first considerations would be the level of intergenerational mobility and the extent to which ascribed characteristics over which individuals have no control, such as race and gender, predict economic status. "Intergenerational mobility" refers to how the relative economic status of parents and their children compare—it is a measure of whether the economic differences between the children of the poor and the children of the rich are narrower or wider than the differences between their respective sets of parents.

We do not have data on particular families and their children over a time period long enough for us to be able to tell whether intergenerational differentials are narrowing or widening. We began collecting long-term panel data (that is, data on the same set of individuals for multiple time periods) in the late 1960s, and economist Gary Solon has studied perhaps the richest source of such information available, the Panel Study of Income Dynamics, to estimate a father-son correlation of economic status of between .4 and .5.[16] We, of course, have only a limited idea of what such a correlation would be were we able costlessly to change it. We presume that families with above-average resources hope for and expect a positive correlation, and that those with below-average resources hope for, but probably do not expect, a negative correlation. Regardless, because resources can be used effectively, we expect that an optimal correlation would be positive, but perhaps would not be "too high." Note that both a zero correlation and a correlation of one indicate that nothing the family does matters. In the zero case, all have the same chance of success regardless of background, while with a correlation of one, economic status is inherited.

We believe that Solon's estimates are indicative of a highly mobile society. Instead of using the two boundaries, we use the midpoint, .45, for the father-son correlation. This correlation is the simplest measure of the expected carryover from one generation to the next. For example, if the economic statuses of two men differ by a specified amount, then the expected difference between their sons' economic statuses is .45 of that amount. To continue to other generations, the correlation is raised to the power by which the generations are separated, so that we square the correlation to calculate the part of the difference in status between two men that is expected to carry over to their grandsons.

This, of course, only gives us the expected differential; the variation about it gives us the possibility of reversal. For concreteness, consider fathers A and B such that, within their generation, A's economic status exceeds the average by one-half of a standard deviation, while B's is short of the average by an equal amount. If economic status follows a bell curve, 38.3 percent of the population will have a status between that of A and B. With this assumption, A is effectively on the boundary of the upper third of the population, while B is on the boundary of the lower third. With a father-son correlation of .45, the expected difference in status

[16] See Gary Solon, "Mobility within and between Generations," in Welch, ed., *The Causes and Consequences of Increasing Inequality*.

between A's and B's sons is .45 times the standard deviation; between A's and B's grandsons the difference is .2025 times the standard deviation. By assumption, A's status exceeds B's, but because the father-son correlation is imperfect, the probability that A's son has superior status to B's is only 63.9 percent, in contrast to a probability of 36.1 percent that B's son has superior status. The grandsons are closer still; the probability that A's grandsons have superior status is 55.8 percent, in contrast to a probability of 44.2 percent that B's grandsons outperform A's.[17] Solon's estimate implies that while there is nontrivial carryover from father to son, the grandsons are essentially on even terms.

This brings us to the extent to which easily identifiable demographic factors predict economic status. In Section V, we use a familiar index, the percentile location, to trace the movement of black men and women and of white women through the wage distribution of white men. The idea is like test-score comparisons: if the average wage percentile of women in a particular year is 25, this means that if each woman is given a percentile score and these scores are then averaged, then on average, 25 percent of the men had lower wages than women while 75 percent had higher wages. Presumably, most are familiar with the basic fact that there has been marked improvement in the relative status of black men and of both black and white women. The calculations we present in Section V are one way of illustrating the gains. We might also consider the following: The median wage is the 50th percentile. At the beginning of the period we

[17] Results for the bivariate normal distribution (see Morris H. DeGroot, *Probability and Statistics*, 2d ed. [Reading, MA: Addison-Wesley, 1986], 300–303) imply that if a father's and son's economic statuses are each distributed normally with the same mean, μ, and standard deviation, σ, and with a correlation of .45, then the son's economic status, denoted S, is related to the father's economic status, denoted F, according to

$$S = \mu + \sigma[.45(F - \mu)/\sigma + z(1 - .45^2)^{1/2}],$$

where z is a standard normal random variable independent of F. Thus, the expected value of a son's economic status, given his father's economic status, is

$$E(S|F) = \mu(1 - .45) + .45F.$$

This further implies that the expected value of a son's economic status, given his father's economic status is half a standard deviation above the mean (i.e., one can substitute $\mu + (1/2)\sigma$ for F), equals $\mu + (.45/2)\sigma$. Likewise, the expected value of a son's economic status, given his father's economic status is half a standard deviation below the mean, equals $\mu - (.45/2)\sigma$. Thus, the expected difference in these two sons' economic statuses is $[\mu + (.45/2)\sigma] - [\mu - (.45/2)\sigma] = .45\sigma$. For grandsons the correlation is $.45^2 = .2025$; hence, the expected difference in economic status is $.2025\sigma$.

The probability that the economic status of A's son, denoted S_A, is higher than the economic status of B's son, denoted S_B, equals the probability that $S_A - S_B$ is greater than zero. The difference in these two normal random variables is distributed normally, with a mean of $.45\sigma$ and a variance of $2(1 - .45^2)\sigma^2$. The probability that this difference is greater than zero can be recovered from a cumulative standard normal probability table; it is 63.9 percent. For grandsons, the calculation uses .2025 for .45, and the resulting probability that the economic status of A's grandson is higher than that of B's grandson equals 55.8 percent.

examine, 1967–69, 18 percent of black men earned wages in excess of the median for white men; by 1996–98 the proportion had increased to 31 percent. Gains for women are more impressive, but begin from a lower base. For black women, at the beginning of the period, only 6 percent exceeded the median for white men, in contrast to 27 percent at the end of the period. For white women, at the beginning of the period, only 9 percent exceeded the median for white men, in contrast to 33 percent at the end of the period.

On seeing these numbers, we expect that many will wonder how much of the improved relative economic status of women and black men is due to real growth in productivity and how much is due to affirmative action and antidiscrimination legislation and its enforcement. The short answer is that we do not know, but we think that productivity growth dominates.[18]

IV. Increasing Wage Inequality and the Response to Incentives

In this section, we use data from the 1968–99 March Current Population Surveys to examine changes in wage inequality and its impact. The Current Population Survey (CPS) is a monthly survey of approximately fifty thousand U.S. households administered by the U.S. Census Bureau. The data from these surveys are used by the Bureau of Labor Statistics to produce the monthly national unemployment statistics, as well as to provide information for other reports and for use by researchers. The March CPS includes an Annual Income and Demographic Supplement that asks households about each member's earnings and employment during the previous calendar year. All of the wage measures presented below are based on weekly labor earnings for full-time work (i.e., 35 or more hours per week), and include wage imputations for those who work part-time or not at all.[19] Other information collected by the CPS includes age, race, gender, educational attainment, and sources and amounts of unearned income.

[18] See James P. Smith and Finis Welch, "Affirmative Action and Labor Markets," *Journal of Labor Economics* 2, no. 2 (1984): 269–301. Concentrating on the 1960–80 wage convergence between black and white men, Smith and Welch observed that the gains by black men were pervasive throughout the economy and were not concentrated disproportionately in those parts of the economy where government contractors were monitored by the Office of Federal Contract Compliance Program or where larger firms (which report to the Equal Employment Opportunity Commission) were concentrated.

[19] Wages for an individual are calculated as annual earnings (before taxes) in the previous year divided by the number of weeks worked during that year. The wage calculations thus refer to the years 1967–98. An important consideration when examining increases in inequality is what happened to the wage opportunities of men who do not work. In order to include all men in the calculations, we imputed the wages of those who worked fewer than 35 hours per week or who worked fewer than 14 weeks (including zero), using a regression based on various characteristics including age, education, marital status, race, and how much they did work (if working). For women, whose wages we compare to men's in Section V, the imputation of wages for those who do not work is a difficult issue and is not done; only women working full-time (at least 35 hours per week) for at least one week in a year are included in the calculations in Section V.

TABLE 1. *Wages of white men relative to the median at selected percentiles of the wage distribution*

	Percentile				
Year	10 (%)	30 (%)	50 (%)	70 (%)	90 (%)
1969	46	78	100	126	184
1983	39	69	100	137	208
1996	38	69	100	141	231

Table 1 documents the increase in wage inequality among white men over the last thirty years.[20] Wage inequality is illustrated by showing how the wage at selected percentiles of the wage distribution compares to the wage at the median, or 50th percentile. The years reported in most of the tables (Tables 1 through 6 and Table 9) refer to the midpoints of five-year periods—in Table 1, for instance, the first row, denoted 1969, refers to wages for 1967–71, while the second and third rows refer to wages for 1981–85 and 1994–98, respectively.

During 1969 the wage at the 10th percentile averaged 46 percent of the median wage, while the wage at the 30th percentile was 78 percent of the median. At the high end, wages at the 70th and 90th percentiles were 126 percent and 184 percent, respectively, of the median wage. Over the next thirty years, wages below the median lost ground relative to the median, while wages above the median gained. By 1996, the wage at the 10th percentile had lost 8 percentage points vis-à-vis the median, and the wage at the 30th percentile had lost 9 percentage points. The wages at the 70th and 90th percentiles had gained 15 and 47 percentage points, respectively, relative to the median.

The large increase in wage inequality over the last thirty years has attracted significant attention, but note that a large majority of this increase has occurred in the top half of wages, especially most recently. Over 85 percent of the increase in the spread between wages at the 90th and 10th percentiles, as measured by percentage points of the median, resulted from the 90th-percentile wage gaining with respect to the median. Between 1969 and 1996 the 90th/10th differential increased from 138 (= 184–46) to 193 (= 231–38), for a change of 55 percentage points. This 55-point increase was comprised of a 47-point (85.5 percent of the total) increase in the 90th/50th differential and an 8-point (14.5 percent) increase in the 50th/10th differential.

[20] All of the wage calculations here include only white men, one to forty years out of school, in order to focus on wage changes for a relatively homogenous group. Section V compares the wages of black men and black and white women to the wages of white men.

TABLE 2. *Growth in real wages at selected percentiles of the wage distribution*

	Percentile				
Period	10 (%)	30 (%)	50 (%)	70 (%)	90 (%)
1969 to 1983	−19	−14	−4	5	9
1983 to 1996	1	1	2	4	13

Note: Real wages are calculated using the GDP deflator for personal consumption expenditures.

Table 1 also shows that the importance of the top half of the wage distribution with respect to increasing inequality is even more pronounced from the early 1980s to the present. Wages in the bottom half of the wage distribution remained stable from 1983 to 1996, with virtually all of the increase in wage inequality being due to increases in wages above the median.

Besides increases in wage inequality—changes in the value of individuals' wages relative to those of others—another well-known and much-discussed fact about wages over the past thirty years is the decline in their real value, or purchasing power. Table 2 documents this change for the same percentiles of the wage distribution.

Between 1969 and 1983 there was a sharp decline in real wages at the 10th and 30th percentiles, with a smaller decline at the median. During the same period, real wages above the median increased. More recently, however, real wages have increased throughout the distribution. Between 1983 and 1996 real wages increased by a small amount at the median and below, with larger increases above the median, especially at the 90th percentile. Referring to the discussion of Pareto optimality above, the wage changes over the past fifteen to twenty years have, absent envy, made all better off.

The changing incentives and opportunities resulting from the increasing wage inequality and changing real wages over the past thirty years have led individuals to change their behavior. From the early 1980s to the present there is a good story—investments in education have increased substantially as individuals have capitalized on opportunities created by the increased demand for skill. From the late 1960s to the early 1980s the picture is darker—men, especially those with only low-wage opportunities, were less likely to work. Part of the reason for this drop in work, however, appears to be the availability of income from sources other than labor earnings. We turn now to discussing sources of the increase in wage inequality, and then we will examine how individuals have responded to these changes in wages.

With reference to the above discussion of the basics, individuals' wages differ because of differences in endowed abilities (including the ability to develop skill) and acquired skills. We can add luck to this list, and perhaps include endowed abilities as part of luck, noting that luck has both transitory and permanent components. Although there are many ways of measuring the import of these factors of interest, the one that is used most often is the proportion of differences in wages that is attributed to each factor. Consider the following equation describing the natural logarithm of an individual's wage:

$$\log(\text{wage}) = a + b\,\text{education} + c\,\text{experience} + \text{other things}.$$

The letters a, b, and c represent unknown parameters, where a is the expected wage of someone with no experience or education, and b and c measure the wage impact of incremental additions to education and experience, respectively. The parameters b and c will change over time if there are changes in the market value of education or experience. Education, typically measured by years of schooling, and experience, typically measured by years since leaving school, represent the observable aspects of skill-acquisition. "Other things" includes endowed abilities, luck, measurement error in wages, and, importantly, the portion of skill-acquisition and effort not captured by either the years-of-schooling or years-of-experience measures.

Using wages, years-of-schooling, and years-of-experience measures for white men (wages here being the same as those used in Table 1), our regression suggests that differences in schooling and experience account for about 30 percent of wage variation. We know, however, that about 20 percent of wage variation is transitory, due either to mismeasurement of wages or temporary blips in actual wages, so that measured differences in schooling and experience account for a somewhat larger proportion of persistent differences in wages.[21]

The shares of wage variation attributable to measured education and experience differences and to differences in "other things" have remained roughly constant over the past thirty years, so that wage inequality among individuals with matching years of schooling and years of experience also has increased. Table 3, which is analogous to Table 1, documents the increase in wage inequality within education and experience levels for white men. As was the case for total wage inequality, a majority of the increase in inequality within education and experience levels has occurred above the median, and wage inequality in the bottom half of the distribution has been virtually unchanged since the early 1980s.

As can be inferred from the discussion above, "other things" account for between 60 and 70 percent of the persistent differences in wages. Is

[21] The figure for transitory wage variation comes from noting that the distribution of a two-year average of wages has a variance that is about 80 percent as large as the variance of the distribution of a single year's wages.

TABLE 3. *Wages within education and experience levels relative to the median at selected percentiles of the residual wage distribution*

	Percentile				
Year	10 (%)	30 (%)	50 (%)	70 (%)	90 (%)
1969	55	81	100	122	164
1983	47	76	100	128	179
1996	46	75	100	130	190

this "too much"? Recall that an important component of this wage residual is skill-acquisition not reflected in the years-of-education or years-of-experience measures. Consider a world in which "other things" play no role in determining wages: an individual makes only one decision—when to leave school—that affects his wage; after that, wages follow the experience path no matter what. There is nothing in the years-of-education measure to capture the quality of education, what was learned or what was retained, or an education's applicability to the job producing one's wage. There also is nothing in the years-of-experience measure to represent the quality or continuity of the work career and nothing regarding the career's applicability to one's present job. And, finally, there is nothing for initiative or effort. It is clear that our measures of education and experience are poor proxies for skill-acquisition and that the role of investments in explaining wage differentials is much larger.[22]

Let us consider an increase in wage inequality attributable to increased variance of the measured education and experience components. We begin by holding constant the distribution of education and experience in the population and examining increases in the parameters b or c, reflecting increases in the value of education or experience (with compensating reductions in the intercept, a, to hold the average wage constant). If the value of work experience increases, then those with below-average years of experience lose relative to those with above-average amounts. But there are no losers. Those of above-average experience gain immediately because their wages increase and will remain higher than they otherwise would have been throughout the remainder of their careers. For those with below-average experience, including future labor-market entrants, what is lost in the early career is made up in the late career. There is a different implication for increases in the value of education. Those in the

[22] One suspects that the opposite is probably true of job amenities, however. See Robert E. B. Lucas, "Hedonic Wage Equations and Psychic Wages in the Returns to Schooling," *American Economic Review* 67, no. 4 (1977): 549–58.

current workforce with below-average years of schooling lose relative to those with above-average amounts. Future workers gain, however, because they can take advantage of the increased value of education by making a greater investment in schooling, to which we now turn.

A. The good: education responds to incentives

As the wages of those with more education have increased relative to those of people with less, levels of education have increased in response. Table 4 presents changes in years of schooling for men who recently entered the labor market and the relationship between these changes and changes in the value of education, as measured by the average wage premium received by college graduates compared to those with only a high school diploma.

After declining somewhat during the 1970s, the wage premium received by those with a college degree increased sharply during the 1980s.[23] This increase continued, though at a slower pace, into the 1990s, with the recent premium at 65 percent, a full 26 points higher than it was at the end of the 1970s.[24] On the heels of this substantial shift in relative wages, the education levels of new labor-market entrants also went up. Thirty-nine percent of the recent entrants in 1979 had at least one year of college, while seventeen years later, in 1996, half of the recent entrants had some college.[25] The younger cohorts have capitalized on the increased value of education by deciding to stay in school longer.

In fact, there has been a renewed focus on education at all levels during the last fifteen to twenty years. Although the Coleman report warning of students falling behind came out in the 1960s,[26] it appears to have taken the substantial increase in the market value of educational investments from 1980 onward to prompt the heightened interest in schools, from elementary through university, and in school accountability.

[23] The wage premium for college graduates is calculated including solely those that only have a bachelor's degree. If those with a postgraduate education are included in the category of college graduates, the premium rises from 46 percent in 1979 to 89 percent in 1996.

[24] While the average wage of college graduates is higher than, and has increased relative to, the average wage of high school graduates, education is not a guarantee of a higher wage. The significant inequality in wages among those with the same years of education implies that there is overlap between the wages of high school graduates and the wages of college graduates. In the late 1960s, the probability that a randomly selected high school graduate had a wage higher than a randomly selected college graduate was about 30 percent. After increasing slightly during the 1970s, this probability was again about 30 percent in the late 1990s.

[25] The enrollment rate for all 18- to 24-year-olds (men and women) in postsecondary-education institutions shows a similar pattern—the rate was 25.7 percent in 1970, 25.7 percent again in 1980, 32.0 percent in 1990, and 36.5 percent in 1998. See U.S. Department of Education, National Center for Education Statistics, *The Condition of Education 2000* (Washington, DC: U.S. Government Printing Office, 2000), 114.

[26] James S. Coleman et al., *Equality of Educational Opportunity* (Washington, DC: U.S. Government Printing Office, 1966).

TABLE 4. *Education wage premiums and educational investments over time*

Year	College/High School Wage Premium (%)	Percentage of Men 1–5 Years out of School with More than a High School Education (%)
1969	44	38
1974	41	41
1979	39	39
1986	55	44
1991	61	48
1996	65	50

B. The bad: men's work-time responds to incentives

Schooling is not the only variable to respond to wage changes. Table 5 shows the changes over the last thirty years in average annual hours worked by men for the percentiles of the wage distribution reported in Tables 1–3. Average hours fell throughout the wage distribution between 1969 and 1983, and then increased for each wage percentile between 1983 and 1996. Over the entire period, however, this drop and rebound did not occur evenly across the wage distribution. As a result there has been an increase in "hours inequality" that mirrors the increase in wage inequality. Hours worked at the lower wages have fallen rather substantially, while hours at the highest wages have increased. At the 10th- and 30th-percentile wages, average annual hours fell between 1969 and 1996 by 278 and 241 hours, respectively, with each decline equivalent to more than six 40-hour weeks. At the 90th-percentile wage, average annual hours increased by 83 hours—more than two 40-hour weeks. The difference in

TABLE 5. *Annual hours worked by men at selected percentiles of the wage distribution*

	Percentile				
Year	10	30	50	70	90
1969	1,672	2,041	2,154	2,211	2,286
1983	1,296	1,693	1,931	2,081	2,250
1996	1,394	1,800	2,049	2,181	2,369

TABLE 6. *Components of annual hours worked by men at selected wage percentiles*

	Percentile				
Year	10	30	50	70	90
Panel A: Percentage Not Working at All					
1969	12.1%	3.4%	1.5%	0.9%	0.7%
1983	21.8	11.1	6.2	2.9	1.4
1996	21.7	10.4	5.3	3.1	1.5
Panel B: Average Annual Hours among Those Who Work					
1969	1,902	2,112	2,187	2,232	2,301
1983	1,657	1,903	2,058	2,143	2,283
1996	1,782	2,008	2,164	2,251	2,404

average hours worked between those at the 90th-percentile wage and those at the 10th-percentile wage increased by a striking 361 hours (or more than two full-time months) from 1969 to 1996.

The increased disparity in annual hours worked by those with higher wages compared to those with lower wages documented in Table 5 has two components: changes in the percentage of men not working at all, and changes in average hours for those who do work. Recall that the wage distributions we are analyzing include all men, with wages imputed, based on individual characteristics, for those not working or working only part-time (see note 19). Thus it is possible to determine the percentage of men who do not work at each percentile of the wage distribution. Table 6 reports the two components of the changes in average hours presented in Table 5. Panel A reports the average percentage of men who do not work at all during the year, for each wage percentile and period, while Panel B reports the average annual hours of those who do work. Note that the figures in Table 5 can be obtained from the figures in Table 6, except for rounding error, by multiplying the fraction who work by the average hours of those working (e.g., $1{,}672 = (1 - .121) \times 1{,}902$).

Between 1969 and 1983 there was an increase throughout the wage distribution in the percentage of men reporting no work at all during the previous year, as well as a decrease at all wage percentiles of the average hours worked by those who did work. The increase in nonwork and the decrease in hours for those working were much larger at lower wages than at higher wages; both contributed to increasing hours inequality.

The story is different for the changes between 1983 and 1996. The average hours of those working increased by over 100 hours at each wage percentile. In fact, as a percentage, the average hours of those working increased the most (7.5 percent) for those at the lowest, or 10th-percentile, wage. This rebound in average hours by those working did not spill over to men not working at all. The percentage of men not working was virtually unchanged between 1983 and 1996. In 1996, more than 1 in every 5 men at the 10th-percentile wage and more than 1 in every 10 men at the 30th-percentile wage did not work even one week during the year. Compared to 1969, an additional 9.6 men in each 100 at the 10th-percentile wage and another 7 men in each 100 at the 30th-percentile wage were not working at all. Over the same period, there was an increase of only 0.8 men in each 100 at the 90th-percentile wage not working.[27]

The pattern of changes in average hours for those who do work, both across wage percentiles and through time, suggests that changes in real wages, and not increasing wage inequality, have played the primary role in affecting work hours. The different time patterns for average hours of those working and for the percentage who do not work suggest that there is more to the story of nonwork than just changing wages.

Flush with the phenomenal post–World War II success of sustained economic growth at unparalleled rates,[28] and with heightened social conscience arising from the civil rights movement of the early 1960s and the subsequent women's movement, Americans set about "fixing" things on many fronts. Judicial decisions such as *Brown v. Board of Education* and legislation such as the Civil Rights Act, the Voting Rights Act, the Equal Pay Act, and Executive Order 11246 moved to try and ensure equal opportunity (or at least improved opportunities) to groups traditionally denied opportunities.[29] At the same time, the Great Society and the associated War on Poverty moved to provide a social safety net for those still without or unable to take advantage of opportunity.

In 1967 the federal government paid $6.2 billion (1998 dollars) to disabled workers under the Social Security Disability Insurance Program. By 1998, with a working-age population that was 58 percent larger, federal payments to disabled workers had increased tenfold in real terms (to $66.3 billion) under the Disability Insurance and the Supplemental Secu-

[27] The wage distribution for all men includes wages imputed for those men who are not working. Thus, nonworking men can have wages at any percentile of the wage distribution, though the imputed wages of nonworking men are concentrated at the lower percentiles. See note 19 for a discussion of the wage-imputation procedure.

[28] See Michael R. Darby, "Postwar U.S. Consumption, Consumer Expenditures, and Saving," *American Economic Review* 65, no. 2 (1975): 217–22.

[29] *Brown v. Board of Education*, 347 U.S. 483 (1954), declared that state-sanctioned segregation of public schools was unconstitutional. The Civil Rights Act of 1964 prohibits employment discrimination based on race, color, religion, sex, or national origin. The Voting Rights Act of 1965 was designed to enforce the Fifteenth Amendment, which granted blacks the right to vote. The Equal Pay Act of 1963 prohibits sex-based wage discrimination between men and women working in the same establishment and performing under similar working conditions. Finally, Executive Order 11246, administered and enforced by the U.S. Department of Labor's Office of Federal Contract Compliance, prohibits federal contractors from discriminating, in employment decisions, on the basis of those characteristics listed in the description of the Civil Rights Act.

TABLE 7. *Average income in 1995–97 for nonworking men and men working full-time and full-year, by age*

	Ages 25–34		Ages 35–44		Ages 45–54	
	No Work ($)	FTFY ($)	No Work ($)	FTFY ($)	No Work ($)	FTFY ($)
Household Income:						
Earned	18,072	51,975	11,702	62,159	13,520	71,756
Unearned	9,581	3,088	12,854	4,196	15,530	6,150
Total	27,653	55,063	24,556	66,355	29,050	77,906
Individual Income:						
Earned	0	32,386	0	44,765	0	50,544
Unearned	3,813	822	6,740	1,701	10,482	2,969
Total	3,813	33,208	6,740	46,466	10,482	53,513

rity Income (SSI) programs combined.[30] There were similar expansions in other public-assistance/welfare programs as the social safety net expanded. What has been the result? In 1967, fewer than 3 percent of men one to forty years out of school did not work at all during the year. Since 1974 (the first year of SSI), this percentage of nonworking men has been above 6 percent in every year, above 7 percent in all but two years, and averaged 8 percent.[31]

How well does nonwork pay? Table 7 compares incomes between men who do not work at all and men who work full-time/full-year. The comparisons are made between the men as individuals as well as between the households in which they reside, and are separated by age group.

Average household income for the men who do not work is below the household income for men working full-time and full-year, but ranges from being more than one-third as much at the older ages to one-half as much at the younger ages. The composition of household income for the nonworking men varies from about 35 percent unearned income at the younger ages to over 53 percent at the older ages.

Average total individual income for the nonworking men (which includes zero earned income by definition) is, of course, lower than the average income of the full-time/full-year workers, but ranges from about 11 percent of the full-time/full-year amount at the younger ages to 20

[30] This data is taken from U.S. Social Security Administration, *Social Security Bulletin Annual Statistical Supplement 2000* (Washington, DC: U.S. Government Printing Office, 2000), tables 4.A6 and 7.A4.

[31] These percentages are calculated from the same data used for Panel A of Table 6.

percent at the older ages. Household incomes of the nonworking men are closer to those of their full-time counterparts—about 50 percent for men 25–34 and about 37 percent for both cohorts of older men. The household income of nonworking men is relatively unlikely to be provided by a spouse; the odds that nonworking men are married is only about one-fourth to one-third as large as the odds of marriage for men working full-time and full-year. Note that older nonworking men have less other household income than do younger nonworkers, but have more of their own (unearned) income. While it is certain that some of the men in the 45–54 cohort who are not working are unable to work, it is nonetheless striking that older nonworking men have, on average, individual incomes that are 20 percent of the average income for similarly aged men working full-time for the entire year.

Table 8 compares recipiency rates for various forms of public assistance for men who do not work and men who work full-time/full-year. The comparisons are again made at both the men's household level (i.e., someone in the household receives the aid) and for the individual men (i.e., they receive the aid). Some types of aid, such as food stamps and energy assistance, are reported at only the household level.

There are large differences in recipiency rates both at the household and individual levels. The last row of the table, which reports the percentage of the individual men who receive at least one of the listed sources of aid, provides perhaps the greatest contrast. While one-third of the younger nonworkers and over one-half of the nonworkers 35 and above receive at least one of the forms of public assistance, only 2 to 3 percent of the full-time/full-year workers receive any of this aid.

Coincident with the rapidly expanding sources of support for nonworkers that began in the mid-1960s, the incidence of nonwork more than doubled between the late 1960s and the mid-1970s, and tripled by the early 1980s. From the early 1980s onward, the average annual hours of those who work rebounded substantially, but nonwork remained high. *The cost of attempts to reduce inequality can be high—the support for nonwork is both safety net and magnet.*

V. Increased Fairness: Reduced Wage Inequality across Race and Gender

In Section I we noted that equality of opportunity implies that differences in achievement—in observable outcomes such as wages and incomes—arise from differences in what individuals do rather than from factors over which they have no control. Perhaps the simplest indicator of whether the economy has become more or less "fair" as wage inequality has increased is whether simple characterizations of individuals by characteristics such as race and gender, over which they have no control, have

TABLE 8. *Percentage of nonworking men and men working full-time and full-year receiving public assistance, by age for 1995–97*

	Ages 25–34		Ages 35–44		Ages 45–54	
	No Work (%)	FTFY (%)	No Work (%)	FTFY (%)	No Work (%)	FTFY (%)
Anyone in Household Receives:						
Medicaid	43.3	10.4	49.5	7.5	38.2	6.5
Medicare	23.9	4.3	39.6	5.2	40.8	5.6
Food stamps	26.6	4.2	29.7	2.4	22.9	1.5
Energy assistance	7.3	0.9	8.9	0.6	7.8	0.4
Rent subsidy	3.2	0.5	3.7	0.3	3.9	0.1
Housing subsidy	9.6	1.7	10.1	1.0	9.3	0.6
Social Security	27.8	5.0	44.9	5.8	48.4	6.4
SSI	22.0	1.2	25.6	1.3	21.4	1.5
Welfare	13.9	1.9	14.6	1.1	9.6	0.8
Individual Receives:						
Social Security	14.1	0.2	28.5	0.3	36.9	0.3
SSI	15.4	0.1	18.2	0.1	15.8	0.1
Welfare	5.1	0.2	7.9	0.1	4.4	0.1
Public workers compensation	3.0	1.2	5.8	1.2	5.2	1.2
Veteran's benefits	0.5	0.5	3.0	0.8	8.2	1.9
Public education assistance	6.0	1.1	1.9	0.3	1.0	0.3
Any of the above forms of public assistance	33.5	2.4	51.0	2.2	57.8	3.0

become a better or worse predictor of economic status. Let us augment the simple wage equation above with indicators for race and gender:

$$\log(\text{wage}) = a + b\,\text{education} + c\,\text{experience} + d\,\text{race/gender} + \text{other things.}$$

In the 1967–71 time range, the proportion of the differences in wages for all men and women that was attributed to differences in race and gender was 18 percent.[32] The proportion of differences in wages attributed to differences in years of schooling and years of experience combined was 23 percent. It is rather striking that thirty years ago race and gender were comparable to schooling and experience in explaining differences in wages.

In the 1994–98 time range, the proportion of the differences in wages for all men and women that was attributed to differences in race and gender was only 4 percent. The proportion of wage variation attributed to differences in measured schooling and experience was 29 percent. Today, wages depend much more on what an individual does than on how an individual looks.

Table 9 provides a more detailed picture of how differences in wages across race and gender groups have become more equal. For each race/gender combination, the table reports the average percentile location of the group in the wage distribution of white men. As the reference group, white men are always located at the 50th percentile on average.

On average, black men and white and black women in 1969 had wages at the 27th, 21st, and 15th percentiles, respectively, of the wage distribution of white men. Over the next thirty years, there were fairly steady gains for each group. By 1996, the average percentiles had increased by between 10 points (black men) and 20 points (black women). To use a different measure, the percentage of black men with wages among the top two quintiles (40 percent) of white men's wages has approximately doubled to 23 percent over the past thirty years, while the percentages of white women and black women in these top quintiles have more than tripled, to 23 percent and 17 percent, respectively. These impressive gains are even more noteworthy given that they occurred while the reference distribution, white men's wages, was becoming more unequal. From Table 1, we see that wages at the midpoints of the top two quintiles (i.e., the 70th and 90th percentiles) increased relative to the median wage by 15 and 47 percentage points, respectively, between the late 1960s and the late 1990s.

Though wage inequality within race and gender groups has increased substantially, the increase in equality between these groups has led to a

[32] Recall that, unlike for men, there are no wage imputations for women—only women working at least 35 hours per week for at least one week in a year are included in these calculations. Also, there are three race categories in the calculations (white, black, and other), leading to a total of six race/gender combinations.

TABLE 9. *Average percentile location of race/gender groups in the wage distribution of white men*

Year	White Men	Black Men	White Women	Black Women
1969	50	27	21	15
1974	50	31	23	20
1979	50	33	26	24
1986	50	34	34	30
1991	50	35	37	33
1996	50	37	39	35

more just, more equitable society. Far from being a calamity, these trends in wage (in)equality have been in the right direction.

VI. Conclusion

The title of this essay links inequality, incentives, and opportunity, and we have endeavored to explain these linkages and document their implications. There has been a tremendous increase in wage inequality in the United States since the 1960s. But inequality, or increases in inequality, are not necessarily bad. Wages play an incentive role in signaling relative labor scarcity and surplus, and substantial gains in efficiency and national output result when individuals respond to these incentives. Inequality in wages, such as the higher wages of college graduates relative to high school graduates, provides individuals with opportunities for increased achievement—by investing more in education, for example. Without inequality, there are no incentives, and without incentives, there are no opportunities for increased achievement and efficiency.

We began our empirical work by documenting the increase in wage inequality between the 1960s and the 1990s. Closer inspection revealed that most of this increase (about 85 percent) occurred in the upper half of the wage distribution, and that there was virtually no increase in wage inequality below the median after the mid-1980s.

We then turned to wages and education as an illustration of the incentive role of wages and the ensuing response. During the past twenty years, the college/high school wage differential increased by two-thirds, from 39 percent to 65 percent, and during this same period the proportion of young men who have more than a high school education increased by more than a quarter, from 39 percent to 50 percent. The increase in college enrollment for all 18- to 24-year-olds was also large, from 25.7 percent to 36.5 percent. Many have taken advantage of the opportunity for higher wages that is afforded by a college education.

But incentives can work in negative ways as well. We showed that the increase in the "pay" of nonwork resulting from the expansion of the social safety net in the 1960s, alongside declines in wages in the lower portion of the wage distribution, almost doubled the fraction of men with the lowest wage potential who do not work at all. This loss in output suggests that, from society's perspective, the costs of reducing measured inequality often exceed the benefits.

As overall wage inequality has increased, the wages across race and gender groups have become more equal. Since the 1960s, black men and black and white women have each gained between 10 and 20 percentile points in the distribution of white men's wages. The decrease in wage inequality associated with differences in these ascribed characteristics, alongside the increase in wage inequality associated with differences in achievement, suggest that economic opportunities have become more equal even though measured economic outcomes have become less equal.

The United States has been through a prolonged period of increasing inequality in wages that too often has been characterized as just another example of more for the rich and less for the poor. While we have no trouble in visualizing changes that we would have preferred, we feel that a fair evaluation of what has been is that increasing inequality within groups specified by race and gender is both good and bad, and that the story between races and genders is unambiguously good. Holding average wages constant, we see no reason to argue that the wage distributions of thirty years ago are superior to those of today.

Economics, Texas A&M University
Economics, Texas A&M University

MISUNDERSTANDING DISTRIBUTION*

By Young Back Choi

I. Introduction

Inequality in income and wealth distribution in society is said to be a great concern to many social critics. Rarely is the issue of inequality in income or wealth distribution, as such, a concern for the majority of Americans as individuals, however. The Nobel laureate James Tobin, an economist, has expressed his amazement at Americans' general lack of concern for the issues of unequal distribution of income and wealth:

> American attitudes toward economic inequality are complex. The egalitarian sentiments of contemporary college campuses are not necessarily shared by the not-so-silent majority. Our society, I believe, accepts and approves a large measure of inequality, even of inherited inequality. Americans commonly perceive differences of wealth and income as earned and regard the differential earnings of effort, skill, foresight, and enterprise as deserved. Even the prizes of sheer luck cause very little resentment. People are much more concerned with the legitimacy, legality, and fairness of large gains than with their sheer size.[1]

The concern about inequality is a political concern especially pronounced among intellectuals or social critics rather than among the general population. For many social critics, inequality in income or wealth distribution is a sign of something gone wrong. For them, the presumptive ideal is equality. Consequently, an increase in inequality is usually viewed negatively and vocally, and a decrease in inequality is often met by silence, indicating an implicit approval. For example, when growing inequality in the late 1980s and the early 1990s was noted, the trend was nearly universally denounced as an evil outcome of the market

* I should like to thank Israel Kirzner, Mario Rizzo, Sanford Ikeda, Richard Miller, David Schmidtz, and Ellen Frankel Paul for their helpful comments and suggestions regarding this essay. The research for this essay was supported by a grant from the Earhart Foundation.

[1] James Tobin, "On Limiting the Domain of Inequality," *Journal of Law and Economics* 13, no. 2 (1970): 263–64.

system.[2] Many predicted that it would become worse. Documenting growing inequality and proposing remedial measures became a growth industry in academia. Unfortunately for the industry, the pattern of distribution has stabilized since the mid-1990s.

Why do many social critics single out individual differences in income or wealth as a special public concern? Not all inequalities command such critical attention. Few show similar concerns about the unequal distribution of other valued attributes, such as height, good looks, intelligence, and athletic ability. Nor do many think it appropriate to demand their equalization. Most people appear to regard the individual differences in these attributes as natural (in the sense that no one can be blamed for the differential outcomes). Why, then, do the critics regard the existing inequality in income or wealth distribution as bad, when they know that the bulk of individual income and wealth in the United States is generated from voluntary exchanges and is a product of individual conduct? What is wrong with unequal distribution of income or wealth?

I believe that there are, broadly speaking, three problems that critics associate with inequality in income and wealth distribution: (a) that the existing inequality is excessive; (b) that inequality leads to increasing polarization because the rich have an inherent advantage over the poor;[3] and (c) that inequality is a sign (or product) of injustice. I believe that each of these views is based on a certain misunderstanding of both facts and the economic processes that generate the income and wealth distribution. It is not that I am proposing some original insights, but that many critics act as if they are oblivious to some elemental facts. In the remainder of this essay, I will try to explain how this is the case.

The outline of the essay is as follows: In the next two sections, I analyze the view that the existing inequality is excessive. Though income and wealth are related and one can be converted into the other, I find it convenient for expository purposes to consider them separately—first income, and then wealth. Sections IV and V will examine, respectively, the views that the rich have an inherent advantage over the poor and that inequality is unjust. I end the essay with some concluding remarks.

[2] For example, see Peter Passell, "Economic Scene: The Rich Are Getting Richer, Etc., and It's Likely to Remain That Way," *New York Times*, March 28, 1996, D2; Paul Krugman, "The Right, the Rich, and the Facts: Deconstructing the Income Distribution Debate," *American Prospect* 3, no. 11 (1992): 19–31; Paul Krugman, "The Income Distribution Disparity," *Challenge* 33, no. 4 (1990): 4–6; and Edward N. Wolff, *Top Heavy: A Study of the Increasing Inequality of Wealth in America* (New York: Twentieth Century Fund Press, 1995).

[3] An associated view is that the rich have disproportionate political influence that undercuts the general welfare. While I do not explicitly examine this view in this essay, I do not believe that it is correct, especially in a democracy with universal adult suffrage and where the rich have a hard time fending off confiscatory taxes. For example, the highest statutory marginal tax rate in the United States was 94 percent in 1954. After several decreases, the rate was reduced to 28 percent in the Tax Reform Act of 1986, but raised again to 39.6 percent in the Taxpayer Relief Act of 1997—over this period, an increasing proportion of national income was collected as taxes.

TABLE 1. *Shares of household income of quintiles*

	Lowest (%)	Second (%)	Third (%)	Fourth (%)	Highest (%)
1998	3.6	9.0	15.0	23.2	49.2

Source: U.S. Census Bureau, *Money Income in the U.S.—1998* (Washington, DC: U.S. Government Printing Office, 1999), xv, table C.

II. EXCESSIVE INEQUALITY: INCOME

Many critics try to show that the existing inequality in income distribution is excessive, in the sense that collective action is needed to reduce it. Of course, in the absence of an acceptable standard, any such judgment is purely arbitrary. Therefore, in arguing that the perception of excessive inequality is a mistake, I do not intend to introduce an arbitrary standard of my own. That would be futile. All that I wish to argue is that critics often convey the impression that inequality is greater than it actually is.

The most commonly used data on American income distribution is from the Current Population Survey (CPS), conducted each year by the U.S. Census Bureau. In trying to demonstrate the extent of inequality, critics commonly use the CPS data to show how the highest-earning segment of the population compares with the lowest-earning segment. For example, Table 1 shows that in 1998 the share of national income that went to the highest quintile was 49.2 percent, nearly 14 times as large as the lowest quintile's 3.6 percent.

Presenting data in this manner, however, conveys an impression of the degree of inequality that is greater than is actually warranted. CPS data measures the money income of households in a year, before taxes and excluding capital gains. Given the specific definition adopted by the Census Bureau to measure income, the failure to net out taxes that higher-earning households pay from income, or to add in the values of noncash transfers that low-income households receive, leads to an overstatement of the degree of inequality.[4] There are also other factors (such as differences in household size, the age of the primary earner, costs of living, etc.) that, if not taken into consideration, tend to overstate the degree of inequality. Let us briefly consider all of these factors in turn.

A. Adjusting income

Since the early 1980s, the Census Bureau has provided estimates of the effects on income distribution of various adjustments such as (realized)

[4] Noncash transfers include food stamps, rent subsidies, free and reduced-price school lunches, and the value of Medicare and Medicaid.

TABLE 2. *Shares of household income of quintiles, 1998*

	Lowest (%)	Second (%)	Third (%)	Fourth (%)	Highest (%)
Official Census data	3.6	9.0	15.0	23.2	49.2
After all adjustments by the Census	4.9	10.7	16.0	23.0	45.4

Source: U.S. Census Bureau, *Money Income in the U.S.—1998*, xix, table F and 48–53, table 12.

capital gains (or losses), the imputed return on home equity net of property taxes, the value of employer-paid health benefits, federal and state income taxes, Social Security and Medicare taxes, the earned income credit (a refund of Social Security taxes for qualifying low-income people), and the values of noncash transfers.[5] Not all adjustments are in one direction, but the dominant factors are the taxes higher earners pay and the noncash subsidies lower earners receive.[6] The overall result of the adjustments, accounted for in Table 2, clearly shows that the official measure of income overstates the degree of inequality. After the adjustments are made, the highest quintile's income share in 1998 falls from 49.2 percent to 45.4 percent, while the lowest quintile's share rises from 3.6 percent to 4.9 percent. The ratio of the share of the richest quintile to that of the poorest falls from almost 14 to slightly above 9.

B. Household size

The CPS reports *household* income, and in the survey household size ranges from one to seven or more. To the extent that household size is not randomly distributed across quintiles—it is not—it must be taken into consideration in any judgments about inequality. As shown in Table 3, in 1998, the average size of households with annual income between $5,000 and $9,999 was 1.74. The average size of households with annual income over $100,000 was 3.25. That is, the size of the households with annual income over $100,000 was almost 90 percent larger than the average size of households with annual income between $5,000 and $9,999. Moreover, there is a positive relationship between household income and household

[5] I would argue that the Census Bureau's analysis is still insufficient, even given these adjustments, because it leaves out the value of tuition assistance, especially at the college level; this is increasingly provided on the basis of need, as many middle-class and upper-middle-class families with college-bound children are acutely aware.

[6] In 1996, noncash transfers accounted for 75 percent of welfare expenditures in the United States. See Vee Burke, *Cash and Noncash Benefits for Persons with Limited Income: Eligibility Rules, Recipient and Expenditure Data, FY 1994–96* (Washington, DC: Congressional Research Service, 1997), 16, 18.

TABLE 3. *Average size (in people) of households at different income levels, 1998*

	Less than $5,000	$5,000 to $9,999	$10,000 to $14,999	$15,000 to $24,999	$25,000 to $34,999	$35,000 to $49,999	$50,000 to $74,999	$75,000 to $99,999	$100,000 and Over
Size	2.06	1.74	1.98	2.23	2.45	2.72	2.97	3.18	3.25

Source: U.S. Census Bureau, *Money Income in the U.S.—1998*, 5, table 2. The average size of all households is 2.61 people.

size.[7] Therefore, drawing inferences about inequality without making an adjustment for the differences in the size of households clearly exaggerates inequality.

How should we make an adjustment? The simplest way is to count one person as one person. Policy analysts Robert Rector and Rea Hederman report that, when adjustments are made on 1997 Census data so that each quintile contains approximately the same number of persons, the income share of the lowest quintile rises from 5.6 percent to 9.4 percent, and that of the highest quintile falls from 45.3 percent to 39.7 percent; see Table 4.[8] Accordingly, the ratio of the income share of the highest quintile to that of the lowest falls from almost 14, in the official data, to a little over 4.

Alternately, one may use an "equivalence scale," a scheme of discounting multiperson households, as is done in the federal government's calculation of the poverty guidelines.[9] With the use of an equivalence scale, the reduction in the measured degree of inequality should be less than that implied by Rector and Hederman. But the question of the specific nature of adjustment regarding household size is not important for our purpose, for the point is made clear: if one does not adjust for differences in household size, income data overstates the degree of inequality.

[7] The only exception is the class of households with less than $5,000 annual income; most of this class's income is government cash transfers. I would guess that single moms disproportionately head these households.

[8] Robert Rector and Rea Hederman, *Income Inequality: How Census Data Misrepresent Income Distribution* (Washington, DC: Heritage Foundation, 1999), 4–5.

[9] Paul Ryscavage, *Income Inequality in America: An Analysis of Trends* (Armonk, NY: M. E. Sharpe, 1999), 30–33. The equivalence scale implicit in the federal government's poverty-line calculation in 1996 is as follows:

Size of family	1 person	2 persons	3 persons	4 persons	5 persons	6 persons	7 persons
Equivalence scale	1.000	1.279	1.565	2.010	2.370	2.680	3.040

TABLE 4. *Shares of household income of quintiles, 1997*

	Lowest (%)	Second (%)	Third (%)	Fourth (%)	Highest (%)
Official Census data	3.6	8.9	15.0	23.2	49.4
After all adjustments by the Census	5.6	10.8	15.8	22.5	45.3
After quintiles are also adjusted to hold same number of persons	9.4	13.3	16.5	21.2	39.7

Source: Rector and Hederman, *Income Inequality*. Due to rounding, not all rows in this table sum to 100.0. Figures in Table 4 are based on 1997 CPS data. All other income figures in this essay are based on 1998 CPS data. There are slight discrepancies between the 1997 and 1998 figures.

C. Income fluctuation and age differences

The Census data measures yearly income. There are two reasons why using yearly-income data overstates the degree of inequality. One is that household income fluctuates from year to year—through occasional unemployment and business failure.[10] It is easy to see how three people with identical lifetime income may nevertheless have unequal distributions of yearly income, depending on who has good fortune and who has a bad break.

The other reason is as follows: an individual goes through different phases of life—young, middle-aged, and aged—and a young person's income tends to increase as time passes (and as he or she gains in experience and skill) and then fall off upon retirement. A population of three people at different phases in life, but otherwise identical, may, therefore, be portrayed as having a high degree of inequality, even though their incomes are equal over their lifetimes. It would be unacceptable in this case to infer from the data that income distribution is highly unequal.

Indeed, higher-income households tend to be headed by individuals in their prime working age, say 35–54; see Table 5. Poorer households tend to be headed by older or younger people. Therefore, if we are to draw a fair inference about the degree of inequality in income distribution, we must also adjust the data for differences in the age of householders (assuming that they are primary earners).

The fact that using yearly-income data leads to overstatement of inequality, due to yearly fluctuation of income and differences in the age of earners, can be addressed if income is measured over a longer period of

[10] Boarding schools, for example, know this—they grant financial assistance yearly because family income fluctuates from year to year.

TABLE 5. *Age of householder at different income levels, 1998*

	Less than \$5,000 (%)	\$5,000 to \$9,999 (%)	\$10,000 to \$14,999 (%)	\$15,000 to \$24,999 (%)	\$25,000 to \$34,999 (%)	\$35,000 to \$49,999 (%)	\$50,000 to \$74,999 (%)	\$75,000 to \$99,999 (%)	\$100,000 and Over (%)
15–24	14.6	7.9	8.3	9.1	6.9	5.6	2.9	1.5	1.1
25–34	20.0	11.4	14.7	17.3	21.4	21.0	21.8	17.2	11.5
35–54	32.1	23.2	23.8	29.2	37.0	45.0	52.7	57.6	61.4
55–64	14.6	13.8	10.7	10.9	12.3	12.5	12.9	15.3	16.8
Over 65	18.7	43.7	42.5	33.5	22.4	15.9	9.7	8.4	9.2

Source: U.S. Census Bureau, *Money Income in the U.S.—1998*, 5, table 2.

time. Indeed, a study shows that considering income over a seventeen-year period reduces inequality by about 30 percent.[11]

D. Differences in costs of living

The judgment on the present degree of inequality must be further modified by the fact that different localities have different costs of living. There are fifty different states in the United States, and they differ considerably in average income and costs of living. For example, according to the Census Bureau, the median household incomes in New Jersey and Arkansas are \$49,297 and \$27,117, respectively. Therefore, the median-income household in New Jersey is placed in the fourth income quintile, and its Arkansas counterpart, in the second. To conclude that the median-income-earning New Jersey household earns some 80 percent more than its Arkansas counterpart would be rash, however, for the costs of living are much higher in New Jersey than in Arkansas.

From our discussions thus far, it should be clear that if all these factors (i.e., taxes, noncash transfers, capital gains, size of household, age of primary earner, and costs of living) were properly accounted for in income data, the degree of measured inequality would be much lower than people commonly infer from careless presentations of the data. It is hoped that at least some people who think that the existing inequality is "excessive" might change their minds after discovering how their judgments are based on an overestimation. However, there are additional factors that must be taken into consideration if the discussion of inequality in income

[11] Peter Gottschalk, "Inequality, Income Growth, and Mobility: The Basic Facts," *Journal of Economic Perspectives* 11, no. 2 (1997): 37. His estimate is based on the University of Michigan's Panel Survey of Income Dynamics.

TABLE 6. *Characteristics of families at different income levels, 1998*

	Less than $5,000	$5,000 to $9,999	$10,000 to $14,999	$15,000 to $24,999	$25,000 to $34,999	$35,000 to $49,999	$50,000 to $74,999	$75,000 to $99,999	$100,000 and Over
Family size	3.00	2.97	3.00	2.91	3.02	3.18	3.27	3.39	3.39
Mean number of earners	0.58	0.69	0.86	1.02	1.34	1.67	1.98	2.19	2.22
% of family earning	19.3	23.2	28.7	35.1	44.4	52.5	60.6	64.6	65.5
% of earners working full-time[a]	8.0	9.9	27.7	35.7	48.9	59.2	70.1	75.6	75.6

Source: U.S. Census Bureau, *Money Income in the U.S.—1998*, 17–18, table 5.
[a] Percentages in bottom row refer to those working full-time for more than fifty weeks a year.

distribution is to go beyond strictly statistical issues and into the issue of equalization through redistribution.

E. *Differences in the amount of work and skills*

Once we adjust for the factors of the previous subsections, a good part of the remaining inequality is likely to be accounted for by differences in the amount of work families perform and the skills they offer. First of all, families differ in the number of people working and the amount of hours they work. Indeed, higher-income families tend to have more people working, and working longer hours, than do lower-income households. For example, compare households in two different income levels—say $5,000 to $9,999 and $100,000 and over. Families in the latter level have over three times as many people working than families in the former do, and earners in the latter level are over seven times as likely to work full-time; see Table 6.

Also important is the fact that a worker with more highly valued skills tends to generate a higher income. A person's skills have definite relationships with age and education. The impact of age on income distribution was briefly addressed in Subsection C. Now consider the impact of the differences in educational attainment (standing in part for skills). The relationship between family income and the educational attainment of families is obvious from Table 7. Counting only people 25 and over, more than 60 percent of the families with yearly income over $100,000 have a member with a bachelor's degree or better. Only 4 percent of such families do not contain at least one individual with a high school diploma. In contrast, almost 40 percent of the families with less than $15,000 in yearly income lack any individuals having a high school diploma.

TABLE 7. *Educational attainment of peak individuals in families at different income levels, 1998*

	Less than $5,000 (%)	$5,000 to $9,999 (%)	$10,000 to $14,999 (%)	$15,000 to $24,999 (%)	$25,000 to $34,999 (%)	$35,000 to $49,999 (%)	$50,000 to $74,999 (%)	$75,000 to $99,999 (%)	$100,000 and Over (%)
Less than 9th grade	12	21	20	14	9	5	2	1	1
9th to 12th grade[a]	24	23	19	17	12	10	5	3	2
High school graduate[b]	37	32	35	37	40	38	33	25	14
Some college	20	18	20	23	26	30	31	29	22
Bachelor's degree or more	7	6	6	9	13	17	29	42	61

Source: U.S. Census Bureau, *Money Income in the U.S.—1998*, 17–18, table 5. Measure of educational attainment is restricted to people 25 years old and over.

[a] No diploma.

[b] Including equivalency.

Given the relationship between income on the one hand and the amount of work and education (standing in part for skills) on the other hand, our inference about inequality should therefore be even further modified, especially if the inference is being used to motivate a redistribution scheme. (One must also consider the possibility that the remaining inequality may be largely attributable to differences in energy, risk-taking, prudence, and ingenuity.)

What I have argued thus far is that regardless of what critics think the appropriate level of inequality is, the inferences based on unadjusted official data overstate the actual degree of inequality. Critics often do not take necessary care in presenting and interpreting the data. I will not speculate unduly on cause. Perhaps these critics are careless about numbers (even though the critics include some well-known economists); perhaps they run with numbers that seemingly conform to what they want to believe.

F. Inequality without redistribution

Before we discuss wealth distribution in Section III, it is important to address one more issue: how much worse the distribution of income would be without the redistribution schemes currently in place. I am not about to propose a specific figure, but I am inclined to observe that the extent of inequality that might prevail is commonly overestimated.

TABLE 8. *Shares of household income of quintiles, 1998*

	Lowest (%)	Second (%)	Third (%)	Fourth (%)	Highest (%)	Gini Coefficient
Official Census data (1)	3.6	9.2	14.9	23.3	49.0	.446
(1) – cash transfers + capital gains + employee health benefits	1.0	7.1	14.2	23.4	54.1	.509
After all adjustments by the Census[a]	4.9	10.7	16.0	23.0	45.4	.399

Source: U.S. Census Bureau, *Money Income in the U.S.—1998*, xix, table F. Due to rounding, the percentages in this table's rows do not always sum to 100.0.
[a] See Subsection A of Section II above.

To see this, consider Table 8. The Gini coefficient for the 1998 official data is .446.[12] By excluding cash transfers from the official data, and adding capital gains and the value of employee health benefits, Census Bureau analysts estimate the Gini coefficient would have been .509 if there had been no government-sponsored redistribution. They then compare this to the Gini coefficient one gets after all the Census adjustments are made, including those for capital gains, employee benefits, taxes, and both cash and noncash transfers: the result is a Gini coefficient of .399. The Census Bureau analysts conclude that the Gini coefficient with redistribution is .399, and .509 without it.

Unfortunately, the analysts seem to ignore a basic lesson of economics—namely, that when a tax on a good is increased or a subsidy on it reduced, the price of the good neither increases by as much as the tax does, nor decreases by as much as the subsidy does.[13] Accordingly, if existing taxes were eliminated, a taxpayer's income would not go up by the amount of the taxes that he used to pay. By the same token, if existing government transfers were eliminated, a transfer recipient's income would not decrease by the amount of transfers that he used to receive. Therefore, it seems that

[12] The Gini coefficient measures the degree to which income distribution departs from perfect equality. If income distribution is perfectly equal, the Gini coefficient is 0. On the other extreme, if no household except one had any income, the Gini coefficient would be 1. It should be noted that since the Gini coefficient summarizes an entire distribution with one value, a Gini coefficient is compatible with any number of distributions. Consequently, an income distribution with a lower Gini coefficient may not necessarily be preferable to one with a higher Gini coefficient.

[13] For example, if the taxes on cigarettes (say, $2 a pack) are eliminated, the out-of-pocket cost of cigarettes (the price of cigarettes plus any taxes) will decline by less than $2. The reason is that at the no-tax price, there would be an excess demand for cigarettes, causing the price to rise. Similarly, if college tuition subsidies are eliminated, college tuitions will not decline by the amount of the subsidies eliminated.

estimating what the Gini coefficient would be without redistribution by simply eliminating taxes and subsidies results in an overestimation of the inequality that might prevail in the absence of government-sponsored redistribution.

III. Excessive Inequality: Wealth

Critics commonly observe that wealth is even more unequally distributed than income. Again, I have no intention of disputing the fact that distribution of wealth is unequal. I merely wish to suggest that careless inferences from commonly available data overstate the degree of inequality. The reason is that the Federal Reserve Board's triennial Surveys of Consumer Finances (SCFs), the best-known data source on household wealth in the United States, exclude from wealth consideration such important items as the value of expected Social Security benefits, the future tax liabilities on unrealized capital gains, and the value of human capital.

A. Value of Social Security and other entitlements

The SCFs define household wealth as net worth (NW), current marketable or fungible assets minus the current value of debts. By focusing on marketable assets, the definition excludes such nonmarketable assets as expected Social Security benefits. However, including the value of retirement benefits from private sources—for example, corporate and union pensions, and individual retirement provisions such as 401(k)s—as a part of one's wealth while excluding the equivalent from Uncle Sam introduces a bias to the extent that Social Security benefits are a more important part of the wealth of the less well-off.[14] The extent of this overstatement is clear from Table 9, which compares the 1992 median net worth of different income classes with and without the estimated present value of Social Security benefits as a part of household wealth. Excluding Social Security benefits, the ratio of the net worths of the median household with more than $100,000 in income and that with less than $10,000 in income is 493 to 1. Including the values of Social Security benefits reduces the ratio to 19 to 1.[15] Appropriate inclusion of the values of other social entitlements—for example, the present value of expected disability benefits—should further reduce the degree of inequality.

[14] Some may try to justify the exclusion of "Social Security wealth" on the ground that the Social Security system, as a pay-as-you-go system, is unfunded. This ignores the fact that not all pensions are fully funded. More importantly, the majority of Americans organize their lives based on the belief that Social Security wealth is real. One should ask politicians whether any of them would be willing to argue that such wealth is not real.

[15] Estimates of the values of expected Social Security benefits are based on algorithms supplied by the Social Security Administration.

TABLE 9. *Median household wealth at different income levels, 1992*

Household Income	NW without Social Security Wealth ($1000)	NW with Social Security Wealth ($1000)
$9,999 or less	1.7	56.4
$24,999 to $10,000	28.3	108.6
$49,999 to $25,000	117.9	231.5
$99,999 to $50,000	279.3	444.6
$100,000 or more	837.8	1,052.3

Source: Arthur B. Kennickell and Annika E. Sunden, "Pensions, Social Security, and the Distribution of Wealth" (working paper, Federal Reserve Board—SCF, 1997), table 3; document available on-line at http://www.federalreserve.gov/pubs/feds/1997/199755/199755abs.html.

Instead of modifying the data to get a more accurate picture, some seem to modify the data to further accentuate the degree of inequality. For example, consider economist Edward Wolff's study of wealth distribution in the United States.[16] He proposes to modify the definition of wealth from NW to the even more narrow measure of financial wealth (FW): "NW minus net equity in owner-occupied housing."[17] He justifies the exclusion of an important American asset on the ground that "it is somewhat difficult to liquidate one's housing wealth in the short term."[18] But there is a certain inconsistency here: FW excludes the value of owner-occupied housing, but not the value of other real estate properties. Is there any evidence that the latter is more liquid than the former? Wolff does not say. But Wolff's definition of wealth in terms of FW results in a further overstatement of inequality in that owner-occupied housing is a more significant part of the wealth of middle-class households, while other real estate properties are a more significant part of the wealth of more well-off households.

B. Tax liabilities on unrealized gains

Also significant is the exclusion of the future tax liabilities on unrealized capital gains, especially during booming asset markets. The effect is to grossly overstate the net worth of more well-off households. For example, suppose that Mr. A bought a vacation house for $10,000 in cash in 1970. He now learns that the property can be sold for $500,000. In the

[16] Edward N. Wolff, "Recent Trends in the Size Distribution of Household Wealth," *Journal of Economic Perspectives* 12, no. 3 (1998): 131–50.
[17] Ibid., 133.
[18] Ibid.

SCFs, the full half-million will be counted toward his household wealth. But were he to sell his property, the proceeds would be subject to taxes for ordinary income under the current tax laws. He may end up paying almost 50 percent taxes on his nominal net gain of $490,000.[19] Therefore, on the day of the survey, the real value of the vacation house—net of the tax liabilities—should be something like half that reported in the SCFs.

This reasoning should generally apply to all unrealized gains that are counted as part of one's wealth. For example, suppose 50 percent of the value of the financial assets of the very well-off is unrealized capital gains. The future tax liabilities on these appreciated assets (supposing that all future gains are subject to preferential long-term capital gains tax rates) add up to about 40 percent—say, the 28 percent alternative minimum tax and about 12 percent in state and local taxes (as in New York City).[20] The result is that if one disregards these future liabilities, one overstates the financial wealth of the very well-off by about 25 percent. This is, of course, just one example, and there is no simple way to estimate the extent of overstatement. But the direction of overstatement is clear. The larger the proportion of unrealized capital gains in the very well-off's NW, the greater the exaggeration.

C. *Value of human capital*

Failure to include in household wealth the value of "human capital," which is the source of most future earnings (especially for professionals), understates the wealth of the young and the middle class. Consider the example of a newly minted surgeon. The SCFs would record his or her net worth as negative, given the large debt incurred to finance medical training. Compare this young surgeon with a 30-year-old invalid with an annuity valued at $500,000 thanks to a generous uncle. (The annuity pays the invalid, say, $45,000 a year until he dies.) The SCFs would record the invalid's net worth at $500,000. Careless inference would lead one to count the invalid as rich and the young surgeon as poor, even though the young surgeon expects to earn, say, $300,000 a year for the next thirty years, based on his human capital.[21]

[19] Under the current tax codes, capital gains on a vacation home are treated as ordinary income. The highest federal marginal income tax rate, which applies to a joint return above $278,450, is 39.6 percent. For a New York City couple, the state and local marginal income tax rates add up to 11.785 percent. Even if the state and local taxes were fully deductible against federal income tax, which is doubtful, the effective state and local marginal tax rates in this case would be roughly 7 percent. The combined marginal tax rates would thus be over 46 percent. This of course does not include the sales tax on the property.

[20] I am using here the example of the very well-off, who would easily become subject to the alternative minimum tax, which is basically a 28 percent flat tax with virtually no deductions. (The only exceptions are mortgage interest and investment expenses.)

[21] In divorce courts, the value of human capital is often recognized for what it is.

D. Fluctuation of net worth

An additional point to consider is that household wealth is customarily measured at a moment in time. To the extent that the net worth of households fluctuates through time and changes through the life-cycle (for reasons similar to those presented in Subsection C of Section II above), this convention significantly overstates the degree of inequality.

E. Consumption vs. savings and investment

There is one more factor that should be considered if one is to draw inferences about the degree of inequality in wealth distribution. The net worth of an individual at a point in time depends much on his or her income stream, consumption (and savings) pattern, and investment strategies. That is, two individuals who are identical in many respects—such as income, years worked, inheritance, and so on—may end up with vastly different net worths at a particular moment.

For example, consider two retired middle managers, X and Y, with identical salary histories. Suppose X's net worth is $2,000,000 and Y's is zero. Are we to conclude that X is infinitely richer than Y and that wealth distribution is very unequal? Not necessarily. Upon a closer look, one may discover that X is an elderly miser who never got married out of fear of spending money on a wife or children. He has had coarse meals all his life, and has methodically saved and invested with a moderate rate of return. On the other hand, Y, with zero net worth, may have had an enjoyable life, supported his wife, and raised his many children well, by prudently spending all his income. To observe that X is infinitely richer than Y, and therefore to recommend that X's wealth be redistributed, would be a very strange and unjust suggestion. Most of X's wealth may be merely postponed consumption, with him getting token rewards (that is, interest payments) for his discipline in saving. Who knows what kind of future consumption plans X has up his sleeve?[22]

I have thus far discussed some misunderstandings about "facts" of income and wealth distribution, misunderstandings that—through careless uses of data—make the distributions look much more unequal than they really are. Let us now turn to analyze social critics' other views about the economic processes that generate income and wealth distribution. In the following section, I will address the view that inequality leads to

[22] In 1995, Oseola McCarty, an 87-year-old black woman from Hattiesburg, Mississippi, donated $150,000 to a local college for a scholarship fund for black youths. She spent all her life as a seamstress earning minimal wages; in her youth, she earned nickels and dimes a day. Nevertheless, she managed to amass a fortune. Her lifetime accumulation was $250,000, as the donation represented 60 percent of her wealth; the rest was distributed among her relatives and her church. It is incredible, but it happened. See Sharon Wertz, "Oseola McCarty Donates $150,000 to USM" (article from the University of Southern Mississippi's Office of University Relations, July 1995), available on-line at http://www.pr.usm.edu/oola1.htm.

TABLE 10. *Gini coefficient of income inequality over time*

Year	1967	1970[a]	1975	1980[a]	1985	1990	1995[b]	1996	1997	1998
Gini coefficient	.399	.394	.397	.403	.419	.428	.450	.455	.459	.456

Source: U.S. Census Bureau, *Money Income in the U.S.—1998*, xiv–xv.
[a] The method of data collection changed in 1970 and 1980.
[b] Increases in 1993 in the limits applied by the Census Bureau when counting some income sources resulted in measured income for the highest-income households rising by considerably more than did their actual income. That is, the method of income-data collection used since 1993 is different from that used prior to 1993.

increasing polarization because the rich have an inherent advantage over the poor. The view that inequality is a sign (or product) of injustice shall be analyzed in Section V.

IV. The Inherent Advantage of the Rich

Many critics appear to have the strong suspicion that the rich have an inherent (and unfair) advantage over the poor, and that this advantage is accentuated by cutthroat competition in the market. They feel that the rich are bound to get richer and that the poor are condemned to increasing misery.

This deeply held suspicion was rekindled by reports suggesting that inequality in income distribution increased in the 1980s and the early 1990s. For example, Table 10 shows that the Gini coefficient of income inequality increased from .397 in 1975 to .419 in 1985, .428 in 1990, and .450 in 1995.[23] Many social critics were convinced by the reports of increasing inequality that their view of the inherent advantage of the rich and the inherent disadvantage of the poor was validated, and that the United States was becoming a polarized society of the haves and the have-nots.[24]

Of course, this was not the only possible interpretation of the reports of growing inequality in measured income or wealth. Volumes have al-

[23] Many people regarded this trend as real enough despite those shortcomings of income and wealth measurements that I noted in Sections II and III. They felt that even a faulty measure, if used *consistently*, could still give a fair sense of change. Even so, one should be mindful that the measurement of income changes over time for various reasons. For example, in Table 10, the big increase in the Gini coefficient between 1990 and 1995, from .428 to .450, is more a reflection of changes in the ways in which income is measured than of changes in income distribution; see Table 10, note b. As noted in the table, there were changes in income measurement in 1970 and 1980 as well.

[24] Economist Paul Krugman, one of the most vocal critics of the trend toward income inequality, was so sure of its causes that he suspected that any individuals who proposed to examine the validity of the thesis of the disappearing middle class had to be "hired guns of the Right." Paul Krugman, "The Spiral of Inequality," *Mother Jones*, November 1996, 47. See also Paul Krugman, "What the Public Doesn't Know Can't Hurt Us," *Washington Monthly*, October 1995, 8–12.

ready been written to explain the reasons for the trend toward growing inequality.[25] The main aim of this section, therefore, is not to add another explanation for the trend, nor to attempt to deny that the trend is real. The main aim of the section, rather, is to analyze the validity of the social critics' understanding of the way the economy works, the understanding that led the critics to believe that they (or their views) were vindicated by the reported trend of growing inequality.

Surely, one can easily think of many advantages the rich have over the poor. For example, the rich have a higher savings rate than the poor, with the poorest saving virtually nothing. Even if the rich and the poor earned the same rate of return on their savings, it is inevitable that the wealth of the rich will grow at a higher rate. Accordingly, the gap between the rich and the poor may grow over time.[26] Another possibility is what economists Robert Frank and Philip Cook regard as the modern tendency of small differences in ability (and resources) to translate into large differences in income (and wealth).[27] They call the process "winner-take-all," and see the real source of rising inequality in its spread.

But is the putative advantage of the rich truly the dominant feature of the process of generating income and wealth in a market economy? I do not think so. The advantage of the rich is more pronounced in the short run. In the longer run, however, it becomes less clear. The reason is that there are other, more important factors in determining income and wealth in the future than the ownership of currently valued assets. The most important of these is entrepreneurship.[28]

However, it is not easy to argue in the abstract. A better way to see that the critics' claim that the rich have an advantage is mistaken is to see whether its implications are consistent with our experience. If it were true that the rich have an inherent advantage, then (a) the distribution of income and wealth should become increasingly polarized over time, and (b) we should observe little mobility. But we observe the contrary. Let me explain.

A. Relative stability of distribution

The first implication, that of an ever-increasing polarization of income and wealth distribution, is not consistent with the evidence. According to economic historians, the pattern of the distribution of earnings among American males in the last 150 years is "marked by long periods of

[25] For a good survey of the literature, see Frank Levy and Richard J. Murnane, "U.S. Earnings Levels and Earnings Inequality: A Review of Recent Trends and Proposed Explanations," *Journal of Economic Literature* 30, no. 3 (1992): 1333-81.

[26] Herbert Inhaber and Sidney Carroll, *How Rich Is Too Rich?: Income and Wealth in America* (New York: Praeger, 1992), 82-89.

[27] Robert H. Frank and Philip J. Cook, *The Winner-Take-All Society* (New York: Free Press, 1995).

[28] For a more detailed discussion, see Young Back Choi, "On the Rich Getting Richer and the Poor Getting Poorer," *Kyklos* 52, no. 2 (1999): 239-58.

relative stability and shorter periods of substantial change."[29] In fact, the pattern of income distribution does not vary much across ages or different economic systems.[30]

What about the recent much-discussed trend of growing inequality in income distribution?[31] Though the increasing inequality in the 1980s has drawn much attention, many economists believe that much of it had to do with changes in demography, labor-market conditions, and industrial structure.[32] The supply of young and less-educated males increased (relative to that of the more educated), reflecting a low premium on education during the preceding decades. At the same time, the relative demand for the labor of less-educated males declined in the 1980s, when the strengthening of the dollar accelerated the restructuring of industries and increased both the industrial migration to high-tech/service sectors and the relocation of manufacturing overseas. Another factor was the increased competition in the labor market brought about by women, who had marked gains during the period under consideration. Changes in the characteristics of families (the proportion of single-head households increased, as did the proportion of the elderly in the population) and of

[29] Levy and Murnane, "U.S. Earnings Levels and Earnings Inequality," 1340. One should note that the periodic changes have not all been in the direction of increasing inequality, and that the overall stability is in the very long run.

[30] International (as well as intertemporal) comparison of income dispersion is difficult because of data incompatibility. Still, economist A. B. Atkinson ventures to say that "within the group of industrialized countries the degree of dispersion is broadly the same," despite differences in economic structures. A. B. Atkinson, *The Economics of Inequality* (Oxford: Clarendon Press, 1975), 27.

[31] The alleged increase in wealth inequality rests on a shakier ground than does the trend of income inequality, in that comparability of data over time with respect to wealth is even more questionable than it is with respect to income. For example, in Wolff, "Recent Trends in the Size Distribution of Household Wealth," Wolff shows that wealth distribution in the United States worsened between 1983 and 1995 (and shows how unfavorably it compares with wealth distribution in European countries and Japan). However, A. B. Kennickell and R. L. Woodburn show that using different weights meant to correct sampling biases can alter the survey results dramatically, especially for the wealthiest segment of the population. A. B. Kennickell and R. L. Woodburn, "Consistent Weight Design for the 1989, 1992, and 1995 SCFs, and the Distribution of Wealth" (working paper, Federal Reserve Board—SCF, 1997), available on-line at http://www.federalreserve.gov/pubs/oss/oss2/method.html. For example, using the revised weights, "the share of the top $\frac{1}{2}$ percent in 1989 is *lower* than that in 1983"; using the original weights "showed a dramatic increase" during the same period (ibid., 2). Kennickell and Woodburn therefore caution against drawing inferences about the trend in wealth distribution by comparing the 1983 and 1989 surveys, which used the original weights, and the 1989 and subsequent surveys using the revised weights. They explicitly cite Wolff's earlier attempts to make cross-country comparisons as strongly inadvisable, given the sensitivity of data to weights and the inconsistency of weights used in different countries.

[32] Levy and Murnane, "U.S. Earnings Levels and Earnings Inequality," 1340–41; Finis Welch, "In Defense of Inequality," *AEA Papers and Proceedings* 89, no. 2 (1999): 1–17. It should be noted that much of the significance of the reported increase in inequality in the 1980s and the early 1990s arises from a common mistake people make: thinking that people in the lowest quintile (and other quintiles) in 1980 are the very same people in the lowest quintile (and other quintiles) in 1990. This is certainly not the case. Somehow, the discussion of the "shares" of certain classes of people seems to conjure up the image of identifiable groups of people.

immigrants (over three-quarters of whom now have less than a high school education) also contributed to the increased statistical dispersion of income distribution. Whatever the cause was, there is no good ground to project the recent trend into the future. Indeed, since the mid-1990s, the income distribution has become stable; see Table 10.

B. *Mobility*

The implied lack of economic mobility is also contrary to the evidence. Relatively few remain chronically poor, within a lifetime or across generations.[33] Intragenerational mobility deals with the degree to which the income status of an individual at a moment in time is determined by his or her economic status at another moment in time. Much of intragenerational mobility has to do with the life-cycle of the individual—the fact that, given a career path, the income of the young increases over time as they gain experience and skills, and falls off upon retirement, as discussed in Subsection C of Section II above. Another source of intragenerational mobility is changes in one's career path.

A study based on the University of Michigan's Panel Survey of Income Dynamics (PSID) shows much intragenerational mobility; see Table 11. The chance that one in the poorest quintile in 1974 improved one's situation by 1991 is 58 percent, and that person's chance of being in the top two quintiles is 21 percent. Given that we are considering intragenerational mobility, mobility is substantial.[34] Noting that there is a good deal

[33] Greg J. Duncan, *Years of Poverty, Years of Plenty* (Ann Arbor: University of Michigan Press, 1984), 41–43, 91. Duncan found substantial mobility and observed that only about 2.6 percent of the population appeared to be chronically poor.

[34] A study based on U.S. income tax returns shows even greater intragenerational mobility. Table A shows that over 85 percent of those in the poorest quintile in 1979 improved their situation by 1988, and 40 percent found themselves in the top two quintiles. Indeed, the chance of someone in the poorest quintile in 1979 remaining there after nine years is the same as him or her joining the highest quintile.

TABLE A. *Percent of each 1979 income quintile in 1988 income quintiles*

1979 Quintile	Lowest (%)	Second (%)	Third (%)	Fourth (%)	Highest (%)
Lowest	14.2	20.7	25.0	25.3	14.7
Second	10.9	29.0	29.6	19.5	11.1
Third	5.7	14.0	33.0	32.3	15.0
Fourth	3.1	9.3	14.8	37.5	35.4
Highest	1.1	4.4	9.4	20.3	64.7

Source: Chris Frenze, "Income Mobility and Economic Opportunity," in Edwin Mansfield, ed., *Leading Economic Controversies of 1996* (New York: W. W. Norton, 1996), 10–45. Due to rounding, not all rows in this table sum to 100.0.

This study has been criticized for suffering from certain sampling biases, as it includes only individuals who filed income taxes both in 1979 and 1988.

TABLE 11. *Percent of each 1974 income quintile in 1991 income quintiles*

1974 Quintile	Lowest (%)	Second (%)	Third (%)	Fourth (%)	Highest (%)
Lowest	42.1	22.8	14.3	13.0	7.8
Second	28.7	36.0	19.3	9.2	6.7
Third	14.7	20.6	32.1	20.5	12.0
Fourth	9.7	12.0	24.2	32.4	21.7
Highest	3.1	7.3	10.2	25.4	53.9

Source: Peter Gottschalk, "Inequality, Income Growth, and Mobility." Due to rounding, not all rows in this table sum to 100.0.

of mobility in the United States, economist Alan Blinder says, "While ghetto dwellers rarely trade places with Rockefellers, ours is not a stratified society."[35]

Intergenerational mobility, which is perhaps of greater interest to many concerned with the unfair advantages of the rich, deals with the degree to which income status is transmitted from one generation to another. Many economists have found evidence for high intergenerational mobility, that is, little correlation between the incomes of fathers and sons.[36] Gary Becker, a Nobel laureate in economics, observes that in rich countries, including the United States, "low earnings as well as high earnings are not strongly transmitted from fathers to sons."[37]

Economist Gary Solon, however, argues that the impression of a highly mobile America is based on flawed studies overestimating intergenerational mobility. According to a study by Solon based on the PSID, the intergenerational income correlation is .4 or higher, "indicating dramatically less mobility than suggested by earlier research."[38] Solon's estimate certainly implies a higher degree of transmission of earnings status across generations than do earlier estimates (for example, William Sewell and Robert Hauser's estimate that the correlation is .18).

But what does it mean? Does the father/son earnings correlation of .4 represent a lack of mobility? Hardly. Consider the following: Given the

[35] Alan S. Blinder, "The Level and Distribution of Economic Well-Being," in Martin Feldstein, ed., *The American Economy in Transition* (Chicago: University of Chicago Press, 1980), 454.

[36] William H. Sewell and Robert M. Hauser, *Education, Occupation, and Earnings: Achievement in the Early Career* (New York: Academic Press, 1975), 72.

[37] Gary S. Becker, "Family Economics and Macro Behavior," *American Economic Review* 78, no. 1 (1988): 10.

[38] Gary Solon, "Intergenerational Income Mobility in the United States," *American Economic Review* 82, no. 3 (1992): 393–408.

father/son earnings correlation of .4, the expected differences in earnings among sons will be only 40 percent of the differences in earnings among their fathers, and the expected differences among grandsons will be only 16 percent of the differences among their grandfathers. Alternately, consider two individuals, X and Y, with earnings such that roughly 15.8 percent of the population earns less than X and 15.8 percent earns more than Y—that is, X is in the lowest quintile, and Y is in the highest.[39] Assuming a standard normal distribution, the chance of Y's son doing better than X's son is 78.8 percent, compared to a 21.2 percent chance of X's son doing better than Y's son. The respective chances are 62.6 percent and 37.4 percent in the grandsons' generation, and 55.1 percent and 44.9 percent in the great-grandsons' generation.[40] Even with a father/son earnings correlation of .4, the economic prospects of the third-generation descendants of someone in the lowest quintile are not much inferior to those of descendants of one in the highest quintile. The degree of mobility in the United States is rather striking.[41] Some people might argue that anything short of equality between the probability of the poor becoming rich and the probability of the rich becoming poor is insufficient. Millions of prospective immigrants wish to vote to the contrary with their feet.

What about mobility among the richest in America? Since one of the major difficulties of using large-scale data is its underrepresentation of those at the highest level of income or wealth, it would be of great interest to get a glimpse of the degree of mobility at the very top of the wealth scale. Mobility among the richest is of added interest in the context of my discussion; if the alleged advantage of the rich really exists, it should be more pronounced among the richest. Table 12 presents the ten richest Americans in 1995 and their prior and subsequent rankings. It should be noted that all, save the Waltons, are self-made. (In 1999, thirty-seven out of the top fifty richest Americans were self-made.) In 1983, only twelve years before, five out of the ten were not even ranked among the richest four hundred. By 1999, only four years later, some of them were already elbowed out by newcomers. Mobility among the richest is high, indeed.

Of course, there are Rockefellers, DuPonts, and Mellons who have carefully husbanded their inheritances and remain among the richest. However, their fortunes pale compared to the newly found fortunes of

[39] Assuming a normal distribution, the positions of X and Y are such that their incomes are one standard deviation away from the mean on either side.

[40] This may be an underestimate of intergenerational mobility, as Solon admits that his model ignores the possibility of differential intergenerational transmission across income strata. The possibility is not idle. Solon discusses the fact that it is possible that the earnings correlation is higher for the highest quintile (.48) and lower for the lowest quintile (.34). If that is the case, "'riches to rags' may occur less frequently than 'rags to riches.'" Solon, "Intergenerational Income Mobility in the United States," 404.

[41] Peter Bauer notes a high degree of mobility in the supposedly stratified Great Britain. Peter Bauer, *From Subsistence to Exchange* (Princeton, NJ: Princeton University Press, 2000), 125–38.

TABLE 12. *The ten richest Americans in 1995 and their prior and subsequent rankings*

Name	Source of Wealth	1983 Rank	1989 Rank	1995 Rank	1999 Rank
W. H. Gates III	Microsoft	n/a	43	1	1
W. E. Buffett	Investments	31	2	2	3
J. W. Kluge	Metromedia	100	1	3	14
P. G. Allen	Microsoft	n/a	86	4	2
S. M. Redstone	Viacom	n/a	3	5	19
R. M. DeVos and J. Van Andel	Amway	102	268	6	152
S. I. and D. E. Newhouse	Media holdings	19	6	7	42
Waltons	Wal-Mart (inheritance)	2	17	8	6
R. O. Perelman	Investments	n/a	5	9	61
L. J. Ellison	Oracle	n/a	98	10	18

Source: Forbes lists of wealthiest Americans, various years.

Bill Gates (Microsoft), Larry Ellison (Oracle), Warren Buffett (Berkshire Hathaway), Michael Dell (Dell Computer), Jerry Yang (Yahoo!), and the like. Moreover, few heirs of great fortunes from the Roaring Twenties are still counted among the richest.[42] Obviously, the rich do not always stay on top.

Evidence considered thus far contradicts critics' claims that the rich have inherent advantages over the poor and that, as a consequence, income and wealth distribution will become increasingly unequal. Instead of finding increasing polarization of income distribution and little or no mobility, we see both long-term stability in the pattern of income distribution and much mobility. Other forces—the most important of which is entrepreneurship—counter the putative advantage of the rich, allowing some of the poor, with all their disadvantages in resources (e.g., poor manpower, difficulty in raising capital, lack of connections, etc.) somehow to supplant the rich, while causing many of the rich, with all their putative advantages, to fall from their dominance. To believe that the advantages of the rich are predominant in competitive economic pro-

[42] Some may remain skeptical, believing that old fortunes are skillfully hidden from the probing eyes of *Forbes* researchers (and, more importantly, from those of the IRS). Of course, there are limitations to the "Forbes 400," as there are with most data. But the suspicion is an unfalsifiable speculation. For what evidence (that can stick in court) is there, when solid evidence would enable an ambitious politico to build an outstanding career?

cesses is to display a profound misunderstanding of economic processes that generate income and wealth distribution.[43]

V. Inequality Is Unjust

Many critics seem to think that inequality in income and wealth distribution is a sign of (or a product of) injustice. They hold onto this belief even when there is no evidence of wrongdoing that is punishable under the law. I believe that the idea of the injustice of inequality in the absence of such evidence is ill considered and largely based on a misunderstanding of the process of income and wealth generation.

If there is evidence that someone gained through unjust acts, our grievance should be against the unjust acts and should have little to do with the gain. Someone either committed injustice or not. The fact that someone is poor should not exonerate him or her from charges of wrongdoing. Otherwise, we exempt all unjust acts that failed to be lucrative. Therefore, the distinction between rich and poor (or the issue of inequality) is tangential to the issue of injustice.

When there is no evidence of injustice, what can be the grounds for the suspicion that inequality is a sign of injustice? If we lived in a country that was lawless (or had unjust laws), the suspicion might well be justified. In that country, few things would be regarded as legitimate. The extant distribution there would hang delicately on the distribution of naked force. But in a country where the law is tolerably upheld, so that whenever evidence of wrongdoing surfaces, the legal system is mobilized to address the wrong, the basis for suspicion is less clear.

The belief that inequality signifies injustice, even when there is no evidence to this effect, seems to be grounded on four kinds of views about economic processes: (a) that one man's gain is necessarily at the expense of others; (b) that voluntary exchanges may be mutually beneficial, but the gains from exchanges are unfairly distributed; (c) that all above-average gains are undeserved; and (d) that there are negative pecuniary externalities. Let us briefly consider these claims in turn.

A. One man's gain is at the expense of another

The belief that one man's gain is necessarily at the expense of another—as is the case when dividing a pie—is deeply rooted in the human psyche. Whatever the origin of the belief, it is not valid when applied to voluntary exchanges, which is what a market economy is largely about. One of the most valuable insights of economics suggests that voluntary exchanges are value-creating and mutually beneficial—otherwise, the exchanges would not have taken place. Nevertheless, the erroneous perception of

[43] See Choi, "On the Rich Getting Richer and the Poor Getting Poorer."

economic processes as a zero-sum game has found expression through the ages in denouncements of trade as unproductive and parasitic. Even today, in the age of universal commerce, the suspicion persists against gains, especially large gains.

Not all large gains are held in suspicion, of course. For example, I have not heard social critics charging that the baseball slugger Mark McGwire's decamillion-dollar income is at someone else's expense. The critics can see that McGwire can hit the ball over the fence better than anyone else alive and that his fans gladly pay to see him play. The same point applies to star entertainers such as singers, actors and actresses, and other sports players. The fantastic gains of inventors also seem to be easily understood and excused.

But when a nondescript businessman or an entrepreneur makes big gains, critics wonder whether someone else is not cheated, exploited, or even robbed. The suspicion has a lot to do with misunderstanding the nature of profit. Profit in the competitive market does not arise from routine practices, but from discovering and exploiting opportunities overlooked by others. The source of profit, in other words, lies in superior knowledge and hunches about market conditions. Social critics, not being privy to the sources of profit, generally see no ground for profit.[44] Since the sources of profit are obscure, the critics suspect some sort of injustice—if not illegal actions, then perhaps highly immoral ones.[45]

Even when the critics come to learn, ex post, about the sources of profits, they often feel that the sources are too trivial to merit the gains—ignoring the fact that the whole informational advantage lies in having these sources before others. (Timing is a crucial factor here. Aren't we all smart in hindsight?) Critics, who usually view themselves as intellectually capable, cannot see how so much profit can be justified by such trivialities.[46] Since the critics fail to see justifiable causes for profits, they do what is "logical," suspecting wrongdoing on the part of entrepreneurs, however unproven. Once they convince themselves that the rich have gained unjustly, they have few qualms about demanding redistribution, which is really only demanding justice as far as they are concerned.

[44] Otherwise, they might have taken an action and captured the profit themselves. Of course, if they valued other things (such as academic pursuits) more highly than the profit, and ignored the profitable opportunity that they were certain of, it was their choice. In this case, they paid the implicit price of the expected profit to engage in their nobler pursuits. The blaming of others for taking profit that the critics themselves could have, then, amounts to the critics blaming others for not sharing the critics' interests.

[45] Young Back Choi, "Entrepreneurship and Envy," *Constitutional Political Economy* 4, no. 3 (1993): 331–47. See also F. A. Hayek, *The Fatal Conceit: The Errors of Socialism* (Chicago: University of Chicago Press, 1989), 89–105.

[46] Furthermore, the source of much American wealth is mundane as well. Many American millionaires own small, nonglamorous businesses, including junkyards, insurance agencies, and small manufacturing concerns. See Thomas J. Stanley, *The Millionaire Mind* (Kansas City, MO: Andrews McMeel, 2000); and Thomas J. Stanley and William D. Danko, *The Millionaire Next Door* (Atlanta, GA: Longstreet Press, 1996). See also Andrew Hacker, *Money: Who Has How Much and Why* (New York: Scribner, 1997), 76–77.

Those critics who suspect injustice in the extant distribution of income, without probable cause, merely because it is unequal, fail to see that the race to discover neglected opportunities—however trivial they may seem in retrospect—is what drives entrepreneurs constantly to bring out new and better products at lower prices. It is a race from which mankind has benefited immeasurably. These critics also fail to see that whatever gains entrepreneurs have, they are what the entrepreneurs' customers voluntarily gave them, because they too benefit in the process.

B. Gains from trade are disproportionately captured by the rich

Critics who would accept in principle the proposition that voluntary exchanges are mutually beneficial may still argue that the gains from trade are not equally or fairly shared if one party—usually the rich and powerful one—has superior knowledge or bargaining power. In Section IV, I argued that the idea of the inherent advantage of the rich is more apparent than real. The key issue here, however, is who should decide what division of gains is fair, if not the parties to the transaction themselves at the time of the transaction. Parties to a potential transaction consider all options available to them at the moment, and the transaction will only be agreed to if both parties believe that the terms of the transaction are superior to any other alternative available to them. The desire of the rich and powerful to dictate their terms to get a lion's share of the gains from trade in a transaction will be frustrated, for if the terms offered by the rich and powerful are indeed lopsided, then there should be offers of superior terms by bargain hunters.

I acknowledge that individuals make mistakes occasionally or even often. But to err is to be human. I assert that society would have a much greater problem if all transactions were made open for renegotiations, in the corrective light of added information and changed circumstances (or at the urging of bystanders), at some time in the future. For then gains from trade would become completely uncertain. Few, if any, would try to trade at all. The consequence would be a reversion to barbarism and meager living for everyone.

C. Inequality is unjustified

Many critics also seem to hold that inequality as such is unjustified, in the sense that there is no good justification for someone having more than others do. This argument comes in two flavors—that above-average income (or wealth) is unearned, and that it is undeserved.

1. *The unearned.* Many critics feel that only income from labor is earned. Income from other sources—rent, interest, and profit—is often regarded

as unearned.[47] This distinction is taken to mean that what is unearned is unjustified. Since the rich are viewed as deriving the bulk of their income from nonlabor sources, their income is seen as unjustified.

But a view such as this is based on much ignorance and confusion. First of all, even if only labor income is earned, the earned income would be distributed unequally, as some people work more, harder, smarter, and with more skills than others. Second, the critics ignore the fact that the majority of households in the United States derive their income from various nonlabor sources—through their pension funds invested in stocks and bonds, through their savings (from past earnings) that earn interest, through the appreciation of the value of their homes, and so on. Under these circumstances, the question is not whose income is earned and whose is not, but who has proportionally more or less "unearned" income.

The answer to this question, however, is not necessarily directly correlated with one's income or wealth. For example, a retired couple that relies on pensions and rents out a couple of rooms in their house, though not rich, would have nearly all of their income coming from nonlabor sources. On the other hand, Chrysler once paid Lee Iacocca a few hundred million dollars a year, which put him as one of the top earners in the world at the time; that income should be classified as earned. Chrysler had hired him to turn around the troubled firm, so the compensation was mostly for his labor, though very highly priced.

But more importantly, why regard income from sources other than labor as unearned in the first place? The view is based on the belief that only labor creates value, and that other factors of production, or rather, their owners, merely partake in the value created by labor. This view ignores the fact that labor alone, without other factors of production, is not very productive. Consider the productivity of millions of souls in Uganda, Somalia, or the Sudan, each of whom could create much value, and earn accordingly, if he or she could relocate to industrialized countries where other factors of production are abundant; this disproves the claim that only labor is productive. The view also ignores the question of how the current owners of other factors of production came to their ownership. Upon consideration, it should become clear that the bulk of the ownership comes from savings and investment, which take much labor, ingenuity, and discipline.

The same critics would regard inherited wealth as also unearned. But there are other inheritances—genetic makeup, upbringing, and so forth. Why single out inheritance of money (or near-money) assets as unearned? What about other inheritances such as intelligence, talents, temperament, disposition, upbringing, looks, and strength, each of which is a valuable asset and in due time can be turned into money or near

[47] Even the U.S. government adopts this sort of terminology when it uses the category "earned income credit."

money? There is no good reason. As if to be consistent, however, some critics have chosen to question the legitimacy of the above-average inheritance of nonmoney assets as well, as we shall see below.

2. *The undeserved.* Even "earned income" is not all justified or deserving in the eyes of discerning critics. Much of the individual differences in income and wealth has to do with differences in endowments (e.g., skills, talents, drive, etc.). But what did the individuals who enjoy above-average income do to *deserve* the valuable assets denied to others? Critics cannot think of any good justification for the good fortune of having the valuable resources (money or otherwise) that are responsible for some individuals doing better than others. Put in another manner, who can justify what they have as merited? All that most reasonable people can say is that it happens to be that way. For critics, then, the inequality in income and wealth distribution is largely a matter of luck, in the sense that one has little control over the outcome.[48] And no one deserves to be lucky, or luckier than others.

It is perverse reasoning to say that to keep what one has, one must be able to explicitly justify one's possession. I wonder whether many can explicitly justify their existence (or longevity or health) so as to satisfy the standard demanded by the critics for the ownership of one's own intelligence, talent, drive, will to excel, and so on. Would the critics dare to suggest that those who fail to justify their existence must forfeit their lives or health?[49] Why must the burden of justification be placed on inequality? I believe that the burden should rather fall on those who, against all things natural, hold equality as the ideal.

The critics' argument that, unless the "luck" of having more than others can be justified (to the satisfaction of the critics), no one deserves to have more than others (that is, everything must be shared equally), is perverse in another way. According to social psychologist Helmut Schoeck, the concept of luck was invented as a means of diverting the envy of others (i.e., their suspicion that you gained unfairly and that therefore you should be sanctioned) by declaring your innocence.[50] Schoeck argues that the origin of the word "happiness" reveals the role of luck in mitigating the envy of others. "Happiness" derives from the Old English word "hap," meaning accident or luck. Earlier people tried to lessen others' envy by describing an extraordinary success as a fluke or as fortuitous (i.e., by disclaiming any unfair action on their part).[51] The fact that over time

[48] Viewing matters in this way, the critics assume a simple form of materialism, denying any efficacy of human agency.

[49] The logic may run as follows: "I am dying of kidney disease. But you have two. What did you do to deserve two sound kidneys when I am doomed? Since you did not do anything to deserve your good fortune, we should equalize. It is only fair that you give me one of your kidneys."

[50] Helmut Schoeck, *Envy: A Theory of Social Behaviour* (Indianapolis, IN: Liberty Press, 1987).

[51] Interestingly, the word for happiness in Chinese, *hsing fu,* with the literal meaning of "good luck," must have a similar origin.

people have come to express the state of being well as being happy indicates that the means of mitigating envy have been more formally institutionalized.[52]

Now, critics propose that luck is unfair. In the hands of the critics, this concept of luck has itself become an instrument of envy, justifying redistribution. The matter has become implicitly one of negative pecuniary externalities.

D. Negative pecuniary externalities

In economics, "negative externalities" are by-products of economic transactions that harm individuals who are not parties to the transactions. Air pollution is a prime example. "Negative pecuniary externalities" occur when some individuals gain from their own economic activities, but others who have nothing to do with these activities feel harmed by the sight of the participants' relative gains. In this mind-set, how well off you are in absolute terms matters not. All that matters is whether anyone is better off than you are. If others are relatively better off than you, then you are injured. In this mind-set, people would be content, even if everyone had meager living conditions, as long as no one were better off.

This is a pure expression of envy. Envy is man's desire to eliminate others' relative gains even if he would become absolutely worse off in the process. Envy is appeased only at equality, regardless of the absolute level of consumption. Only those societies that have been able to develop sufficient means to mitigate the destructive forces of envy have been able to build civilizations and prosper. Anthropologists have documented that two of the most distinguishing features of poor societies are the relative free expression of envy and the universal fear of envy on the part of those who come to have above-average gains.[53]

[52] Leda Cosmides and John Tooby, "Cognitive Adaptations for Social Exchange," in Jerome H. Barkow, Leda Cosmides, and John Tooby, eds., *The Adapted Mind: Evolutionary Psychology and the Generation of Culture* (New York: Oxford University Press, 1992), 212–20. Evolutionary psychologists argue that the human brain is hardwired to invoke a sharing norm in circumstances where the variability of individual success (e.g., successful hunting) is greater than that of the collective, the connection between individual success and individual merit is uncertain, and there is no means of storing food. This description applied to the sort of hunter-gatherer society from which human beings have emerged only relatively recently. But the norm became less compelling as human beings went through successive stages of economic development—agriculture, handicraft, manufacturing, and so on, with an ever-expanding network of exchanges—where the connection between individual success and merit is more direct, individual gains can be stored, and people can pool risks through various insurances.

[53] See Eric R. Wolf, "Types of Latin American Peasantry: A Preliminary Discussion," *American Anthropologist* 57, no. 3 (1955): 452–57; Y. A. Cohen, "Four Categories of Interpersonal Relationships in the Family and Community of a Jamaican Village," *Anthropological Quarterly* 28, no. 3 (1955): 121–47; and Audrey I. Richards, *Land, Labour, and Diet in Northern Rhodesia* (London: Oxford University Press, 1939).

VI. Conclusion

In the United States, social critics are much more concerned about unequal distribution of income and wealth than the general public is. To these critics, inequality is wrong and undesirable; collective actions are needed to reduce it. I have discussed the critics' concerns on three broad topics—that inequality is excessive, that market competition is rigged in favor of the rich, and that inequality is unjust—and tried to argue that each is based on a misunderstanding of the facts. First, when official statistics are properly adjusted (for such missing items as taxes, noncash transfers, the value of Social Security benefits, the size of households, the age of primary earners, differences in costs of living, etc.), inequality in income and wealth distribution is much lower than the critics portray. The remaining inequality of income is largely attributable to differences among workers in their amounts of labor and skill; in the case of wealth, inequality reflects differences in consumption behavior and success of investment, as well as differences in income over time.

Second, the idea of the rich having an inherent advantage over the poor is more apparent than real. Its implications—increasing polarization of income and wealth, and lack of mobility—are not supported by the facts. The idea itself reflects a profound misunderstanding of the process of market competition.

Third, the attitude of regarding inequality in income and wealth distribution as a sign of injustice arises in a large measure from the critics' inability to understand the sources of profit. The sources of profit are often obscure and the critics cannot imagine its justifiable causes. Unjustified gains, it is reasoned, must be a sign of injustice, even when there is no evidence. If the critics understood the nature of profit, and how the race for profit has brought forth many of the good things in life, they would not regard profit and inequality as signs of injustice.

The association between income (or wealth) distribution and justice (or fairness) may be triggered by the word "distribution." Distribution (or, more formally, "frequency distribution") is a method of organizing and summarizing data whereby individual observations are distributed in accordance with the few distinct values that the variable can take. Hence, we speak of (frequency) distributions of income, wealth, height, weight, age, and so on. Even so, the word "distribution," in connection with income and wealth, tends to conjure up in the minds of many an image of someone apportioning a set of resources, as in a family. This tendency reflects the habits of mind the bulk of humanity acquires in being brought up in families. The strength of the appeal of equality as the ideal rests largely on these habits of mind. Unfortunately, it is the wrong imagery for modern economic processes that operate beyond family, beyond one's own local community, and even beyond national boundaries. The mistaken imagery of a "national family" conjures up obligations and entitlements that are only appropriate within a *real* family.[54]

Though many people have a vague longing for equality, once it is stated explicitly they easily recognize its absurdity as a practicable goal. Equality is impossible to achieve, and attempts to achieve it would produce many undesirable results. Incentives are perverted if in the name of reducing inequality money is taken away from those who work and given to those who do not, or if money is taken away from those who make available the goods that consumers want (when and how they want them) and given to those who do not render any service to others. If a society tries to redistribute constantly (as it will be bound to do if it is to keep inequality at a low level), not only will that society become much poorer through the perversion of incentives, but it will become increasingly arbitrary and oppressive as well.

Nevertheless, critics maintain that it is necessary and desirable that the opportunities that individuals face be equalized, especially for the young. Many social programs are motivated by such a belief. However, equalization of opportunities is not any easier than equalization of income or wealth. People, as bundles of characteristics, differ along many dimensions. Trying to equalize along only one dimension (measurable income or wealth, for example), disregarding all others, is arbitrary and reckless if we do not know individuals' values along that dimension and how those values might change in the near or distant future. A poor farm boy may grow up to be a millionaire sports star or a businessman, while another boy born with a silver spoon in his mouth may grow into an imbecile, squandering a fortune and becoming penniless. A redistribution to equalize the recorded income or wealth during these individuals' boyhoods would in fact be transferring wealth from the poor (the imbecile, poor in human capital) to the rich (the farm boy, rich in human capital). One can go on and on.

The real problem with the attempt to equalize income or wealth distribution stems from failing to realize that the vast majority of income or wealth is obtained as a result of voluntary transactions among individuals. Income and wealth are typically the cumulative result of market prices received for certain services rendered (to someone). Income and wealth both support and result from the role of the price signals that most economists readily recognize as crucial in the working of the market, channeling resources to those activities that benefit consumers. To become indignant that income or wealth is unevenly distributed is akin to becoming incensed that a car fetches a higher price than a banana. Demanding that inequality in income or wealth distribution be reduced

[54] Note also that many who hold equality as the ideal have a peculiar view of equality that stops well within a national boundary. The fact that the poorest in a given critic's own country may be far better off than the rich in another country is often viewed with surprising detachment.

substantially is like demanding that the price difference between a student violin and a Stradivarius be reduced substantially.[55]

The politics of equalization would entail severe restrictions on what individuals can or cannot do, beyond the general rules of conduct, as economic processes would have to be fitted to conform to some acceptable level of equality. Consequently, if redistributive measures are at all successful, they will produce a stagnant economy through regulations and discouragement of economic activities, and a society with more rigid class distinctions through a diminution of mobility. The end result will be far from what the social critics imagine.

Economics, St. John's University

[55] If this demand were put into practice, Stradivarius violins would disappear in no time.

CAN ANYONE BEAT THE FLAT TAX?*

By Richard A. Epstein

I. Introduction: Are Proportionate Taxes Just?

The inequalities of wealth and fortune form a central part of the human condition, and these over time have been a constant source of social unease. Whether they should be praised and preserved or endured or corrected is an issue that produces uniform discord. One source of this difficulty in analysis stems from the possible ways in which these persistent inequalities arise. It is easy to condemn any differences in wealth created by the victor's expropriation of the vanquished's honest toil. It is far more difficult to condemn those identical differences when they are attributable to the thrift and foresight of the successful relative to the laziness or self-destructiveness of the impoverished. Furthermore, most find it morally ambiguous how best to respond to differences between persons that are the result of luck or chance, such that they do not reflect positively or negatively on either the character of those who have done well or those who have done poorly.

The first and second scenarios tend to generate relatively clean responses. In the first case, the use of aggression to acquire the possessions of another individual should be rectified under principles of corrective justice. The victim ought to secure the return of what has been taken from him or compensation for the loss. The close connection between injurer and victim, moreover, does not offend, as far as I can see, any utilitarian concern about how the tort law might, for example, be used to advance overall economic efficiency. The victim is likely to have the most information about the injurer's wrongful conduct and the extent of his own injuries, and ordinarily can best defend his own conduct should it become a matter of dispute. However straightforward this sort of case is from a moral point of view, it is tangential to the central concern here, for the condemnation meted out under a corrective-justice theory is undiminished even if it is the poor who use violence against the rich. Whatever the popular appeal of a romanticized Robin Hood, Aristotle captured the tough-mindedness of the orthodox position by noting that corrective jus-

*I have benefited from comments made at the Work in Progress Workshop at the University of Chicago in June 2000. I should also like to thank Albert Alschuler, Bernard Meltzer, and David Schmidtz for their comments on this essay. David Weisbach directed me to the relevant tax policy literature and helped me greatly by giving me an extensive critique of an earlier draft of this essay. My thanks also to Robert Alt (class of 2002 at the University of Chicago Law School) for his thorough research assistance.

tice does not take notice of "whether a good man has defrauded a bad man or a bad man a good one,"[1] and the same point surely carries over to wealth. Aristotle did not give us an exhaustive account of corrective justice, but by fair implication it appears that he believed that the concern with rectification was separable from disputes over the fair distribution of wealth and opportunities at stake here.

Similarly, the results are generally straightforward under the second sort of case, that of self-inflicted harm, whether by act or omission. Under principles of corrective justice, in these cases the victim and injurer are rolled into one, so that no relief against another should, or could, be granted. This position carries over to modern schemes of no-fault compensation such as workers' compensation, where individual employees cannot recover for deliberately self-inflicted harms even though their own negligence does not bar or reduce their recovery for unintentional harms.[2]

So the test cases for theories of redistribution arise when the differences in circumstances are not brought about by the misconduct of the unfortunate person, or indeed of anyone else in society. In this context, individual rectification makes no sense because we cannot identify any putative wrongdoer. But leaving the losses where they lie misses the possibility of acting for the benefit of all by equalizing wealth for persons under conditions of uncertainty. Such actions could in principle be justified on the ground that a marginal dollar is worth more to the poor person than to the rich one, or, alternatively, on the ground that any differences in talents and ability result from a natural lottery and should therefore be rejected as morally arbitrary. A still more aggressive stance could argue in favor of equal incomes across the board, so that the amount of wealth one receives is unrelated to the amount that one earns. Whatever the soundness of these various positions, one point remains clear: the simple lawsuits that achieve corrective justice cannot bring about a wholesale realignment of economic interests. Use of larger social mechanisms is required.

In this essay I wish to address the possible use and soundness of one such mechanism for achieving this goal: taxation. Taxation may serve multiple functions: it may provide for the provision of classic public goods, or it may be used as a vehicle of redistribution of wealth from one group in society to another, or it may be used for some combination of

[1] Aristotle, *Nicomachean Ethics*, in Richard McKeon, ed., *The Basic Works of Aristotle* (New York: Random House, 1941), 1132a2–3.

[2] For an early description of the basic system, see *Ives v. South Buffalo Ry. Co.*, 201 N.Y. 271, 285, 94 N.E. 431, 436 (1911), which noted that "every employer who is engaged in any of the classified industries shall be liable for any injury to a workman arising out of and in the course of the employment by 'a necessary risk or danger of the employment or one inherent in the nature thereof; . . . provided that the employer shall not be liable in respect of any injury to the workman which is caused in whole or in part by the serious and willful misconduct of the workman.'" ("Classified industries" here referred to those typically dangerous trades that were covered under the early versions of the workers' compensation laws.)

both. One effective lens for understanding the question of whether differences in wealth between individuals matter—and matter morally—is to examine the conflict between libertarian and social-welfare conceptions of taxation. In assessing this conflict, I shall not explicitly address the claims of an egalitarian position: so long as one can show the weakness of the more moderate claims of the social welfarist, then the more aggressive position of the egalitarian must, *a fortiori*, fail.

To show the social welfarist's weaknesses, it is necessary to revisit the perennial debate, which shows signs of heating up anew, over the proper function and form of taxation.[3] On the former issue, the question is whether the role of taxation is to facilitate the provision of public goods and services that voluntary markets cannot provide. On the latter, the question is whether the redistribution of wealth across individuals is an appropriate function of government. The two questions are, of course, closely connected, but not necessarily so. It is therefore no accident that the defenders of limited government generally view state-mandated redistribution with suspicion and thus gravitate toward the flat tax on ordinary income.[4] The defenders of the welfare state have an equal attraction to progressive taxes as part of a more comprehensive system of income redistribution. The issues of tax equity and tax efficiency that are raised by this deliberation emerged long before the dawn of the new millennium; indeed, they predate the adoption of the first federal income tax in 1913.

The outer parameters of this debate are not all that difficult to identify, and I have touched on them elsewhere.[5] In a strong libertarian world, the only obligations that may be imposed on individuals are those voluntarily assumed and those created when an individual trespasses or commits private wrongs against other citizens for which they are called upon to answer. Even as a private law matter, however, this scope of individual obligation seems to be too narrow to embrace the entire field of potential liability. For example, the law of restitution deals with the question of "unjust enrichment," where benefits have been conferred on a defendant

[3] Some of the classic works relevant to this debate are Edwin R. A. Seligman, *Progressive Taxation in Theory and Practice*, 2d ed. (Princeton, NJ: American Economic Association, 1908); F. W. Taussig, *Principles of Economics* (New York: Macmillan, 1911); and Walter J. Blum and Harry Kalven, Jr., "The Uneasy Case for Progressive Taxation," *University of Chicago Law Review* 19, no. 3 (1952): 417–520. For a more modern treatment, see David Gauthier, *Morals by Agreement* (Oxford: Clarendon Press, 1986).

[4] Just by way of clarity, the discussion of the flat tax here has nothing in common with the proposals to switch to what amounts to a rather novel form of consumption tax. My proposal is one that assumes the current income base and then imposes a unified rate over the base from first to last dollar. For an exposition and exposé of the new flat tax, see Marvin Chirelstein, "The Flat Tax Proposal—Will Voters Understand the Issues?" *Green Bag*, 2d ser., 2 (1999): 147–61. "Briefly stated, the Flat Tax (Forbes/Kemp/Armey etc. version) is not an income tax at all, flat or otherwise. Rather, it is a Value Added Tax with a rebate to low-wage workers." Ibid., 150.

[5] Richard A. Epstein, "Taxation in a Lockean World," *Social Philosophy and Policy* 4, no. 1 (1986): 49–74.

under circumstances that require that the thing be restored to the plaintiff, or require that the defendant compensate the plaintiff for the thing's value.[6] Thus, restitution sometimes requires an individual to pay when his property has been rescued by the intervention of third parties under circumstances of dire necessity in which he was not in a position to defend his property himself.[7] In other cases it is obligatory to return something that has been obtained by mistake (e.g., too much change in the supermarket).[8]

This law of restitution, as it applies to cases of necessity, gives rise to a clear public law analogy. The libertarian system, with its exclusive emphasis on the prohibition of force and fraud, contains no mechanism to secure the public enforcement of private obligations that is itself required by the libertarian state. As a comprehensive system of public funding cannot be coordinated through voluntary participation, the theory of restitution offers the best justification for having the state collect taxes from the individuals who benefit from its protection.

As a matter of principle, this analogy is far from perfect. What is preserved is the idea that individuals can be required to pay the state for the benefits conferred on them by state protection. But the reasons why they can be required to pay differ, for in the public law case the problem is the difficulty of arranging for voluntary coordination of payments from a large number of beneficiaries, *not* the bargaining breakdown that hampers certain difficult two-party transactions. Yet nonetheless the analogy has bite because in both cases high transaction costs (stemming from different reasons in each case) block voluntary transactions, and thus justify the state's use of force in ways that work to the benefit of the parties from whom the exaction is obtained. The theory of restitution thus supplies a justification for the use of coercion, and also places limitations (in the form of the requirement of the return benefit) on the use of coercive power.

Once this structural concession is made, then the pure libertarian theory no longer binds in public affairs any more (or less) than it binds in private affairs. Someone must figure out a way to determine not only the size of the government budget, but also a rule that allocates a fraction of that budget among all the individuals who benefit from the service paid for by that money. This task demands that the state use coercion against its citizens. This use of force in turn opens up the risk that the system of taxation will be abused and perverted and thus transformed into an instrument of confiscation that some individuals can wield against others—unless the requirement of the return benefit is strictly enforced. One could

[6] See generally *Restatement (Third) of Restitution* sec. 1, cmt. a (preliminary draft, October 1998): "Liability in restitution is triggered by receipt of a benefit, under circumstances such that the recipient is not justified in retaining the benefit without paying for it."

[7] Ibid., secs. 19–21.

[8] Ibid., secs. 5–12.

easily throw up one's hands and hold that the protection against this risk, if it is a risk, lies with the political branches of government, which must respond to any nascent concerns for fairness sensed by a majority of citizens. Alternatively, one might argue that the risk of disguised confiscation justifies constitutional limitations on the sovereign power to tax—limitations, for example, like those in the United States that require tax uniformity across geographical regions.[9] But in order to rely on political or constitutional institutions, or some combination thereof, to limit potential abuses of discretion, it is first incumbent to identify the contours of the just (or, if one prefers, efficient) tax so that we can add flesh to the twin substantive concerns of confiscation and abuse of discretion. This task requires a normative theory of taxation that can be invoked to either support or condemn, in political or constitutional terms, any particular regime of taxation.

In order to make this inquiry tractable, I shall concentrate largely on the personal income tax, and leave to one side the full range of other taxes that are part and parcel of the modern state. Thus I do not take into account the system of double taxation on corporate income (once when the income is earned, and again when it is distributed as a dividend). I also ignore the complications associated with any death or estate tax, which operates as a second tax on accumulations that have been previously taxed. Furthermore, I ignore the sales tax and similar taxes on specified transactions. Finally, I also ignore the imposition of Social Security and Medicare taxes; the former is flat up to a certain level, and the latter operates as a flat tax on all earned income.

Any system of practical reform has to ask how these various taxes should be integrated with the income tax. But before these technical issues are examined, it is critical to understand how the system of taxation works if all income, on both labor and capital, is taxed at the same rate. Under this assumption, I wish to argue that the flat tax is superior to all others because it is compatible with a wide range of visions of the proper role of government. It works quite well with the limited-state libertarian model as a rough (indeed the only serviceable) proxy for a benefits theory of taxation. The case for the flat tax remains strong, however, even in a system that for utilitarian reasons favors some degree of redistribution.

[9] U.S. Constitution, art. 1, sec. 8: "The Congress shall have Power To lay and collect Taxes, Duties, Imposts and Excises, to pay the Debts and provide for the common Defence and general Welfare of the United States; but all Duties, Imposts and Excises shall be uniform throughout the United States." It has been held that "uniform" here refers to geographical uniformity, as may be implied from the last phrase, "throughout the United States." But even here the rule has been read, wrongly in my view, to allow for deviations from the geographical norm, as when the U.S. Supreme Court allowed the U.S. Congress to exempt Alaskan oil from the Crude Oil Windfall Profit Tax of 1980; see *United States v. Ptasynski*, 462 U.S. 74 (1983). The removal of the constraint creates too much discretion for too little good purpose. There is no reason to modify an excise tax to subsidize the production of high-cost Alaskan oil. (There was no reason to impose this tax in the first place, either.)

The ideal level of redistribution can be too great as well as too small, and the flat tax system does a good job in limiting the amount redistributed without choking it off altogether.

It is difficult to choose between a strong and a qualified defense of the flat tax in the abstract, for so much depends on how much wealth and liberty is lost to achieve any given unit of redistribution. But as a matter of general political philosophy, the best approach seems to be this: First, try to find ways to encourage voluntary exchanges. Next, develop public institutions that help replicate the gains obtainable by private contract, that is, by inducing legislatures to enact laws that promote, to the extent possible, across-the-board improvements. The easy cases for public intervention rest on the desire to create Pareto improvements by coercion. Only after these gains have been completed should one move down the dangerous path to redistribution—that is, cases in which social intervention produces gains for one individual or group only at the expense of losses to another individual or group. Operationally, this means that we should first seek to remove impediments to voluntary transactions in order to expand production before we turn to issues of redistribution. With wealth expanded, more resources are available for redistribution, and fewer individuals will have claims on them. How far down the redistributivist path we should travel once market mechanisms are given their due gives rise to genuine difficulties that I cannot answer here. But even if I cannot make the case for categorical prohibitions against efforts to redistribute wealth, I do think that the potential social benefits of most redistributivist strategies are limited. And in any event, the size of those potential gains depends at least in part on the success of any legal system in removing the regulations and obstacles that impede sensible voluntary transactions.

In order to establish the case for the flat tax, I hope to show that it functions well *whether or not* one accepts the case for some social redistribution of wealth. Section II investigates the reasons why private partnerships gravitate toward an analog to the flat tax—the pro rata division of losses—and why this position has appealed to the broad run of small-state libertarian thinkers. Section III then sets out the imperfect case for the flat tax. Section IV examines the extent to which it is proper to draw on private analogies (of partnership) to understand social institutions (of taxation), and then uses those analogies to explain the superiority of the flat tax over the head tax (i.e., a tax of so much per person, regardless of income). Section V examines the extent to which redistribution can and should take place under the flat tax. Section VI then explores the relationship between progressive taxes and redistribution. Deductive victories and necessary truths escape the defenders of the flat tax. But it is a robust second-best alternative, one that comes out first-best in any world that worries about the mix between theoretical conceptions and practical implications.

II. Private Partnerships and Social Surplus

Setting out the appropriate regime for taxation is necessarily a structural inquiry that comprises a determination of what forms of wealth may be taxed and what rate structure should be imposed. Once we are forced to recognize that government must use force to support its own efforts, what general principles are left to guide its imposition? At the most general level, a social contract theory may be invoked to set the parameters of taxation. Here both the words "social" and "contract" have to be given their due weight. The idea of exchange lies at the core of contract.[10] The motivation for exchange is mutual gains through trade. As has been said countless times before, each participant parts with what he values less in order to obtain what he values more.[11] Voluntary exchange therefore is in expectation a positive-sum game, even if in some fraction of cases either or both sides regret the transaction after it has been consummated. The secret of contractual success rests in the fact that the property received in one transaction can be resold in the next, wherein a new round of gains can be achieved. In this system, the key point is to reduce the level of transaction costs so as to increase the speed and frequency of beneficial transactions.

Social contracts, like actual contracts, seek mutual gains for all the parties that are said (hypothetically) to enter into them. But in social contracts, the large number of parties makes it impossible to overcome the transactional obstacles to voluntary exchange. Social infrastructure—from law and order to roads—cannot be funded or created by millions of ordinary bilateral contracts. What is needed is an overarching transaction to coordinate the efforts of millions of people so as to develop the infrastructure that all require. At this point, the needed exchanges must be coerced by the state. In this context, the critical limitation on state power under the orthodox restitution theory set out above is that each person is supposed to receive more from the protection and services supplied by the state than he is called on to surrender to it. The same pattern of gains

[10] There are important exceptions to this principle. A firm offer—I agree, gratis, that you should have ten days to decide whether to purchase my home for $100,000—should be binding for a limited period of time even though the offeree has not supplied consideration in exchange. Such offers are made in order to induce a greater study by the offeree and thus should be treated as a part of the exchange process. The more difficult questions arise in connection with promises to make gifts; these promises are often not enforceable in the absence of formalities, such as seals, notarization, or witnesses. But these important side points do not detract from the overwhelming centrality of exchange relationships in the law of contract.

[11] For the judicial pronouncement, see *Coppage v. Kansas*, 236 U.S. 1, 17 (1915):

> Indeed a little reflection will show that whenever the right of private property and the right of free contract co-exist, each party when contracting is inevitably more or less influenced by the question whether he has much property, or little, or none; for the contract is made to the very end that each may gain something that he needs or desires more urgently than that which he proposes to give in exchange.

and losses that one finds in voluntary contracts should carry over to these social contracts. Stated otherwise, when voluntary contracts are not possible, the fallback position allows property to be taken only when just compensation is provided to each person from whom it is taken. When particular pieces of land are taken for public use, then the compensation can be provided in cash. But that cash has to be raised by general tax revenues. A comprehensive social contract theory requires that the win/win condition be sought not only with respect to the individual whose property is taken for public use, but also with respect to the full range of citizens whose wealth is collected in order to fund the purchase in question.[12] However difficult this ideal is to achieve in practice, the goal remains clear: government coercion is justified only to the extent that it provides net benefits to those individuals subjected to coercion.

Even this condition may not be sufficient, for it leaves open the possibility of a skewed distribution of gains: some individuals will benefit greatly from state coercion, while others will benefit only a small bit. To help counteract against this possibility, most legal systems have locked into a traditional focal point that calls for the pro rata division of gains and losses derived from any common venture[13]—a rule that has its origins in the default provision for private partnerships since the earliest times.[14] Observing this constraint tends to reduce private incentives to jockey for an advantageous position, and simultaneously helps curtail the abuse of discretion inherent in the exercise of (monopoly) government power. In a sense, therefore, the ultimate test of a social improvement is more rigorous than that required under the standard tests of Pareto superiority. Not only must it be the case that at least one person will be left better off and no one will be left worse off, but in principle every individual must be made better off to the same degree, that is, receive the same rate of return on his proportionate investment in social infrastructure. At the abstract level, then, social contract theory combines and extends the common law rules of restitution (compensation must be provided for benefits conferred under conditions of necessity) and partnership (pro rata division) to forge a coherent conception of the system of limited government.

Social contract theory then seeks to make the system of state coercion imitate the patterns of gains and losses that are found in voluntary associations. As a result, the element of pro rata gain from collective action becomes one of the hallmarks of a system of limited government. The question then arises as to how this theory is applied to the general theory

[12] For a fuller discussion of the implications of this principle, see Richard A. Epstein, *Takings: Private Property and the Power of Eminent Domain* (Cambridge, MA: Harvard University Press, 1985).

[13] For a more detailed discussion of this rule, see Richard A. Epstein, *Bargaining with the State* (Princeton, NJ: Princeton University Press, 1993), 91–103.

[14] See Gaius, *Institutes*, bk. III, 150.

of taxation. In this regard there has been a very broad consensus among classical liberal thinkers in favor of the flat or proportionate tax as a method of funding essential government services. The stage is set, in a sense, by Aristotle, who in speaking of distributive justice generally notes, abstractly, that "[t]he just, then, is a species of the proportionate."[15] This broad conception is thereafter linked to taxation by John Locke, who writes, "'Tis true Governments cannot be supported without great Charge, and 'tis fit every one who enjoys his share of the Protection, should pay out of his Estate his proportion for the maintenance of it."[16] Similarly, Adam Smith writes in *The Wealth of Nations* that "[t]he subjects of every state ought to contribute towards the support of the government, as nearly as possible, in proportion to their respective abilities; that is, in proportion to the revenue which they respectively enjoy under the protection of the state."[17] The economist Frédéric Bastiat listed progressive taxation as a form of legal plunder that represents a perversion of the law to improper ends.[18] Finally, Hayek wrote, "[A] person who commands more of the resources of society will also gain proportionately more from what the government has contributed,"[19] and thus should be taxed proportionately. I have taken the same position myself.[20]

For my purposes here I pass over some equivocation in these various formulations. Smith, for example, does not explain the equivalence between apportionment by abilities and apportionment by revenues. Nor does he clearly show how each of these stands in relation to the return benefits conferred by state action. While a fuller theory must resolve these issues, the obvious question remains: why the convergence of our hardy band of libertarian, small-government thinkers to the proportionate tax?

[15] Aristotle, *Nicomachean Ethics*, 1131a30.

[16] John Locke, *Second Treatise of Government*, in Locke, *Two Treatises of Government*, ed. Peter Laslett (1689; reprint, Cambridge: Cambridge University Press, 1999), 362. Locke then goes on, evasively, to write, "But still it must be with his own consent, *i.e.*, the Consent of the Majority, giving it either by themselves, or their Representatives chosen by them." Ibid. Of course, the difference between individual consent, which renders taxation nugatory, and decision by majority rule, which could make it mischievous, is of fundamental importance. But for Locke it was a detail, for from his next sentence it is clear that his true target was dictatorial imposition of taxes: "if any one shall claim a *Power to lay* and levy *Taxes* on the people, by his own authority, and without such consent of the People, he thereby invades the *Fundamental Law of Property*, and subverts the end of Government." Ibid. (emphasis in original). Matters get much more difficult once we have rejected dictatorship and confine our search to the ideal democratic formula.

[17] Adam Smith, *The Wealth of Nations* (New York: Modern Library, 1937), 777.

[18] Frédéric Bastiat, "The Law," in Bastiat, *Selected Essays on Political Economy*, ed. George B. de Huszar, trans. Seymour Cain (Irvington-on-Hudson, NY: Foundation for Economic Education, 1950), 22.

[19] Friedrich A. Hayek, *A Constitution of Liberty* (Chicago: University of Chicago Press, 1960), 314.

[20] Epstein, "Taxation in a Lockean World," 69. For the full catalogue of supporters of proportionate taxation, see Barbara Fried, "Why Do Libertarians Love Proportionate Taxation?" (manuscript); and Barbara Fried, "The Puzzling Case for Proportionate Taxation," *Chapman Law Review* 2, no. 1 (1999): 157–95.

In order to understand how it is that we move in that direction, it is important to return again to fundamentals, and to note that within the classical liberal state the function of the government is to provide those standard public goods that markets cannot generate. These goods have two familiar characteristics.[21] First, once the good is supplied to one individual, it cannot be kept from the next individual. The classic example is the streetlight that benefits all who walk along the public way. Second, there is (within broad limits) a nonrivalrous consumption of the good, such that the benefit obtained by one citizen using the good is not reduced when that benefit is shared by a second. Streetlights and national defense both meet this definition. Under a theory of limited government, the set of public functions is limited to the provision of these classical public goods, and—or so I shall assume provisionally for the moment—does not include a redistributivist function whereby wealth is transferred coercively from some group of individuals to another; this includes all transfers from rich to poor.

III. The Imperfect Case for the Flat Tax

Operating within this narrow assumption, how strong is the case for the proportionate tax over, as Smith says, revenues derived from all the sources of income, rents, profits, and wages?[22] Here, the usual starting point for many public relationships is what passes for analogous private relationships. Smith himself makes this point quite forcibly, for immediately after he announces his preference for a general rule of proportionate taxation, he reverts to a private law analogy—the presumptive rule of proportionate contribution—to justify it: "The expence of government to the individuals of a great nation, is like the expence of management to the joint tenants of a great estate, who are all obliged to contribute in proportion to their respective interests in the estate."[23] At one level this conclusion could be criticized as exhibiting little more than an ad hoc love of symmetry that does not respond to any important social needs. But in truth I think that Smith's analysis gains traction the more that complications are introduced.

To understand why, start with the simple case of two individuals who wish to split the cost of a trip. Just to make it basic, assume that the only input that they are required to make to this joint venture is a cash con-

[21] For an early influential exposition, see Mancur Olson, Jr., *The Logic of Collective Action* (Cambridge, MA: Harvard University Press, 1965).

[22] Smith, *The Wealth of Nations*, 777.

[23] Ibid. This point was anticipated by Aristotle in the *Nicomachean Ethics*, when, in speaking about proportion, he writes, "For the justice that distributes the common possession is always in accordance with the kind of proportion [i.e., geometrical] mentioned above (for in the case also in which the distribution is made from the common funds of a partnership it will be according to the same ratio which the funds put into the business by the partners bear to each other)." Aristotle, *Nicomachean Ethics*, 1131b30.

tribution: there are no contributions of labor that might differ in time, quality, or degree, and therefore no need to develop some metric by which to assess different kinds of contributions. Assume that the full trip costs $100. How should the costs of this trip be allocated? The instinctive answer of the ordinary citizen is to split the costs evenly between the two parties, such that each pays $50. The mutual acceptance of this pro rata or equal division would offer a strong assurance that the condition of mutual gain was satisfied.

The more troublesome question, however, is whether we are confident that this even distribution of expenses is "fair" as between the parties. Answering that question is nonproblematic if we assume that the two parties are identical in all respects (i.e., in terms of wealth, attitudes toward risks, valuation of the venture) so that each attaches the same subjective value to the trip, which we will (in violation of strict utilitarian canons of ordinality) assume to be $75. In this case, the pro rata rule yields low bargaining costs and an even division of surplus. Nothing could be less problematic from a theoretical point of view.

But from this point forward, the more insistent the analysis, the murkier the results. Suppose that we strongly suspect that the utilities of the two parties differ with respect to the trip, such that it gives A a monetized utility of $100 and B one of only $75. The purist might object that there is no way to quantify this result because utilities are always incommensurate across people. But in this case, at least, we can think of an effective test to smoke out the difference between A and B. If the cost of the trip were $80 per person, then A would accept the equal division while B would not. Hence, the question here is whether we should in principle rejigger the cost allocation between the two parties to reflect differences in subjective utility that by hypothesis both parties know to exist.

How might this be done? One possible way is to try to equalize the net gains in utility that each person gets from the venture. In this case, we know that we have $75 in potential gains (assuming once again that the total costs of the trip equal $100, and that its value is $100 and $75 for A and B, respectively). To make sure that each party enjoys an equal gain, it would be necessary to reduce B's contribution to $37.50 and to raise A's to $62.50, leaving A with a gain of $37.50 ($100 – $62.50) and B with the same gain ($75 – $37.50). But here we have no ironclad assurance that the parties themselves would adopt this allocation, since B would receive a 100 percent return on his investment ($75 for $37.50), while A would receive only a 60 percent return ($100 for $62.50) for his. Alternatively, it could be possible to equalize the subjective rate of return that both parties get on their investments. To do this here, A must contribute $57.14, while B must contribute $42.86; each side will realize a 75 percent return on his initial investment ($100 / $57.14 = 1.75 and $75 / $42.86 = 1.75). I am not clever enough to figure out which division of gain works best in this case, but I suspect that no one else is, either.

The real problem raised by these examples can be stated in more general form: Let the initial points for A and B be a and b, respectively, such that they begin at (a, b) and can move to a set of points all of which lie to the "northeast" of that point (i.e., with $a' > a$ and $b' > b$). Deciding which of these points (a′, b′) should be is not dictated by any of our homespun intuitions. In the easy case where $a = b$, we could opt for equal outcomes: $a' = b'$ as with our initial case. But if $a \neq b$, then all bets are off. We could continue to move upward at a forty-five-degree angle so that the initial inequality is preserved, or we could try to move back toward a point on the northeast frontier (that is, the range of points indicating the outcomes achievable if all the possible surplus is split between the parties) that more closely approximates equality. Thus, if we started with both parties at 3, then we should divide a surplus of 6 equally between them so that both are at 6. But if we start with A at 4 and B at 2, it is an open question whether the addition of 6 units should result in an outcome with A at 8 and B at 4, or A and B both at 6, or A at 7 and B at 5, or some other combination in which the wealth held by A and B equals 12, $a' > 4$, and $b' > 2$.

No one has found a reliable way to choose between these alternatives, or other sets of alternatives that can be identified, even though the problem has been long and extensively explored in the game-theory literature.[24] If the skeptical mind can now recognize that introduction of the simplest asymmetry of position in a two-person cooperative game makes it difficult to find out just how far north and how far east we should go, then what hope is there of getting a coherent theory for the division of surplus when dealing with matters of general taxation across large portions of the population?

One obvious response to this impasse is to try to solve the two-person scenario by positing the one-shot game as part of a larger set of transactions. Suppose it turns out that we have two individuals who go on many trips. Here it is possible to envision two scenarios. In the first, player A always gets more of the surplus value than does player B. Here, nothing makes the situation any worse than it is in the single-shot version of this game—but things might be a bit better. If each run is an exact duplicate of the single run, then the size of the stakes may make it worthwhile to contract explicitly away from the default provision. The gains from contracting grow larger as the number of transactions under consideration rises, but the costs of contracting are not likely to rise as rapidly; hence, as more transactions are considered, there is a greater likelihood of a bargain that alters the initial set of default provisions so as to improve the joint welfare of the parties.

The more likely scenario, however, is one in which there is some variation in the rates of return from the various trips, so that in some trans-

[24] See R. Duncan Luce and Howard Raiffa, *Games and Decisions: Introduction and Critical Survey* (New York: Wiley, 1957), chap. 6, esp. sec. 6.8.

actions the larger surplus lies with A, while at other times it lies with B. In this repetitive-game situation, the impulse to keep with the original pro rata solution will in general only get stronger. While there are no guarantees, the constant repetition of the same game suggests that over time the surplus will tend to even out if the parties simply stick to the equal division. The case for this position becomes still stronger once it is clear that in many cases neither party knows its reservation price; all each party knows is that the trip is worth more than $50 to him, such that he has decided to participate. (After all, how many people who shop at the supermarket know, or bother to determine, their reservation prices for most of the goods they purchase?) At this point the equal division is even more attractive: it reduces A's need to assemble the information and to persuade B of his (A's) true reservation price, and vice versa. So the even division endures because it operates as a true focal point, even though the equal division of the costs does not necessarily generate an equal division of the surplus.

We thus have a reason as to why equal division serves as a powerful default rule, but it remains important to understand why it is a default rule instead of a conclusive presumption. To see why this is the case, assume that the trip still costs $100, but now B has a maximum reservation price of $40 while A has a maximum reservation price of $75. Here it is quite clear that the total gains from the trip equal $15 ($75 + $40 – $100). If, however, equal division of costs is required, then the trip will not take place at all: B will decline to participate in the venture because he would suffer a net loss of $10. In these circumstances, if B can convince A of his (B's) true reservation price, then it might be possible to alter the respective contributions so that they still sum to $100, but with B paying less than $40 and A paying less than $75.

Three caveats apply, however. First, there is no unique division of costs that covers this situation, just as there was no unique division when both parties valued the trip at over $50. More specifically, the deal will go through so long as we set the cost for B between $25 and $40 and the cost to A between $60 and $75. (Only when the cost figures fall within these respective ranges will both sides end up ahead.) Second, even in this case the possibility of repetitive dealing might well induce the first player to accept equal division, even for a $10 loss, in order to minimize the bargaining costs and to preserve any long-term gains from the relationship—at least if he can expect to hold substantial surplus in future transactions. Third, here, as in the earlier cases, it is not clear whether it helps the parties to have the power to renegotiate with each other. Suppose that B is only *pretending* that his reservation price is $40; we could then have a situation where A and B have the same reservation price but make different contributions toward the cost of the trip. From the ex ante perspective, an external rule that prohibits any renegotiation (and thus forces each party to contribute equal amounts) works better than one that allows it—which helps explain why partnership renegotiations are often so painful. The full range of responses shows that even in the easiest of circumstances, the divide-the-surplus game is fraught with indeterminacy and may lead to skewed outcomes.[25]

The most obvious extension of this two-party game is one that includes three or more parties; this is closely akin to Smith's example, mentioned above, of the division of expenses for a large estate. Here the basic dynamic of the situation is as it was before: the sensible contract has to ensure gains to all parties to it, and the stabilization of gains again points to an easy generalization of the principle of equal division: require equal contributions from all n players. The possible asymmetries only increase in likelihood: player C could have a reservation price of $55 or one of $150, or anywhere in between. Choosing a specific formula to answer this sort of difficulty is certainly no easier in the n-person case than it is in the two-person case, and it may well get harder still. One great advantage of the equality system is that it is robust over an expansion in the number of players: those who find that the costs of a joint venture do not exceed the benefits simply do not have to participate, or may sell out their interests if they are already involved. In a voluntary setting, then, the principle of equal division does quite well over a wide range of transactions even if it cannot realize in an abstract sense the equalization of subjective gains for all participants over all rounds.

It should be noted that the principle of equal division does not apply only to situations in which multiple players have all made equal contributions. In an ordinary partnership, it is possible to divide gains pro rata to the (unequal) amounts contributed by each of the partners. This division allows people to make investments of different sizes in the same business without having to face the risk of net loss that would emerge if all investors, no matter the size of their investment in a venture, received the same, equal-dollar division of the venture's gains.

IV. From Partnership to Taxation: Do Public/Private Comparisons Work?

It seems that the simple partnership model has some serious implications for a general scheme of taxation when the social contract theory again calls, in principle, for some ideal division of surplus. However, this

[25] It is in part for this reason that I am skeptical of the game-theoretical derivations for the pro rata rule that characterizes David Gauthier's work. See Gauthier, *Morals by Agreement*, 137. Gauthier derives the rule through use of the principle of "minimax relative concessions," which provides "that given a range of outcomes, each of which requires concessions by some or all persons if it is to be selected, . . . an outcome [should] be selected only if the greatest or *maximum* relative concession it requires, is as small as possible, or a *minimum*, that is, is no greater than the maximum relative concession required by every other outcome." Ibid. (emphasis in original). I am not the only one to find this formulation obscure, but the payoff seems to be pro rata concessions by persons with unequal shares of wealth—that is, a flat tax on income.

claim can be attacked, as has been perceptively done by Barbara Fried, as an effort to use a model of the rates of return obtained in competitive markets to understand the behavior of parties in the very different setting of an n-person monopoly, in which there are no viable alternatives that help shape the distribution of surplus.[26] After all, only a competitive market provides a unique allocation of surplus as a by-product of its (the market's) unique equilibrium price. But the whole point of the *normative* argument is *not* to predict how people would in fact bargain to agreement on an infinite time horizon in a situation in which a single holdout could doom the operation of the state. Rather, as in the general theory of regulation of natural monopoly, the object of the normative argument here is to deduce a set of constraints that induce the monopoly players—here, each individual citizen—to behave, to the extent that laws can do it, as if they were in a competitive market.[27] The pro rata formula championed by Smith does not do this ideally, but it certainly is preferable to the decision to bask in the indeterminacy of complex bargaining models.

In light of the limitations noted above, the Smith quotation has to be reinterpreted to say that revenue received by the state should be, ideally, a perfect proxy for the utility that this revenue generates for the contributing parties. Yet the private analogies show that nothing guarantees that this outcome will hold. The same amount of cash generates different utility levels for different persons. The situation is made more difficult by the fact that the total gains that an individual receives from the protection of the state include more than what Smith refers to as rents, profits, and wages; they also include the imputed income that falls outside the tax system entirely, which covers not only the market value of goods that have been produced within the household, but also the full range of benefits, both psychic and social, that arise from living in a society protected by the rule of law. Thus, an individual's total gains cover the protection of both individual liberty in noneconomic contexts—bodily integrity, friendship, and marriage—as well as the financial transactions to which it is possible to attach estimates of gain or loss.

Assuming that much of these gains derive from state protection, the question then arises as to how we should structure taxes to satisfy the basic condition of the social contract theory—that is, we must ask how one can use coercion in a way that leaves all parties better off than they were before the imposition of state protection. In stating this particular rule, it is important to recognize a deep ambiguity in how the pre-state

[26] See Fried, "The Puzzling Case for Proportionate Taxation," 165–68.

[27] On the theory of regulation, see Robert S. Pindyck and Daniel L. Rubinfeld, *Microeconomics*, 2d ed. (New York: Macmillan, 1992), 350, where it is noted that responding to a natural monopoly by using a system of optimal price regulation produces the competitive solution. For a judicial account of rate regulation, see *Duquesne Light Co v. Barasch*, 488 U.S. 299 (1989). For one analysis of the relevant difficulties, see Richard A. Epstein, *Principles for a Free Society: Reconciling Individual Liberty with the Common Good* (Reading, MA: Perseus Books, 1998), chap. 10.

baseline should be defined. One possibility is to treat it as a (Hobbesian) state of nature in which no individuals have any rights whatsoever. In this case we are generally confident that the overall level of wealth and income will be low. But we must be clear about the source of wealth and income, because no accepted definition of legal rights and duties forces people to back off the relentless pursuit of their own self-interest. In the Hobbesian vision of the world, the state of nature gives you all that you can grab by aggression and deceit, used alone or in cooperation with other people. Yet in dealing with taxation, the prohibition against redistribution is *not* intended to preserve the relative shares that all individuals have in the absence of legal order. Rather, it takes for its baseline the basic insight of the Lockean tradition—namely, that individual rights to liberty and property can be well-defined in a state of nature even if they can be only imperfectly defended without some centralized political force.[28]

The point here is that the conceptual move from Hobbesian liberty—do what you can get away with—to Lockean liberty—respect the person and property of others—will have profound consequences. In this situation we should expect a substantial increase in the overall size of the pie, whether measured in terms of wealth or utility. But by the same token, some few unidentifiable individuals may perceive themselves as worse off by virtue of the loss of their prior ability to engage in acts of aggression against others. At this point, however, the correct response is to ignore this perceived imbalance, on the ground that the overall gains swamp any distributional losses. In addition, it is hard to identify in the abstract which hardy individuals, if any, lose by the creation of a civil order; we thus have no prospect of finding out which individuals should receive compensation in cash and from whom they should receive it, even if such compensation could be tendered. Certainly there is no sensible reason why any state should wish to encourage people to maraud against their neighbors in the hopes of squeezing compensation out of others as the price for establishing the social order. We should also note that if there is any redistribution at the initial stage of social formation that disfavors would-be aggressors, it can be defended on any one of three grounds. First, it may be justified by advancing a morally defensible conception of individual autonomy and property. Second, we can say that the losses of

[28] Here is not the place to indicate why some defense of territory and liberty is indeed possible even under Hobbesian assumptions, but the core of that defense relies on the insight that in equipoise, a good defense beats a good offense. Hence, if two individuals or families are of equal strength, normally neither can take the other: they therefore divide territories. The actual advantage that is needed to secure dominance can easily be quite large, so that even a powerful adversary could relent in its pursuit of a weaker rival. This tendency is increased because sharply aggressive actions against one group will expose even the winner, after its resources have been depleted, to incursions by a third group that stood aside during the initial encounter. Hence, two adversaries may well develop a steely truce that with time can harden into a boundary. But lots of blood will be spilled along the way.

would-be aggressors are fully compensated for by that share of the overall social improvements that goes to the losers. Third, we could claim that these losses are not worth compensating because of the political dangers that are invited by trying to create a system of compensation for any dislocations created by some move out of the state of nature.[29]

The instrumental question is how to move from a world without centralized enforcement of rights to one with organized, and limited, state power. On this point, we can easily see how taxation is required, but even after this point is conceded, we must then deliberate about taxation's form. One common proposal is that the prohibition against redistribution through state action militates in favor of a head tax. The argument here is that each individual has to pay for his fractional share of the overall cost of the venture. It is like saying that a member of a joint association has to treat the assessments for common expenses as a lien against his property, which is commonly the case.

The head tax has provoked a fierce opposition politically. The most famous example in recent times comes from England, where in 1990 Margaret Thatcher's Tory government sought to replace a local real estate tax based on assessed valuation with a head tax on each adult in the region. The response was instant political annihilation and a quick but bloody retreat.[30] This episode shows that the head (or poll) tax has no political traction. But we must be careful about what inferences we draw from this event. The narrow conclusion—head taxes should not be used to support general revenue functions—is correct. But it is wrong to think that this conclusion embarrasses the general test announced above, namely, that individuals should benefit, to the extent practicable, from any use of state coercion against them.

Sometimes it is said that "[a] head tax is 'efficient' because it is unavoidable and does not change the behavior of any taxpayer."[31] Yet this proposition only applies if we assume that all taxpayers have sufficient wealth to cover both the head tax and their personal living expenses, which they may not. More generally, the principled objections to the head tax become apparent if we assume that all individuals can divide their resources between two stylized goods, one being their private possessions and wealth and the other being their share of services and amenities

[29] By way of contrast, winners gain relatively little from a system of progressive taxation, which reduces the stock of wealth as it seeks to improve its overall distribution. See Section VI of this essay.

[30] For a brief account, see Joel Slemrod and Jon Bakija, *Taxing Ourselves: A Citizen's Guide to the Great Debate over Tax Reform*, 2d ed. (Cambridge, MA: MIT Press, 2000), 49.

[31] Joseph Bankman and Thomas Griffith, "Social Welfare and the Rate Structure: A New Look at Progressive Taxation," *California Law Review* 75, no. 6 (1987): 1913. For a parallel, it could be assumed that taking out a home mortgage does not change the behavior of the holder of the equity interest. This may well be true when the value of the property is far above the lien, but it is demonstrably false when the property's value is equal to or less than the lien. In such cases, quick foreclosure is necessary to hold back rapid deterioration of the underlying asset.

in the public domain. The basic condition that each person wishes to establish is equivalence at the margin, such that the last dollar taken in public expenses gives a (diminishing) marginal utility equal to that of the (diminishing) marginal utility of one's private expenditures. The explanation for this position depends on the simple proposition that each person seeks to maximize personal welfare. If public and private expenditures are not in equilibrium at the margin, then an individual can reduce his expenditures by $X on private (or public) expenditures, and devote that sum of money to public (or private) expenditures. Although the total expenditures remain the same, the net increase in utility justifies the shift in spending.

The head tax does not begin to equate the utility of public and private expenditures. To see why, let us consider the position of A, who has earned $1,000 in one year in a society that contains (to keep the numbers simple) one thousand people. If social earnings here equal $10 million, then the average person has earned $10,000 per year. Assume further that public expenditures equal 10 percent of total wealth, or $1,000,000. A head tax would require A to contribute 1/1,000th of that total, or his entire earnings of $1,000, leaving nothing over for food, clothing, and shelter. It is quite clear that when A dies of starvation he is not made better off by participation in the social contract. The first dollars spent on food, clothing, and shelter have a far greater marginal value to him than the last dollars spent on public goods. The use of a head tax therefore leaves this person worse off than before.

So the head tax is always bad in light of the general criterion that justifies state coercion only insofar as it benefits all the parties so coerced. But once we scale down A's contribution to his pro rata share of the overall pie—$100—then we have to make up the missing $900 elsewhere. We could try some elaborate formula that spreads it across many people, but the simplicity of a pro rata rule seems evident in its relative immunity from political machinations. Alternatively, we could try blending a partial head tax with a flat tax, but again the heavily regressive nature of the head tax leaves much of the bad aftertaste, and does little to guarantee those at the bottom a pro rata share of the gain from government expenditures. In addition, some political institutions have to decide how to set the head tax, and must pick a number that is large enough to justify the imposition of a second system of taxation, but small enough to avoid ruination for those at the bottom. In principle, someone might try to avoid these difficulties by keeping a head tax for part of the revenue needs of government and supplementing it with a flat tax for the rest. But no one knows where these lines should be drawn (or why), which means that complex systems including both sorts of taxation are always difficult to organize within a political framework. In general, the added complexity does not seem to be worth the candle. Better to stick with the flat tax across the board.

Once simplicity wins out, then, we are back to the flat tax as a consistent, safe, second-best alternative to some ideal of taxation in which the rate of return that each citizen receives from his tax contributions is equalized. Here, the flat tax is not a default presumption that the parties can reverse using contrary contractual terms. The fixed nature of this exaction thus creates important differences between the flat tax and the ordinary business partnership. Citizens do not pick their fellow citizens. Nor can they opt out of any public arrangement when the benefits that they derive from government services are less than their proportionate share of the tax burden. Successful citizens are therefore more vulnerable to expropriation in political associations than they are in voluntary ones. In this context, the flat tax offers them a modest source of protection in a setting where the exit option is no longer available.

V. Redistribution under the Flat Tax

Thus far the discussion of the flat tax has proceeded on the assumption that it tends to eliminate redistribution of income between individuals. The factual predicate of this assumption is hard to evaluate, but on balance it seems likely that a flat tax system contains a limited redistributivist skew in favor of the poorer members of society, even if public revenues are spent solely on classic public goods.

Assume for the moment that individuals have two kinds of private wealth: nonpecuniary interests, such as those involved in bodily integrity, liberty, and personal relationships, and pecuniary interests, such as the rents, profits, and wages that Smith identifies as the proper objects of taxation. By definition, any system of income or wealth taxation does not touch these nonpecuniary interests, no matter how great their magnitude. Now if the value, subjectively conceived, of individuals' nonpecuniary goods were proportionate to the value of their pecuniary goods, then the shrinkage of the tax base would have few long-term consequences for the overall distribution of wealth across persons. The use of the narrower tax base would privilege nonpecuniary goods over pecuniary ones, so we would expect all persons to shift from productive labor to what economists call, somewhat misleadingly, leisure (which all too often is idleness), or more precisely, goods and services that are outside of the tax system. Although this shift is theoretically problematic, from an administrative point of view, the alternative of trying to use the broader base is simply worse given the enormous intrusions needed to track nonpecuniary benefits: do we give tax deductions for divorce or death, or impose surtaxes for marriages and childbirths? No one wishes to be mired in this swamp, so we retreat to the smaller tax base because we cannot (and do not want to) monitor the larger one.

The shift, however, has more profound consequences in those cases where the nonpecuniary forms of wealth do not move in lockstep proportion with measurable forms of wealth. There is good reason to believe that the relationship between these two components is skewed across individuals. It seems plausible to suppose that individuals have a higher variation in their levels of pecuniary wealth than in their levels of nonpecuniary assets: even the poorest person attaches a very high subjective value to staying alive. The total wealth schedules for people therefore do not vary by a factor of a million or more. Rather, they are compressed into a much smaller range. To take a simple example, suppose that two persons had pecuniary economic incomes of $10,000 and $100,000 respectively. This would indicate a one to ten split under the flat tax. But if the first person values nonpecuniary benefits at $50,000 and the second values them at $260,000, then the overall tax split is no longer tenfold, but is now reduced to sixfold ($60,000 to $360,000).

Therefore, on plausible assumptions, a flat tax on pecuniary income appears to work a systematic redistribution to the rich from the poor, and thus paves the way to the adoption of some form of regressive taxation. But this particular issue is not discussed in the writings of Locke, Smith, Bastiat, and Hayek, all of whom devote their attention to the pecuniary tax base (Smith's rents, profits, and wages), and embrace the flat tax within the context of that framework.

But even if we decide to take nonpecuniary benefits into account, it is far from clear that we should gravitate to any form of regressive taxation. There are two important arguments on this issue; the first involves the administration of the tax system. Setting tax levels is not only a matter of ideal theory; it also involves practical estimates made during the political process. Any deviation from the flat tax on pecuniary income requires the state to estimate specifically the ratio between pecuniary and nonpecuniary benefits for each individual separately, or to resort in part to the questionable head tax. Even for strong libertarians, the opposition to redistribution of wealth is only one source of anxiety; this fear has always been paired with the worry that new forms of government discretion will pave the way to greater political abuse. Consider here Adam Smith's insistence that the "[t]ax which each individual is bound to pay ought to be certain, and not arbitrary."[32] The dangers of arbitrary taxation are multiplied when any number of regressive (or progressive) tax schedules are on the table. Endorsing the flat tax represents a judgment, perhaps inarticulate, that having stable distributions of burdens, even if skewed in favor of the poor, is in a sense more important than maintaining a constant ratio of benefits to burdens across all taxpayers. We accept, in other

[32] Smith, *The Wealth of Nations*, 778. He then goes on to note: "Where it is otherwise [e.g., when taxes *are* arbitrary], every person subject to the tax is put more or less in the power of the tax-gatherer, who can either aggravate the tax upon any obnoxious contributor, or extort, by the terror of such aggravation, some present or perquisite to himself." Smith thus focuses on the discretion of the individual tax-collector, but a similar, albeit lesser, mischief arises when there is discretion with respect to overall rates.

words, the same kinds of imperfections in taxation that we accept in the allocation of the expenses involved in running a joint tenancy. Proration of costs can proceed without precise knowledge of benefits, and yields a stable focal point in a world where focal points are hard to come by and should not be casually abandoned.[33] It is therefore not necessarily a failure of the antiredistributivist nerve to endorse the flat tax even though it works some redistribution from rich to poor. It could also count merely as a sensible concession to the administrative complexities that hamper the implementation of any philosophical ideal.

The second argument anticipates the next part of this essay. Most people believe—even if they cannot prove—that wealth has diminishing marginal utility. They believe it with respect to their own incremental levels of wealth, and they believe it with respect to differences of wealth between people. (If there were no such belief, the case for progressive taxation would collapse.[34]) One advantage of the flat tax is that it allows a limited realization of this redistributive concern, one that is subject to a built-in constraint that is necessarily cast aside whenever a progressive system of taxation is allowed: the total amount of redistribution is neatly constrained by the flatness of the tax. If this is the case, then we have a way to have a bit of our cake and eat it, too. The flat tax advances administrative convenience, limits the scope of political discretion, and undoes the complex incentive structures of a progressive or regressive tax. Given this, so what if it builds in a limited amount of income redistribution?

VI. Progressivity and Redistribution

Thus far this discussion has proceeded by assuming that the function of the state is to solve the coordination problems in the provision of classical public goods, not to secure redistribution of wealth across individuals. The mission is to use government coercion to secure what look like general Pareto improvements. The great advantage of this approach is that it reduces faction, curbs discretion, and increases overall output by searching for win/win situations in the political environment. Yet as the previ-

[33] See Fried, "The Puzzling Case for Proportionate Taxation," 6–8.

[34] People in fact do accept some progressive taxation. See, for example, Blum and Kalven, "The Uneasy Case for Progressive Taxation," 420, where the authors accept a system of "degressive taxation" whereby the first tier of income is wholly exempt from taxation. Similar sentiments are found in Hayek, *A Constitution of Liberty*, 314. This sort of system is, of course, not a flat tax system, but a two-tier system. From here it is easy to insist that if there are two tiers, then twenty would be permissible as well. See Fried, "The Puzzling Case for Proportionate Taxation," 161. The right response, in my view, is to retract the move to a two-tier system. It is important, I think, that all persons be subject to first-dollar tax constraints of some sort, if only for the way they influence individuals' political participation. It is just ever so much more difficult to vote for spending measures if you will be required to help fund them.

ous paragraph indicates, it is hard to ignore the common claim that the diminishing marginal utility of wealth offers a reason for the state to redistribute wealth, through taxation, from its more fortunate citizens to its less fortunate ones.[35]

This redistributivist position is of course not without its detractors, and it is important to review the objections to it. The most obvious line of criticism is that redistribution of wealth, when consciously done, counts as little more than theft initiated by the state. No poor individual can claim as of right the wealth of a richer person. The common law theories of restitution and unjust enrichment merely allow state-mandated exchanges to be used to overcome various obstacles to voluntary transactions; they cannot be used to support any comprehensive program of redistribution. So why then allow the state to do for poor individuals what they are not allowed to do for themselves?

One possible answer is that the interposition of a public entity severs the one-to-one correspondence between those who give and those who receive, and thus neutralizes the private law analogy to theft. But why does this clever device alter the traditional conclusion that A's poverty does not in itself create a legal claim against B's resources? Certainly it is possible to recreate the matching that links up this A to that B. Any political pooling arrangement can be disentangled using clear accounting conventions. The intermediary thus does nothing to either strengthen or weaken the claims for redistribution. If the theft charge is sound, then anonymity and impersonality will not defeat it. More substantive considerations have to be raised.

One alternative response is to deny that the transfer payments made by the state are redistributivist in the first place. Here the argument takes a leaf from the work of John Rawls and holds that these payments should be looked at from behind the veil of ignorance as a form of social insurance. In private insurance systems, individuals with identical profiles ex ante almost always generate different payouts ex post. To the extent that these skewed payments are the outgrowth of (actuarially) fair contracts, however, the charge of redistribution is fully negated. Unfortunately, however, the concept of "social insurance" suffers the same fatal ambiguity that is found in the world of taxation. In principle, social insurance schemes could be designed to follow the same pattern as that exhibited by a system of proportionate taxation in a libertarian state: the state would exact payments from each individual in proportion to the risk that it covered, such that the pooling would make each person better off than he had been before. Alternatively, however, social insurance could operate as a set of disguised subsidies that require individuals with different risk pro-

[35] For one recent defense of steep progressivity, see Martin J. McMahon, Jr., and Alice G. Abreu, "Winner-Take-All Markets: Easing the Case for Progressive Taxation," *Florida Tax Review* 4, no. 1 (1998): 1-81.

files to make identical contributions or require individuals with the same risk profiles to make different contributions. At this point social insurance no longer embodies Pareto-efficient forced exchanges; instead, it works redistribution in disguise, both by intention and effect.[36] Indeed, the tax increases of the Clinton administration and the elder Bush administration were in response to political pressures and the perception that the rich were not paying their "fair share" of taxes, where the only operative definition of "fair" required the rich to pay a larger fraction of the total than they were paying.[37] The social insurance line is so powerful that it could justify, without more, any regime of taxation. We are thus back to square one.

The third line of argument abandons the false allure of social insurance. In its place the defenders of progressivity argue that the intervention of reasoned state power creates a high public purpose that makes it impossible to equate public redistribution as a large-scale form of theft. In their view, three features distinguish redistributive taxation from garden-variety theft: (1) theft consists of random individual acts of depredation, which gives rise to a sense of unfair singling out when one person is robbed while his neighbor is untouched, whereas redistributive taxation involves an orderly transfer through the tax system, a transfer justified by an important public purpose; (2) redistributive taxation achieves gains far larger than those achievable through theft; and (3) unlike a system of redistributive taxation, garden-variety theft generates massive uncertainty and forces citizens to take extensive steps to defend themselves. But even after these substantial differences are taken into account, one still needs to justify what is essentially a lesser state offense, for redistributive taxation itself creates substantial political uncertainty that in turn causes factional struggles; these problematic aspects of taxation emerge even if we do not have to face those arbitrary decisions of the individual tax-collector that so upset Adam Smith.[38] On balance I would adopt the basic proposition that we should not give the state powers on behalf of one group of citizens that those citizens have never had on their own vis-à-vis some other group. This strong line condemns the progressive

[36] See, for example, Alain Enthoven, *Theory and Practice of Managed Competition in Health Care Finance* (New York: Elsevier Science Publishing, 1988), 2–4, advocating the obligation to provide "decent minimums," which includes the "moral obligation to help the poor." For my criticism of the Enthoven position, see Richard A. Epstein, *Mortal Peril: Our Inalienable Right to Health Care?* (New York: Addison-Wesley, 1997), 27–37.

[37] For this account, see Jeffrey A. Schoenblum, "Tax Fairness or Unfairness? A Consideration of the Philosophical Bases for Unequal Taxation of Individuals," *American Journal of Tax Policy* 12, no. 2 (1995): 221–22. The difficulty with this sort of political argument is that it has no stopping point at all. Start with a flat tax, and then assume that "the ability to pay" of the rich is greater than it is for the poor. Now new tax increases will be progressive. Keep the same assumption and the next tax cut will concentrate on the poor. This cycle can go on indefinitely so that progressivity becomes ever more steep with each change in rate structure. The optimal-tax literature, whatever its weaknesses, does not make this mistake, for it offers an idealized tax structure that could be used to condemn current rates as either too progressive or too regressive.

[38] See the quotation from Smith in note 32 above.

income tax even if by some indisputable measure of social welfare it does increase the welfare of the poor more than it hurts the welfare of the rich. The purpose of the state is exhausted with its initiation of forced exchanges that lead to Pareto improvements. Shifts in wealth that help some and hurt others are so dangerous a mission and so fraught with risk that they ought to form no part of the state's general program.

This hard line dovetails nicely with the standard notion that interpersonal comparisons of utility are not possible. On this account, it is not possible to add utilities across persons any more than it is possible to add dollars to marks without knowing the exchange rate between them.[39] But this claim seems to be false, or at least overdrawn. As a general empirical observation, wholly apart from government intervention, we see that parents compare utilities for their children, and that many individuals make gifts on a person-to-person basis, or through charitable intermediaries. All of these transactions are predicated on the possibility of interpersonal comparisons made not by a neutral observer, but by a participant in the social scene. But it hardly follows that because these transactions have been made privately and voluntarily, they should be made collectively and coercively as well. Private individuals can choose their donees, and the overlap between their utilities of donors and donees in these cases will certainly reduce any wealth slippage that might otherwise occur. It is hard to postulate deadweight loss resulting from a voluntary gift transaction. Indeed, to the extent that donors identify closely with their recipients, and obtain a (derived) benefit from giving, the ability to make charitable transactions should create incentives for productive labor.

This view, however, leaves a large gulf between voluntary redistribution within close-knit groups and legislative redistribution on a grand scale. In the latter situation, the element of coercion raises questions concerning the abuse of discretion that are foreign to private, voluntary transactions, even when these transactions are partially subsidized by tax deductions for charitable contributions. And the lack of close connection between the parties who pay and those who receive may impose a high implicit tax on the wealth so transferred. Nonetheless, the modern public-finance literature does not falter over these points, but rather works on different models of social-welfare function. These models assume that interpersonal comparisons of utility can be made between strangers, that charitable activities do not matter much in the overall picture, that variations in administrative costs are small under all relevant systems of taxation, that the aggregation of wealth for investment purposes does not depend on the choice of taxation regimes, and that public-choice problems do not create serious impediments to sound government policy.

[39] For more on this idea, see Brian R. Binger and Elizabeth Hoffman, *Microeconomics with Calculus* (Glenview, IL: Scott, Foresman, 1988), 104.

At this point the models quickly assume technical complexity beyond my grasp. But their major feature is that they treat as their *sole* relevant consideration the trade-off between the diminishing marginal utility of wealth, on the one hand, and the reduced incentives to produce wealth, on the other. The sharper the decline in the marginal utility of wealth, the stronger the case for progressive taxation (assuming that levels of charitable donations do not rise in response to this common knowledge); but the more corrosive the incentive effects of higher taxation, the stronger the case for flat or regressive taxes. Quite simply, any effort to redistribute wealth will necessarily have some negative impact on the willingness of people to create it. But this simple relationship does not begin to capture the complexity of tax planning in the real world. Once high marginal rates are imposed on earned income, upper-income taxpayers have more options open to them than simply cutting back on their work. They can seek to take advantage of obscure provisions of the Internal Revenue Code that allow them to defer the recognition of gain, or that allow them to have the income taxed to another person. They can devise corporate transactions that allow them to have some of their earned income taxed at lower capital gains rates. These activities carry hidden costs because transactions that are reshaped for tax reasons are likely to be less efficient economically than the simpler business structures that they displace. Such tax planning is not the sole source of evasive activity. Tax lobbying never comes cheap, and the quest for loopholes becomes ever more urgent as the marginal rates of taxation increase.

These activities on the private side induce responses from those determined to make good on the promise of progressive taxation. The law therefore has to develop doctrines that prevent income-splitting over time and within families, and that bear the public costs of deciding, and then redeciding, just how progressive the system is in the first place. Ordinary people have little reason to concern themselves with the fine points of these doctrines, but the richest taxpayers will invest as much to save a dollar of taxes as they would to make a dollar in income.

The costs of progressive taxation have real bite, for while political rhetoric routinely claims that the "rich" (the top 1 percent) never pay their fair share, the standard models rightly eschew this type of argument and treat it as a given that the level of progressivity can be too high as well as too low. From a public-choice perspective, the likely error is that taxes will be too high, if only because in the short run the median voter will perceive himself as benefiting from a progressive system, and in addition often believes, falsely, that every rich person can shield income behind a wide array of tax shelters.[40] Some measure of the social losses taxation imposes is found in the relevant elasticities of higher taxation. These

[40] See Slemrod and Bakija, *Taxing Ourselves*, 61 ff., where it is noted that the ordinary American thinks that the tax rate of a family that earns $50,000 is 14 percent and that the rate of a family earning $200,000 is only 7.5 percent. As Slemrod and Bakija point out, the actual rates paid by these families are, respectively, around 12 and 21 percent.

elasticities are commonly estimated as being close to 0.4, which means that each 1 percent increase in marginal taxes reduces output by 0.4 percent. But this result is subject to the further caveat that the elasticity of income is higher (0.57) for persons whose income is over $100,000, so a better estimation is that each 1 percent increase in marginal taxes reduces output by 0.57 percent.[41] In addition, the elasticities get even higher for two-income families—roughly around 1.0—because the second spouse (usually the wife) faces both high marginal income tax rates and Social Security taxes on her first dollar of earned income.[42]

In light of this welter of offsetting considerations, it seems fair to assume that since progressive taxation is directed toward individuals and families whose taxable income is well over $100,000, the output losses in question could be quite great. In this regard, economist Arthur Okun's metaphor of the leaky bucket captures the situation quite well.[43] (In the metaphor, the bucket starts out with a gallon of water taken from the reservoir of the rich, but may transfer only one or two quarts to the storage containers of the poor.) The loss in output caused by transfers could come from many sources: some individuals may just cut back on work (and as the percentage of freelance workers continues to rise, this possibility could become more important); other individuals might decide to retire early; still others will use inefficient tax-driven transactions to defer the recognition of gain or convert ordinary income into capital gains; and in still other cases, old-fashioned evasion and deferment could displace the more subtle forms of avoidance. The combined effects are not easy to measure, but by any account they are too large to ignore.

Of course, this wealth loss has global consequences that lie outside the model. After all, if the United States has a weaker aggregate economic position, this could have unfortunate consequences in dealing with foreign affairs, since it could lead to reductions in defense spending in settings where God favors big battalions. But the difficulties with respect to wealth loss are typically examined in a narrower focus, solely as they relate to the trade-off between work and utility. The upshot of these models goes as follows. The ideal tax system is sometimes said to consist of two features.[44] The first is a built-in "demogrant," whereby each citizen receives some fixed sum of money if he earns zero revenue during the

[41] Jon Gruber and Emmanuel Saez, "The Elasticity of Taxable Income: The Evidence and Implications" (NBER working paper), available on-line at http://papers.nber.org/papers7512. A lower estimate of the relevant elasticity, placing it at 0.1 to 0.3, is quoted in Bankman and Griffiths, "Social Welfare and the Rate Structure," 1923.

[42] For the 1.0 figure, see Bankman and Griffith, "Social Welfare and the Rate Structure," 1926.

[43] Arthur Okun, *Equity and Efficiency: The Big Trade-Off* (Washington, DC: Brookings, 1975).

[44] For a detailed defense of this ideal tax system, see Bankman and Griffith, "Social Welfare and the Rate Structure," 1945 ff. The standard model of this form derives from James A. Mirrlees, "An Exploration in the Theory of Optimum Income Taxation," *Review of Economic Studies* 38, no. 2 (1971): 175–208.

year. The size of this grant is reduced at relatively high marginal rates as the first dollars of income are earned, such that a grant of $10,000 may be reduced by $1 for every $2 earned, an effective marginal tax rate of 50 percent. Once one has made enough income at the higher tax rate to pay back the grant, the rates one pays on further income are reduced to some lower amount—say 30 percent. The large size of the demogrant keeps the overall rate structure progressive, but creates low marginal rates for highly productive taxpayers.

The second, and most striking, feature of the system is its starting point, which allows individuals to receive something for nothing: those who are capable of working but choose not to nevertheless receive an income large enough to meet the minimum necessities of life. It seems quite clear that this position in and of itself dooms the program for both political and moral reasons. The popular impulse favoring the redistribution of income through government arose from traditional norms of benevolence. These norms do not state, nor does anyone really think, that any able-bodied person should receive unconditional subsidies. The Biblical injunction "By the sweat of your brow you shall eat your bread" finds continued resonance in the modern sentiment that rails against giving a 22-year-old $10,000 per year for living at home with his parents and hanging out with his friends. Such a program will not survive, even if only a small fraction of the recipients engage in what most ordinary people regard as abusive activity. The long tradition of philanthropy has never denied the imperfect obligations of benevolence, that is, those that stem from an awareness of our common humanity, but which are enforced only by conscience or informal social sanctions. But that said, the traditional conception of benevolence diverges powerfully from the model of separable and additive social utilities. It sees moral obligations of common humanity such that, in the words of Pufendorf, "[I]t is not right to destroy food when we have had enough, or to sop up or conceal a spring of water when we have drunk our fill, or to destroy navigation guides or road signs after we have made use of them."[45] These duties all involve situations in which someone has to expend effort to deny a common good to others. This "do no affirmative harm" moral duty is widely regarded as unproblematic. Morality, as it were, is ratcheted up to a higher level when it requires a genuine sacrifice by one individual for the benefit of another. In these cases, the dynamics are harder, but we are told:

> The amount of these benefits and their distribution depend on the condition of the giver and of the recipient. The caution to be observed here is that our generosity should not actually do harm to

[45] See Samuel Pufendorf, *On the Duty of Man and Citizen According to Natural Law* [1673], ed. James Tully, trans. Michael Silverthorne (Cambridge: Cambridge University Press, 1991), 64.

> those whom we think we are helping and to others; that our kindness should not exceed our capacity; that we should take into account each man's dignity and should give above all to those who are deserving; and that we should give where our help is needed and with due regard for the degree of personal relationship.[46]

This position does not have a lot of traction to decide particular cases, but such an open-textured understanding is not a vice in a system where the duties of benevolence are enforced by conscience and not by law. What is clear, however, is that the idea of the "deserving poor" carries with it the caveat that no gift of assistance should be made in unconditional fashion.[47] Some investigation should be made of the condition of the recipient, and some restrictions should be imposed on the way in which the gift, whether in cash or kind, is used. Such restrictions do in fact exist in many legal systems; in some cases they limit the kinds of goods and services that can be bought with the gift (e.g., food stamps or vouchers for education), and in other cases individuals are required to work, or seek work, as a condition of the grant. The whole idea is one of moral instruction, which requires grants for limited purposes. The simple utility trade-offs between equity and efficiency do not capture much of the huge program of state-run redistribution undertaken to give "society" leverage to impose its set of values on its recipients. The model of atomistic individuals with separable but additive utility functions is no part of this overall picture.

That said, however, it may well be that something can be salvaged from the combination of the social-welfare tradition and the traditional conception of benevolence. It is not possible to make any intelligent assessment of the redistributivist tendencies of the tax system without some knowledge of how the revenues obtained are spent. Suppose, for example, we were to introduce a system of vouchers that gave specific grants for education to all youngsters in the general population and their families. Combine this system with a general flat tax and the program starts to have some resemblance to the recommendations of the public-finance specialists who think that a system of demogrants and flat taxes is the ideal tax regime. All this only shows the difficulty of making any generalizations about demogrants in the first place. If a fraction of low-income persons receives various categorical programs, then this could count as a reason for the social welfarist to gravitate toward the flat tax as a second-best solution, even though it becomes impossible to have a uniform system of transfers that treats all persons

[46] Ibid.

[47] This is one of the main themes in, for example, Marvin Olasky, *Compassionate Conservatism: What It Is, What It Does, and How It Can Transform America* (New York: Free Press, 2000). At ibid., 19, Olasky notes the importance of "challenging" people to stretch and transform their character.

who receive the same income in exactly the same fashion. For those of us who believe in the strong Paretian norm, the difficulty of integrating taxation with spending programs counts as a strong argument for the elimination of public transfers in the first place. But even if this objection is entirely waived, a system of conditional grants does not fit easily with the social-welfarist conception that models the level of progressivity on separable and additive utilities.

The difficulties with the proposed ideal tax structure do not stop even if the demogrant survives these criticisms. One unhappy feature of the supposed ideal tax structure is that it imposes a very high marginal tax rate on those individuals with the least income. The effect of this is to deter individuals from entering the workforce—and if they do not make it to this first rung of the ladder, they might not be able to make subsequent advances in the workplace. At the other end, the relatively high levels of elasticity among those with high incomes makes a stiff progressive tax something of a dubious proposition. In principle, however, the loss of output such a regime would cause could be offset if we posited that there is a steep decline in the marginal benefits of additional wealth.

For example, a model championed by Joseph Bankman and Thomas Griffith, two professors of taxation, postulates that "the marginal utility of an additional unit of either income or leisure is inversely proportional to the amount already owned," such that a tenfold difference in wealth between a rich person and a poor one means that a marginal dollar gives a rich recipient one-tenth the utility it would give to a poor one.[48] The necessary implication of this position is that utility levels in a no-tax world are quite compact, for all individuals are assumed to derive equal utility from their equal amounts of leisure time. In the specific hypothetical world Bankman and Griffith describe, as wages double from $10 to $20, utility increases from 7.272 to 7.966; as they double again from $20 to $40, utility increases to 8.659. A group of three individuals containing one member at each of these income levels would have a summed utility of 23.897.[49] The ideal tax transformation of this data is said to result from a tax rate of 31 percent with a demogrant of $70.88. This system yields a utility schedule of 7.614, 7.982, and 8.491, for an overall improvement in utility to 24.087—an increase of less than 1 percent.[50]

The utility compression from top to bottom in this system moves from around 16 percent to about 10 percent, but the shift in hours worked is far more dramatic, as total work output drops by about 25 percent, with the least-paid worker producing around 43 percent less than before and the richest worker increasing his output by only 7 percent. These numbers

[48] Bankman and Griffith, "Social Welfare and the Rate Structure," 1951–52.
[49] Ibid., table 1, p. 1953.
[50] Ibid., table 2, p. 1954.

assume that the quality of work and leisure is the same for each level of workers, but we should note that commonsense assumptions go the opposite way on both points. First, it seems likely that individuals with high-income, creative jobs receive consumption value from work that is not shared in equal proportion by lower-income workers. It is not quite clear how this cuts on the question of overall elasticity. It could keep high-income workers in high-pressure jobs, or it could lead the $1 million lawyer to become the $100,000 law professor. Second, Bankman and Griffith's model assumes, falsely, that the value of leisure time is the same regardless of the amount of wealth for expenditures in those time periods. It is a good guess that in the Bankman-Griffith scenario, the utility of leisure will fall with the radical increase in leisure time, not to mention the potential loss in the formation of human capital, which will have adverse effects on the long-term vitality of the labor market. These caveats suggest that Bankman and Griffith's model overstates their ideal tax plan's meager utility gains. In the end, I am happy to treat their mathematical illustrations as the poster-children against progressivity, since whether predicted or delivered, the incremental amounts of additional utility generated by their plan seem trivial compared to the huge risks (even in utility terms) that it promises.

The criticisms cut deeper. Even if we ignore the collateral complications, the key assumption of the Bankman-Griffith model—that the utility of a marginal dollar varies inversely to wealth—seems wrong in its own terms. The source of this intuition is as follows. The decline in the marginal utility of an additional steak after you have already eaten one may be very high. But wealth is convertible into any number of different goods, so in each case the decline in utility has to be measured by referring to the utility of the most desired good as yet unpurchased. This simple fact suggests that the utility of wealth will decline far more slowly than the utility for specific goods. This interpretation is bolstered by the endless hours that well-to-do people put into their start-ups, family businesses, law firms, and investment banks; these hours of work cumulatively suggest that entrepreneurs ascribe a high marginal utility to wealth, just like ordinary members of the population. Therefore, the decline in output caused by a progressive tax is somewhat reduced, but the loss in utility associated with such a tax is somewhat higher than the standard models presuppose.

The matter becomes still more complicated when the utility attached to wealth is thought in some sense to depend on the relative standing of one individual to the others. One line of thought is that the quest for status encourages a form of wasteful competition and that superhigh forms of progressivity should be used to counteract the tendency of people to become business magnates or entertainment superstars. The argument here is that ostentatious displays of consumption and use represent the economic equivalent of an arms race, which could be conveniently suppressed by a system of severe progressive taxation.[51] This argument is then reinforced by the indisputable observation that the recent prosperity in the United States has further skewed both income and wealth in favor of the rich.[52]

The relationship of this observation to the theory of taxation is obscure, however. First, even proportionate taxation increases the share of the common burden that is placed on the well-to-do, which means that the less fortunate have more funds released for private expenditures without there being any compromise in the quality of the public goods provided. Second, there is no reason why the positive utilities from improvements in relative status should be disregarded, even if they require large sums of money to achieve. The neoclassical theory can be adopted to say that status goods imply an increasing marginal utility of wealth.[53] This conclusion could be attacked on the ground that certain forms of utility should not count as legitimate preferences, but at this point the ostensible purity of the economic model is necessarily negated, so the case for high progressive taxation rests ultimately on the discomfort that some have with the wealth of others. But once again these external effects are far from uniform. Even if we put aside the external economic benefits that are created by captains of industry, dot-com wonders, athletes, and entertainers, we (or some of us) might be quite happy to encourage their activities because of those activities' positive externalities: the richness and vibrancy that they contribute to popular culture. Why penalize Michael Jordan or Tiger Woods, who generate so much more excitement than the runners-up in basketball or golf? It is all too easy to let deeply held puritanical instincts dominate discussions of both taxation and popular morality, but the irony here is that people of great wealth can only consume a tiny fraction of their worth, no matter how great their appetites. The value of conspicuous items, such as fancy houses, is little more than a rounding error in their fortunes.[54] To dwell on consumption is to ignore the true badge of the ultrarich, which is how much they are worth, not how much they consume.

[51] For the origins of this line of thought, see Robert H. Frank and Philip J. Cook, *The Winner-Take-All Society* (New York: Free Press, 1995); and Robert H. Frank, *Luxury Fever: Why Money Fails to Satisfy in an Era of Excess* (New York: Free Press, 1999). For the direct connection to progressive taxation, see McMahon and Abreu, "Winner-Take-All Markets."

[52] Slemrod and Bakija, *Taxing Ourselves*, 57–61.

[53] See, for example, Gary S. Becker, Kevin M. Murphy, and Ivan Werning, "Status, Lotteries, and Inequality" (working paper of the George J. Stigler Center for the Study of the Economy and the State), available on-line at http://gsbwww.uchicago.edu/research/cses/documents/GSCworkingPapersPDFs.htm.

[54] See Ahmad Diba and Noshua Watson, "America's Forty Richest under 40," *Fortune*, September 18, 2000, 114: "To our surprise, we found that the value of residences was immaterial [to the rankings]. The home may be the biggest asset for most of us mere mortals, but to an Internet company founder, even a $10 million mansion is just a random tick in the company's stock."

Worse still, perhaps, this fixation on consumption or wealth leads us to ignore the positive spillover effects that only high status and genuine distinction can confer. The situation here is what I have called the preference for soft selective externalities.[55] The resentments and envy that some poor individuals may have toward some rich individuals are duly taken into account, but the positive experience that ordinary people derive from watching the exploits of the rich and famous is systematically ignored. A dynamic society, however, needs its stars as well as its foot soldiers, and a regime of progressive taxation cannot be justified as a means to thin the ranks of the former.

VII. Conclusion

I think that I have said enough to show the genuine uncertainties that plague the overall case for progressive taxation. But in closing, it is important to stress that this debate has continued for as long as it has precisely because no one has been able to conjure up a single knockdown argument either for or against that tax regime. But the case against the progressive tax *can* be put in this form: Make the tax steep, and the incentive effects are likely to dominate the purported gains of redistribution. Make the progressivity shallow, and the administrative costs will undermine whatever gains the system promises. Rather than incur the political costs of establishing and reestablishing the optimal tax structure, stick with a program that comes off as a robust second-best. Use the flat tax because it advances the cause of tax simplification, avoids the pitfalls of regressive taxes, and offers a useful partial constraint on government behavior that forces the state to articulate the reasons for its redistributivist programs. The flat tax might perhaps be found inferior to the optimal system of progressive taxation, if we could determine what that optimal system is, but since no one can, the flat tax offers a robust second-best choice for public finance, which counts as first-best in an imperfect world.

Law, The University of Chicago

[55] See Richard A. Epstein, "Externalities Everywhere? Morals and the Police Power," *Harvard Journal of Law and Public Policy* 21, no. 1 (1997): 61–69.

WHY JUSTICE REQUIRES TRANSFERS TO OFFSET INCOME AND WEALTH INEQUALITIES

By Richard J. Arneson

I. Introduction

If an array of goods is for sale on a market, one's wealth, the tradable resources one owns, determines what one can purchase from this array. One's income is the increment in wealth one acquires over a given period of time. In any society, we observe some people having more wealth and income, and some having less. At any given time, some societies have a greater average wealth than others. Across time, we can observe societies becoming richer or poorer and showing more or less equal distributions of wealth among their members. Does it matter from an ethical standpoint whether some people have more income and wealth than others? Does securing a more equal distribution of income and wealth either constitute the achievement of something that is intrinsically morally desirable or serve as a reliable means to the achievement of some intrinsic moral value? If we suppose that justice demands, in many circumstances, the equalization of the income or wealth of persons, what principles of justice generate this demand?

Some philosophers and social critics have made confident pronouncements in response to these questions. Writing about the distribution of money and commodities in contemporary democracies, political theorist Michael Walzer observes that insufficient income excludes a citizen from full membership in society.[1] Since the norm of democratic equality requires that all citizens should enjoy the same full membership, Walzer argues, by one means or another all citizens must be assured a sufficient level of money. Moreover, there are some things that money should not be able to buy: in any society, the social meanings of particular goods rule out their exchange by sale. Neither votes nor the obligation to perform military service should be tradable, and there are numerous other examples of controversial sorts of exchanges that are either prohibited or strictly regulated. If the assurance of sufficient income and wealth guarantees full membership to all citizens, and if the only goods for sale are those goods that should be for sale according to our shared values, then, according to Walzer, "there is no such thing as a maldistribution of consumer goods. It

[1] Michael Walzer, *Spheres of Justice: A Defense of Pluralism and Equality* (New York: Basic Books, 1983).

just does not matter, from the standpoint of complex equality, that you have a yacht and I do not, or that the sound system of her hi-fi is greatly superior to his, or that we buy our rugs from Sears Roebuck and they get theirs from the Orient. People will focus on such matters, or not: that is a question of culture, not of distributive justice."[2] This attractive-sounding position comprises three claims: (1) regarding the distribution of income and wealth, what matters morally is that everyone should have enough, (2) a person has enough when poverty does not block her from being a full member of democratic society, and (3) provided everyone has enough, that some people have more income and wealth than others violates no fundamental principle of justice or morality.[3]

According to this doctrine, the fact that some are better off financially than others is a social-justice concern only if such inequality has the effect of increasing or decreasing the number of people below the line of sufficiency (that is, the number who do not have enough). Inequality in and of itself is not undesirable from the standpoint of justice. For that matter, that people are exactly as well off financially as others is deemed desirable or not from the standpoint of justice depending on the effects of this equality on the numbers of people who reach the sufficiency line. Walzer's position is a version of "sufficientarianism," the principle that the distribution of resources in society is just if and only if everyone has enough. As stated so far, the sufficientarian principle does not resolve the question of whether or not distributions of income and wealth are in and of themselves morally significant. This issue turns on how sufficiency is understood. The good-enough level might be defined in noncomparative terms, in which case whether any given individual has more or less than others is not intrinsically morally significant. For example, it might be held that the good-enough level is the level that enables a person to attain a stipulated amount of pleasure or degree of life-plan fulfillment over the course of her life. Alternatively, the good-enough level might be defined in comparative terms. For example, it might be stipulated that everyone has enough income and wealth when nobody has less than some fraction of the average level. This essay focuses on noncomparative versions of the sufficiency doctrine. My reason for doing so is that these versions are more interesting and plausible than their comparative counterparts.

[2] Ibid., 107–8. Walzer here mentions his notion of "complex equality," which he contrasts with "simple equality." Simple equality obtains in a society if everybody has the same amounts of goods or is treated identically. Complex equality obtains in a society if each person is treated within each separate distributive sphere according to norms that reflect the shared values for that sphere held by the society's members. Walzer endorses complex equality and repudiates simple equality.

[3] I do not here trace these claims back to Walzer's master principle of justice, that the practices of a society are just when they conform to the shared values of their participants. I am interested in a truncated, bowdlerized version of Walzer's views that strikes me as more interesting and compelling than the master principle.

Sufficientarianism attracts distinguished advocates. Philosopher Harry Frankfurt has argued forcefully for components of this doctrine.[4] Philosopher Elizabeth Anderson defends a democratic-equality conception of justice that develops Walzer's version of sufficientarian doctrine.[5] Philosopher Martha Nussbaum identifies the level of sufficiency as being a good-enough level of positive freedom. On her account, the person who has enough possesses the capability to function at an acceptable level in all of the ways that are individually necessary and together sufficient for a decent quality of human life.[6]

In a rough-and-ready way, the sufficientarian approach conforms to the antipoverty focus of the welfare policies adopted by modern governments. On their face, the aim of these policies tends to be to define a minimal acceptable standard of living and to prevent people from falling below this standard; they do not aim to make the worst off as well off as possible or anything of the sort.[7] In recent years these welfare-state policies have attracted criticism, and some governments have reduced their commitment to them. But the criticism for the most part challenges the efficacy of these policies, not their normative rationale.[8] To the extent that welfare-state policies (and their replacements directed toward the same goals) implement most voters' values regarding the amelioration of poverty, we might suspect that the commonsense moral views of most people are congruent with sufficientarianism.

[4] Harry G. Frankfurt, "Equality as a Moral Ideal," in Frankfurt, *The Importance of What We Care About: Philosophical Essays* (Cambridge: Cambridge University Press, 1988), 134–58. I should note that while Frankfurt argues against economic egalitarianism and urges that what matters is not that people have the same income and wealth, but that in these respects they have enough, he does not address the issue of what justice requires, all things considered. In a footnote he states, "The fact that some people have more than enough money suggests a way in which it might be arranged for those who have less than enough to get more, but it is not in itself a good reason for redistribution." Ibid., 147–50 n. 19. Whether there are any good reasons for redistribution, and if so, what they might be, are topics into which Frankfurt does not delve, beyond the statement just quoted.

[5] Elizabeth Anderson, "What Is the Point of Equality?" *Ethics* 109, no. 2 (1999): 287–337. For discussion, see Richard Arneson, "Luck Egalitarianism and Prioritarianism," *Ethics* 110, no. 2 (2000): 339–49.

[6] Martha Nussbaum, "Aristotelian Social Democracy," in R. Bruce Douglas, Gerald M. Mara, and Henry S. Richardson, eds., *Liberalism and the Good* (New York: Routledge, 1990), 203–52; Martha Nussbaum, "Human Functioning and Social Justice: In Defense of Aristotelian Essentialism," *Political Theory* 20, no. 2 (1992): 202–46; Martha Nussbaum, "Women and Cultural Universals," in Nussbaum, *Sex and Social Justice* (Oxford: Oxford University Press, 1999), 29–54. For discussion, see Richard Arneson, "Perfectionism and Politics," *Ethics* 111, no. 1 (2000): 37–63; and Martha C. Nussbaum, "Aristotle, Politics, and Human Capabilities: A Response to Antony, Arneson, Charlesworth, and Mulgan," *Ethics* 111, no. 1 (2000): 102–40.

[7] For the idea that social justice requires a set of institutions that brings it about that the worst-off members of society are made as well off as possible, see John Rawls, *A Theory of Justice*, rev. ed. (Cambridge, MA: Harvard University Press, 1999).

[8] See Charles Murray, *Losing Ground: American Social Policy, 1950–1980* (New York: Basic Books, 1984).

In this essay I shall argue against the Walzerian version of sufficientarianism and also against the more general doctrine. Neither provides a morally sound way of determining when justice requires forced transfers from more wealthy to less wealthy persons. I will suggest a more promising approach to the justice of transfers.

A preliminary point: this essay assesses sufficientarianism as a candidate fundamental moral principle—as a statement of what ultimately matters morally. But the sufficientarian doctrine that everyone should have enough might be proposed at a lower level of abstraction and intended to serve as a rough-and-ready public-policy guide. The idea of this practical sufficiency norm would be that whatever exactly a just society is, it does not allow people to languish in readily avoidable abject misery and poverty; the norm thus implies that we should strive to get everyone to a threshold of decent existence. If various plausible fundamental moral outlooks converge in endorsing practical sufficiency in many settings, perhaps we can be confident that this norm is sensible even if we are uncertain about what fundamental moral principles should be embraced. Moreover, the advocate of the practical sufficiency norm might cheerfully allow that what counts as "enough" will vary from context to context and may not be determinable without some arbitrary specification. The reader who inclines toward interpreting the sufficiency doctrine as a practical guideline will regard my critique that follows as misplaced overkill: I am attacking a signpost as though it were a theory.

Yet the sufficiency doctrine provides an answer to the question of when (if ever) governmental transfers of income and wealth are permitted or required by justice only if sufficiency is construed as a fundamental moral principle. Moreover, as indicated above, political philosophers have proposed sufficientarianism as appropriate at this fundamental level. In this construal, the doctrine is interesting and plausible and apparently has a lot going for it. My critique of sufficientarianism, pitched at this fundamental level, is not an attack on a view that no one defends or that is on its face indefensible. Furthermore, some of the difficulties I locate in the sufficiency doctrine seem to me to be present also in the usage of it as a rough-and-ready guide, though I shall not develop this point in what follows.

II. The End of the Story

The discussion of sufficientarianism in this essay follows a serpentine path. It may be worthwhile to indicate where it ends. This is easy to do, because my view of why justice requires transfers is simple. People's lives can go better or worse on the whole. Just transfers of distributable resources improve the lives of recipients or others indirectly affected.[9]

We should distinguish between short-term and long-term effects of transfers. In the short run, transferring resources away from a person usually makes the person's life go worse, if she would have used the transferred resources to her benefit. The recipient of a transfer is usually better off, depending on what she does with the resources and what she would have done without them. Transfers, especially if repeated over time as predictable policy, will have effects on people's motives and behavior that might lead to desirable or undesirable outcomes in the near or long term. If income is progressively taxed and redistributed to others, those who are subject to the tax may opt for more leisure and less productive employment, or they may seek to engage in income-producing activities beyond the reach of the tax collector. In the nineteenth century, the social critic John Stuart Mill observed that in calculating the overall benefit that accrues to the recipient of transfers, we should distinguish between "the consequences of the assistance itself, and the consequences of relying on the assistance." [10] The latter he deemed bad, often so bad as to bring about a net loss. He supposed that reliance on assistance is undesirable because it inhibits the useful motive of self-help. One might imagine the motivational effect as different: a person who is ground down by circumstances but is then given the assurance of aid may well gain pluck as well as greater energy to make further gains. At any rate, I hold that to qualify as just, a transfer must have desirable consequences on the whole over the long run. (Right-wingers and left-wingers tend to disagree about what the long-term consequences of proposed transfers would be.)

Three factors determine the value of consequences for distributive-justice purposes. First, it is better if a person's life goes better rather than worse. A life that goes better has higher well-being, a magnitude fixed by the objective value of the goods that an individual attains, not her subjective attitudes or opinions regarding them. Second, the lower that a person's well-being over the course of her life would be absent a benefit we could secure for her, the greater the moral value of getting her a given gain in well-being. Third, the more one is reasonably held responsible for one's present plight by virtue of the contribution of one's voluntary choices and conduct in producing it, the lower the moral value of securing a given gain in well-being (if one is being proposed as a recipient of a transfer) or the greater the moral disvalue of bringing about a loss in one's current well-being prospects (if one is being proposed as a source of

[9] For simplicity, I ignore the case of transferring resources to one in the expectation that the resources will be redistributed, as when we get resources into Mother Theresa's hands with the aim of aiding the poor of Calcutta.

[10] John Stuart Mill, *Principles of Political Economy*, in J. M. Robson, ed., *Collected Works of John Stuart Mill* (Toronto: University of Toronto Press, 1965), 3:960.

resources to be transferred to others). I claim that just institutions, social practices, and actions are those that maximize the moral value of consequences as measured by a scale that integrates the three factors of well-being gain, prior lifetime well-being expectation, and responsibility. This view, which accords priority to gaining benefits for the worse off, particularly those not responsible for being worse off, is called the "priority view."

To embrace this simple view of just transfers, one must embrace the idea that the fact that one could act in a way that would create a benefit (or avoid a loss) for another person is a reason to perform that act. The worse off the person is in terms of lifetime well-being, the stronger the reason to help now. Also, the strength of the reason to help can be amplified or dampened by the degree to which the person's present plight, if bad, came about as a result of fate dealing her a bad hand rather than as a result of her negligent playing of the cards that fate has dealt her.

The simple view just sketched excludes many factors that might be thought to shape the moral principles that determine the circumstances under which transfers are just. At the level of principle (though perhaps not at the level of practical policy), priority rules out the possibility that morality permits or requires giving special weight to the goal of ameliorating the life conditions of disadvantaged people who are fellow members of one's nation-state or political community. My moral claim that someone owes me a just transfer is not strengthened just because the person happens to be a fellow citizen or community member rather than a distant stranger. Philosopher Ronald Dworkin writes, "No government is legitimate that does not show equal concern for the fate of all those citizens over whom it claims dominion and from whom it claims allegiance." [11] On this view a legitimate government need not extend equal concern past national borders. The simple view I espouse rejects this moral judgment.

The sufficiency doctrine, the proposal that distributive justice requires that everyone have enough, can be interpreted either as a cosmopolitan or as a community-centered doctrine. That is to say, the doctrine might assert (1) that distributive justice requires that each community bring it about that all its members have enough, or (2) that distributive justice requires that everyone everywhere have enough. On the latter construal, sufficientarianism might seem far too expansive in its view of what we owe each other. But even on the expansive construal, at least obligation gives out once everyone reaches the sufficiency threshold. In contrast, the

[11] Ronald Dworkin, *Sovereign Virtue: The Theory and Practice of Equality* (Cambridge, MA: Harvard University Press, 2000), 1. For an interesting argument that supports Dworkin's position that the requirements of distributive justice to help those afflicted by unchosen disadvantage are stronger among fellow citizens than among strangers, see Richard W. Miller, "Cosmopolitan Respect and Patriotic Concern," *Philosophy and Public Affairs* 27, no. 3 (1998): 202–24.

priority view appears much too demanding and open-ended in the obligations it imposes on us to improve people's lives around the globe. Compared to the priority view, the sufficiency doctrine appears to be more moderate, so it invites a careful examination.

III. Consumption above the Line of Sufficiency

For now, let us just assume that we can specify the level of a good-enough or decent quality of life in a satisfactory way. (Later I shall challenge this assumption.) The question then arises, why is what happens to people above the line morally unimportant, at least so far as distributive justice is concerned?

Walzer's examples of consumption above the line of a good-enough existence are rhetorically persuasive. The examples he mentions are cases in which it is far from clear that the person with more money uses it to effect a significant improvement in his life. Such cases are common; all of us use money in this way sometimes. We use available resources to satisfy the strongest desires of ours that these resources allow us to satisfy. Often these urgent desires are tenuously, if at all, linked to anything we would be prepared to call our good. With a little cash, we get doughnuts; with more cash, more and fancier doughnuts.

But it is not a necessary and inevitable feature of the satisfaction of desires above what Walzer identifies as the sufficient level that it fails to advance our good. If he had written that it does not matter from the standpoint of distributive justice, once everyone has a decent existence, that extra cash enables one person but not another to live for an extra twenty healthy, active years, to complete a life's ambition by writing a fine novel, to attain a thorough understanding of contemporary physics, or to get through a bad patch in a relationship with a partner one deeply loves without ruining the partnership, we would balk. These things and myriad others that are above what anyone would mark as the minimal level of a decent existence do matter. Such goods matter to those who attain them as well as to those who strive and fail to get them, and distributive justice should be responsive to these nontrivia.

So despite Walzer's rhetoric, we should note that what happens above the line of sufficiency might be morally significant.[12] To my mind, the features of people's circumstances that are germane to distributive justice are those that have an impact on their well-being. The ultimate concern of

[12] Readers might be puzzled at this point, because the text proceeds on the assumption that if something matters morally, it matters from the standpoint of distributive justice. But can't a consideration matter morally from some standpoint distinct from that of justice, such as a standpoint of human compassion or human decency? In my perhaps idiosyncratic usage, "justice" considerations encompass all of the serious moral obligations that people owe to each other. Distributive justice encompasses all significant moral requirements having to do with the distribution of goods and evils, except for further requirements that are triggered by wrongdoing.

distributive justice, and hence the measure of someone's condition for purposes of applying distributive-justice norms, should be the objective welfare, well-being, or utility that the person attains (or perhaps, is enabled to attain) over the course of her life. Actions, practices, and institutions are to be assessed by the objective quality of life they deliver (or make possible) for those they affect. As a matter of practical policy, we need to be guided by standards of assessment that employ observable and administrable proxies to measure those elements of objective welfare that we cannot feasibly gauge directly. We should care about the distribution of money for its overall impact on the quality of people's lives.

IV. Does One's Comparative Position Matter?

Inequality might be deemed good or bad for its effects. But leaving aside such instrumental value and disvalue, we may wonder if how one person's condition compares to another's might itself be intrinsically morally desirable or undesirable. For example, one might hold that it is intrinsically morally better, all other things being equal, if all persons are equally well off. For another example, one might hold that it is intrinsically morally better if saints are better off than sinners.

These are difficult, unsettled issues, in my view. But there is something intuitively plausible on its face about the sufficientarian's denial that how one person's condition compares to that of another is intrinsically morally important. To illustrate the thought, suppose it is discovered that there are more people who have ever lived than we previously believed. For instance, suppose we have painstakingly calculated the overall moral significance of each person's life having gone as well or badly as it in fact went, but then discover that a million years ago a million people lived on Jupiter. If how one person's condition compares to the condition of others is intrinsically morally important, we have to redo the calculations. It may then turn out that, all things morally considered, it was morally bad that my life went as well as it did, given how my life compares to the lives of the ancient Jupiterians. The moral judgment about the moral significance of my existence that we made in ignorance of Jupiterian history may be reversed once that history is accessible to us. This last claim follows from the position that it is intrinsically morally important how one's condition compares to that of others. The claim may conceivably be true, but is hard to swallow.

V. Enter Sufficientarianism

The preceding reflections might seem to set the stage for an easy victory for the sufficientarian doctrine. If how well I am doing as compared to how well others are doing does not intrinsically matter, it might seem natural to suggest that what does matter morally is that each person should have enough (where "enough" is not a fixed minimum percentage of the aggregate that people, or people in one's community, get).

Frankfurt points out that philosophers arguing for the moral importance of equality express themselves in ways that strongly suggest that concern about inequality is not what really elicits the concern they voice.[13] Let us call this the "argument from egalitarian confusion." Egalitarians urge that significant inequality is bad by pointing to situations in which there is a large gap between the conditions of well-to-do people and poor people and in which the poor face grim prospects, leading lives that are horrible or that lack significant sources of satisfaction. Frankfurt correctly notes that examples of this sort do not really force the judgment that inequality per se is bad. In responding to the examples as described, we should note the possibility that we are appalled above all by the grim badness of the lives that these poor people lead. But this grimness does not necessarily attach to the fate in which one gets the short end of the stick (is worse off than others). There are sticks and *sticks*: some are much longer than others, so the short end of one may not be bad. If it were simply the gap in economic circumstances or well-being between poor and well-off people that troubled us, then we should be equally troubled by a similar gap between the conditions of the rich and the superrich. But we are not, nor should we be. The suggested conclusion is that what is morally objectionable is not that some people's conditions are worse than the conditions of others, but rather that some people face grim life conditions that fall below any reasonable threshold of a decent quality of life.

With respect to inequalities in the income and wealth that different persons have, the idea would be that it is not morally problematic that some have more and others less. What is morally problematic is that some people have less income and wealth than they need to meet the standard of sufficiency. What counts as enough money for a given individual depends on that individual's total set of circumstances along with her aims, ambitions, and preferences. Determining the extent of one's need for money requires a careful assessment of one's comprehensive present and likely future circumstances and wants. Merely to compare how much income and wealth one has compared to what others have is a distraction. To become preoccupied with such economic comparisons is to become alienated from an orientation toward what really matters for the success of one's life.

[13] Frankfurt, "Equality as a Moral Ideal," 146–48. Frankfurt cites two instances of affirmations of inequality's disvalue that exhibit the confusion he notices—those expressed in Ronald Dworkin, "Why Liberals Should Care about Equality," in Dworkin, *A Matter of Principle* (Cambridge, MA: Harvard University Press, 1985), 206; and in Thomas Nagel, "Equality," in Nagel, *Mortal Questions* (Cambridge: Cambridge University Press, 1979). Frankfurt's criticism of Dworkin appears at Frankfurt, "Equality as a Moral Ideal," 147, and his criticism of Nagel is at ibid., 149–51. Nagel revisits this issue in Thomas Nagel, *Equality and Partiality* (Oxford: Oxford University Press, 1991), 69–71.

Frankfurt explores the idea of economic sufficiency: under what circumstances does an individual have enough income and wealth? Frankfurt's suggestion is that one has enough money when one is reasonably content with the amount one has, and one can be content in this way either because one's life is already going well enough or because more money would not help remedy its shortcomings. Frankfurt adds that he understands being content in this context as being compatible with recognizing that more money would improve one's life. Being content with the amount of money one has here means that one does not have "an *active interest* in getting more";[14] a person in this state does not find further improvement in his economic condition important. In other words, for a person to be contented with his economic circumstances means "that he does not resent his circumstances, that he is not anxious or determined to improve them, and that he does not go out of his way or take any significant initiatives to make them better."[15] To this account we should add the qualifier that what counts is that the person would be reasonable to have the attitude toward his economic circumstances just described. We do not want the requirements of distributive justice as provision of sufficiency to vary depending on people's whims or overweening ambitions, so that if one desperately wants the moon and the stars, one does not have "enough" without them.[16]

Note, however, that tying the notion of the good-enough level of income and wealth to the attitudes it would be reasonable for a person to adopt toward her circumstances brings it about that the notion of the good-enough level entirely floats away from the idea of sufficiency invoked by the argument from egalitarian confusion. That argument implicitly identifies a person's level of sufficiency as being the level of a minimally but acceptably decent quality of life. But one might have far above that level by anyone's lights, yet still reasonably be desperately anxious to improve one's circumstances and quite ready to take aggressive steps to secure improvements. By itself, this difficulty might not be daunting. Perhaps it merely means that the best articulation of the sufficiency ideal requires abandonment of the argument from egalitarian confusion.

But setting that argument to the side, we still find that the Frankfurt strategy, taken on its own terms, is implausible. Notice first that a person who correctly anticipates that her life conditions will be impoverished and grim might reasonably work to adopt a Stoic attitude of indifference to the prospect that she will fail to enjoy many important components of a good life and that she will fail to command those normally important

[14] Frankfurt, "Equality as a Moral Ideal," 153.
[15] Ibid., 154.
[16] This reasonableness qualification is my suggestion. Frankfurt mentions the possibility of such a qualification as is described in the text, but remains noncommittal regarding it; see ibid., 152 n. 24.

means to the good life, adequate income and wealth. She could train herself not to care about such matters. Suppose she is successful. Then she will be content with the paltry income and wealth she has and will find nothing unsatisfying or distressing about how her life goes, even though, in objective terms, the life is gruesome. We are supposing that the development of these attitudes is part of the person's best strategy of response toward her life conditions and that the attitudes she develops are in that sense reasonable.

There is another problem with Frankfurt's strategy. A person at the high end, facing terrific life prospects that include immensely favorable economic circumstances, might reasonably develop very ambitious life goals that require for their fulfillment piles and piles of money in addition to the immense stock of money he now enjoys. Let us call this person "Bill Gates." He might be the richest man in the world. Nevertheless, contemplating his economic circumstances, Bill is immensely and actively interested in gaining far more money, and reasonably so. He needs that extra cash in order to fulfill his very ambitious life goals. Note that these goals, while ambitious, are not unreasonably so. Indeed, developing an immense, focused, strong concern for bettering his economic circumstances and regarding that concern as important to his life may be the most effective means available to Bill to give him the best chance of achieving his rational life plan. Frankfurt's construal of what it is for a person to have enough money then yields the conclusion that in this sort of case the richest man in the world might not have enough.

Both of these cases illustrate the problem with Frankfurt's strategy—the subjective attitude toward getting more money for herself that it is reasonable for a person to develop in view of her total circumstances does not help to identify a notion of having enough that would be a useful tool for a theory of distributive justice. We evidently need to take another tack.

Perhaps this dismissal of Frankfurt's proposal (that to have enough is to have an amount that a reasonable person would be content to have) is too brisk. Suppose we say of the person who adapts to horrible life prospects by cultivating an attitude of contentment that to identify the good-enough level we ignore strategic adaptations of that sort. And suppose we say of a person whose excellent prospects spur her to greater ambition that while it is not unreasonable for her to develop ambitions that preclude contentment, in her circumstances contentment would also be reasonable. The good-enough level would then be the lowest level of good that it would be reasonable to be content with. On this construal, one has enough when it is the case either that more resources would not help or that one's life is going sufficiently well that it would be reasonable to be content with its course, with the stipulation that the reasonableness of being content that is in question is fixed only by one's response to the qualities of one's life and not by the consideration that strategically refraining from becoming content might improve it.

This response fails to rescue the Frankfurt proposal. The attempt to characterize the measure of a good-enough quality of life has led us in a circle. When does one have enough? When one, contemplating one's life, would reasonably be content. When would one reasonably be content? When one's life is going well enough. In order to apply the contentment test, one must already be in possession of a way of determining when a life is good enough, but this measure is just what we were seeking in the first place.

There is yet another difficulty that afflicts the Frankfurt proposal. Frankfurt supposes it can be reasonable to be content with one's life, where this includes not being disposed to take steps to make it better even though one sees it can be improved. This supposition is aligned with philosopher Michael Slote's claim that rationality can consist in "satisficing" rather than optimizing.[17] One satisfices by taking steps that will produce a satisfactory outcome, where a satisfactory outcome need not be the best outcome that is reachable. For instance, facing a sequence of offers to purchase a car that one wants to sell, one might adopt the strategy of deciding on a satisfactory sale price and accepting the first offer that meets the chosen target.

Slote associates the idea of satisficing with the different idea of moderation. Satisficing is a strategy of choice; moderation, as Slote explains it, seems to be a matter of having modest appetites.[18] Slote's moderate individual seeks and accepts an outcome that is less than the best that she could get for herself. Having had one snack, she rejects a second, even though taking it would render her better off, because she is content with an outcome that is less than the best attainable. Setting aside choices that put the agent's own interests in conflict with the interests of other agents, Slote supposes that it is rational to be moderate and rational to be a satisficer rather than an optimizer.

Taking steps to improve one's condition typically involves costs to the agent, including the cost of calculating the costs and benefits of further actions one might take. Furthermore, many choices one might take to improve one's condition are risky or uncertain, and carry a (possibly unknown) chance that the outcome will render one's condition worse. Given these considerations, satisficing can in fact be an optimizing strategy for agents with finite information-gathering and choice-making capacities who face alternatives whose outcomes are risky or uncertain. Seeking a satisfactory outcome and not holding out for a better-than-satisfactory outcome is optimal when the expected costs of seeking a better-than-satisfactory outcome outweigh the expected benefits. So to focus on the issue of whether it can be rational for an agent to satisfice,

[17] Michael Slote, *Beyond Optimizing: A Study of Rational Choice* (Cambridge, MA: Harvard University Press, 1989).

[18] See ibid., 10-13. I owe this point, and others, to written comments by David Schmidtz on a preliminary draft of this essay.

and seek a satisfactory outcome, rather than optimize, and seek the best outcome reachable, we should focus on decision problems in which the imperatives of satisfice and optimize clearly yield different directives. Suppose an agent is choosing among life plans, and there is nothing that relevantly distinguishes plan A and plan B except that A will yield a superior outcome; suppose also that the agent knows this fact about A and B. If both A and B will certainly yield outcomes that are above the satisfactory level, the Slote position is that a fully rational person might select B rather than A, on the ground that B, though inferior, is good enough. In the same vein, Frankfurt would say that an agent whose life course is following B but who knows that she could costlessly switch to A and reach a better outcome with certainty can be reasonable to be content with B and not switch course on the ground that B is good enough.

The issue posed here about the nature of rationality is delicate and controversial. I merely note that anyone who shares my intuition that satisficing is just plain irrational when it is not rationalizable as optimizing under given constraints has an extra reason to reject the Frankfurt proposal for determining the threshold of sufficiency. (In the same spirit, I find Slote's moderate individual, who rejects the second snack even though taking it renders her better off at no cost to others, just plain irrational.)

Let us go back to the task of finding a criterion that will enable us to tell when a person's life is going well enough on the whole. We need a way of picking one level of quality of life as being the good-enough level.

VI. Sufficiency and Triage

The sufficientarian principle of justice says that institutions and practices should be arranged and actions chosen so that of those people who will ever live, as many as possible reach the sufficient level. This formulation leaves it open how to define the sufficient or good-enough level.

In defining sufficiency, my bias is to employ a standard of objective well-being. Such a standard measures how well off or badly off someone is, for purposes of determining whether he attains the good-enough level, by looking to the objective well-being or welfare level that he reaches (or perhaps, is enabled to reach). One might opt for a standard of subjective well-being or of something that has nothing to do with well-being, but it is unclear why we should care about whether the person is doing well or badly according to such nonobjective measures. If the measure we use can tell me that I am doing well when my life is going badly or doing badly when my life is going well, why should we care that people do well in that measure's refined sense? But if the measure is deemed to be the well-being the person (objectively) gets or is enabled to get, it becomes mysterious why there is supposed to be one special level of well-being that is all-important. Why is it acceptable for justice to exhibit a tunnel vision that pays no mind to anything except the numbers of people that reach a particular welfare level?

We might approach this topic by reflecting on a type of situation in which something like a sufficiency approach does seem morally appropriate. If soldiers and civilians are wounded in battle, and medical personnel and equipment cannot treat adequately all who need care, a triage morality has intuitive appeal.[19] Suppose we identify being well off or badly off in this context with the severity of one's medical condition. A leximin approach, which bids us as a first priority to do all that we can to improve the condition of the very worst off, strikes us as uncalled for. There may be precious little we can do to aid the very worst off, and it may well be that caring for them as a leximin approach decrees would involve lavishing huge amounts of scarce medical resources on people who will gain very little from these huge infusions of care. Allotting each wounded person an equal share of scarce medical resources (tailored to each patient's specific needs) also strikes us as implausible. Some of the wounded may be hardly wounded at all, some will die soon no matter what we do for them, and some will live only if we quickly give them a larger-than-per-capita share of available resources.

Consider this norm: Distribute scarce medical resources so as to save as many lives as possible. This norm states a sufficientarian approach, with the level of sufficiency identified as avoiding near-term death. "Saving lives" is a vague goal. We might wonder if one who could be kept alive for a few days if treated, but cannot be healed, should be counted as having reached the threshold level if he is enabled to live for those few days. I leave aside here the task of suitably refining the statement of the sufficientarian goal.

Saving as many lives as possible will dictate giving no treatment to those who cannot be saved no matter what. It also dictates giving no treatment to someone who could be saved only by an expenditure of resources that would save more lives if deployed to other potential patients. Furthermore, it forbids giving aid (at least during the postbattle emergency) to those who will live even if untreated. If this policy dictated leaving me untreated to die of my wounds, I might well complain, but it seems reasonable for medical personnel to reply, "We are leaving you untreated in order to save as many lives as possible."

I do not claim to have shown that sufficientarianism as described, applied to the battlefield scenario, is the morally preferred policy. I merely want to sketch a context in which sufficientarianism has some prima facie

[19] I borrow the idea that battlefield triage represents one understanding of sufficientarianism from an unpublished essay by John Roemer, though I do not think he would endorse the lesson I draw from the comparison.

plausibility and does not seem obviously counterintuitive. In my view, the underlying reason that the battlefield triage scenario fills this bill is that saving a life is arguably far more important morally than alleviating suffering for a few days or helping to make the death of those who are dying more comfortable. The difference between dying in the aftermath of battle and being enabled to emerge alive from one's wounds for the foreseeable future also seems far more significant than the difference between living but losing a limb and living and retaining the limb. At the limit, if we regarded all possible outcomes for potential patients of receiving greater or lesser medical treatment as insignificant except the outcome in which a person whose life is threatened is saved from death, we would unequivocally embrace the sufficientarian principle in this application as we have interpreted it. If we think that, for example, alleviating the pain experienced by people in their dying hours is utterly insignificant compared to the saving of a life, then we should not channel medical resources to alleviate the deathbed hours of even an infinite number of potential patients if this outcome must be purchased at the cost of leaving one person who could be saved to die. If we think that *anything* we might achieve by expending medical resources pales into insignificance in just this way in comparison with the value of saving a life, then the triage policy—use medical resources so as to maximize the number of lives saved—makes perfect sense.

I do not think that in any actual battlefield triage scenario, the possible utility gains would shape up as I have characterized them, such that nothing matters at all except the number of lives saved. What one should notice is that in the special imagined circumstances in which sufficientarianism would be a plausible and arguably correct policy, it yields the same recommendations as other views. Utilitarianism, for instance (along with variants of utilitarianism that give extra but not infinite weight to securing utility gains and avoiding utility losses for those who are worse off), would also support the triage policy as described. Hence, the battlefield scenario is not a good example on which to focus our thoughts as to whether sufficientarianism is a superior morality to these other views. To adjudicate among these views we need to examine examples in which the different views yield different implications concerning what we should do.

We should also note that if we relax the very special factual assumptions that we packed into the characterization of the battlefield example, we find that sufficientarianism loses its aura of plausibility. We can do this by making the battlefield example more realistic. It is not in fact true that saving a life is of transcendent importance compared to any other goal that we might achieve in situations where there are numerous patients in dire need and scarce medical resources with which to treat them. In some cases, the life that we could save would be so damaged as to be barely worth living or perhaps even not worth living at all. Suppose Smith is severely injured. We can keep him alive, but he will stay in a coma for ten years and then emerge to live a short life of a few hours of intense, irremediable pain before finally dying. Suppose Jones is on the verge of death from his wounds. We can save him, but he will never recover: he will be confined to a hospital and will never again have the use of reason. These cases show that saving a life encompasses many possible outcomes that vary greatly in their moral value. Some of these possible outcomes even have negative moral value. On the other hand, we might at a very tiny cost of resources be able to alleviate the pain of many dying patients. Surely this is a great possible gain, not an inconsequential one. To take another example, consider a patient who will live regardless of whether she is treated or not, but who will have the full use of her limbs only if she is treated. It is unnecessary to consider further examples. Even in battlefield triage situations, our beliefs about the relative value of various possible expenditures of resources prevent the sufficientarian principle from seeming morally compelling.

VII. What Is Wrong with the Sufficiency Doctrine?

The idea that the first priority of justice is to bring all persons to the level of an acceptable quality of life, so far as this is possible, sounds attractive. The sufficiency norm seems to combine a kind of special concern for the worse off with a moderate limit on that concern. Once we have brought someone to the good-enough level, what happens above that level is not the concern of justice. It might be that an acceptable quality of life requires ready access to a functioning car, but it does not matter from the standpoint of justice that I drive a Chevy and you drive a Ferrari. Moreover, the sufficiency doctrine weaves together individual responsibility with a moderately demanding conception of distributive justice. Once all are sustained above the line of sufficiency and a fair framework of terms of interaction is established, each individual is responsible for how she chooses to live her life and for the level of well-being that she gets as a result. The individual above the line of sufficiency is responsible for her life in the sense that she will bear the costs of the choices she makes: if she meets an unfortunate outcome leaving her above the sufficiency threshold, this will not trigger a justified claim for further compensation.

The rub comes in specifying the sufficiency threshold in a nonarbitrary way. The relevant standard for determining when the sufficient level is reached cannot focus just on one aspect of the quality of a person's life, but must somehow integrate the value of various goods that we find significant in a human life. In broad terms, we need a way of making interpersonal comparisons of utility or welfare. This is a tall order, but for present purposes let us suppose we have the theoretically best interpersonal welfare measure on hand. It is not cheating to make this assumption in the present context of argument, because I am trying to refute the sufficiency doctrine; to clarify where the doctrine goes wrong, it is best to grant controversial assumptions that the doctrine shares with a great many approaches to distributive justice. If interpersonal comparisons of welfare make no sense, then the entire theory of distributive justice is in trouble, not just the sufficiency doctrine.

With the theoretically best standard in hand, we will find a continuum with an infinite number of gradations of well-being. (We get qualitatively the same result if we have a very large finite number of degrees of well-being.) A person's life can range from horribly gruesome to wonderfully rich in fulfillment, with indefinitely many stops existing between these extremes. Although moralists have proposed various putatively nonarbitrary ways of slicing into the continuum and declaring some particular point the good-enough level (some suggestions will be reviewed below), my claim will be that there is no good reason for picking these points rather than others.

Wherever the level of sufficiency is set, the doctrine of sufficiency must face two objections. The sufficientarian norm holds that we ought to bring it about that as many as possible of the people who will ever live reach the sufficient level, defined over the course of their lives. The objections respond that the norm gives bad advice in two types of situations. If the line of sufficiency is set lower, the first problem is exacerbated; if the line is set higher, the second problem becomes worse.

The sufficientarian norm tells us what to do only if our actions can affect the number of people who reach the good-enough level. One type of problematic case involves conflicts of interest between those who can be moved to sufficiency or enabled to stay there and those who will remain above the line whatever we do, but whose welfare will be affected by our choice. Giving strict priority to increasing the numbers of people who meet sufficiency means that even if a huge number of people who are securely above the threshold can be enabled to secure immense gains in well-being, such gains do not outweigh the moral priority of bringing it about that one person moves from just barely below the threshold to just barely at it. Suppose we can move millions and millions of people from moderate fulfillment to absolute bliss. These huge welfare gains count as nothing against the alternative option of moving a single person from just below the threshold to the threshold level. The question then arises, what makes the level selected as sufficient so morally special that the extreme discounting of those gains and losses that do not bear on sufficiency makes sense?

A second type of problematic case involves conflicts of interest between those just barely below the threshold level and those who are unavoidably leading subthreshold lives but who can be significantly aided nonetheless. Suppose millions of people are leading lives of hellish quality, perhaps at the level of concentration camp victims. Suppose further that they can be raised to at best a moderate quality of life, close to the threshold, but that some constraint exists preventing us from enabling any of these people from advancing to the threshold level. Still, we can bring about huge improvements in quality of life for huge numbers of people. We have one alternative choice: we could instead take one individual whose prospects are currently just below the threshold level and boost her prospects by a tiny bit, so as to place them at the threshold. On the sufficientarian view, we must choose the latter option—and again, the moral urgency attributed to the goal of getting people to the sufficient level is counterintuitive.

The two problems have a common structure. Sufficientarianism accords lexical priority to the goal of getting as many people as possible to the good-enough level. This strict priority ranking makes sense only if everything that can befall an individual pales into utter insignificance from the standpoint of morality besides the single matter of whether she does or does not lead a life that reaches (on the whole) the threshold level. From an individual standpoint, of course, people might care about many other things. To revert to Walzer's image, I might care a lot about whether I buy my rugs from Sears Roebuck or from the Orient. But moral evaluation is supposed to impose, as it were, the priority of need over desire.

But as already mentioned, if you substitute other possible differences in people's conditions for the ones Walzer mentions, the idea that all such comparisons are irrelevant from a moral standpoint begins to look worse than dubious. The sufficientarian is forced to say that if neither of us can be brought to sufficiency, it does not matter that you die a painful, lingering death at age 10 whereas I die a quick, painless death at age 20. She must also say that if we are both above sufficiency, it does not matter that I suffer from chronic arthritis and die at age 60 while you stay in the pink of health until you die at the ripe old age of 100. But only commitment to a bad theory would incline anybody to say such things, for they are as plainly false as any moral claims ever are.

To imagine a world in which sufficientarianism would be acceptable, we must conjure up one in which no gains in the quality of people's lives that might occur either above or below the line of sufficiency have any importance at all in comparison with the moral urgency of getting as many people as possible to the line of sufficiency. In such a world, either people themselves evaluating their own lives reasonably give strict lexical priority to attaining sufficiency, or people do not make such assessments but morality, for reasons of its own, overrides their assessments in the sufficientarian manner. Neither possibility is remotely credible.

VIII. Attempts to Specify the "Good Enough" Nonarbitrarily

Walzer suggests plausibly that in a market society, possession of money confers some level of membership in that society. The good-enough level is then set as the amount of economic resources that is necessary for full membership in society. So long as adequate access to cash and the other conditions needed to sustain the status of "equal democratic citizen" are met, economic inequality above the line of sufficiency is not a concern of justice.

One might quibble with the claim that there is some minimum income and wealth one must have to be a full member of a democratic society. One can imagine personal talent and charm substituting for a secure income. Imagine a brilliant homeless mathematician who lives as a guest in the homes of one and then another of her mathematical colleagues, who offer hospitality in order to have the opportunity to collaborate on research projects with the guest. Not having the wherewithal to purchase anything at the supermarket does not make the itinerant mathematician a social outsider. But for most of us, Walzer's claim that access to money is a prerequisite for belonging to society is roughly correct. What is less plausible is the claim that there is some amount of economic resources (perhaps different for different persons) possession of which places one at a threshold of full membership. The membership in market society that money confers admits of many degrees. Once again the problem arises, how does one select a point on the line in a nonarbitrary way?

Even if we could surmount the difficulty of arbitrary line-drawing, full membership in society, however exactly that is construed, need not coincide with having very much by way of access to a good quality of life. The financial requirements for sustaining a nonillusory feeling of belonging to the community one inhabits may be very low in an impoverished society, but membership in that society might not provide access to the goods of civilization.

Nussbaum decomposes the idea of "living well enough" into a number of functionings (or doings and beings); attainment of all of these is deemed necessary and sufficient for a good-enough quality of life. Nussbaum adds that justice requires that everybody should be sustained in the opportunity to attain all of these functionings at the good-enough level. If one of the functionings is romantic fulfillment, one might have the capability to achieve this functioning but decide to live one's life as a celibate monk. If one of the necessary functionings is being adequately nourished, one who has the capability to be adequately nourished but voluntarily embarks on a sustained religious fast is not thereby the victim of injustice. On this account, an individual reaches the threshold of sufficiency when over the course of her life she has the opportunity or capability to attain each of the functionings necessary for a good life at a good-enough level.

The idea that the good life for a person can be understood as the achievement of a number of independently important dimensions or kinds of good makes sense. Nussbaum's efforts to specify the items that belong on this objective list of human goods are admirable. By itself, however, this account leaves unsolved the problem of specifying a nonarbitrary sufficiency level for each of the goods that is postulated to be on the list. One might have hoped that breaking the problem down into parts in this way would make the difficulty of arbitrary line-drawing tractable. Take the example of learning to ride a bicycle or learning to swim. There is a stage of floundering and wobbling, and then a jump to a basic competence.

But even with regard to these examples, it is far from obvious that the level of basic competence is unambiguous (suppose I can ride on a wide level path but cannot maintain control on a narrow downhill track, or that I can dog-paddle a little but cannot master a range of strokes), and it is doubtful that whatever level is specified to be good enough has special ethical significance. Moreover, with many significant functionings, such as becoming educated, enjoying good health and fitness, and developing friendships, it is clearly futile to try to specify a sufficient level such that achievements below the threshold and above it have far less moral value than those bringing one over the threshold. Finally, when we evaluate a person's overall level of functioning, what matters is the appropriately weighted sum of all of her significant beings and doings. High achievements on one dimension can offset a low attainment on another, so that someone can be sustaining a very good quality of life even though one or another of her functioning (or capability, if you prefer) scores is subpar. Once again we are back to the idea of comprehensive welfare or well-being, which admits of indefinitely many gradations, none of which has any particular claim to be deemed the all-important threshold of sufficiency.

I have attempted to rebut the most plausible attempts in the literature to work out the notion of a good-enough level of quality of life.[20] I have no general proof that this notion cannot be specified in a satisfactory way to fulfill its role in a sufficientarian ethic. The doctrine of sufficiency as understood by its proponents puts enormous theoretical pressure on the notion of the good enough. My hunch is that this pressure cannot be contained in a satisfactory way. Put another way, the hunch is that the appeal of the sufficiency doctrine dissipates as the doctrine is worked out in detail.

IX. Sufficiency and Responsibility

There is another objection against the sufficiency doctrine, one that by itself only suggests the need to qualify the doctrine rather than reject it. In this sense the criticism to be adumbrated is less fundamental than those developed in the previous sections. Still, the necessary qualification is nontrivial.

[20] For another interesting attempt to specify the sufficient level, see Arthur Ripstein, *Equality, Responsibility, and the Law* (Cambridge: Cambridge University Press, 1999), chap. 9. Ripstein urges that when distributive justice is done, a fair background is in place that secures each individual the resources needed for meaningful agency. My response by now should be predictable. Meaningful agency (under any plausible construal) comes in degrees, and there is no unique level of agency that generates distributive-justice imperatives. Also, a person who can exercise meaningful agency might still face unchosen life conditions that offer her grim prospects for a decent quality of life, prospects so bad that others have a justice-obligation to ameliorate them.

As I have been construing it, the sufficiency doctrine requires that we bring as many people as possible of all those who shall ever live to the level of sufficiency. One judges whether someone is at the sufficiency level by assessing that person's entire life. The aim that is proposed is that the person's life, taken as a whole, should meet the sufficiency level. There are questions raised by this formulation about how to interpret the sufficiency of a life. Suppose that an individual is far above the sufficiency level for most of her life but sinks below it for a time toward the end of her life. We might judge that as a whole this individual did not attain sufficiency because such attainment requires that the good-enough level be maintained at each moment of one's life. Alternatively, we might say that over her life as a whole this person did attain sufficiency because such attainment requires merely that one's life should be at the good-enough level on the average over time, a condition she meets. Finally, we might think we need rather to make a single holistic judgment that takes account of various factors that affect the character of the individual's life taken as a whole, factors that cannot simply be considered as though they are goods that accrue at particular discrete times of one's life. I leave these complications aside and just suppose that we have some acceptable way of assessing whether or not a person's life as a whole reaches the good-enough level.

The responsibility-based objection to sufficientarianism argues that some ways in which a person's life as a whole might fail to reach sufficiency are properly ascribable to the person, as her responsibility, not the moral responsibility of society. That is to say, the moral obligations set by a reasonable theory of social justice do not require society to guarantee or do everything in its power to ensure any level of welfare for any individual. The most that society is required to do is make it possible for individuals to attain the "just" level of welfare if they put forth suitable effort. Let us assume, contrary to the arguments of the previous sections, that we have a compelling account of the good-enough level that justice requires us to secure for as many people as possible. Suppose that a society dedicated to achieving sufficiency for all provides me with a level of resources and education that would enable me to get to the good-enough level if I were to conduct my life in a reasonably prudent way, but that I nevertheless do not conduct my life prudently. Instead, I squander my opportunities and am on a path that will take me to the gutter. Since the sufficientarian principle of justice imposes as a first priority that as many as possible be sustained at the good-enough level, society on this view is obligated to supply me with extra resources to make up for my imprudence, at least so long as doing so does not prove to be an inefficient use of resources from the sufficientarian standpoint. But then suppose I squander these resources again, and again, and again. Perhaps there are good reasons to adopt a forgiving line on responsibility, such that we should provide a person second, third, and fourth chances to get her life into decent shape even if she has thoroughly ruined her first, second, and third chances. But in principle the sufficientarian obligation never runs out. Under sufficientarianism, society is always committed to the proposition that the first priority of justice, taking lexical priority over any other duty that might compete with it, is that as many as possible should be brought to have the good-enough level. This goes too far. There should be a moral division of responsibility between society and the individual, one that at some point permits society to say to the individual that enough has been done for him regardless of the lifetime welfare level he experiences.

There is a flip side to this responsibility objection. If the sufficiency doctrine holds that as many people as possible be sustained at the good-enough threshold over the course of their lives, it follows that if we accept the doctrine, we should restrict individual liberty in self-regarding matters whenever doing so increases the numbers who are sustained at the threshold. Consider, then, dangerous activities that are dangerous only to their voluntary participants and that are highly valued by them. It is likely, for example, that those who engage in mountain climbing would not be reduced to a subthreshold existence if they were prohibited from engaging in the sport. Yet some youthful participants will suffer premature death or irremediable severe disability from climbing injuries. These unlucky participants end up below the sufficiency threshold. (Note that for the purposes of considering this objection I am supposing that my previous arguments denying that a reasonable, nonarbitrary sufficiency level can be specified are unsuccessful.) It follows that banning mountain climbing, if we can police the ban without excessive cost, would boost the number of people who are sustained at the good-enough level. According to the sufficiency doctrine, then, we ought to enact and enforce such a ban.

I am not opposed in principle to all paternalistic restriction of liberty,[21] but the sufficiency doctrine goes overboard in this regard. In the example just described, the practice of mountain climbing might generate large welfare gains for those involved in it, despite the unfortunate accidents that befall a few. The sufficiency doctrine would recommend banning the activity when virtually any remotely plausible alternative ethic would reject this counsel. This is another instance of the implausibility of treating all welfare gains that can be achieved—no matter how large, no matter the numbers of people affected—as morally insignificant (for all practical purposes) when the gains lie above the line of sufficiency.

X. A Wider Sufficiency Doctrine?

The discussion to this point is directed at a particular interpretation of the idea that justice requires that everyone have enough. The interpreta-

[21] A paternalistic restriction of liberty is a restriction of a person's liberty against her will for her own good. It is also paternalistic to restrict the liberty of one person in order to prevent harm to another when the person being harmed or threatened with the risk of harm voluntarily consents to be affected by the first party's action.

tion holds that justice accords strict lexical priority to the aim of bringing it about that as many as possible of the people who shall live reach the level of sufficiency. Perhaps, one might argue, the trouble lies not in the general idea of sufficiency, but in the uncharitable gloss I have given it.

One possibility is to relax the stipulation that the aim of attaining sufficiency for as many as possible takes lexical priority over other values of justice. One aim has lexical priority over another just in case one should refuse to sacrifice even the smallest degree of fulfillment of the first aim in order to secure any degree whatsoever of fulfillment of the second. Suppose we assert that attaining sufficiency is important, but does not merit strict lexical priority.

The core of my objection against sufficiency is that it demands discontinuity, a jump in our moral response, in an area where no basis for this discontinuity can be found. The assertion that the aim of sufficiency ought to get less than lexical priority should attract the objections I have already made, but they will apply to a lesser degree corresponding to the reduced strength of the asserted priority for sufficiency. At the limit, just asserting that attaining sufficiency would be nice is not a claim strong enough to be objectionable.

Another adjustment to sufficientarianism lets it avoid the objection that the doctrine favors one individual's tiny but threshold-breaching change in well-being over any gains, however large, that could be obtained for people whose lives are hellishly bad but could be significantly improved, albeit to a subthreshold level, at modest resource cost. This revised sufficiency doctrine says that the top priority of distributive justice is to bring about improvements in the lives of those who are below the threshold of sufficiency. Below the threshold, priority goes to obtaining benefits for those who are worse off, whether or not they can be brought to sufficiency. This priority might be interpreted as more strict or less strict. The character of this revised version of sufficiency can be indicated by considering the version of it in which priority is maximally strict. Under this doctrine, one should always give strict lexical priority to bringing about gains (or preventing losses) for the worst off, up to the threshold of sufficiency. This version of revised sufficiency may be described as "leximin with a cap."[22]

Revised sufficiency consists of two elements. One is that we should give priority to bringing about gains (and preventing losses) for the worse off. The second is that the priority for the worse off is shaped by the threshold of sufficiency: bringing about gains for those below the threshold has absolute priority over bringing about gains for those already above the threshold, and for those above the threshold, priority for the worse off ceases to obtain.

Of these two elements, only the second strikes me as objectionable. Giving priority to the worse off is fine. Determining the appropriate

[22] I thank David Schmidtz for suggesting this version of revised sufficiency.

strength of this priority is beyond the scope of this essay; we can say, however, that the extreme leximin version of this priority is too strict. To hold, as leximin insists, that achieving a benefit of any size, however small, for the worst-off person takes precedence over achieving any benefit, however large, for any number of next-worst-off persons is surely excessive.

Though the priority element of revised sufficientarianism is plausible, shaping priority by the threshold of sufficiency is not. As I have urged, we should not forgo an opportunity to secure sizable benefits for large numbers of individuals above the sufficiency threshold merely because we face a situation in which those benefits can only be obtained if we allow for incremental losses for small numbers of individuals below the threshold. For example, preventing lethal diseases that strike only those above the threshold could be morally more cost-effective than achieving tiny pleasures for subthreshold individuals. Also, priority for the worse off, to the extent that it matters at all, does not cease to matter altogether when one has to resolve conflicts of interest among individuals who are above the threshold to different degrees.

Some of the subthreshold individuals whom the revised view gives priority to aiding will be very poor transformers of resources into welfare. They can be helped, but an enormous infusion of resources will provide them very little benefit. Such people become basins of attraction for resources under the revised view. This defect attaches to the sufficiency doctrine itself, but when we move to the revised view, the problem worsens. This is so because the revised view recommends channeling resources to poor transformers even when they cannot be brought to sufficiency, so long as further infusions of resources will produce some further gain in their condition.

XI. Prioritarian Justice

I hope the critical discussion of sufficientarianism above paves the way for a sympathetic appreciation of a rival doctrine that to my mind absorbs the strengths of sufficientarianism without also taking on its weaknesses. Recall Frankfurt's disparagement of the advocates of equality. Philosophers such as Dworkin and Thomas Nagel are presented as invoking the contrast between the impoverished lives of poor people and the enormous material privileges enjoyed by many citizens of the world's most prosperous nations. It is bad, they say, that some are so badly off while others are prospering to so great an extent, at least if we suppose that the situation is remediable. The prosperous could shift resources to the needy, or failing that, the morally minded state could compel the prosperous to disgorge some of their advantages to aid the truly needy. The contrast between grim suffering and extreme opulence is supposed to persuade us, Dworkin and Nagel seem to suggest, that inequality per se is morally undesirable. But if inequality per se were what is undesirable in the described scenario, Frankfurt notes, we would equally be appalled by the similar degree of inequality between the very prosperous and the super-prosperous. But in fact this latter inequality strikes us as a "don't care." Hence, what is undesirable in the first scenario is not inequality per se.

What is most plausible in Frankfurt's disparagement of Dworkin and Nagel is his claim that everyone's having the same amounts of things is not intrinsically morally desirable. A broader claim is also plausible: how well one person's life goes is fixed by the weighted sum of objective goods one attains, not by how the sum of one's goods compares to the sums of others. But it is a long jump from these claims to the doctrine of sufficiency. In particular, agreeing with the observation that the gap between the life prospects of the hopelessly destitute and the moderately well off matters a lot more than the similarly sized gap between the life prospects of the very well off and the incredibly well off does not compel agreement with the claim that nothing matters other than avoiding grim conditions of life and attaining sufficiency. We can account for the observation without countenancing the dubious notion of the good-enough quality of life.

Consider the weighted utilitarian or prioritarian moral principle, which holds that the moral value of securing a benefit (or avoiding a loss) of a given size for a person increases as the size of the benefit increases as measured by a utility or welfare scale, and also increases as the level of utility or welfare that the person would have reached over the course of her life in the absence of that benefit (or loss prevention) decreases. (My formulation here assumes that cardinal interpersonal comparisons of utility or welfare make sense, though in given circumstances they might be difficult or unfeasible to make.) This principle includes a family of positions that vary depending on the relative weight that each assigns, in calculating the moral value of benefits, to (a) size of benefit and (b) prior welfare level of its recipient. Prioritarianism, as a form of act-consequentialism, holds that we ought always to maximize moral value so defined.

For the prioritarian, what matters morally when getting a benefit to a person is in the offing is not how badly off that person is in comparison to others. What matters is the degree to which the person is well off or badly off as measured on an absolute or noncomparative scale. To see this point, consider two possible situations in which we might confer a small benefit on Smith. In each case the world contains one hundred people and Smith is the worst off of all of them. The two possible worlds differ in this way: In one, Smith is very badly off, with a well-being level of −100, a hellish condition. The other ninety-nine people all have lives worth living, with well-being levels above the zero point. In the second world, by contrast, while Smith is still the worst off, the differences in well-being between Smith and the others are minuscule. Smith is at −50.0002, for example, and the other ninety-nine people are at −50.0001. In this second case, it hardly matters at all whether it is Smith or one of the others who obtains the benefit, whereas in the first case, it is morally a big deal that the benefit should if possible be channeled to Smith rather than to any of the others. What is morally significant in determining what we should do is the absolute well-being level of the persons we might aid or harm, not their relative positions.

Return to Frankfurt's argument from egalitarian confusion. First of all, we should agree with Frankfurt that the amounts of income and wealth one has are not in and of themselves ethically important. What matters is the quality of life that one's income and wealth, together with one's other circumstances, enable one to attain. According to prioritarianism, it is morally valuable to give a single unit of well-being improvement to a very badly off person rather than to a moderately badly off person, less important to secure a comparable benefit for a moderately well off person rather than for a decidedly well off person, and still less important to channel a similar benefit to an extremely well off person rather than to someone who is far better off, even if in each case the inequality in well-being between the two potential recipients is exactly the same. The prioritarian weighting secures this result. Accounting for what is plausible in the argument from egalitarian confusion does not require us to posit the idea of a sufficient or good-enough level and the norm that the top priority of justice is to maximize the number of people who get to this good-enough level. We have seen that these latter ideas turn out to be problematic when examined, so it is a welcome result that the argument does not pressure us in the slightest to embrace them.

Eschewing leximin priority rankings, the prioritarian will in practice espouse a moderate egalitarianism. By this I mean that the priority accorded by the prioritarian to securing gains for the worse off is not absolute, but varies depending on the amount of benefit that can be secured for both the better off and the worse off. Leximin says that we should prefer a penny's worth of benefits to the worst off to any amount of foregone gains for others, no matter how great and no matter how many better-off persons could be helped. Prioritarianism rejects this rigid and doctrinaire priority ranking.

In other respects, however, prioritarianism is a radical morality. Whether prioritarian ends should be achieved through coercive means or through noncoercive means should be decided strictly according to the calculation that fixes which policies would deliver better consequences, as assessed by prioritarianism, in the long run. At the level of first principle, there is no special moral presumption against coercion and compulsion.

Like any impartial consequentialism, prioritarianism bids us to pay no heed in principle to distance in space and time, to national boundaries, or to special ties such as those of family, friendship, or community. One's obligations toward distant strangers and persons who will exist in the future are the same as those one has to fellow members of a particular current society near at hand. It may be that it is infeasible or impossible for me to do anything that would make a difference to the lives of distant persons, but possible and feasible for me to do a lot for those close by. If so, the prioritarian principle limits its focus to the near at hand—but only to the degree that this extreme assumption actually holds true. It may be that it is much more difficult for me to become sufficiently informed about distant people and places than it is for me to learn about my own neighborhood, with the upshot being that it is hard for me to form reliable views as to how to help faraway strangers and avoid harming them. Again, if this is really so, then my judgments about how I should act toward distant strangers should be discounted by their uncertainty. In principle the prioritarian moral imperative to help the needy varies in strength only with people's neediness and the costs and benefits of alternative actions, not with the strength of the special ties one has to particular persons.

A subtler issue arises once one notes that the prioritarian "ought" is a thin notion. From the fact that I ought to do X it does not follow and may not be true that if I fail to do X I should be punished, even merely by internal pangs of conscience. Bringing it about that punishment accrues to those who act wrongly might itself be a wrong act by prioritarian standards. The social planner implementing prioritarianism would not wish to make war against human nature by raising the practical standard of obligation so high that people would be socialized to punish themselves and others for those violations of duties that natural selfishness strongly inclines people to perpetrate all the time. At least, the ideal social planner would not make war against human nature in this way if, as is likely, doing so would make the expected outcome worse by the prioritarian moral standard. So from the fact that well-off people morally ought to give away much of their wealth toward the amelioration of global poverty and act morally wrongly if they do not, it does not immediately follow that people should be made to feel obligated to act in this way if being obligated involves being liable to punishment for noncompliance.

XII. Responsibility-Catering Prioritarianism

One further wrinkle demands straightening. Even if prioritarianism only incorporated priority to the worse off, it would still give rise to an instrumental norm of individual responsibility. By holding people responsible for their conduct, in the sense that people will be made to bear some of the costs that their conduct creates for other people and themselves, we bring it about that over the long run more moral value is achieved than would be if we refrained from enforcing some such norm of responsibility.

But quite aside from the instrumental value of holding people responsible, I believe that bringing it about that a benefit of a given size goes to someone who is badly off through no fault or choice of her own is intrinsically morally better than bringing it about that a similarly sized benefit accrues to someone who is equally badly off but has brought about her own unfortunate condition through her own fault or choice. By the same token, if someone is well off by sheer luck, and another is well off by dint of morally commendable effort on behalf of worthy goals, it is intrinsically morally better to secure a gain (or prevent a loss) for the second person rather than the first if we must choose between them.

Even if one agrees with these last claims, the question arises how much moral value responsibility contributes to outcomes apart from its instrumental uses. Also, one might wonder whether the intrinsic importance of responsibility, whatever it should turn out to be, has much by way of implications for practical policy, given the futility of trying to devise governmental policies that would vary treatment of individuals according to their lifetime responsibility levels. I have optimistic hunches that we can gauge the importance of responsibility and that it will not turn out to be irrelevant to practical policy guidance, but I do not claim to have done anything in this essay to substantiate these hunches.

XIII. Conclusion: Yachts, "Hi-Fi," and Rugs from the Orient

Against Walzer's moderate and sane-sounding view, I have claimed that it might well matter from the standpoint of distributive justice that one person's recreational boats, stereo equipment, and rugs are superior in quality to those of others. Some individuals have more and better than other people. Such an inequality might be morally significant, and this might be so even if it is conceded that all people have "enough" according to the sufficiency doctrine.

Eliminating some inequality might improve the well-being of the worse off, even at some cost to the better off, so that well-being, if weighted to favor the worse off, would rise. If so, and if the policy that promotes equality would not dampen incentives so as to lessen weighted well-being in the long run, then, other things being equal, prioritarian justice favors the elimination of the inequality.[23]

The correct account of how one person comes to have more and better than another might indicate that sheer unchosen luck creates the discrepancy, not the moral quality of people's choices. If this happens to be so, then considerations of responsibility do not block the presumption in

[23] Of course, in some circumstances prioritarian justice would deliver the result that resources should be transferred from worse off to better off. (Suppose that if Bill Gates had even more money than he currently has, he would do things with the extra cash that would bring about more weighted well-being in the long run than would come into existence if the cash transfer to Bill were not made.) My point in the text is that according to priority, there is sometimes a straightforward and compelling case for transfers to reduce inequality.

favor of egalitarian transfer that is established if it is the case that the transfer would boost weighted well-being over the long run.

Being worse off than another does not matter morally in and of itself, but being well off or badly off does matter, and if the urgency of a person's moral claim to our aid becomes stronger the worse off the person is, then it will turn out that being worse off than another will put one ahead in the queue of justice. One's comparative position is the shadow of what really matters.

Philosophy, University of California, San Diego

THE IMPORTANCE OF BEING SUFFICIENTLY EQUAL*

By James K. Galbraith

> The liberal reward of labour, therefore, as it is the necessary effect, so it is the natural symptom of increasing national wealth. The scanty maintenance of the labouring poor, on the other hand, is the natural symptom that things are at a stand, and their starving condition that they are going fast backwards.
>
> —Adam Smith[1]

> He hated unemployment because it is stupid and poverty because it is ugly.
>
> —Joan Robinson, on John Maynard Keynes[2]

I. Introduction

Neither income nor wealth should be too highly unequal. But there is a fundamental distinction between pay for work and the ownership of capital assets. The reasons to moderate these inequalities therefore differ, and the arguments are best considered separately.

The case for sufficient equality in pay is aesthetic and pragmatic. Too much inequality is unpleasant and dysfunctional.[3] Because it is associated with high rates of poverty, it is ugly. Because it leads to unemployment and the evils thereof, readily avoided by simple, proven methods, it

* I thank my student associates in the University of Texas Inequality Project (http://utip.gov.utexas.edu) for their phenomenal research into aspects of the inequality issue, in particular Amy Calistri, Anindya Chaudhuri, Pedro Conceição, Pedro Ferreira, Vidal Garza Cantú, Lu Jiaqing, Hyunsub Kum, and Wang Qifei, who served as coauthors of papers with me and helped to compile the data set on which this essay is based.

[1] Adam Smith, *An Inquiry into the Nature and Causes of the Wealth of Nations* (London: Dent, 1970), book I, chap. 8, p. 65.

[2] Joan Robinson, "What Has Become of the Keynesian Revolution?" in Milo Keynes, ed., *Essays on John Maynard Keynes* (Cambridge: Cambridge University Press, 1975), 128.

[3] What *degree* of equality should be considered "sufficient"? This is an important question, but determining it is not the central task of this essay. The purpose of phrasing my argument as a case for *sufficient* equality is to frame the general issue in a precise way, that is, to argue that the shape of the distribution of income matters—that more equality has advantages, that inequality can be excessive. It is also to avoid the trap, into which philosophers and economists sometimes fall, of centering the argument at the extreme cases. There is no practical case for perfect equality, for Cambodia under the Khmer Rouge, just as even the most extreme conservative would not defend Mobutu in the Congo. The practical question is posed within the framework of modern capitalist social democracy. It is: should we care whether inequality rises or falls?

is stupid. More equal societies have less unemployment, fewer poor, less crime, and better public services; they are on the whole more prosperous and stable and more peaceful places to live.

The case for sufficient equality in the distribution of wealth relates mainly to the construction of political life. Highly unequal societies are always dominated by the rich. Whatever the legitimacy of great wealth, it is sordid (an aesthetic consideration) to weight political influence by asset value. And speaking practically, deeply unequal societies cannot function as coherent social units; they cannot govern themselves on legitimate terms. Rather, they fracture and they fractionate. A sufficient degree of wealth equality is thus necessary for any collection of individuals properly to be considered as a society in the first place, and for such a society to function as a democracy.

This essay will take up the pay and then the wealth dimensions of the case for sufficient equality. Since aesthetic issues are mainly matters of taste, it will concentrate on the pragmatic arguments. The issues related to income and pay especially need careful consideration, for conventional theoretical treatments of equity and efficiency typically presuppose the conclusion that there exists a trade-off between these two values. And the conventional empirical treatment of the efficiency/equity relationship has also been flawed for other reasons, reasons that are partly conceptual and partly related to gross deficiencies in the interpretation of available data. These have led to widespread misinterpretation of the actual experience of America, Europe, and the developing world in recent years.

II. The Distribution of Pay

A. Theory: the market myth

The elementary textbook view of markets, wages, profits, and employment states a theological position. *From all according to their average product, to each according to his marginal product.* That is the rule. Everything that is required in order to make the rule hold, including constant returns to scale, perfect competition, a smoothly differentiable production function with well-defined factor inputs (with capital and labor measured in efficiency units and with well-behaved factor-price frontiers[4]), and full employment of resources, is assumed. The rule then implies that an optimum of efficiency and a Pareto maximum of social welfare will be achieved.

It follows that anything that interferes with the market mechanism, so to say, *artificially*, will produce a decline in efficiency. In particular, inter-

[4] For a definition of production functions and factor-price frontiers and a discussion of the technical issues involved in these assumptions, see Geoffrey Harcourt, *Some Cambridge Controversies in the Theory of Capital* (Cambridge: Cambridge University Press, 1972).

ference in the price mechanism will certainly do so. Any increase in my wage—the price of my labor—relative to my marginal product can only discourage my employer from demanding my services. The resulting fall in my employment can only reduce average product, generating a "deadweight loss" under the demand function. This is the "efficiency/equity trade-off": equality *produces* unemployment, and so reduces output and wealth below what they would otherwise be.

A *moral* argument for more equality can still be made. But it is an argument from the heart, not from the head. Those who espouse it are taking a stand against the greater wealth of the larger number. They are suggesting that the price of compassion should be paid. Against this view, there will stand the rigorous conservative, the inveterate logician, to make the case for more output, more accumulation, and a higher growth rate. And under the assumptions, the conservative is not wrong. Given a long enough run, everyone is better off with more output; the power of compound growth trumps the short-run solace of progressive tax and transfer schemes every time.

Usually, by the time a student has been brought along, through enough symbolic reasoning and mathematical derivation, to take seriously all the restrictions on the underlying model and its implications, he or she barely notices that nonsense is being slapped on nonsense.[5] For the entire construct is artificial to begin with. In a world that never was, under conditions designed *a priori* to achieve the ideal, in which, among other things, unemployment is ruled out by construction, change will of course make things worse. An exceptionally scrupulous teacher may remind the student that none of this has application to the world in which we actually live. But such scruples would undermine the incentive to learn the model, and so they are usually relegated to footnotes; the student perceives, first and foremost, the ideological lesson lying in plain view.

This is an academic issue, but only in part. For the elementary textbook view actually dominates popular and policymaking thinking about the great issues of social order in the industrial world today: inequality in America and unemployment in Europe. Rising inequality in America is regrettable, almost everyone claims to agree. But the textbook view tells us that this increase is the result of a changing pattern of marginal products, of "skill-bias" in technological change, a by-product of our informa-

[5] One odd feature of the simple textbook theory is that while it is often used to defend inequality, it actually predicts perfect *equality* of wage rates under the ideal conditions of the model. For if "labor" is a single homogenous input to production, all units of labor should be remunerated at the unique "marginal product of labor." (This is the *law of one price*.) Theorists escape this embarrassment by postulating that differences in pay are due to differing endowments of "human capital"—that they are in fact a form of profit rather than wage income. But that only raises another question, that of how human capital endowments are decided.

tion age.[6] It is therefore the price we pay for full employment. Any effort to regulate pay inequalities would only cost us jobs.[7]

In European discussions, by application of the same principle, unemployment is the price of the welfare state. European rightists, led by tart-tongued organs like the *Economist*, maintain that "a good sign of an efficient job market is a wide gap between the highest and the lowest paid";[8] Europe, they say, is not efficient, and the blame lies with the trade unions and the social democrats and their stubborn resistance to pay cuts. European leftists respond by defending their culture against barbarism *à l'amèricaine*. If unemployment is the price of civilization, they say, so be it! Meanwhile, up to 20 percent of the working-age population of Spain is left unemployed for over twenty years.

In truth, though, not even simple microeconomic theory supports the notion that there is necessarily an efficiency/equity trade-off according to which cutting prices or boosting wages necessarily cuts output. At the start of the Second World War, American price controllers realized that slapping restrictions on prices and controls on high-end wages—radically equalizing the pay structure and the real wage—did not reduce output.[9] Quite to the contrary, production soared, even of civilian goods. A little bit of monopoly-model reasoning helped to explain why: when price controls were imposed, production went from the monopoly-profit maximum toward the competitive-profit maximum, which is higher.[10] In other words, the theoretical idea of the efficiency/equity trade-off *depends* on the competitive-market assumption. But there are no perfectly competitive

[6] The concept of "skill-bias" in technological change is now fading from the economic literature; a thorough appraisal and critique of the concept is given in James K. Galbraith, *Created Unequal: The Crisis in American Pay* (New York: Free Press, 1998), chap. 2.

[7] And so inequality is, as U.S. Federal Reserve chairman Alan Greenspan once testified to Congress, "*outside the scope, so far as I am concerned, of the issues with which we deal.*" Alan Greenspan, testimony to the House Banking Committee, Subcommittee on Domestic and International Monetary Policy, March 5, 1997, quoted in ibid., viii (italics mine).

[8] "Economics Focus: Rich Man, Poor Man," *Economist*, July 24, 1993, 71 (p. 73 in the magazine's UK edition).

[9] Among these price controllers, notably, was the late Walter Salant of the Brookings Institution, a veteran of the Office of Price Administration, from whom I heard this interpretation at a conference in the early 1980s. This argument is of course not intended to explain the full degree of productive expansion during the war; it merely points to the contribution of controls. A recent and dramatic example of the same principle operating in reverse arose in the winter of 2000–2001 in the California electric power crisis. In that case, deregulation and freeing of prices *failed* to produce needed increases in investment and output, and Californians suffered from the predictable consequences of introducing monopoly conditions into what had been a successfully regulated industry.

[10] In the textbook monopoly model, a firm chooses output so that marginal revenue is equal to marginal cost, and prices at the rate the market will bear. This produces the restriction on output, high prices, and excess profits characteristic of classical monopoly. Price controls, however, eliminate the capacity of the firm to raise prices by restricting output; in effect, they flatten the marginal revenue curve. Thus, when subjected to controls, monopolistic firms can be expected in principle to find a new profit maximum at a higher level of output.

markets in real life, and under any other market structure, output and efficiency may increase instead of fall when equality increases.[11]

Larger theoretical issues—macroeconomic issues—also hang over the trade-off idea. John Maynard Keynes's *The General Theory of Employment, Interest, and Money* forced a generation of economists to abandon the assumption that full employment would prevail under free markets.[12] The "paradox of thrift" meant that efforts to increase savings—the exercise of the Victorian virtues of parsimony and abstinence—would only reduce effective demand, consumption, business investment, national income, and so savings itself. Thus, policies to concentrate wealth in the hands of those who would not consume it were misguided. The right thing to do was to drive *down* the rate of profit by forcing *up* the pace of investment, and to do that by spreading out purchasing power and effective demand. As the Cambridge economist Joan Robinson explained:

> The whole elaborate structure of the metaphysical justification for profit was blown up when [Keynes] pointed out that capital yields a return not because it is productive but because it is scarce. Still worse, the notion that saving is a cause of unemployment cut the root of the justification for unequal income as a source of accumulation.[13]

Keynes provided, in other words, a macrotheoretical underpinning for the efficiency of equal distributions. His idea was that the benefits of full employment would prove transcendent.[14] And he saw the reduction of idle financial accumulations, through a more equal distribution of pay and a reduction of the share of profits in total output, as the central element in a policy aimed at full employment. The objective should be to raise spending, not saving. For this, purchasing power had to be delivered to those who would spend freely. This could be done by governments directly, of course, if individuals willing to shoulder the burdens could not be found. But if individuals and households would do it, so much the better:

[11] A similar monopoly/monopsony argument underpins David Card and Alan Krueger's explanation as to why increasing minimum wages does not reduce employment. See David Card and Alan Krueger, *Myth and Measurement: The New Economics of the Minimum Wage* (Princeton, NJ: Princeton University Press, 1995).

[12] John Maynard Keynes, *The General Theory of Employment, Interest, and Money* (London: Macmillan, 1936).

[13] Joan Robinson, *Economic Philosophy* (London: Pelican, 1964), 72–73.

[14] The idea that full employment should be the fundamental policy objective was, of course, always opposed by conservative economists, who in the late 1960s constructed a formidable theoretical argument according to which high rates of unemployment should be accepted in order to avoid runaway rates of inflation. The experience of the late 1990s finally discredited this proposition, and the concepts of a "natural" rate of unemployment and its close relative, the "nonaccelerating inflation rate of unemployment" (NAIRU), have now largely been abandoned.

> Therefore, O patriotic housewives, sally out tomorrow early into the streets and go to the wonderful sales which are everywhere advertised. You will do yourselves good—for never were things so cheap, cheap beyond your dreams. Lay in a stock of household linen, of sheets and blankets to satisfy all your needs. And have the added joy that you are increasing employment, adding to the wealth of the country because you are setting on foot useful activities, bringing a chance and hope to Lancashire, Yorkshire and Belfast.[15]

There is no general reason in economic theory to favor grossly unequal distributions, and there may well be, on several grounds, a pragmatic preference for more equal distributions. But the issue cannot be left as a matter of taste between alternative versions of economic theory. The next question is: which works better in practice?

B. Evidence: equality, employment, and growth

1. Inequality and unemployment across Europe. Take the case of Denmark.[16] It is a small country, nestled in the north of Europe. Unlike its near neighbors Norway, Great Britain, and Holland, it is not floating on seas of oil or gas. Unlike Belgium, which grew rich on the rape of the Congo, Denmark never had major colonies; Greenland is a dud. Unlike Switzerland, Denmark was occupied in World War II; it did not prosper by laundering German money. Denmark also lacks major industry and, apart from fundamental contributions to twentieth-century theoretical physics, it is not a technological power.

And yet Denmark is today the third-wealthiest country of Europe,[17] evidence of strong, consistent, stable economic growth over the decades. It is also roughly the most equal. And it enjoys roughly the lowest unemployment rate in Europe, as well as one of the highest ratios of employment to active population.

Denmark is a prima facie counterexample of the efficiency/equity tradeoff. It is, indeed, a test case for the Keynesian propositions that equality is good for employment and that steady full employment is the key to

[15] John Maynard Keynes, "Economy (1931)," in Keynes, *Essays in Persuasion: The Collected Works of John Maynard Keynes* (London: Macmillan, 1972), 9:138.

[16] I am grateful to Bengt-Aage Lundvall, Sven Larson, and Per Gunnar Berglund for their various insights on the Danish case.

[17] After Norway and Switzerland, judging by per capita gross domestic product (GDP). According to the Luxembourg Income Studies, Denmark's inequality of net household income clocked in at about .24 on the Gini scale in the early 1990s, compared to a value of .34 for the United States at the same time. See the table at Luxembourg Inequality Study, "Income Inequality Measures," available on-line at http://lisweb.ceps.lu/keyfigures/ineqtable.htm. Unemployment rates in Denmark in recent years have been at or below 4 percent.

growth and wealth. Moreover, Denmark is *not* an exception to any rules. There are no tricks of policy here—such as the "active labor-market policies" and flexible work hours often given credit for relatively low unemployment rates in the Netherlands.[18]

Denmark is, rather, the endpoint on a continuum that covers most of the countries of Europe. The rules of this continuum are straightforward. First, lower unemployment means higher income. The high-income countries of Northern Europe systematically enjoy lower rates of unemployment than their less wealthy Southern cousins. Second, lower inequality means lower unemployment. The strong welfare states of Northern Europe have higher employment rates and lower unemployment rates than the relatively inegalitarian countries of the South. These rules apply across all of Europe, as my associates and I have shown in other work.[19] Denmark, about the most equal of them all and one of the richest, merely sets the standard from which other countries of Europe may be judged.[20]

How does this equality/employment connection work, opposed as it is to the logic of the supply and demand model? The answer is truly simple, once you see it. Unemployment is, in part, an expression of stress and of discontent. Measured unemployment rates reflect the desire, and the ability, of people who would otherwise be peasants or on the dole to seek better employment at better pay. When there are few jobs and major pay gaps, it is normal for large numbers of people to go hunting for the few available good jobs. Long queues are the inevitable result.

But in a fairly equal society, low-productivity workers are already being paid well—within shouting range of their more productive compa-

[18] The Netherlands is commonly cited for low unemployment rates, but it has a lower employment-to-population ratio than Denmark, and many fewer hours worked, indicating that part of the Dutch success lies in discouraging people from seeking work, rather than from providing it. The concept of "active labor-market policies" generally refers to training people for appropriate positions, but in the Dutch case the more important element appears to be accommodating the structure of jobs—through short time and flexible hours, for instance—and the attitudes of the population to a low absolute level of employment.

[19] See James K. Galbraith, Pedro Conceição, and Pedro Ferreira, "Inequality and Unemployment in Europe: The American Cure," *New Left Review*, no. 237 (1999): 28–51, also published in James K. Galbraith and Maureen Berner, eds., *Inequality and Industrial Change: A Global View* (Cambridge: Cambridge University Press, 2001). These sources also provide a detailed statistical evaluation of the relationship between income, inequality, and unemployment.

[20] In 1998 Denmark had a GDP per hour of only 92 percent of the average for Organization of Economic Cooperation and Development (OECD) states, well below European norms; moreover, unlike the Japanese, Danes do not work abnormally long hours. They benefit from a larger working population, a higher labor-force participation rate in the population, and low unemployment, and together these factors raise Denmark's GDP per person to 103 percent of the OECD average. Deplorable performance on the same factors explains why the EU-14 as a group yields 103 percent of the OECD average in output per hour but nevertheless has only 90 percent of the OECD average in per capita GDP. See Bart van Ark and Robert H. McGuckin, "International Comparisons of Labor Productivity and Per Capita Income," *Monthly Labor Review* 122, no. 11 (1999): 33–41. (The OECD includes most countries of Western Europe and North America as well as Japan, Korea, Australia, and New Zealand.)

triots. They have, therefore, much less incentive to search for a better job. And highly equal societies subsidize many of the amenities of life, from education to health care to housing. That being so, who wants to leave a pleasant and undemanding low-productivity job? In an equal society, people stay employed where they are, often for a working lifetime. The resulting society may well lack excitement. But it is very capable of producing high levels of output and economic well-being, and it is not an accident that Denmark is both egalitarian and rich.

2. The United States and Europe. Moreover, the laws of economics are the same on all inertial continents. The United States and Europe are not at opposite ends of an inequality/unemployment spectrum. Contrary to what many believe, the United States did not reach full employment by cutting the wages of the poor. To the contrary:

- Were we living under an iron efficiency/equity trade-off in the United States, rising minimum wages would cause unemployment, but as economists David Card and Alan Krueger demonstrated, they do not. California and New Jersey raised minimum wages in the 1980s and unemployment fell; the same thing happened when the national minimum wage was raised in the 1990s.[21]
- Were we living under an iron efficiency/equity trade-off, less skilled workers should be more heavily employed, relatively, in the United States than they are in Europe, but as economist Richard Freeman demonstrated, they are not.[22] The United States and Europe employ roughly similar proportions of skilled and unskilled workers.
- Were we living under an iron efficiency/equity trade-off, then in the United States unemployment should have fallen when inequality rose in the early years of the 1980s, and pay inequalities should have gone up when unemployment fell in the 1990s. But the exact reverse is the case. Unemployment and inequality rise and fall together, month by month and year by year. Using a measure of inequality that relies on manufacturing wages, my associates and I have shown that this relationship holds monthly as far back as January 1947,[23] and annually as far back as 1920.[24]

[21] Card and Krueger, *Myth and Measurement*, marshals this evidence.

[22] Richard Freeman, "The Limits of Wage Flexibility to Curing Unemployment," *Oxford Review of Economic Policy* 11, no. 1 (1995): 63 ff.

[23] James K. Galbraith and Vidal Garza Cantú, "Inequality in American Manufacturing Wages, 1920–1998: A Revised Estimate," *Journal of Economic Issues* 33, no. 2 (1999): 735–43, also published in Galbraith and Berner, eds., *Inequality and Industrial Change*.

[24] Thomas Ferguson and James K. Galbraith, "The American Wage Structure, 1920–1947," *Research in Economic History* 19 (1999): 205–57, also published in Galbraith and Berner, eds., *Inequality and Industrial Change*.

Indeed, the relationship between pay equality and employment is so close[25] as to raise the question of whether these two phenomena are really anything other than different ways of measuring the same underlying economic condition. Unemployment is a measure of the distress of those at the bottom of a statistical distribution of economic outcomes. Measures of pay inequality reflect the divide among those who remain at work. Anything that increases the distress of those at the bottom, weakening the access of low-wage workers to employment, should in principle also weaken the grip of the remaining low-wage workers to their pay—reducing their hours worked each week, and weeks worked each year, as well as their average rate of pay for each hour. And the historical evidence suggests that this is exactly what does happen.

There is thus a continuum between those who are least successful in their working lives and those who do not work at all.[26] This continuum implies that inequality and unemployment should rise and decline together; ample empirical evidence now supports this proposition.[27] Inequality produces unemployment. Unemployment produces inequality. Measures that reduce inequality also reduce unemployment, and measures that reduce unemployment also reduce inequality.[28]

Equality, then, is good for employment and vice versa. But how does this square with the perception that the United States is a low-equality, high-employment country, while Europe has chosen a "high road" of good jobs but high unemployment?

Apart from the matter of capital income,[29] the key to this puzzle lies in another problem of data and perception. The comparison of pay and income inequality between the United States and Europe is always done on a country-to-country basis. For example, the United States might be compared first to Germany, then to France, then to Spain.

And indeed, the United States is more unequal in its distribution of pay than almost any European country: much more so than the Nordic countries or Germany, somewhat more so than France or Britain, and slightly

[25] Economist Sonmez Atesoglu finds that time series of these two variables are highly co-integrated, and that "in the long run there seems to be bi-directional causality between [them]." Sonmez Atesoglu, correspondence with author, July 9, 2000.

[26] As Marx once put it, "[T]he general movement of wages are [*sic*] exclusively regulated by the expansion and contraction of the industrial reserve army, and these again correspond to the periodic changes of the industrial cycle." Karl Marx, *Capital* (London: Lawrence and Wishart, 1974), 1:596.

[27] See Galbraith, *Created Unequal*.

[28] The *Economic Report of the President* (Washington, DC: Government Printing Office, 2000) contains an effective discussion of the relationship between inequality and macroeconomic performance, and admits that this relationship calls into question past assumptions that rising inequality necessarily accompanies improved technology or expanding trade. See ibid., 23–40.

[29] Of which the United States has more than Europe, because the United States has fewer state-owned productive assets and has enjoyed a sustained profits boom in the past decade.

more so than Italy. Thus, a country-to-country comparison can lead to a trade-off view in which the European countries mostly have less inequality and more unemployment. This leaves only a few cases (such as Denmark and the Netherlands) to be explained as anomalies or as users of enlightened interventions such as active labor-market policies.

But we have already noted the presence of a systematic relationship *across* Europe between unemployment and income levels. The richer countries have had, ever since the late 1970s, lower rates of unemployment and higher employment-to-population ratios. Unemployment is minimal in Norway, serious in Germany, harsh in France, and catastrophic in Spain.

The fact that there is a systematic statistical relationship between unemployment rates and national per capita income levels is, in itself, proof of the integration of the European economy in practice. Spain is not an independent and isolated national economy anymore. There are no barriers to trade, or capital flow, nor any formal barriers to the movement of labor throughout Europe. There is now, as well, a single currency unit across the entire region. It is therefore necessary, from a statistical and practical point of view, to measure inequality and employment at the European level and not at the national level.

When this is done, the notion of Europe and the United States being at the opposite ends of an employment/equality spectrum disappears. Inequality within countries of Europe is relatively low. But inequalities between them are very high; much higher than those across comparable distances in the United States. Adding together the two components, inequality within and between countries, one finds that overall inequalities of pay are actually higher in Europe than they are in the United States. Taking account only of pay, Europe, for the present, is both *more* unequal and *less* fully employed than the United States.[30]

To put the matter in another way, low-income European *regions* now behave very much as do lower-income *population groups* in the United States. To be Spanish as opposed to German, for instance, is statistically similar to being black as opposed to white in America: in each case, the former group has roughly 60 percent of the income, and twice the unemployment rate, of the latter. And there is nothing that the Spanish, by themselves, can do about it. Only a reduction of the income gap between Spain and the rest of Europe will reduce the gap in unemployment. And

[30] I have explored the policy implications of this for Europe in other papers, notably Galbraith, Conceição, and Ferreira, "Inequality and Unemployment in Europe." Adding Mexico to the United States would tend to even the comparison, of course, but it would not change the analytical point: along with higher inequality, adding in Mexico would raise the measure of unemployment on the North American land mass. (Adding in Canada, a much smaller country than Mexico, would in past years have reduced measures of inequality and unemployment for North America slightly, but Canadian inequality figures seem to have converged toward U.S. values in recent years.)

a reduction of the income gap can only come about through an expansion of the transfer mechanisms of the European Union (EU).[31]

The larger macroeconomic questions mentioned at the end of the previous, theoretical subsection emerge clearly when Europe as a whole is compared to the United States. How did the United States achieve full employment? In part, it did so by recycling savings and profits into consumption and investment. The technology sector, for instance, has been a mechanism for recycling stock valuations into the employment of young professionals. But equally, and much more important, housing-price increases have been routinely leveraged, through mortgages and home equity loans, into consumption spending, so that ratios of household debt to income reached a historic high of 165 percent in the early part of the year 2000. The household sector, in other words, undertook the expansionary borrowing that the government sector, bent on balancing its accounts, declined to do. The United States does not suffer from any paradox of thrift.

Europe, on the other hand, does suffer from a massive paradox of thrift, made especially intractable by the fact that it falls across national lines. Germany, in particular, is afflicted by an older generation that never recovered from the frugalities of war and postwar reconstruction. That generation has been accumulating vast, unexpected wealth, which it does not know how to consume. And yet there are no adequate means to transfer this purchasing power to Spain, Portugal, Greece, Italy, and Turkey, where there are entire worlds to build, and thirty million unemployed men and women who might be available to build them. Indeed, the residual national identities and separation of populations within traditional boundaries serve as powerful barriers, for the time being, against private recycling of German money to Spain.[32] This in one sentence is the

[31] Presently the EU engages in significant fiscal transfers to national and regional governments; the EU contribution to Portugal, for instance, is on the order of 3 percent of Portugal's GDP. But transfers through the central mechanism of the EU to individual citizens of Europe—the model pioneered in the United States by the Social Security system—are lacking. Such transfers, because they are automatic entitlements and very cheaply administered, are a much more efficient means of reducing income disparities than programs requiring the design and execution of development projects such as highways and housing. It is worth noting, too, that while in accounting terms these systems appear to be transfers from richer to poorer countries, the economic effect is, rather, to mobilize resources that would otherwise be unemployed in the poorer countries, and it is by this means, and not an actual transfer of wealth, that inequalities are mainly reduced. In other words, giving Euro-denominated purchasing power to the elderly in Spain will lead largely to the employment of other Spaniards in caring for the elderly, not in the physical movement of goods and services from Germany to Spain. The proposal, in other words, is for the EU to assume certain responsibilities that the fiscal restrictions of the European Treaty prevent national governments from effectively assuming on their own.

[32] Why are Germans not making mortgage loans on a large scale in Spain? First of all, precisely because Spaniards are too poor! But also because privately managed German capital is as mobile as any other, and in recent years the highest returns have been first in Asia, then in New York and California. Concentrating European resources on European problems will require public mechanisms dedicated to that task.

tragedy of European integration, European inequality, and European unemployment.

3. Inequality and growth in the developing world. Another large area of practical misconception concerns the relationship between economic inequality and economic growth, particularly in the developing world. The great Harvard economist Simon Kuznets long ago hypothesized that in the earliest stages of economic development economic growth might generate increases in inequality. But after the transition to industrialization got underway, Kuznets argued, further increases in total income would tend to bring inequality down. Thus the project of economic development would bring about for poorer countries what it had already achieved in rich ones: the creation of a unified and relatively egalitarian industrial middle class.

This optimistic view has not fared well with recent researchers, and a new consensus has largely rejected Kuznets's conjecture. In a new paper, David Dollar and Aart Kraay of the World Bank note that there is in the recent development literature a "striking absence of any correlation between (changes in) income and (changes in) inequality," and go on to affirm this result in their own analysis.[33] The practical implication is exactly as conservatives argue *a priori*: that a pro-growth strategy need not concern itself with inequality; raising the absolute living standards of the poor at the average growth rate is the best one can do.

But on what is this conclusion based? It is based on a large collection of household-income inequality statistics, assembled by Klaus Deininger and Lyn Squire at the World Bank from virtually every substantial household survey conducted over the postwar period. This data set is now being used in many papers that attempt to assess the role of inequality in economic development. Yet it turns out that Dollar and Kraay are able to find, in this mass of data, just 245 acceptable observations of household-income inequality, covering eighty countries, to match to measures of change in economic growth. This is an average of just three five-year intervals per country—often spaced over very long and erratic intervals of time.

The World Bank's data set is not reliable, not consistent, and not representative of the world economy. Only a handful of countries regularly report income inequality data. Outside of this handful (the United States, the United Kingdom, Sweden, Japan, and Taiwan), the data set is based on estimates that are highly inconsistent through time, simply because social science researchers operating at widely separated intervals on a subject as complex and sensitive as income inequality—without coordinating their efforts, for the most part—are unlikely to come up with estimates that can be sensibly compared. The new consensus finding that

[33] David Dollar and Aart Kraay, "Growth Is Good for the Poor" (working paper of the World Bank Development Research Group, March 2000), 12.

there is no relationship between changes in inequality and changes in growth may either be due to the fact that no such relationship exists, or to the inadequacies and inconsistencies of the data set.

The World Bank's data set is also at variance with facts of common observation. It appears to show, for instance, Spain emerging as the most equal country in Europe in the 1990s. In the 1980s, India is shown as a low-inequality country, in the same ranking quantile as Finland. Between the 1980s and the 1990s, if these data are to be believed, inequality declined in half the countries for which data pairs exist in both decades. This is, of course, complete nonsense.

The only way to examine inequality better is to find better data. In a comprehensive adaptation of major international data sets on industrial employment and payrolls, my colleagues and I at the University of Texas Inequality Project (UTIP) have done exactly that. We have produced a data set capable of showing annual changes in earnings inequality, in manufacturing, for 103 countries over up to thirty-four years, 1963–97—a total of 2,539 separate observations, just over ten times the number of data pairs in the Dollar/Kraay analysis. We have also produced *monthly* estimates of changing earnings inequality over long time periods for Mexico, Brazil, Canada, and the United States.

Analyzing the relationship between changes in inequality and changes in growth in our data set is slow work. So far, though, we have found a systematic negative relationship between inequality and growth in annual data for each of nine large countries in Latin America, with the further finding that actual declines in per capita GDP almost always coincide with increases in inequality of earnings.[34] Contrary to the explicit assertion of Dollar and Kraay, crises are very bad for income distribution. We also find a very striking linear, negative relationship between inequality and growth using measurements based on monthly observations for Mexico and Brazil, and for Mexico we document that currency crises, associated with sharp devaluations of the peso, have drastic effects on distribution of pay.[35]

In contrast to a finding of no relationship, a consistent, stable *negative* relationship cannot be attributed to bad data. Bad data can destroy relationships. But unless there is a showing of systematic bias in measurement (for which no rationale exists in the present context), bad data cannot forge a relationship that is not real. We therefore conclude that the evidence supports what Kuznets argued decades ago against what the

[34] James K. Galbraith and Vidal Garza Cantú, "Grading the Performance of the Latin American Regimes, 1970–1995," in Galbraith and Berner, eds., *Inequality and Industrial Change*. Similar findings have recently been made for about twenty Asian countries, with just a few exceptions.

[35] Paulo Du Pin Calmon et al., "The Evolution of Industrial Wage Inequality in Mexico and Brazil," *Review of Development Economics* 4, no. 2 (2000): 194–203, also published in Galbraith and Berner, eds., *Inequality and Industrial Change*.

World Bank is arguing today. Economic growth is good for equality, and reductions in inequality are generally associated with higher growth.[36]

The UTIP data pose a challenge to the emerging consensus among some development economists that increases in inequality can be disregarded. This emerging consensus is, indeed, rapidly passing into the folk wisdom. Jagdish Bhagwati, an eminent insider in the economics profession, has articulated it forcefully:

> The United Nations Development Program and the World Bank have fallen prey to repeating endless condemnatory variations on the theme that globalization has led to greater income inequality. But even if such a causal relationship could be established—and it has not been—they do not explain why it should matter, given that inequality's consequences will differ hugely across countries, from negative to positive effects.[37]

The UTIP data do not establish a per se relationship between globalization and inequality. But the reason for this is only that the word "globalization" lacks a precise definition, and we cannot evaluate what we cannot measure.[38]

What we do show is that in the overwhelming majority of countries, economic inequality increased drastically in the 1980s and 1990s, most of all on the Eurasian land mass as the Communist economies and their near neighbors collapsed. We further show that these increases in inequality are strongly associated with declines in GDP growth.[39] Our complaint, therefore, is not with globalization alone, but also with the failure of globalized economic institutions to deliver strong and stable economic growth. These failures are indisputable. The serious question is whether they are *necessary* attributes of globalization, or whether better institutions might not produce better results.

[36] All rules have exceptions, and the important one in this case is not the lowest-income countries (as Kuznets supposed) but rather the very highest income countries, those that supply capital goods to the rest of the world economy. In the cases of the United States, the United Kingdom, and Japan, there is a weak positive association between growth and pay inequality, attributable to the fact that the strongest growth rates occur in the investment boom at the start of an expansion.

[37] Jagdish Bhagwati, "Globalization in Your Face," *Foreign Affairs*, July/August 2000, 134–39.

[38] In analyses postdating the drafting of this essay, we do find two mutually distinguishable effects, both of which increase inequality in the global economy. The first is declining national rates of GDP growth, and the second is a dramatic and systematic general increase in inequality levels around the world, beginning in 1981 and persisting through the end of our data set in 1998. We think the most likely explanation for this rise in inequality levels independent of changing GDP is the rise in global real interest rates that took effect in 1981.

[39] Further evidence for this relationship is provided by the nations of Southeast Asia. Unlike most of the rest of the world, inequality in these nations fell in the 1980s and 1990s—at least prior to 1997—but this decline was associated with strong economic growth.

And, contrary to Bhagwati's assertion, there are essentially no cases where rising *pay* inequality—leaving aside the effects of a profits boom on capital valuations—can be shown to have had positive effects on economic development. The policy failures of the era of globalization have produced, and are continuing to produce, economic and social disaster.

C. *What is to be done?*

Within the advanced industrial countries, the mechanics of maintaining a sufficiently equal distribution of pay and income are well worked out. To maintain wages at the bottom of the pay structure, a decent minimum wage is essential; in the United States in recent years, this has been supplemented effectively by the earned income tax credit (EITC).[40] Progressive taxation is the main check on pay at the top of the structure; unions provide an egalitarian impulse at the middle. Social security programs put a floor under the living standards of the elderly and others who are unable to work; public health care (for the elderly only, in the U.S. case) reduces the risk of poverty from catastrophic depletion of savings. Public education and subsidies to higher education complete the picture in most advanced countries. The point to appreciate is not that these institutions exist and function: they plainly do. It is, rather, that they contribute to *improved efficiency* as much as they contribute to *sufficient equality*. They are not, as simple-minded economic theology would sometimes have one believe, mysteriously originating impediments to the achievement of some much richer society that could be achieved through the supposed magic of the market.

To achieve sufficient equality across national lines is a much more difficult problem. The failure to solve this problem is, indeed, the crippling inadequacy to date of the EU. The gap between Spain, Portugal, Greece, and Italy on one side, and Norway, Germany, Denmark, and Sweden on the other, must be narrowed. In other work, I have suggested the steps Europe might take: a "European Pension Union," a continental "topping-up scheme," and a European Morrill Act leading to the establishment of a network of European universities.[41] The usual reaction is that these suggestions are far-fetched and unrealistic. But those reacting

[40] The minimum wage and an EITC scheme (called "topping up") were both recently introduced in the United Kingdom.

[41] James K. Galbraith, "European Unemployment: What Is the Solution?" (remarks presented at the Learning2000 Conference, Lisbon, Portugal, June 6, 2000). A European Pension Union would supplement the national pension payments of lower-income regions and countries, thus working toward the same convergence already achieved for creditors in financial markets through the common currency and equalization of interest rates. A topping-up scheme would amount to a tax credit for working Europeans with relatively low wages. A European Morrill Act would be the European analogue of the American Morrill Act of 1862, the Civil War legislation that established the U.S. system of land grant universities.

in this way rarely have plans of their own for bringing thirty million Europeans into productive employment.

And of course, difficult as it is to secure equality throughout Europe, it is all the more difficult to secure it between the developing countries and the West. But there are periods of time that experienced better results on this latter score than have been achieved in recent decades. In the Bretton Woods period (1945–71), exchange rates rarely changed, and those countries that were parties to the Bretton Woods agreements had access to an international pool of liquidity to support full employment. The resultant financial stability permitted developing countries truly to develop—at growth rates that were characteristically in the neighborhood of 5 to 8 percent per year throughout the developing world. Since the early 1970s, the rise of free capital markets (as a result of the large-scale dismantling of capital controls and the return of private commercial banks to the predominant position in international lending) and floating currencies have cut this norm by half. It is not hard to see the general direction that a corrective policy should begin with. Successful development in the context of reasonably open trade relations requires a firm and stabilizing national and international framework of control over capital flows.[42]

D. A note on inequalities of pay and profit income

Readers may be perplexed by the claim that inequality *declined* in America during the long boom of the 1990s. Didn't reports of rising inequality dominate the news during this time? Weren't liberal commentators (especially) always speaking of the paradox of rising inequality amidst general plenty, and of the plight of those left out? Didn't the "digital divide" emerge as a central issue of recent years?

The resolution of this puzzle lies in the distinction between labor income ("pay") and capital income ("profit"). The former is related to work effort, and is the right construct for any consideration of a systematic relationship between equality and output. The latter is related to patterns of capital ownership. Since these patterns can take any form at all in principle, there is no *a priori* relationship between a shift of aggregate income from wages to profits and the inequality of distribution.

The effect of a shift between wages and profits in the aggregate on inequality depends on who owns capital, and on the sectoral distribution

[42] The construction of such a stabilizing framework in practice will require action in three broad domains: national policy in the developing countries, particularly large countries like China and India that have effectively maintained capital controls; global international policy, in the form of support from the International Monetary Fund and the World Bank for regime stabilization; and probably also regional international policy, in the form of the development of a new network of regional financial authorities, such as the Asian Monetary Fund proposed by Japanese vice-minister of finance Eisuke Sakakibara in the wake of the 1997 Asian financial crisis. Regional monetary funds would administer capital controls for member countries when the latter are too small or practically weak to handle the job alone.

of increases in capital value. In a socialist country, capital is owned by the state, and a shift toward profits would *increase* equality, at least notionally, by raising the relative share of income held in common.

In the United States, some forms of capital are widely held (housing, for instance). Social Security wealth—a form of capital so intangible it is rarely counted, even though it is perhaps the largest form of private wealth in America—is held in common by every working and retired American, and it rises with every increase in Social Security benefit obligations. But financial wealth remains highly concentrated, and common stocks perhaps most of all.[43] Thus, a boom in housing will tend to decrease the inequality of wealth, while a boom in stocks—the defining characteristic of the late 1990s—will increase inequalities in wealth. A boom concentrated in a new-technology sector (by definition closely held) will increase inequality most of all.[44] And the profits boom of the 1990s did in fact increase measured inequalities of income, due to the rising share of capital in total income. As my UTIP colleagues and I show in other work, receivers of sharply higher incomes in the United States were remarkably localized in a handful of counties spread across the country: New York County, King County (Washington), and Santa Clara County (California) were prominent among them, for reasons that will not surprise anyone with a grasp of industrial geography in the United States.[45]

But none of these changes in capital-asset valuation has anything to do with work effort, the productivity of work, or the efficiency of economic life for most Americans.[46] For most Americans, it is *pay equality* that matters for the pragmatic questions of the factitious efficiency/equity trade-off. And pay inequality did decline with the decline of unemployment in the 1990s, improving economic efficiency and social welfare in measure. The inequality of the distribution of wealth, on the other hand, has mainly political implications, to which we now turn.

[43] Familiar statistics show, for instance, that ownership of financial assets in the United States is highly concentrated: the top 1 percent of households held 38.93 percent of net worth and 48.17 percent of financial wealth in 1989, according to Edward N. Wolff, *Top Heavy: A Study of the Increasing Inequality of Wealth in America* (New York: Twentieth Century Fund, 1995), 11. However, these numbers are sensitive to fluctuations in the valuation of corporate stock and housing (as Wolff shows), and also to the inclusion or exclusion of such intangibles as Social Security wealth. See also the important work of Lisa A. Kiester, *Wealth in America: Trends in Wealth Inequality* (Cambridge: Cambridge University Press, 2000), 87 ff.

[44] In the late 1990s, furthermore, the increasing use of stock options to pay high-level managers in the technology sectors caused a distinct blurring of categories, as rising capital values led to perceived increases in the inequality of measured *earnings* in the manufacturing economy.

[45] See the UTIP website at http://utip.gov.utexas.edu for illustrations.

[46] Had the shares of Microsoft been redistributed by Judge Thomas Penfield Jackson from William Gates to all past purchasers of his operating systems—truly a suitable antitrust penalty—then any further rise in Microsoft's share prices would have had an equalizing rather than a monopolizing effect on the distribution of measured wealth. Nothing else, apart possibly from the patterns of residential development on the shores of Lake Washington, would have changed at all.

III. The Distribution of Wealth

A. Equality and political participation

A basic theory of the relationship between wealth equality and the legitimacy of political life can be drawn from the philosopher John Rawls.[47] On his account, inequality is a form of information.[48] A more unequal society defines its members more sharply in terms of their positions in the distribution: the poor know that they are poor, the rich know that they are rich. Thus they are, and thus they will remain.

To be born into a society with a relatively *equal* distribution of capital wealth is therefore (and conversely) akin to being brought up behind the famous veil of ignorance about one's own future position in that society. As Rawls argues, only from behind such a veil can one make appropriate decisions and judgments about the rules of political life—including of course the appropriate distribution of capital assets.

Furthermore, as political scientist Thomas Ferguson has argued in a scathing blend of political theory and topical observation, the elementary economics of the savings function assures that only those with access to substantial capital income will participate fully in political life.[49] Usable capital assets are for the rich. For the middle classes they are largely illiquid: one cannot commit one's home or pension fund to a political cause. For working people they are largely hypothetical, and apart from trade union dues they cannot be mobilized effectively for political use. That being so, modern politics in the United States substantially excludes the nonrich populations, and boils down instead to competitions and coalitions among groups from the investor classes.

In a highly unequal society, therefore, there is a presumption of illegitimacy about social arrangements. These have been made with full regard to the political position and the wealth of particular competing industrial and financial groups, and with each of these groups fully knowing the direct effect, to them, of alternative outcomes. Only a strong dimension of countervailing power[50]—something far more visible in America fifty years ago than it is today—can assure participation by lobbies of labor, the elderly, racial minorities, and so forth. And no one speaks effectively for the unorganized worker or the truly poor, and partly for this reason such individuals do not find it worthwhile even to vote.

[47] John Rawls, *A Theory of Justice* (Cambridge, MA: Harvard University Press, 1971).

[48] From a mathematical standpoint, measures of inequality are actually derived from measures of information. See the discussion in James K. Galbraith and Pedro Conceição, "Constructing Long and Dense Time Series of Inequality Using the Theil Statistic," *Eastern Economic Journal* 26, no. 1 (2000): 61–74, also published in Galbraith and Berner, eds., *Inequality and Industrial Change*.

[49] Thomas Ferguson, *Golden Rule* (Chicago: University of Chicago Press, 1998).

[50] See John Kenneth Galbraith, *American Capitalism: The Concept of Countervailing Power* (Boston: Houghton Mifflin, 1952).

These considerations are matters of plain common sense, but it may still be useful to consider them from a more abstract point of view. Why is it that a coalition of bankers, say, cannot be trusted with the larger public interest? The answer lies not in the specific moral deficiencies of banking, as such. Rather, it lies in the dynamics of any small group that operates in its own self-interest within the larger public domain.

As political participants, people have multiple identities. They are members of a neighborhood, citizens of a state, professionals or laborers of a certain type, members of a trade union, members of a particular ethnic group, members of a particular gender. Why do some identities come to dominate and others to recede? Why do bankers generally form a cohesive political force while retail clerks do not? Why, in America, do certain racial minorities (blacks, in particular) form a fairly cohesive political identity while the ostensible racial majority (whites) consists in fact of a mosaic of distinct and fairly rivalrous subgroups?

The answer lies in the ability of a group to *differentiate* itself from the median identity of the society as a whole. Identity *is* distinctness. "White" is not a distinct identity to most people who happen to be white in America (and among Northerners, at least in certain circles, the term carries a certain stigma). Whites are white to nonwhites but not, particularly, to themselves. Black, on the other hand, is an identity that those who are black cannot generally escape, even should they want to.

But while people may have many identities, surely the most powerful differentiator of otherwise similar individuals is capital wealth. This is because the *creation* of identity requires resources. Retail clerks—with every good reason to mobilize themselves politically in favor of, for instance, mandatory vacations or a higher minimum wage—lack the resources to create such an identity for themselves. Bankers, on the other hand, have both the motive and the means.

Anyone with experience of the politics of banking law[51] understands the consequences of this form of economic organization. Banking legislation is about the legal authority of banks vis-à-vis their clients, their depositors, and competing financial institutions. Of these three foci, typically the latter predominates. Why? Because it entails decisions among *competing* groups of the wealthy and powerful—between banks and investment banks (historically, over the terms of the Glass-Steagall law separating commercial and investment banking[52]), between banks and savings and loan institutions (over the terms of regulation historically

[51] The present author spent a number of years as the staff economist for the Committee on Banking, Finance, and Urban Affairs in the U.S. House of Representatives.

[52] The Glass-Steagall Act was enacted in 1933; it prohibited commercial banks from undertaking the functions of investment banks, and vice versa. Thus it separated the functions of lending to and evaluating business operations from speculative intervention in corporate ownership and control, and formed an important safeguard against the financial abuses that had led to the crash of 1929 and subsequent Great Depression.

favoring the latter), and so on. Issues relating to the rights of consumers (for instance, privacy legislation) or of neighborhoods (for instance, the Community Reinvestment Act[53]) play a far smaller role in the life of a banking legislator in the U.S. Congress.

An interesting case of constructed political identity in America (one that so far has not spread to other nations) can be found in the emergence over twenty years of the "information economy." Prior to 1980, this term was never heard; famously, the "technostructure" was considered an element of the large corporation—the intelligentsia of AT&T or International Business Machines.[54] But in the late 1980s a distinct identity emerged, and with it a political agenda, centered first on protecting U.S. electronics firms from Japanese competition, and later on such industry-specific national issues as immigration requirements for skilled programmers, the penetration of the Internet into schools and libraries, a tax moratorium on electronic commerce, and so on. Skillful political figures have not been slow to appreciate the fund-raising potential of this new and highly concentrated center of wealth; much of the adulation focused on the "new-economy entrepreneurs" can be seen as a form of flattery aimed at consolidating their political support, or at least preventing them from defecting to the other side.[55]

It may be that the political agenda of a particular sector will be narrow and of little direct concern to the larger public. It may be, in the case of the information industry's agenda, that the effects are more on the *form* of civic life than on the general well-being of the population. Nevertheless, all such agendas entail political choices. The drive to accommodate software companies on immigration comes into direct conflict with the desire of a particularly powerless group—recent immigrants from poor countries—to take advantage of the priority under existing law for family reunification. The pressure to exempt electronic commerce from state and local sales taxation creates a powerful incentive to buy on the Internet, and a corresponding drain on state and local tax coffers. School and library spending on computers, and the technicians to maintain them, comes directly at the expense of books, art supplies, and musical instruments. In all of these cases, a powerful and wealthy element is pitted against a diffuse and much more weakly organized one, and the preferences of the powerful element are likely to prove dispositive in the political system.

[53] The Community Reinvestment Act (CRA) imposes certain requirements on banks to make loans in neighborhoods from which they draw deposits, and to provide public accountability for their use of depositors' funds. Senator Phil Gramm (R-TX), formerly chair of the Senate Banking Committee, has declared that the CRA requirements are "worse than slavery." Even allowing that this quotation may reflect the good Senator's benign view of that antebellum institution, it is a particularly strong sign of the power of banking interests over banking law.

[54] John Kenneth Galbraith, *The New Industrial State* (Boston: Houghton Mifflin, 1967), 71.

[55] The elaborate courtship that attends a figure like William Gates on any appearance in Washington—notwithstanding his legal difficulties—is, of course, a premier case in point.

It follows generally that one cannot expect for a group organized along sectarian lines and distinguished by great wealth to have a larger interest in mind. Wealth entails separation, separation entails special interest, special interest entails conflict—or at the least the risk of conflict—with the common well-being.

B. Inequality and the welfare state

Possibly the most severe consequence of the separation and distinctiveness engendered by highly unequal wealth distribution is felt by the welfare state. What is the welfare state? It is a set of public institutions that provide in common and on a universal basis for a number of goods that can be provided privately in principle and that historically have been reserved to those who could pay by private means. These include basic and higher education, health care, and insurance against disability and old age.

Welfare states exist only in egalitarian societies, and their strength is directly proportional to the equality of the distribution of wealth. In the extreme cases, under Communist regimes, capital assets are not privately held at all, and all social benefits have to be publicly provided.[56] Social democratic governments—the Scandinavians and Germans—elaborately provide the full panoply of welfare benefits from the public budget. But even in countries avowedly devoted to free markets, public provision is the rule. The government of the United States provides the bulk of retirement income to America's elderly, and covers about half of all U.S. expenditures on health care. American states and localities provide the vast majority of education services. Even such an ostensibly capitalist locality as Texas—historically dependent on Eastern capital—funds the major part of its higher education system by using public resources.

Still, the tendency of those with concentrated wealth is to continue to provide for themselves. In the first instance, this leads to the maintenance of private schools, colleges, universities, hospitals, and pension funds, as well as security services and other amenities of life.[57] None of these per se are to be objected to. But the natural next thought of the wealthy person is, if I am paying for all these services for myself, and at premium prices, why should I also pay for them for everyone else? There follows the unremitting pressure of the lobbies against progressive or even proportional taxation, with results that are everywhere in the tax code. We see the Social Security payroll tax capped such that it does not apply to

[56] Often, though, this was achieved through the institutional framework of the state-owned firm, an arrangement that tied the provision of social benefits to the fate of the enterprise when Communism collapsed (as in the Soviet Union) or when reform opened such firms to competition (as in China). The Western social democratic system, which puts education, health care, and most pensions *directly* under the state, has proved the more successful model.

[57] It is not coincidental that private universities—to name an ultimate luxury good—prosper mainly in close geographic proximity to major centers of capital income.

income above $76,200 at present writing. We see the reduced maximum tax rate on capital gains income—a form earned exclusively by holders of capital wealth. We see the pressure to abolish taxation of gifts and estates.[58] We see the pressure against income taxation and in favor of sales taxation, at both the federal and the local levels.

To the extent that these pressures are successful, the burden of payment for public services falls increasingly on the middle class.[59] And because the upper and lower classes are disproportionately large in unequal societies, the middle class finds the burden heavy and hard to take. Thus, excessive inequality in the distribution of capital assets is likely to set up a chain reaction down the bell curve; those in the middle may be motivated to oppose public benefits that they would actually like to have, simply because they cannot afford to provide them both for themselves and for those who cannot pay anything at all.

In this way, excessive and growing inequality of wealth—even in a wealthy country—is a pernicious enemy of public services. It is not an accident that declines in the political base of the welfare state are associated, everywhere, with increasing dispersion in the wealth distribution, nor that the media organs of the wealthy[60] are the most inveterate enemies of public programs.

C. *What is to be done?*

The remedy for all of this is surely not a perfectly egalitarian distribution of wealth. It is not (as was done in China under the Cultural Revolution) the tearing down of professional classes and the ending of economic differentiation. It is also probably not—as many good American liberals suppose—a campaign finance reform package that would somehow eliminate the pernicious influence of great wealth on political life without

[58] The move to repeal the U.S. estate and gift taxes in the summer of 2000 appears to have reflected in part the particular concerns and rising political importance of the new-economy millionaires. Though for the most part this was a party-line issue, repeal had support from Western Democrats and opposition from Eastern Republicans. This suggests a rift between the information economy tycoons, largely from the West, and the insurance companies, headquartered in the East. The former were protecting their newly won paper fortunes, largely tied up in the stock of their own companies, while the latter stood to lose a lucrative line of business insuring small enterprises against estate tax liability. Repeal ultimately passed Congress but was vetoed by President Clinton; the issue is, however, likely to return in the new administration.

[59] In rebuttal to this argument, conservatives sometimes cite the high fraction of federal income taxes that continue to be paid by those in the highest income percentiles. But this is mainly a reflection of the high fraction of total income earned by those in the highest percentiles, and of the fact that the federal income tax is one of the few taxes that are progressive in their incidence. It remains necessarily the case that as taxes are shifted from the upper percentiles toward the middle, the burden decreases on the former and increases on the latter.

[60] For instance, the magazines *Forbes* and the latter-day *Fortune*, as well as the editorial page of the *Wall Street Journal*.

eliminating the concentration of wealth itself. This last measure will not do more than merely mask the influence of the wealthy.

Rather, the answer lies in seeking—as with pay and income, but for different reasons—a *sufficiently* equal distribution of capital wealth. The rich should be taxed. Their charitable gifts and foundations should be strongly encouraged by tax law, including especially estate and gift taxation. They should not be treated with undue deference by those who are not directly fawning over their money. But all this is only part of the solution.

The other part, much more important, lies in creating forms of capital wealth that the rest of society can partake of. Of these—to take the American case as an example—Social Security wealth has been historically perhaps the most important. The capital value of Social Security in the United States is enormous—it measures in the trillions of dollars—and it has lifted the entire elderly population of the country out of poverty since the early 1970s. It is not by accident that the elderly retain one of the more potent political voices in the country not directly tied to any *private* form of wealth-holding. All measures that strengthen Social Security transfer implicit capital wealth to the elderly.

Housing is another form of capital wealth of great importance. This is the middle American family asset. The extension of home ownership to two-thirds of American households by the end of the 1990s was a major accomplishment of the economic expansion of that decade. Unfortunately, however, there was a price: heavy indebtedness, so that in the near term home ownership is not necessarily synonymous with capital wealth. People are "house poor." This can be cured, of course—as it was in the 1960s and early 1970s—by measures of public policy that stabilize or even reduce mortgage debt relative to home value, the most important being a lower and stable interest rate. Indeed, the debates over U.S. monetary policy can be seen as a masked but direct argument over the distribution of wealth: should it be reallocated steadily from debtors to creditors, as a high real rate of interest necessarily implies, or should wealth instead be reallocated back toward the debtor classes—homeowners—through a rate of interest lower than the rate of growth of incomes?

Finally, there is education, the capital asset of the young. Higher education in particular has become the ticket to creditworthiness in the United States; you virtually cannot refuse a mortgage to an applicant with a college degree. At present, 26 percent of the adult population of the United States holds at least a college degree, a proportion not closely rivaled anywhere in the world, except for the Netherlands.[61] Measures that expand access to America's colleges and universities—such as grants and low-interest loans—are well-established, highly effective ways in which class barriers can be, and historically have been, reduced in the United States.

[61] And about half the U.S. adult population has the next best thing—*some* experience with college or university education.

Sufficient equality in the distribution of wealth—sufficient, that is, for a tolerable political life—can be constructed, even in a society characterized and partly dominated by private capital. It is a matter, mainly, of making sure that nonpecuniary forms of capital—social security wealth, housing, and education above all—are generously supported and paid for in good measure from capital incomes. This was, indeed, the mid-twentieth-century solution, though it was badly eroded toward the end. It was a sensible resolution of a classic problem—the reconciliation of capitalism with freedom, equity with efficiency, and democracy with private power—the first in all history, and the only one so far. A better one is not likely to come along.

IV. Conclusion

Sufficient equality in the distribution of income, within a country, is a proper goal of efficient economic policy, and is part of a strategy for shared prosperity and full employment; it is both effect and cause. The means for achieving sufficient equality are varied, but straightforward: minimum wages, collective bargaining, social insurance, and effective public payment of major medical expenses. The main obstacles to these modest goals are political; they are not economic.

Sufficient equality in the distribution of wealth helps to resolve the political questions. If ordinary households have adequate capital assets—education, housing, social security wealth, and a financial reserve—they will and do participate in democratic governance, with a decent respect both for those who have less than themselves and for those who have more.[62] Likewise, a functioning democratic society does not organize its members into ghettos, neither of the poor, nor of the rich.

Across international lines, these issues are more difficult. International lines exist, in part, to preserve inequality. But given global economic relations (or, as in Europe, continental integration), the question of inequality must be dealt with across national frontiers. Here, the essence of the issue is convergence. And the essence of convergence is, simply, getting more rapid economic growth in poor nations than in rich ones. To achieve this, on a sustained basis over decades, must become the task of a new international development architecture, one that includes a new system of international financial stabilization and control. This is no simple matter, but is clearly necessary, as the existing system of free global capital markets has failed.

Lyndon B. Johnson School of Public Affairs, University of Texas at Austin

[62] In a famous old Texas story, Robert Montgomery of the University of Texas Department of Economics was once summoned to explain his views to the legislature of that state. The first question was, "Dr. Montgomery, do you believe in private property?" And the answer came back, "Why yes, Senator, I do believe in private property. I believe in it strongly. And I think everyone in Texas should have some." The hearing is said to have ended at once.

DOES INEQUALITY MATTER—FOR ITS OWN SAKE?

By Alan Ryan

I. Introduction

This is a simple essay. It raises a familiar question about equality, adduces a very small amount of empirical evidence about the social consequences of *equality* as distinct from *prosperity*, and broods on the difficulty of providing a really persuasive answer to the question raised. I begin with the view that there simply cannot be anything intrinsically wrong with inequality, move on to the view that there are extrinsic reasons for anxiety, dividing these into conceptual and empirical reasons, though without any great commitment to the clarity of that distinction in this context, and end with some reflections on recent social and political theory. The essay thus begins with what I hope are clear and (what I am sure are) very simple thoughts, before muddying the water pretty thoroughly thereafter.

II. Inequality Is Morally Unproblematic: Hobbesian Themes

There is a tendency in the literature on theories of justice to assume that equality is the baseline, moral and intellectual, from which all discussion starts. Theories of desert, for instance, that explain desert in terms of providing "ambition-sensitive justifications of departures from equality" assume that equality is the baseline and that departures from it need justification, while equality itself does not.[1] I repudiate that view here, not so much because I think it is simply wrong as because its acceptance would serve no useful purpose. On the one hand, it would beg the question if it were to be construed as saying "Yes, it is true that inequalities are prima facie wrong"; and on the other, it would entangle us in some old and unprofitable arguments about what *sort* of inequality is wrong. Better, therefore, to begin by repudiating the idea that inequality needs justification in a way that equality does not.

The thought behind my repudiation is this: Imagine as a thought experiment that an egalitarian places on two plates identical meals, equal in size, nutritional content, and composition. They are not substantial meals; let us say they each amount to a rare quarter-pound cut of fillet steak, a small helping of French fries, and a little green salad. One plate is set

[1] The phrase is Ronald Dworkin's; see Ronald Dworkin, *Sovereign Virtue* (Cambridge, MA: Harvard University Press, 2000), 23.

before a newborn baby, the other before a hungry truck-driver. Both are outraged, though the latter is more articulate about it than the former. Have we treated them equally? It seems to me that we have. Have we treated them sensibly, properly, fairly, in a utility-maximizing, rights-respecting fashion? It seems to me that we have not.

Now, the egalitarian who thinks that equality needs no defense while inequality does will wriggle his or her way out of this problem by insisting that equality does not mean literal equality, since no amount of wriggling can evade the point that these meals are equally nutritious, identically constituted, and so on and so forth. What equality means to the egalitarian, if it does not mean literal equality, is not easy to say, however. If, for instance, it means that each meal should be equally suitable to the needs of the consumer, the morally relevant element of this is that a meal ought to be *suitable*. That both meals should be *equally* suitable adds nothing to the thought that both should be suitable. The irrelevance of equality can be seen by extending the thought experiment a little. Suppose we can achieve *one* suitable meal only. In this case, we have the ingredients to make a truck-driver's special for the driver, but not the ingredients to feed the newborn. We may regret that we cannot do what we ought for the baby, but we would not think it morally more satisfactory to throw away the trucker's meal and achieve parity of unsuitability. Certainly, on the one hand we must behave fairly, but on the other we must achieve as much good as possible if we are to act in a morally serious fashion. It would be unfair to care less about the baby than the trucker, but equality as such does not in a context such as this compete with other values, such as fairness or efficiency.

Given this thought, I turn to the view that inequalities of income and wealth *cannot* be intrinsically objectionable. Everything hangs on the idea of intrinsic objectionableness, of course, and it may be that many readers will think that I achieve my object by shutting out so many obvious anxieties about inequality that my case reduces to vacuity. It does not matter if I do, because the extrinsic considerations carry as much weight as a rational egalitarianism requires, but I shall take the risk in any event. The grandfather of rational choice theory is, arguably, Thomas Hobbes. Hobbes relies on the thought that human beings are motivated to act by the desire to achieve their own greatest apparent good.[2] Underpinning this thought is Hobbes's physicalist understanding of human beings: according to this, we are self-maintaining automata, whose behavior is governed by the imperative to avoid our own extinction and to maximize the flow of vital motions about the heart; the appearance of the flow of vital motions to us is the psychological experience of happiness.[3] This is not a doctrine of *selfishness* in the ordinary sense, since the goals to which

[2] Thomas Hobbes, *Leviathan* (New York: W. W. Norton, 1997), 32.
[3] Ibid., 32.

we are attracted are not always such as to damage the interests of others in favor of the interests of ourselves. It is a doctrine of *self*-regardingness in the sense that any goal whatever that we are moved to pursue must be part of the set of things that *we* value. An unselfish person is not one whose preferences bear no relation to himself, but one whose desire for the welfare of others motivates his pursuit of his goals. My goals are *my* goals, even if the achievement of my goals does you good.

One interesting feature of the Hobbesian account of these topics that bears directly on the topic of inequality has not survived into recent and more technically sophisticated theorizing. Hobbes suggests ways in which a concern with equality and inequality seeps into our motivations even though he has the same reasons as every other rational choice theorist to leave equality and inequality out of the discussion. One might think that if *we* are concerned with what (truistically) concerns *us*, we need not concern ourselves with how everyone else is faring. My welfare is *my* welfare, my utilities are derived from the satisfaction of *my* preferences, and that is the end of it. But for Hobbes, two things spoil the story. First, Hobbes's value-skepticism leads him to suppose that we want what "appears good" to us; there is no objective condition of something *being* good other than by reference to us. "Calling good" is the fundamental notion, as in Hobbes's claim that "whatsoever is the object of any man's Appetite or Desire, that it is, which he for his part calleth *Good*."[4] Desire projected onto objects of desire produces what one might think of as an optical illusion, the appearance of objective value. Hobbes is in this way a precursor of Bertrand Russell and John Mackie, offering a form of "error theory of value" almost three centuries before they do. But Hobbes also supposes that we are unsure about what we want; since our bodies are in constant motion, our desires are so as well. There is no summum bonum, no condition of felicity in which we are satisfied and at rest; rather, felicity consists in continually prospering.[5] In the absence of agreed objective standards of the good life, we are likely to wonder whether we are prospering as much as we might. Hobbes supposes that we create a surrogate value-objectivity in the objects of our desire by using the envy of others as the test of our own success. Just as, in Robert Nozick's treatment of standards, the basketball player thinks he is really pretty good until the day he encounters the likes of Wilt Chamberlain, so Hobbesian man thinks he is doing pretty well until he encounters the neighbor who is eating a bigger apple or wearing a thicker sheepskin.[6] Once we see what we *might* have, what we actually have is dust and ashes in our mouths; conversely, when we see that our neighbor's satisfaction has turned to dust and ashes, what we have tastes all the sweeter. This is not an exercise

[4] Ibid.

[5] Ibid., 37.

[6] See Robert Nozick, *Anarchy, State, and Utopia* (New York: Basic Books, 1974), 240–42; and Hobbes, *Leviathan*, 69–70.

in pure malice or in wishing ill upon our neighbors. Rather, the natural extension of the search for the things that enhance the flow of vital motions about the heart is the search for a supergood; this supergood is the knowledge that we are the envy of others, and that we *must* be doing well. The process gets out of hand when nothing will satisfy us but the knowledge that we are the envy of everybody. Hobbes is uninclined to complain about human nature, and he thinks nothing a sin unless there is a law—divine, natural, or conventional—against it. Nevertheless, the desire to be preeminent comes close to counting as the fundamental flaw in human nature; "glory" is the hardest of passions for a state to subdue.[7]

The second way in which comparisons enter the argument would for most writers constitute a subject distinct from the discussion of inequalities of income and wealth. This subject is the acquisition of power. Almost all of us distinguish wealth from power. Hobbes, however, gives a perfectly general definition of power as the means we have present to attain some future apparent good, and is quite clear that wealth is power.[8] Since Hobbes places first among human passions a restless striving for power upon power that ceases only with death, it is a central part of Hobbes's argument to explain the search for power and to show how it can be contained. But it is worth pausing momentarily to distinguish Hobbes from almost everyone else in the literature of political theory on this topic. Machiavelli, to take the obvious counterpart, deplored economic inequality because of its political consequences, such as the rise of a self-seeking, vicious, vainglorious, and corrupt aristocracy, whose retainers and hangers-on disturb the peace and make the efficient conduct of war, diplomacy, and commerce impossible. Machiavelli also says that the possession of excessive riches by some will lead others to lose sight of both the military virtues and the private or domestic virtues, and will lead to the downfall of the republic—a theme to which I shall return in due course.

Hobbes has no interest in this argument, famous and long-lived though it is. Hobbes's point is simpler. We seek power because we want to control the future; income and wealth are means to that control, just as the possession of a .45-caliber revolver is. There are not two topics, the one economic inequality and the other its political consequences. Hobbes subsumes the economic in the political, because he sees wealth as essentially comparative, and believes that the basic unit of currency is power. The point of power is control; the unpredictability of nature set to the side, the chief obstacle to *my* control is the will of other men, backed up by whatever resources they can muster. It follows that I am rich to the extent that others are not. If I have $10,000 and nobody else has more than $1,000, then the painting on the wall of your studio is mine for a few dollars; if

[7] Hobbes, *Leviathan*, 56–57.
[8] Ibid., 55 ff.

everyone else has $10,000, the price goes up, my certainty of having the painting goes down, and my utility is so much the less.

Like his successors among the utilitarians, Hobbes thinks that the controlled competition of the marketplace is benign in (most of) its effects, and believes that controlling the use of lethal weapons is a more urgent and more central task for a state than controlling the way we make and spend money. Unlike his successors, he does not draw a sharp distinction between the uncoercive exchanges of the market and the coercive regulation of the state; all he is concerned with is which exercises of "power" have to be controlled and in what way it might most effectively be done. *One* way, besides the familiar methods of social and ideological control that *Leviathan* sets out for Hobbes's sovereign to employ, is to persuade individuals to retain the focus on their own satisfactions that is in some sense natural to us, but from which we can easily be distracted. That is, we must consider whether we are contented by what we have and what we do, not whether we are as contented as others or whether what we have is as good as what they have. Hobbes's emphasis on the conventionality of marks of distinction is intended not only to stop the aristocracy from making unjustified claims to a natural title to govern, but to encourage all of us to suppress status-based or esteem-based appraisals in favor of more sensible ones. The difficulty, of course, is that Hobbes's epistemological skepticism deprives him of a wholly cogent standard of what is sensible.

III. Inequality Is Morally Unproblematic: John Rawls's Argument

We must leap forward now to the most familiar argument in the recent literature to the effect that inequality *in itself* is not a problem. This comes in a work that argues exactly what I have denied, that inequality needs justification in a way that equality does not. In John Rawls's *A Theory of Justice*, the contracting parties hidden behind the "veil of ignorance," making their hypothetical contract with one another, each focus on his or her own welfare alone.[9] In Rawls's terminology, they are mutually disinterested; they derive no pleasure from the success of others, and they derive no pleasure from the failures of others.[10] This is not, of course, an account of the parties' actual motivations, since they are hypothetical persons, and it is not an account of ordinary human motivation in the real world; the real world, with its sins and errors, reappears only late in the narrative. The requirement of mutual disinterest is a way of shadowing into the hypothetical contract-making situation the denial that envy is a morally legitimate motivation in the real world. Similarly, Rawls credits

[9] John Rawls, *A Theory of Justice* (Cambridge, MA: Harvard University Press, 1971).
[10] Ibid., 13 ff.

his hypothetical contractors with a highly implausible degree of risk aversion, not because he thinks we are risk averse in our ordinary lives, but to shadow into the motivation of the contractors the moral requirement that we not take risks with other people's lives and welfare.[11]

So, we have the notion that if we were mutually disinterested, there could be nothing wrong with inequality as such. Each of us is concerned with his or her own well-being, and the well-being of others does not impinge thereon. I think that this is, however elaborately fleshed out, the sum total of the argument. It is what lies behind such familiar defenses of inequality as the reminder that "unless some drive Rolls Royces, none will drive Fords," or as Locke observed, that the day laborer in England lives, lodges, and is clothed better than the Native American chief, although there is no unequal division of the land in "inland America."[12] Rawls, like Locke, insists that we are to look to the welfare of each individual; *what* he or she possesses can be described independently of what anyone else possesses, and we can distinguish between *how well off* we are and *how satisfied we are with how well off we are*. The latter is vulnerable to envy, spite, malice, and all sorts of unattractive motivations—and it should be noticed that it is not only the envy of the poor that comes into the narrative but the pride and self-congratulation of the well off. A person who would choose to have $100 worth of real consumption possibilities so long as others have only $50 worth, rather than $500 worth on the condition that others also have $500 worth, is as misguided as the poor man who would rather have $100 all round than $500 for himself and $1000 for many others.

Rawls's justification of inequality is that unequal rewards to those who take part in economic cooperation is a good bargain for the people at the bottom of the income and wealth distribution, so long as high rewards for some really are a condition of the well-being of all. This is the case exhaustively discussed for the past three decades. It is worth noticing that it is unlike the libertarian case, which sees no cause to justify any distribution whatever, so long as it emerges from the exploitation of "entitlements," which is to say our property rights in ourselves and externals, or, in a larger sense, from luck. It is also unlike the utilitarian case, which from Bentham onwards holds that the target of social policy is overall welfare, that diminishing marginal utility is sufficiently common to make it prima facie right to equalize the distribution of income and wealth, and that the interesting questions are then about the countervailing considerations—issues of incentive above all—that justify departures from equality.[13] Finally, there are "baseline" theories that eschew *equality* as a moral goal, but argue that social

[11] See Rawls's discussion of slavery at ibid., 167 ff.

[12] John Locke, *Two Treatises of Government*, ed. Peter Laslett (Cambridge: Cambridge University Press, 1967), 314–15.

[13] Jeremy Bentham, *Theory of Legislation* (London: Trubner, 1887), 104.

policy should somehow or other ensure that there is a welfare baseline beneath which we do not suffer people to fall. Rawls, utilitarians, and baseline theorists frequently sustain similar policy recommendations in the real world, but they do so for different reasons.

IV. Psychological Effects of Inequality

If inequalities of income and wealth are not intrinsically objectionable, we should consider the extrinsic objections to them, that is, the objections to their effects. An entire tradition of political theory has been devoted to this topic, and it would be all too easy to start with Plato and never emerge from *The Republic*. Accordingly, I shall simplify savagely, and offer abbreviated accounts of some well-known criticisms of the psychological, political, and economic effects of inequality; I will then gesture at some interesting empirical evidence that connects high levels of economic inequality with a generally lowered level of well-being.

The greatest critic of inequality's psychological impact was Rousseau. His seminal essay *Discourse on the Origins of Inequality among Men* was misunderstood by Engels when he declared that it was the first work of historical materialism.[14] Certainly, Rousseau sketches an account of the origin of classes and class conflict that resembles what Engels offered a century and a half later; both accounts are tied to a hypothetical history of the creation of property rights in land (as distinct from informal rights to the undisturbed enjoyment of items of immediate consumption and use).[15] But Rousseau understands his own intentions better when he describes himself as a painter of the human heart. The process in which he is interested is that whereby human beings changed through long historical evolution from creatures indistinguishable from other intelligent animals into rational and moral creatures. This evolution was both progress and regress. It was progress, because Rousseau never doubts that the acquisition of rationality and a moral sense was progress; it was regress because we lost the simple natural balance of animal life and instead made ourselves miserable. "Civilized man is a depraved animal" was one of the remarks by which Rousseau enraged contemporaries like Voltaire.

Rousseau's thought is this: Prior to our historical evolution, we are by nature intelligent creatures well-adapted to our surroundings and to ourselves. We are not exactly happy, because animals do not felicitate themselves on their successes as humans do, but we are not miserable and neurotic. We have two instincts, *amour de soi* and *pitié*; the first is the wish for our own self-preservation, and the second is an instinctive aversion to

[14] Jean-Jacques Rousseau, *Discourse on the Origins of Inequality among Men*, in Rousseau, *The Discourses and Other Early Political Writings* (Cambridge: Cambridge University Press, 1997).

[15] See ibid., 166 ff.

the sufferings of creatures like ourselves. These are *instincts;* we act on them only in the sense that they impel us. We do not adopt them as our guides, and we are not conscious of following them. In the fullest sense, we are not yet conscious at all. We do not know *that* we are human beings, even though we have an instinctive affinity for our species; nor do we know *which* members of that species we are. Comparisons with others are therefore impossible. So are comparisons between our present and our future, or between our past and our present; the concept of a "life plan" is entirely foreign to us. Rousseau insists, and it is what sets him apart from Hobbes, that we must in these conditions have no fear of death. Animals fear danger, but without a conception of their own existence as continuing self-identical entities, they have no conception of their own extinction. The haunting fear of that ultimate end of all our hopes and fears is not something they can experience.

It is not an instinctive fear of violent death that drives us to establish political institutions and the rule of law, but the consequences of the social strains set up by civilization. Rousseau's imaginative skills—much admired by Adam Smith and David Hume—are directed toward the analysis of the way that man comes to live "autrui de lui-même," which is to say the way in which we come to value our own existence only in terms of the impact we make on others and not in terms of our own real welfare. For Rousseau, this is a disaster many times over. The acquisition of language, reason, self-consciousness, and an understanding of time allows us to understand that the moral principles binding on all rational creatures require us to treat one another justly and as moral equals. Yet we also find ourselves flouting these values. The comparisons between ourselves and others on which the recognition of their equal moral standing with ourselves is founded are the same comparisons that incite us to wish to be those others' social, economic, or intellectual superiors. The price of becoming moral is a loss of innocence. Animals act as they do on impulse and without sin; we are divided selves and ridden with guilt. Inequality is both the cause and consequence of this disaster. As soon as we are conscious of others, we wish to cut a fine figure in their sight. We become vulnerable not only to the real ills of existence—such as pain, hunger, death, and loneliness—but to the envy and ill will of other people. Every slight is a little death.

This sort of rivalry makes life much harder for the social theorist than the seemingly more alarming problems of the Hobbesian state of nature do. Once there is peace, Hobbesian man can tolerate the competition Rousseau deplores. For Rousseau, the existence of this competition entails a latent civil war always on the verge of breaking out into open hostility. The Hobbesian sovereign can end the physical war of all against all, but not the psychological one. Hobbes knew this, but thought that once peace and prosperity were assured, most of us would be moderate in our wants and not self-destructively competitive. Rousseau casts a more jaundiced eye on prosperity; prosperity, along with the intellectual advance it promotes and the elaborate social life it brings in its train, creates the psychologically destructive behavior that Rousseau condemns. In a famous note to the *Discourse* he gives a wonderfully chilling account of the inner life of civilized man.[16] Rousseau supposes that the inner life of civilized man is dominated by the fantasy of being able to exercise complete control over the reactions of all one's competitors for esteem, wealth, sexual favors, and so on. The logic of control is Hobbesian. An individual needs more and more power over others so that they shall not resist his demands on them. The ultimate form of control is to kill all one's rivals. This achieved, an individual is a ruler in imagination over a desert in which he is alone and has no one to validate the absurd pride that led him to wish to be the master of everyone else. Rousseau's lesson that despotism internalized is self-defeating and self-destructive recalls Plato and anticipates Freud.

But the lesson provokes an obvious question: how far do inequality and self-destructive vanity feed upon each other, and how great an evil is it if they do? There is no determinate answer to this question. Different kinds of inequality produce different effects, and the vanity of different people varies from the harmless to the lethal. A modern egalitarian such as Ronald Dworkin deplores the fact that the poor have inadequate health care and education, receive less than decent treatment by the criminal justice system, and face various other inequities. The complaint is familiar, and what lies behind it is the thought that one of the advantages that wealth brings is the ability to purchase the good will of politicians and lawyers. The question to pose to Rousseau (and indeed to ourselves) is "Supposing that the less well off were decently supplied with the necessities of life, were treated as equal citizens, and received equal justice, would you still be opposed to inequalities of income and wealth?" Rousseau's answer might come in two parts. The first would be simply to mock the question as absurd. How *could* one suppose that such a world might exist? The second is to insist that poverty is a felt condition rather than an objective matter of having the resources to meet one's needs. Contented precolonization aboriginals in Australia lived lives that to us appear poverty-stricken, dangerous, and altogether intolerable; until our arrival, however, they themselves were content enough with their diet, accommodations, and occupational opportunities. It is the riches of others that turn our sufficiencies into sources of shame and humiliation. To be poor in the demoralizing sense is to be poorer than others.

The rational response to Rousseau is, I fear, boringly pragmatic. *Some* sorts of consumption, in *some* societies, are intended by the consumers and understood by the spectators to function as marks of distinction, and to separate out those who do and those who cannot enjoy these things.

[16] Ibid., 198–99.

Tickets in the Royal Enclosure at the Royal Ascot race meeting have no other function—a fact attested to by the derision with which journalists greet so many of those who are seen there. But not all the things that people enjoy fit this category; many enjoyable things are essentially uniform goods that one can buy more of as one's level of disposable income rises. In the late twentieth century, motor vehicles became something very like this. They were, of course, a fashion item as well as a means of movement, but the variety of fashions they could serve meant that there was no socially recognized status hierarchy. Nevertheless, small symbolic niches certainly existed where the choice of a BMW over a Mercedes or the ostentatious parking of a Harley Davidson outside the office door indicated (if the gesture was successful) that here was a young 50-year-old with fire in his belly or (if the gesture was unsuccessful) that here was a self-deceived 50-year-old who had not noticed that he was past this sort of thing.

If it is a boring response to Rousseau to observe that he is only *sometimes* right, it is worth noticing that he *is* sometimes right. To the extent that he is right, it means that disciples of Rawls must take two things into account. The first is that Rawls's incentive-based arguments for inequality of reward must be taken with a pinch of salt. For instance, the pay of CEOs bears little relationship to their worth to the companies that employ them; for one thing, their worth to the companies that employ them is obscure in the way that the worth of generals to the armies they lead is obscure. Teams need leaders, but what leaders do is difficult to describe. Even if we agree that leaders contribute to the success of the companies they lead, the disparities between leaders and others, in terms of salary and size of share options, are driven by "fancy value" in the Lockean sense (that is, value based on something other than utility).[17] If Jones gets $5 million, Smith sets his sights on $6 million; if Jones had been paid $1 million, Smith would have settled for $1.2 million. Neither salary relates very directly to the companies' achievements, though a CEO's pay will generally have some connection with a company's size and salience in the public eye. If large numbers of high incomes are set by such considerations, Rawls's defense of inequality becomes not shaky in itself, but shaky as a defense of the inequalities we see around us. It is not less morally persuasive, but it is less sociologically relevant.

The second point Rawlsians must consider is that we need to revisit the idea of envy. Rawls, as we know, drives out envy in the first part of *A Theory of Justice*, and then drives it out again in the third part of the book. As noted above, in the first part, envy is eliminated by the device of "mutual disinterestedness," the role of which is to discredit envy. On the general principle of "naturam furca expellas, tamen recurrat" ("you may drive nature out with a pitchfork, but she will return"), however, Rawls argues in the third part of the book for a greater degree of equality than

[17] On "fancy value," see Locke, *Two Treatises of Government*, 316-20, 409-10.

the difference principle would in theory demand, in order to reduce the likelihood of envy, and thus of class warfare and other abrasive social and political phenomena. However, we might turn this argument around and argue that envy is the response that is intended to be triggered by trophy salaries and the ostentatious display of wealth. Moreover, we might argue that we should not care what produces the emulation that drives a free market economy, so long as something does. If envy does it, that is fine, even if many people would like to see the rich brought down from their perch *however little they themselves would benefit*. So long as we can thwart that desire and divert the energy behind it into the productive channels of a competition for high-risk/high-reward employments, we should not moralize about fallen human nature. If not impressed about turning bad motives to useful ends, we might decide that the search for trophy salaries is a sort of social aggression against everyone else, and wish to put a lid on it. Innumerable societies have had sumptuary legislation designed to keep the rich from quarreling among themselves and to keep them from irritating the less well off, and only the most bald-headed libertarian can argue that there is anything wrong with such legislation in principle.

A thought that this argument may inspire is one I shall recur to later. One might think that in a rational world—one that is governed by rules that are designed to secure as much general happiness as possible, on the basis of just terms of social cooperation—individuals would see themselves as at least in part the servants of the public as well as of themselves and their own families. The thought is not that they should be entirely self-abnegating, nor that they have no self-interest. If they had no self-interest, it is not obvious that they would know how to promote the general interest, or have any use for the idea of just terms of cooperation. But there is a difference between getting a fair reward for what we have contributed to the welfare of our society and getting whatever the market will bear. This is not a matter of pointing out that well-crafted incentives increase the general welfare, and that people may ask for what a well-crafted system would allow them to ask for. It is to argue that people are entitled to a reward for service. If we are to advance down this latter track, we will need a conception of fairness in contribution and reward, and a view of the possibilities of motivating the contributors to a modern economy. Rousseau does not advance that discussion very much, nor did the theorists who should have done so in the nineteenth century—Marx and Mill.

V. Political Effects of Inequality

Mention of sumptuary legislation brings up the political dimension of inequality. Assuming that we have decided against Rousseau's view that self-promoting spite and self-destructive envy are to be avoided at all costs, we can turn briefly to the most familiar of all arguments against inequality. From Plato to Dworkin, taking in every representative thinker of a broadly republican stripe on the way, this argument has been the same. It is said that rich people subvert the political system. They do not content themselves with buying Cadillacs, but insist on buying judges, politicians, political parties, and Congress. This is to be distinguished from another famous argument that I shall simply ignore. Tough admirers of Rome and Sparta disliked rich societies because they made their inhabitants soft. They also made them apathetic, so that when rich men stole the political system people were content to be enslaved by them. This fear of majority apathy, and the fear of the loss of military vigor and the effeminacy of the state, are not themes I examine here. The point we should focus on is that among the things that inequalities of income and wealth lead to, one of the most important is further inequality—of power, access to the political system, access to justice, and access to whatever else of importance the political system produces.

There are two branches to the anxiety. The first is that there are some areas in which we think, for whatever reason, that anything other than strict equality is intolerable. We do not propose to give rich men three votes to acknowledge their wealth, nor to allow them three closing speeches in court to acknowledge their possessions; we think that equality before the law is a matter of equality in this if nothing else, and that "one man, one vote" really means one man, one vote. In practice, of course, we put up with the most striking divergences from these principles. It is a familiar fact that in the United States, the death penalty is never carried out on anyone who has the money to hire a halfway competent lawyer, and that in all societies the poor receive worse justice than do the rich. By the same token, the Supreme Court's extraordinary views about free speech lead to a situation in which rich men are encouraged to purchase political office through their ability to purchase the advertising time that will secure name recognition.

The cure for this distortion of the judicial and political processes is easy to imagine, but very difficult to implement. The detachment of money from elections requires tough rules about campaign expenditures, and such rules need to be strictly enforced. If electoral courts erred on the side of suspecting politicians of misconduct, it would have a beneficial effect. This, however, is something that would require a sea change in current American political culture, where the popular belief that most politicians are crooks is not widely shared by politicians and judges.[18] It might be possible in some political systems to ensure that political advertising is prohibited, or that such advertising is limited to a certain amount donated by media outlets, but this simply cannot be done in early twenty-first-century America. By the same token, an effective legal aid system

[18] I do not, of course, mean to suggest that the United States is particularly unusual in this.

could be created for poor defendants in criminal cases, though it would be difficult to run such a system in a way that did not benefit lawyers rather than clients and was invulnerable to abuse by the well off. The chances of such a system being created in the United States are not good.

The second branch of the anxiety emerges from the observation that purchasing political influence is an affront to democracy. Were the process to go unchecked, the result would at best be class government, and at worst government by an unaccountable oligarchy of rich men clustered about the modern equivalent of a royal court. Once again, it is not difficult to think of ways in which this could be prevented by direct political and legal means even if nothing were done to prevent or even reduce the inequalities of income and wealth that allowed rich men to behave in this fashion. The Roman republic—which was a moderated oligarchy, not a democracy—allowed sufficient direct input from the representatives of the common people to hold the rich in check for several centuries; in the end, it came to nothing and the Empire ensued. The American republic showed signs of heading in the same direction in the last quarter of the nineteenth century. Aggressive critics of the present condition of the United States sometimes suggest that we are again heading toward the politics of the Gilded Age.

I will not make any judgment here on the empirical plausibility of these arguments. In other contexts, one might pursue this issue at length, but here I am only arguing that these arguments—which, if well founded, are very powerful arguments criticizing the impact of money on politics—do not suggest that there is any *intrinsic* objection to inequalities of income and wealth. Of course, many critics think that it is neither here nor there whether the objections are intrinsic or extrinsic; for our purposes, however, it is an important distinction.

VI. Economic Effects of Inequality

I will now turn to the economic objections to inequalities of income and wealth, bearing in mind as before that the question is about the *intrinsic* undesirability of these inequalities. I ought now to make one qualification to the sharp distinction between intrinsic and extrinsic considerations that I have hitherto accepted. One point I am about to make concerns inequality's potential impact on the price level and availability of particular sorts of goods. This is not exactly an intrinsic consideration, nor is it exactly extrinsic. To have a higher income than others is to be able to exert more market power than they can. Money is command over the labor of others, and therefore the possession of more of it is the possession of more power over the labor of others.

The familiar argument about the irrelevance of inequality as opposed to poverty is simple and persuasive. If I need one comfortable and reliable car and I have it, it does not injure me if you have six of them. If I need a swift, efficient, benign, and well-trained doctor to cure my ailments, it is fine if I have one who will treat me now and affordably, and neither here nor there if another doctor who is no better than mine will charge you three times the price. If I have no car, I have a problem; if I cannot find a competent doctor, I have a problem. Otherwise, I have no problem. Why, then, does there *appear* to be a problem in the aforementioned cases? The obvious answer is that our measures of poverty are clumsy, and do not catch what we need them to. One alternative answer that I am not disposed to accept is that the logical connection between some contemporary measures of poverty and the existence of inequality means that when there is greater inequality, there must be more poverty. For example, assume that poverty is defined as receiving half the average level of earnings; further assume that inequality increases in such a way that average earnings increase while the wages of the lowest 40 percent do not—this would occur if some of the fairly well off became much better off. In this case, there has been an increase in poverty in the sense that more people will have less than half the average level of earnings, but it is not obvious that the newly "poor" are any worse off than they were before. The "no skin off their noses" argument leaves the situation open for further discussion.

To show that the newly poor are, or might be, worse off, consider something that is easy to sketch informally but beyond me to formalize. Think of the effects that the aforementioned increase in inequality may have on the housing market. The price of the houses that the better off live in will rise, and since housing stocks are inelastic, the price rise will run down through the lower levels of housing, with the effect that the rents of the worse off will rise as well. Alternatively, think of the effects on public transport of a rise in the incomes of persons who want to purchase cars. As the demand for cars rises, the ridership on public transport will decline, and the transport available to the poor will be diminished. The worse off will be forced to buy cheap cars as a defensive reaction to the worsening of what is available to them. This is not the Rousseauian state of affairs in which the rich buy cars "at" the worse off; the rich may feel entirely benign about the poor and buy cars only because they are useful. The effect of their doing so, however, will be to worsen the position of the worse off even if the latter suffer no drop in money income. Their standard of living will drop.

It is situations of this sort that explain the apparent paradox whereby affluent societies' worst-off members, with incomes of $5 to $10 thousand a year, may be poorer than they would be living on a fifth of that amount in a poor country. A doctor's services may be out of their reach in the United States, but would be available in a poorer country; decent housing may be out of reach in the United States, but would not be so elsewhere. The obvious question is what this has to do with inequality, and the answer is that the differences in consumption patterns between the poor and the affluent determine what is produced, and may remove from the marketplace things that the poorer people need. I have been writing as though increased inequality always stems from the better off flourishing and numerous worse-off people staying where they were, and this is one possibility. But there is an equally common situation in which a general rise in prosperity leaves some small part of the population worse off. One explanation for increased homelessness, for instance, has been that once upon a time there was a substantial demand for cheap dormitory-style accommodation, but the places where this would have been provided have been turned into apartments, and nobody reckons to make money by supplying the old style of accommodation. As a result, this explanation suggests, a hole has appeared in the market, and people who would at any rate have found space in a flophouse now camp on the streets. The difficulty about arguments of this sort is always that their empirical adequacy is disputable; if current health and safety regulations were as lax as they were sixty years ago, it seems not unlikely that there would still be flophouses, and if this is right, it is not inequality but regulation that accounts for the homeless on the streets.

Still, there may well be cases where the consumption patterns of the better off remove from the market those things that would benefit the worse off. The use of cars by the affluent deprives the poor of a bus service that would break even only if the affluent also used it. In medicine, the dramatic diseases of the better off attract the efforts of doctors who would do more for human happiness by treating the back pain, fallen arches, and undramatic chronic ailments of the less well off. The place of this sort of effect in my intrinsic/extrinsic categorization is unclear because it is not obvious how we could prevent the effect without removing the cause. But these cases are what we should set in the scales against the argument, made canonical by Rawls, to the effect that the unequal rewards handed out by the market are what sustains innovation and growth and therefore the long-run welfare of the less advantaged. I do not mean that Rawls's argument is invalid, only that there are countervailing considerations with respect to it that are not examined in *A Theory of Justice*.

Some writers discount such side effects on the ground that our right to cause them is implied in the existence of property rights, whether rights in our own labor or rights in external assets.[19] If we have property rights in our own efforts and our own resources, then so long as we do not actively prevent others from using their like rights in their own efforts and resources, they have no ground for complaint. There is an alternative analysis, offered in Mill's *On Liberty*.[20] On this account, the injury done to another by the employment of one's property rights is a genuine injury and should be acknowledged. If two of us compete for a job and I get it,

[19] See Nozick, *Anarchy, State, and Utopia*, 178 ff.

[20] John Stuart Mill, *On Liberty*, in Mill, *"On Liberty" and Other Writings* (Cambridge: Cambridge University Press, 1989), 94–95.

I have damaged you. How much I have damaged you may be hard to tell, and will depend on what other alternatives you have available; nonetheless, my success is your loss. Mill argues that the *practice* of allowing such injuries, when they are caused without fraud or force, is a fair price to pay for the benefits of competition. All the same, the injury is an injury, and our acceptance of the winner's right to inflict that injury on the loser needs the justification that Mill's argument provides. Hence, the impact of the better off on the worse off is to be counted rather than ignored. There is an obvious policy implication. If public services were formerly profitable and needed no subsidy, but became less profitable because of an income-related switch to private provision, one might think that instead of either raising charges or reducing services—the usual reaction to such circumstances in Britain—it would be more appropriate to tax the better off and subsidize the relevant services.

VII. Is Inequality Bad for Us? Some Empirical Issues

Finally, I want to consider some empirical issues and some last observations about inequality and motivation. There is some evidence that inequality, as distinct from absolute poverty, is damaging to social welfare. This evidence is not easy to evaluate, and it is often reported in terms of increases in poverty. This is a confusion if what is meant to be conveyed here is that an increase in poverty is simply the same thing as a rise in inequality. But there is some evidence that societies with more equal distributions of income and wealth have a better record in terms of health and general well-being than do societies whose per capita gross domestic product is higher but less equally distributed. It is very obvious that the United States has strikingly bad health figures when it comes to the lowest income quartile of the population: this group's life expectancy and ordinary levels of health are more like those of a Third World country than those of any European nation. Even at the higher levels of income and wealth, however, Americans at a given level are less healthy than their counterparts in more egalitarian countries. There may be any number of possible explanations, but the mere fact is interesting in itself.[21]

Crossnational comparisons of other indicators of social exclusion, such as antisocial behavior and academic underperformance, exhibit the same patterns found in comparisons of health statistics, suggesting that there is a deterrent to self-care created by the raw fact of living in an inegalitarian society.[22] (Britain seems in this, as in much else, to fall between the United States and the Scandinavian and other northern European countries.) Before concluding that here is the evidence that inequality is intrinsically bad for a society, there are many steps we would need to take. For start-

[21] See Norman Daniels, Bruce Kennedy, and Ichiro Kawachi, *Is Inequality Bad for Our Health?* (Boston: Beacon Press, 2001).

[22] See ibid.

ers, even this sort of evidence is not evidence that inequality is *intrinsically* bad, since what we have is, at the very most, some evidence that the optimistic story that inequality encourages emulation and achievement is false and that the pessimistic story that it discourages self-esteem, optimism, and upward social mobility is right. The purest version of the thought that *mere* inequality cannot be a problem is not touched by such evidence, one might respond; the ill effects must be the result of something else. One might, however, begin to think that this response concedes the crucial point: that inequalities of income and wealth are causally implicated in bad outcomes independently of general prosperity and poverty, and that we must go on to analyze which aspects of inequality cause these outcomes and which do not. One might, for instance, wonder whether racial or class inequalities—inequalities of esteem and social respect rather than inequalities of income and wealth—are the real cause of the damage; if they were, and if we could split these inequalities off from simple inequalities of income and wealth, then perhaps no such damage would emerge. In Britain, for instance, there is a correlation between ill health and geography that has less to do with the income levels of the inhabitants of the given areas than with certain regions' persistent culture of self-neglect, hard drinking, and street violence—a culture that is not healthy for those who are trapped in it. People in different cultures would not be so affected by income inequality.

What we find with respect to health is also plainly true of educational attainment. Within the various ethnic groupings in Britain, the divergence of educational achievement is considerable, even allowing for income levels. Afro-Caribbean children generally underperform West African migrants, just as Bangladeshi subcontinental Indians generally underperform Gujarati migrants from East Africa. The amount of education children receive and the educational level they eventually achieve vary with income and wealth within communities, and the gross impact of income is dramatic and unmistakable; nonetheless, this impact varies greatly according to the cultural predilections of different ethnic groups. Once again, the moral is that *if* we construe our question narrowly enough, we can properly say that it is not inequality of income and wealth that does the damage here, but that this inequality has ill effects only in conjunction with cultural factors that are not themselves simply a consequence of income or wealth inequality.

VIII. Conclusion: Equality for Its Own Sake

Let me present one final thought about the intrinsic undesirability of income and wealth inequalities. If we entertain very different views about our own relations with other people, we might well think such inequalities are undesirable *unless* they reflect differences in need. The slogan that Marx borrowed from the Saint-Simonians—"from each according to ability, to each according to need"—is not a simple egalitarian principle, as Marx himself was at pains to observe. Indeed, the sense in which Marx was an egalitarian is not easy to describe. The "ability-need" formula was the formula that he thought should transcend the "equal rights" formula of his contemporaries, and it is clear that it is intended to accommodate what egalitarians want, but to do so in a form that they had not imagined. If we deplore the view that in economic transactions we are entitled to ask for whatever we can get, subject to some loose constraints on driving extortionate bargains, we might find Marx's view attractive. In essence, the ability-need formula is intended to eliminate inequalities based on bargaining position and allow inequalities that represent "need." The question of what "need" will embrace is not one to be embarked on here; we may, however, take it that anyone who says he needs a sufficient supply of Chateau Margaux to develop his palate in good clarets will not get very far, even though Engels described his vision of heaven as Chateau Margaux 1848. Nor can we say that what we need covers only those things without which our lives will go very badly, because Marx expanded the concept of need to embrace whatever is required to live a truly human life.

In non-Marxian discussion, the notion of need is sharpened by contrasting the necessities of life with unneeded luxuries; Marx, however, was eager to say that by the time that we achieve the rational economic arrangements that lay on the far side of capitalism, we will have expanded our conception of human nature and acquired new and more human needs. In these circumstances, we might not be able to insist that we need an adequate supply of Chateau Margaux, but we are not confined to saying that we merely need *some* education, *some* health care, and *some* decent level of shelter and subsistence. It is simple enough to see that if I have a life-threatening disease, my need for costly treatment will entitle me to a greater share of resources than would be appropriate for someone who has a slight sore throat; it is less easy to see, however, how we are to allocate resources if my need for canvasses and oil paints is to be set against your need for a Latin dictionary. Marx's casual claims about abundance do not meet the demands of a serious discussion of distribution. On the other hand, Marx's contribution principle really eliminates the inequalities that a Rawlsian approach to justifying inequality lets through. Rawls's second principle of justice argues that any degree of inequality is acceptable so long as it improves the welfare of the worst off as much as possible; it therefore presupposes not that I shall contribute according to my ability, but that I shall employ my abilities to the extent that I am induced to do so by my own self-interest. It is, in that sense, explicitly opposed to Marx's principle, which holds that I am obliged to contribute to the best of my ability, simply because that is what I am obliged to do. "Obliged" here perhaps carries too much of the ethical baggage that Marx abandoned, but now that G. A. Cohen has sacrificed Marx's analytical apparatus to preserve his (Marx's) moral convictions, we may perhaps describe Marx as a moralist without undue embarrassment.[23]

We can at last reach an answer to the question we began with—that is, the question of whether inequality matters for its own sake. Inequalities of income and wealth are licit if they reflect discrepancies in needs or in the resources people have to make use of when contributing according to their abilities. Otherwise they are intrinsically wrong. They are not intrinsically wrong because equality takes logical or moral priority over inequality, but because the distribution of income and wealth should reflect the moral commitments of the human beings who produce that income and wealth. These commitments ought—if we can spell out Cohen's doctrine with any persuasiveness—to be broadly egalitarian in their consequences. If we cannot imagine that society would be prosperous and happy if we all behaved decently,[24] we have a problem on our hands, but we still have a reason to say that such inequalities are intrinsically wrong. They may be a necessary evil, but they are an evil nonetheless. To argue that inequalities of income and wealth are intrinsically wrong, one would appeal directly to the postscarcity theory of justice offered by Marx, or to some equivalent moral theory that represents our endowments as gifts to be employed for the good of others. There is no shortage of such non-Marxian perspectives, from the Christian view based on the parable of the talents to the ideals of the Fabians or the English Idealists. To make any of these ideas persuasive would be the work of a different exercise than this, and hence this conclusion is essentially hypothetical: if the perspective with which we began is persuasive, and a rational person focuses his or her attention wholly upon his or her own well-being, then inequality does not matter for its own sake; if the perspective so loosely sketched in the last few paragraphs is persuasive, it does.

Politics, New College, Oxford University

[23] See G. A. Cohen, *If You're an Egalitarian, How Come You're So Rich?* (Cambridge, MA: Harvard University Press, 2000).

[24] This is the disturbing message of Bernard Mandeville, *Fable of the Bees* [1714], ed. Phillip Harth (Harmondsworth, UK: Penguin, 1970).

EQUAL RESPECT AND EQUAL SHARES

By David Schmidtz

I. Introduction

We are all equal, sort of. We are not equal in terms of our physical or mental capacities. Morally speaking, we are not all equally good. Evidently, if we are equal, it is not in virtue of our actual characteristics, but despite them. Our equality is of a political rather than metaphysical nature. We do not expect people to be the same, but we expect differences to have no bearing on how people ought to be treated as citizens. Or when differences do matter, we expect that they will not matter in the sense of being a basis for class distinction. We admire tenacity, talent, and so on, but do not take such features to entitle their bearers to be treated as "upper class." Neither are people who are relatively lacking in these features obliged to tolerate being treated as "lower class." As a society, we have made moral progress. Such progress consists in part of progress toward political and cultural equality.

Have we also made progress toward *economic* equality? If so, does that likewise count as moral progress? Some people have more than others. Some earn more than others. Do these things matter? In two ways, they could. First, we may care about differences in wealth and income on humanitarian grounds; that is, we may worry about some people having less not because less is less but because less sometimes is not enough. Second, we may care on grounds of justice; that is, we may think people would not have less if some injustice had not been done.[1]

What provokes such concerns? One provocation is conceptual: philosophical thought experiments, and so on. We imagine how the world would be in some idealized hypothetical situation, and then ask whether departures from the ideal are unjust, and if so, how they might be redressed. A second provocation is empirical: statistical reports on income inequality, and so on. Statistics paint a picture of how the world actually is, and how unequal it is. We are left wondering whether such inequality is acceptable, and if not, what to do about it.

[1] Some worry about differences in wealth because they believe such differences eventually become differences in political power. (Whether such concerns justify increasing or decreasing the amount of political power that eventually gets put up for sale is a separate question, touched on at the end of this essay.) This worry could be made to fit quite nicely into either of the above two reasons for concern about inequality, or we could call it a third, separate reason.

This essay examines these two provocations. In response to concerns of a conceptual nature, Section II offers a limited defense of distribution according to a principle of "equal shares," explaining how and why even nonegalitarians can and should respect egalitarian concerns and make room for them even in otherwise nonegalitarian theories of justice. As Section III notes, though, "equal shares" is only one way of expressing egalitarian concern. The connection between equal treatment and justice may be essential, but the connection between equal treatment and equal shares is not. Sections IV and V reflect on why the rule of first possession limits attempts to distribute according to principles (not only egalitarian principles) of justice. Finally, in response to empirical concerns, Section VI examines recent studies of income distribution in the United States.

Undoubtedly, egalitarians will think I have not made *enough* room for egalitarian concern. After all, if an egalitarian is someone who thinks many economic goods should be distributed equally, and redistributed as often as needed so that shares remain equal, then at the end of the day, I am not an egalitarian. I am, however, a kind of pluralist. Justice is about giving people their due; if we are not talking about what people are due, then we are not talking about justice. On the other hand, what people are due is a complex, multifaceted, context-sensitive matter. There is a place for equal shares.

II. On Behalf of Equal Shares

Political theorist Bruce Ackerman's essay "On Getting What We Don't Deserve" is a short, engaging dialogue that captures the essence of egalitarian concern about the justice of differences in wealth and income.[2] Ackerman imagines you and he are in a garden. As Ackerman tells the story, you see two apples on a tree and swallow them in one gulp while an amazed Ackerman looks on. Ackerman then asks you, as one human being to another, shouldn't I have gotten one of those apples?

Should he? If so, why? Why only one? What grounds our admittedly compelling intuition that Ackerman should have gotten one—exactly one—of those apples? Notably, Ackerman explicitly rejects the idea that his claim to an apple is based on need, signaling that his primary concern is not humanitarian. Instead, Ackerman's view is that the point of getting one apple is that one apple would have been an equal share. Equal shares is a moral default. Morally speaking, distribution by equal shares is what

[2] Bruce A. Ackerman, "On Getting What We Don't Deserve," *Social Philosophy and Policy* 1, no. 1 (1983): 60-70. My discussion of Ackerman borrows from David Schmidtz, "Finders, Keepers?" *Advances in Austrian Economics* 5 (1998): 277-89; and David Schmidtz and Robert Goodin, *Social Welfare and Individual Responsibility* (New York: Cambridge University Press, 1998). For a skeptical response to Ackerman's thought-experiment methodology from an egalitarian perspective, see James K. Galbraith, "Raised on Robbery," *Yale Law and Policy Review* 18, no. 2 (2000): 387-404.

we automatically go to if we cannot justify anything else. As Ackerman sees it, to give Ackerman an equal share is to treat him with respect. In Ackerman's garden, at least, to say he does not command an equal share is to say he does not command respect.

Is Ackerman right? Looking at the question dispassionately, there are several things to say on behalf of equal shares as an allocation rule, even if we reject Ackerman's presumption in favor of it. In Ackerman's garden, equal shares has the virtue of not requiring further debate about who gets the bigger share. No one has reason to envy anyone else's share. When we arrive all at once, equal shares is a cooperative, mutually advantageous, mutually respectful departure from the status quo (in which none of us yet has a share of the good to be distributed). In short, equal shares is easy. We call it "splitting the difference," and often it is a pleasant way of solving our distributional problem. In the process, we not only solve the problem, but offer each other a kind of salute. In Ackerman's garden, it is an obvious way to divide things and get on with our lives—with no hard feelings at worst, and at best with a sense of having been honored by honorable people.

These ideas may not be equality's foundation, but they are among equality's virtues. Crucially, even nonegalitarians can appreciate that they are virtues. Thus, while critics may say Ackerman is assuming the egalitarianism for which he is supposed to be arguing, the virtues just mentioned beg no questions. Even from nonegalitarian perspectives, then, there is something to be said for equal shares. Therefore, whatever conception of justice we ultimately entertain, we can agree there is a place in a just society for dividing certain goods into equal shares. In particular, when we arrive at the bargaining table more or less at the same time, for the purpose of dividing goods to which no one has made a prior claim, we are in a situation where equal shares is a way of achieving a just distribution.

It may not be the only way. For example, we could flesh out the thought experiment in such a way as to make bargainers' unequal needs more salient than their equality as citizens. But it is one way.

III. An Egalitarian Critique of Equal Shares

Yet there are times when following the equal-shares principle—paying people the same wage, say—would fail to show others equal respect. Suppose an employer routinely expects more work, or more competent work, from one employee than from another, but sees no reason to pay them differently. In such cases, the problem is not raw wage differentials so much as a lack of proportion in the relations between contribution and compensation. The lack of proportion is one kind of unequal treatment. And unequal treatment, and the lack of respect it signals, is what people resent.

Children often are jealous when comparing their shares to those of their siblings—or, a bit more precisely, when comparing shares doled out by their parents. Why? Because being given a lesser share by their parents signals to them that they are held in lower esteem. They tend to feel differently about having less than their richest neighbor, because so long as no one is deliberately assigning them smaller shares, no one is sending a signal of unequal esteem.[3] Here, too, the problem is departures from equal respect rather than from equal shares. Equal shares is not the same as equal respect, and is not always compatible with it.[4] "Unequal pay for equal work" is offensive, but so is "equal pay for unequal work."

Intuitively, we all believe some people deserve more than others. This belief, though, is ambiguous. If I have better opportunities than you do, and as a result acquire more than you do, do I deserve more? Egalitarians will say no. The ambiguity is this: I do not deserve "more than you do" *under this description* because there never was a fair competition between us to determine which of us deserves more. Therefore, I do not deserve to have a central distributor maintain any particular ratio between your reward and mine. Nevertheless, notice what this leaves open. I may well deserve X while you deserve Y, on the basis of my working hard for X and your working hard for Y as we live our separate lives, with nothing in this story even suggesting that $X = Y$. Therefore, even if we were right to suppose that a central distributor would have no basis for judging us to be of unequal merit, and thus could be denounced for deliberately assigning unequal shares, we could still be wrong to infer that the shares we respectively deserve are equal.

Accordingly, there is a difference between unequal treatment and unequal shares. Unequal treatment presupposes treatment; unequal shares do not. If we are being *treated* unequally, then there is someone whom we can ask to justify treating us unequally. It would make sense for an egalitarian such as Ackerman to insist on this. Moreover, in Ackerman's garden, your grabbing both apples arguably is a token of unequal treatment. But what if Ackerman arrives several years after you have grabbed

[3] As children grow up, we expect them to resent their siblings less rather than resent their neighbors more, but this expectation is not always met. A well-known philosopher once complained to me about airline deregulation, not because of safety or quality of service or anything like that, but because it made her unsure of whether she was getting the lowest possible price. She had paid $300 for her ticket, and for all she knew the person beside her paid $200 for the same ticket. I speculated that before deregulation, both tickets would have cost $700. She answered, in a passionate voice, "But at least you knew!" Knew what? Obviously, there was nothing humanitarian in this kind of egalitarianism. This philosopher is not alone. A neighbor of mine recently said she would rather pay $20 for a blanket at K-Mart than pay $8 for the same blanket in the nearby border town of Nogales, because at K-Mart you know everyone is paying the same price, whereas in Nogales, someone else might be getting the same blanket for $6.

[4] As David Gauthier expresses a related point, "impartial practices respect people as they are, the inequalities among them as well as the equalities." See David Gauthier, *Morals by Agreement* (Oxford: Oxford University Press, 1986), 270.

both apples and turned the garden into an orchard? Nonsimultaneous arrival complicates the case, making it harder to see the grab as a token of treatment at all, unequal or otherwise. Suffice it to say, we can be committed to denouncing unequal treatment without being committed to denouncing every unequal outcome as if it were a result of unequal treatment. Ackerman presumes the moral default (in a very general way) is equal shares. Even if, as seems likely, Ackerman is wrong, this is no reason to give up on the idea that the moral default is equal *treatment*.

A. Equal worth and equal treatment

Suppose we have a certain moral worth that is not affected by our choices. That is, although we may live in a morally heroic way or a morally depraved way, how we live makes no difference as far as this moral worth is concerned: there is nothing we can do to make ourselves more or less worthy. If this were true, then we might all, as it happens, be of equal worth.

Now suppose instead that along certain dimensions our moral worth can be affected by our choices. In certain respects, that is, some of our choices make us more or less worthy. In this case, if in certain respects our choices affect our worth over time, it is unlikely that there will ever be a time when we are all of equal worth in those respects.

None of this is a threat to egalitarianism, because only a caricature of egalitarianism would presume that all of us are equally worthy along all dimensions. Instead, part of the point of the liberal ideal of political equality is to foster conditions under which we will tend to make choices that augment rather than diminish our worth along dimensions where worth depends on choice. Liberal political equality is not premised on the false hope that under ideal conditions, we all turn out to be equally worthy. It presupposes only a classically liberal optimism regarding the kind of society that results from putting people (all people, so far as this is realistically feasible) in a position to choose worthy ways of life.

B. Equality and oppression

Humanitarianism is concerned with how people fare. Egalitarianism is concerned with how people fare relative to each other. So says philosopher Larry Temkin. Humanitarians, he says,

> favor equality *solely* as a means to helping the worse off, and given the choice between redistribution from the better off to the worse off, and identical gains for the worse off with equal, or even greater, gains for the better off, they would see no reason to favor the former over the latter. . . . But such people are not egalitarians in my sense if their concerns would be satisfied by a system in which the poor had

access to quality care, but the rich had even greater access to much better care.[5]

Accordingly, what distinguishes egalitarianism from humanitarianism is that a humanitarian would never compromise the care offered to the poor merely to greatly worsen the care offered to the rich, whereas an egalitarian at least sometimes would.[6] Temkin, himself an egalitarian, says the problem with humanitarianism is that it is not concerned with equality.[7] In Temkin's words, "As a plausible analysis of what the egalitarian really cares about, . . . humanitarianism is a nonstarter."[8]

Philosopher Elizabeth Anderson responds, "Those on the left have no less reason than conservatives and libertarians to be disturbed by recent trends in academic egalitarian thought."[9] Academic egalitarians, she thinks, have lost sight of why equality matters.[10] Thus, she criticizes philosopher Richard Arneson for saying, "The concern of distributive justice is to compensate individuals for misfortune. . . . Distributive justice stipulates that the lucky should transfer some or all of their gains due to luck to the unlucky."[11] Along with Arneson, Anderson classifies Gerald Cohen and John Roemer as welfare egalitarians.[12] She contrasts this group with those who advocate equalizing resources rather than welfare, such as Ronald Dworkin, Eric Rakowski, and Philippe Van Parijs.[13] Despite differences between these thinkers, what their works collectively show, Anderson says, is that "[r]ecent egalitarian writing has come to be dominated by the view that the fundamental aim of equality is to compensate people for undeserved bad luck."[14] Anderson, though, thinks that "[t]he proper negative aim of egalitarian justice is not to eliminate the impact of brute

[5] Larry S. Temkin, *Inequality* (New York: Oxford University Press, 1993), 8.

[6] One of Temkin's contributions to the literature is his discussion of what he calls "the Slogan": "One situation cannot be better than another unless there is someone for whom it is better" (ibid., 248). The Slogan's point is to separate true egalitarians (who would say a more equal distribution can be better even when there is no one for whom it is better) from true humanitarians (who would deny this). Temkin, an egalitarian, says the Slogan is false (ibid., 249).

[7] Ibid., 246.

[8] Ibid., 247.

[9] Elizabeth S. Anderson, "What Is the Point of Equality?" *Ethics* 109, no. 2 (1999): 288.

[10] Terry L. Price reaches a similar conclusion in Terry L. Price, "Egalitarian Justice, Luck, and the Costs of Chosen Ends," *American Philosophical Quarterly* 36, no. 4 (1999): 267–78.

[11] Richard J. Arneson, "Rawls, Responsibility, and Distributive Justice," in Maurice Salles and John A. Weymark, eds., *Justice, Political Liberalism, and Utilitarianism: Themes from Harsanyi* (Cambridge: Cambridge University Press, in press), quoted in Anderson, "What Is the Point of Equality?" 290. For a later work in which Arneson abandons egalitarianism in favor of what he calls sufficientarianism, see Richard J. Arneson, "Why Justice Requires Transfers to Offset Income and Wealth Inequalities," in this volume.

[12] For a sustained and circumspect—yet uncompromising—defense of a related kind of egalitarianism, see the more recent Tom Christiano, "Arguing for Equality of Condition" (manuscript).

[13] Anderson, "What Is the Point of Equality?" 293.

[14] Ibid., 288.

luck from human affairs, but to end oppression."[15] Egalitarianism's proper aim, she claims, is to enable us "to live together in a democratic community, as opposed to a hierarchical one."[16]

Anderson says that "democratic equality's principles of distribution neither presume to tell people how to use their opportunities nor attempt to judge how responsible people are for choices that lead to unfortunate outcomes. Instead, it avoids bankruptcy at the hands of the imprudent by limiting the range of goods provided collectively and expecting individuals to take personal responsibility for the other goods in their possession."[17] In contrast, Anderson argues, academic egalitarianism gains some undeserved credibility because we assume anything calling itself egalitarian must also be humanitarian. But although she is an egalitarian herself, Anderson says we cannot assume this connection.[18] Moreover, the academic egalitarian's reasons for granting aid are disrespectful. When redistribution's purpose is to make up for someone's being less capable than others (due to bad luck in the natural lottery), the result in practice is that "[p]eople lay claim to the resources of egalitarian redistribution in virtue of their inferiority to others, not in virtue of their equality to others."[19] Political equality has no such consequence. In the nineteenth century, when women began to present themselves as having a right to vote, they were presenting themselves not as needy inferiors but as autonomous equals—not as having a right to equal shares but as having a right to equal treatment.

We can draw two conclusions from all this. First, egalitarianism cannot afford to define itself by contrast with humanitarianism. No conception of justice can afford that. Second, egalitarians and nonegalitarians can agree that a kind of political equality is called for even when equal shares as a distributive principle is not. Thus, to the conclusion that a pluralistic theory of justice can make some room for equal shares, we can add that a pluralistic theory can make room for a second kind of equality as well, a specifically political kind.

C. *Equality and meritocracy*

Very roughly, a regime is meritocratic to the extent that people are judged on the merits of their performance. A pure meritocracy is hard to imagine, but any regime is bound to have meritocratic elements. A corporation is meritocratic insofar as it ties promotions to performance, and departs from meritocracy insofar as it ties promotions to seniority. A society is meritocratic insofar as, within it, people are paid what their

[15] Ibid.
[16] Ibid., 313.
[17] Ibid., 289.
[18] Ibid.
[19] Ibid., 306.

work is worth. In short, in meritocracies, rewards track performance. The important point is that rewards actually track performance; it is neither necessary nor sufficient that anyone *intends* for them to do so. A corporation's culture of meritocracy is often partially a product of deliberate design, but a corporation (or especially, a whole society) can be meritocratic in some ways without anyone deciding it ought to be.

The idea of meritocracy is vague, to be sure, yet precise enough for academic egalitarians to see conflict between equality and meritocracy. Thus, philosopher Norman Daniels says that claims of merit derive from considerations of efficiency and cannot support stronger notions of desert.[20] Furthermore, regarding job placement, "the meritocrat is committed, given his concern for productivity, to distributing at least some goods, the jobs themselves, in accordance with a morally arbitrary distribution of abilities and traits."[21] Daniels concludes, "Unfortunately, many proponents of meritocracy have been so concerned with combating the lesser evil of non-meritocratic job placement that they have left unchallenged the greater evil of highly inegalitarian reward schedules. One suspects that an elitist infatuation for such reward schedules lurks behind their ardor for meritocratic job placement."[22]

Daniels's view exemplifies what Anderson calls academic egalitarianism, but liberalism also has an older, nonacademic tradition within which equal respect and meritocracy go hand in hand.[23] We see people as commanding equal respect qua citizens or human beings, but not as commanding equal respect in every respect. Egalitarians and nonegalitarians alike appreciate that genuine respect has meritocratic elements, and thus to some extent tracks how people distinguish themselves as they develop their differing potentials in different ways.[24]

Daniels says the "abilities and traits" that individuate people are "morally arbitrary," but I say that if we care about what people contribute to

[20] Norman Daniels, "Merit and Meritocracy," *Philosophy and Public Affairs* 7, no. 3 (1978): 207.

[21] Ibid., 222.

[22] Ibid.

[23] I mean to be speaking here of the liberal tradition in a quite general way, rather than of classical or modern variations on the theme. To put it in terms of stylized history, I mean liberalism as it developed in Europe and America in reaction to monarchy in particular and to social hierarchy in general. For that matter, even the socialist tradition once was in part a meritocratic reaction to a social hierarchy that prevented working classes from being able to earn fair wages.

[24] For a good discussion of this issue, see Richard J. Arneson, "What, if Anything, Renders All Humans Morally Equal?" in Dale Jamieson, ed., *Singer and His Critics* (Oxford: Blackwell Publishers, 1999), 103–28. Temkin too makes room for merit, saying, "I think deserved inequalities are not bad *at all*. Rather, what is objectionable is some being worse off than others *through no fault of their own*" (Temkin, *Inequality*, 17). Unfortunately, the sort of room Temkin tries to make has an awkward consequence. If Bill has more than me because he does better work, then according to the quotation's first sentence the inequality is deserved and therefore not bad at all; at the same time, though, I am worse off through no fault of my own, which is objectionable according to the quotation's second sentence.

our society, then traits that enable people to contribute are not arbitrary. Those traits make people who they are and define what people aspire to be, at least in societies that respect those traits. We encourage people to work hard and contribute to society by truly respecting people who work hard, not by insisting that hard work is morally arbitrary while conceding a need to fake respect in hope of conditioning people to work harder. Incentive structures work better when we see them not merely as incentive structures but also as structures that recognize merit.

For practical purposes, certain kinds of egalitarian and meritocratic elements often go together. As a broad empirical generalization, wherever we find a substantial degree of political equality, we also find a substantial degree of economic meritocracy. Far from being antithetical, the two ideas are symbiotic. A central facet of the traditional liberal ideal of equal opportunity is a call for removing arbitrary political or cultural barriers to economic mobility. After the fact, we need not and do not attach the same value to what people produce. (Obviously, people themselves are not indifferent to whether their plans pan out one way rather than another. If our inventions work, we attach more value to them than we would have if they had not, and we expect the market to do likewise.) Before the fact, though, traditional liberals want people—all people—to be as free as possible to pursue their dreams. That is to say, the equal-opportunity element of liberal tradition placed the emphasis on improving opportunities, not equalizing them.[25] The ideal of "equal pay for equal work," within the tradition from which that ideal emerged, has more in common with the ideal of meritocracy, and with the kind of equal respect built into the concept of meritocracy, than with equal shares per se.

In passing, note that meritocracy is not a synonym for market society. Meritocrats could say the marketplace's meritocratic tendencies are too weak; great talent too often goes unrecognized and unrewarded. Egalitarians could say such tendencies are too strong; Daniels seems to worry that rewards for satisfying millions of customers are larger than they should be. Underlying both complaints is the more fundamental fact that markets react to performance only in the form in which said performance is *brought to market*. So long as Emily Dickinson kept her poetry secret, the marketplace had no opinion about its merits. The marketplace tends to reward a particular kind of performance—namely,

[25] Interestingly, Richard Miller says "people are pervasively victimized by social barriers to advancement in any reasonably efficient capitalist economy. . . . On the other hand, in an advanced industrial setting, some reasonably efficient capitalist system is best for everyone who is constrained by justice" as Miller conceives of it. There is nothing inconsistent about this, although it "depends on facts that would sadden most observers of the modern industrial scene, saddening different observers for different reasons: Central planning does not work, yet traditional socialists were right in most of their charges of capitalist inequality." Richard Miller, "Justice as Social Freedom," in Rodger Beehler, David Copp, and Béla Szabados, eds., *On the Track of Reason: Essays in Honor of Kai Nielsen* (Boulder, CO: Westview, 1992), 38.

wealth-creating performance—and tends to reward that kind of performance in a particular way—namely, with wealth, or sometimes with fame and glory.[26] Markets create time and space within which people can afford hobbies; they can write poetry, if that is what pleases them, without having to worry about whether that particular activity is putting dinner on the table. But the marketplace generally does not judge, and does not reward, what people do with the space they reserve for nonmarket activities.

Let me stress that my remarks about the consistency of, and even synergy between, equality and meritocracy are offered in defense of the proposition that there is room within a pluralistic conception of justice for elements of egalitarianism. If, contrary to fact, it really were true that we had to make a choice between equality and meritocracy, it would be like choosing between egalitarianism and humanitarianism. When egalitarianism allows itself to be contrasted with humanitarianism, it begins to look monstrous. It likewise would be monstrous to reject a system not because it *fails* to recognize and reward merit, but precisely because it succeeds.

D. Pure distribution is rare

In the real world, almost nothing we do is purely distributive. To take from one and give to another does not only alter a distribution. It also alters the degree to which products are controlled by their producers. To redistribute under real-world conditions, we must alienate producers from their products. This alienation was identified as a problem by Marx, and ought to be regarded as a problem from any perspective.

In a world bound to depart systematically from egalitarian ideals, egalitarian philosophy can encourage these alienated and alienating attitudes, although egalitarian philosophy is not unique in this respect. As noted by Anderson, academic egalitarians tend to see luck as a moral problem. A purist meritocrat, though, would agree, saying success should not be mere luck, but ought to be earned. So, if meritocratic ideals had the actual effect of encouraging feelings of alienation in a world bound to depart systematically from meritocratic ideals, that would be regrettable. The general point here is that even when an uncompromisingly radical philosophy is attractive on its face, the psychological baggage that goes with it need not be. A theory of justice can deafen us to the cost of alienating producers from their product. It deafens us by telling us what we want to hear: that the product should be distributed in accordance with our dream, not the producers'.

[26] On this topic, I regard as essential reading Tyler Cowen, *In Praise of Commercial Culture* (Cambridge, MA: Harvard University Press, 1998); and Tyler Cowen, *What Price Fame?* (Cambridge, MA: Harvard University Press, 2000).

Defenders of redistribution sometimes try to justify ignoring this cost. A familiar move is to deny that people are producers. On this account, natural endowments produce. Characters produce. Persons do not. A person's character "depends in large part upon fortunate family and social circumstances for which he can claim no credit,"[27] and therefore, at least theoretically, there is a form of respect we can have for people even while giving them no credit for the effort and talent they bring to the table.

So the story goes. One basic problem with it is that the form of respect it posits is not the kind that brings producers to the table, and therefore that form of respect is, from any perspective, deficient. It is not the kind of respect that human beings value; it is not the kind that makes societies work.

Anderson notes, as many have noted, that egalitarians "regard the economy as a system of cooperative, joint production," in contrast with "the more familiar image of self-sufficient Robinson Crusoes, producing everything all by themselves until the point of trade."[28] She goes on to say that we ought to "regard every product of the economy as jointly produced by everyone working together."[29] By way of response, we all understand that Anderson's article is the product of a system of cooperative, joint production. We all know she did not produce it by herself. Yet we also understand that it is her article, and we would be furious were we to learn that Ackerman had walked into her office one day and said,

[27] John Rawls, *A Theory of Justice* (Cambridge, MA: Harvard University Press, 1971), 104. No one has done more than Rawls in recent generations to rekindle philosophical interest in liberal egalitarianism. Rawls's approach is to set aside as morally arbitrary everything that makes people unequal: that they have unequal talents, that some have better characters than others, that they have differing hopes and dreams, and so on. Crucially, and rather incredibly, he sets aside that some people have done more than others. All of these things, he says, are arbitrary from a moral point of view (ibid., sec. 17). Having done all this, it could hardly be news if the resulting conclusion turned out to have an egalitarian flavor. Many of Rawls's moderate and mainstream readers have been offended by Rawls's apparent denigration of everything that makes a person a person, and by what they see as egalitarianism taken to absurd extremes. But I think these reactions miss the fundamental point. The Rawlsian exercise does not surprise readers by coming to extreme yet plausible egalitarian conclusions. On the contrary, what is newsworthy is that the result is not a strict form of egalitarianism. Even if we resolve to ignore everything that makes people unequal, and indeed everything that individuates them as persons, the door remains wide open for unequal shares. *This* is Rawls's signature contribution. If we understand Rawls in this way, then this essay's objective is complementary to Rawls's. That is, where Rawls argues that even if we stack the deck in favor of egalitarianism, we still find substantial room for unequal shares, I argue that even for beings as unequal in morally nonarbitrary ways as we are, there remains significant room within a pluralistic theory of justice for important elements of egalitarianism.

[28] Anderson, "What Is the Point of Equality?" 321. In passing, the Crusoe image is indeed familiar, even if only in the works of liberalism's communitarian critics. In fact, the classical liberal view is that the legacy of free association is community, not atomic isolation. Humans have been organizing themselves into communities since long before there was any such thing as what we now call the state. See Loren Lomasky, "Nozick on Utopias," in David Schmidtz, ed., *Robert Nozick* (New York: Cambridge University Press, 2001); and Christopher Morris, *An Essay on the Modern State* (Cambridge: Cambridge University Press, 1998).

[29] Anderson, "What Is the Point of Equality?" 321.

"Shouldn't I get half of that article?" We do not start "from scratch." Rather, we build upon work already done. We weave our contribution into an existing fabric of contributions. We contribute at the margin (as an economist would put it) to the system of cooperative production, and, within limits, we are seen as owning our contributions, however humble they may be. This is *why* people continue to contribute, and this in turn is why we continue to have a system of cooperative production.

The most crucial point, perhaps, is that there is something necessarily and laudably ahistorical about simply respecting the abilities that people bring to the table. We need not always dig around for evidence (or worse, stipulate) that people are products of nature and nurture and therefore ineligible for moral credit. Neither must we think of our trading partners as Robinson Crusoes. Often, we simply give them credit, and often simply giving them credit is the essence of treating them as persons rather than as mere confluences of historical forces.

When we do choose to reflect on the historical background of any particular ongoing enterprise, it is appropriate to feel grateful to Thomas Edison and all those people who actually did help to make the current enterprise possible. It would be inappropriate (that is, disrespectful to people like Edison) to feel similarly grateful to people who did not actually do anything to help make the current enterprise possible. (To my mind, one of the most perfectly incredible facts about political philosophy is that, given the premise that thousands of people contribute to the tide of progress that puts individuals in a position to do what they do, we go on to debate whether the appropriate response is to honor those who did contribute or to take their money and give it to those who did not.) When particular people literally contribute to joint projects, they ought to feel grateful to each other and collectively proud of their joint achievement. However, they need not feign agnosticism about the specifics of each partner's contribution in cases where (as it usually works) they are keenly aware of the nature and value of what particular partners have contributed.

Of course, there is much to be said for acknowledging how lucky we are to live within this particular "system of cooperative, joint production" and for respecting what makes it work. My point is only (and my guess is that Anderson would agree) that the room we make for these attitudes must leave room for acknowledging complementary considerations: the kind that bring producers to the table, and the kind involved in treating individual flesh-and-blood workers with genuine respect.

IV. Equal Shares versus First Possession

In Section II, I attributed to Ackerman the view that "equal shares" is a moral default, the distribution rule we automatically go to if we cannot justify anything else. Needless to say, that is not how we actually do it. For various resources in the real world, the principle we go to if we cannot justify anything else is one invoking first possession. If you walk into the cafeteria carrying two apples, we do not begin to discuss how to allocate them. If the apples are in your hand, their allocation normally is not our business.

Ackerman, though, rejects the rule of first possession. He says that "the only liberty worthy of a community of rational persons is a liberty each is ready and willing to justify in conversation with his fellow questioners. To ground rights on first possession is at war with this ideal."[30] But if this is so, why is first possession ubiquitous? In Ackerman's garden, we are offended when you grab both apples. Why is the real world so different—so different that if Ackerman were to walk up to you in the cafeteria and say, "Shouldn't I get half of your lunch?" we would be offended by Ackerman's behavior, not yours?

Evidently, there is some difficulty in generalizing from Ackerman's thought experiment. Why? The main reason why Ackerman's point does not generalize is that in the real world we do not begin life by dividing a sack of apples that somehow, on its own, made its way to the bargaining table. Instead, we start with resources that some people have helped to produce and others have not, resources already possessed and in use by some people as others arrive on the scene. Contractarian frameworks like Ackerman's depict everyone as getting to the bargaining table at the same time; it is of fundamental moral importance that the world is not like that.

In a world where virtually everything at the table is there because someone brought it to the table, it is easy for equal respect and equal shares to come apart. In a world like that—a world like ours—to respect people is to acknowledge what they bring to the table, to respect the talent and effort manifest in what they bring, and to respect the hopes and dreams that lead them to bring what they do. But to respect them in this way is to respect their contributions as *theirs*.

A. Respect in a world of nonsimultaneous arrival

Why do property regimes around the world and throughout history consistently operate on a principle of first possession rather than one of equal shares? The reason, I suppose, starts with the fact that in the real world people arrive at different times. When people arrive at different times, equal shares no longer has the intuitive salience it had in the case of simultaneous arrival. When someone has gotten there first and is peacefully trying to put his or her discovery to use, trying to grab a piece of the action, even if only an equal piece, is not a peaceful act. It is not a respectful act. If Ackerman were to enter a corner grocery and begin discussing how to allocate whatever he can find in the cash register, as if the shopkeeper were merely another party to the discussion, he would not be treating the shopkeeper with respect. Here is a thought experi-

[30] Ackerman, "On Getting What We Don't Deserve," 63.

ment: in a world where Ackerman was not obliged to respect prior possession, how long would shops remain open for business?

Academic lawyer Carol Rose says that a legal rule that confers the status of owner upon the first person unambiguously taking possession of a given object induces discovery.[31] By inducing discovery, the rule induces future productive activity. A second virtue of such a rule is that it minimizes disputes over discovered objects.[32] In short, it enables shopkeepers to make a living in peace.[33]

Recall Ackerman's previous claim: "[T]he only liberty worthy of a community of rational persons is a liberty each is ready and willing to justify in conversation with his fellow questioners. To ground rights on first possession is at war with this ideal." Simply dismissing the other side as at war with the ideal of rational conversation, as Ackerman does here, is itself at war with the ideal of rational conversation. The truth, for millennia, has been that failing to respect prior possession is the stuff of war in an absolutely literal way. Moreover, the central place of prior possession is not a cultural artifact. Virtually any animal capable of locomotion understands at some level that if you ignore the claim of an animal that got there first, you are not treating it with respect.

B. *Xenophobia*

An overlooked virtue of first possession is that it lets us live together without having to view newcomers as a threat, whereas a rule of equal shares does not. If we were to regard every newcomer as having a claim to an equal share of our holdings, the arrival of newcomers would be inherently threatening. Imagine another thought experiment: A town has one hundred people. Each has a lot that is one hundred feet wide. Every time someone new shows up, we redraw property lines. Each lot shrinks by the amount needed to make room for the new person's equal share. Question: how friendly will this town be? Even now, in our world, people

[31] Carol Rose, "Possession As the Origin of Property," *University of Chicago Law Review* 52, no. 1 (1985): 73–88.

[32] Note that the person who establishes first possession need not acquire unconditional permanent ownership. The kind of ownership one establishes by being the first to register a *patent*, for example, is temporally limited. Alternatively, a *usufructuary* right is a particular kind of ownership that lasts only so long as the owned object is being used for its customary purpose. Thus, for example, the first person to grab a particular park bench acquires a right to use that seat for its customary purpose, but only so long as he or she occupies the bench. When the person gets up and leaves the park, the bench reverts to its previous unclaimed status.

[33] Needless to say, history is filled with irreparable injustices, which often boil down to failures to respect claims of those who were there first. The ubiquitous phenomenon of respect for prior possession is mostly an in-group phenomenon. Human groups tend not to respect claims of other groups unless those other groups are capable of defending their claims in battle. So, nothing said by Rose or by me is meant to imply that prior possession has in fact been consistently respected. On the contrary, aboriginal peoples around the world consistently have been brutally subjugated. Had prior possession been respected, many of human history's most tragic episodes would not have happened.

who see the world in zero-sum terms tend to despise immigrants. The point is not that xenophobia has moral weight, of course, but rather that it is real, a variable we want to minimize if we can. Recognizing first possession helps, compared to redistributing according to an equal-shares principle. To say the least, it would not help to tell people that newly arriving immigrants have a right to an equal share. At first, members of the community would clamor for a wall to stop people from getting in. Eventually, the point of the wall would be to stop people from getting out.

Likewise, apropos Ackerman's assertion that a liberty is worthy only if we are each ready and willing to justify it in conversation, imagine a world in which the title to your property was perpetually contingent on your ability to defeat all challengers in debate. In any remotely successful community, quite a lot of the structure of daily life literally goes without saying and needs no argument; this enables people to take quite a lot for granted and allows them to pour their energy into production rather than self-defense, verbal or otherwise.

The central role played by prior possession in any viable culture, across human history, is a problem for egalitarianism, although not uniquely for egalitarianism. Meritocracy is equally in a position of having to defer somewhat to a norm of respecting prior possession. A viable culture is a web of positive-sum games, but a game is positive-sum only if players are willing to take what they have as their starting point and carry on from there. A viable conception of justice takes *this* (along with other prerequisites of positive-sum games) as its starting point.

V. The Zero-Sum Perspective

The obvious moral problem with first possession, of course, is that those who arrive later do not get an equal share. Is that fair? It depends. Exactly how bad is it to be a latecomer? Egalitarian thought experiments such as Ackerman's are zero-sum games. In such models, first possession leaves latecomers with nothing. When you, the first appropriator, grab both apples (or even one, for that matter), you leave less for Ackerman or anyone else who comes along later. Your grab is a preface to pure consumption. Thus, as philosopher Hillel Steiner has noted, in the same way that first-comers would see newcomers as a threat under an equal-shares regime, newcomers would see first-comers as a threat under a regime of first possession.[34] Or at least, newcomers would see first-comers as a threat if it really were true that in a first-possession regime it is better to arrive early than late.

But this is not true. One central fact about a regime of first possession is that over time, as a rule, it is far better to arrive late than early. It would be unusual to meet people in a developed nation who are not substantially more wealthy than their grandparents were at a comparable age. We

[34] Hillel Steiner, conversation with author, September 24, 2000.

have unprecedented wealth today precisely because our ancestors got here first, cleared the land, and began the laborious process of turning society into a vast network of cooperative ventures for mutual advantage. In the real world, original appropriation typically is a preface to production, and then to mutually advantageous commerce with widely dispersed benefits. It is not a zero-sum game. First possessors pay the price of converting resources to productive use. Latecomers reap the benefits.[35] We occasionally should remind ourselves that in the race to appropriate, the chance to be a first appropriator is not the prize. The prize is prosperity, and latecomers win big, courtesy of the toil of those who got there first.

So, when someone asks why entrepreneurs should get to keep the whole value of what they produce, the answer is that they don't. To some people, this will seem obvious. Yet there are some who really do see the world in zero-sum terms. To them, when you grab an apple in Ackerman's garden and start planting apple seeds, it is analytic that no one else will ever benefit from all those future harvests.

A. Structural unemployment

The zero-sum perspective is most tempting when viewing the labor market. Thus, philosopher Robert Goodin can say, "If there are a thousand people looking for work and only one job, one can get work only on condition that the remainder do not. That one person succeeds in getting a job, far from proving that all could, actually precludes others from doing so."[36] Goodin admits labor markets are not really like that, yet he does not retract the claim. Citing philosopher G. A. Cohen, Goodin says, "Marxian economics provides reasons for believing that precisely that is true of the proletarian in any capitalist economy."[37] That is, "If the structure of the situation is such that one can succeed only on condition that not all do, then the freedom of the one is perfectly consistent with the 'unfreedom' of the many."[38] This is what has come to be called "structural" unemployment.

[35] For a state-of-the-art discussion of this issue, see John T. Sanders, "Projects and Property," in Schmidtz, ed., *Robert Nozick*. See also David Schmidtz, "The Institution of Property," *Social Philosophy and Policy* 11, no. 2 (1994): 42–62.

[36] Schmidtz and Goodin, *Social Welfare and Individual Responsibility*, 126.

[37] Ibid., 126 n.

[38] Ibid., 126. Cohen considers the proletariat free to remain or not remain proletarian workers in the following sense: The proletariat is like a group of people locked in a room. There is a key, but it will work only for the first person who uses it. "Each is free to seize the key and leave. But note the conditional nature of his freedom. He is free not only *because* none of the others tries to get the key, but *on condition* that they do not (a condition which, in this story, is fulfilled)." G. A. Cohen, "The Structure of Proletarian Unfreedom," *Philosophy and Public Affairs* 12, no. 1 (1983): 11. Cohen's article is wonderfully provocative. It is easy to see how someone could see it as realistically describing the kind of "key to success" we have when seeking work, although I am not sure whether Cohen himself meant it this way.

Some will see Goodin as stating a necessary truth: when two people apply for the same job, it is as if there were only one apple in Ackerman's garden. Others will say that in developed economies, the salient ratio is not (or not only) the number of jobs per *job-seeker* but the number of jobs per *month*. The former ratio leads people to misinterpret the supply of jobs as a stock rather than as a flow. If the unemployment rate is 10 percent, that does not mean one-tenth of the population is doomed to unemployment. For many, what it means is that their number is called less often than it would be if the rate were lower—unless there is genuine structural unemployment, as in countries where, for example, women are legally or culturally barred from working. But what creates structural unemployment is structure, not the rate of flow in the labor market.

B. Markets are not auctions

If society were a zero-sum game, then the only way for some to have more would be for others to have less. When we see society as actually like this, we are tempted to believe the argument that when some people have more dollars, they bid up prices of whatever is available for purchase, thereby outcompeting cash-poor people and making them worse off. This is an interesting and rhetorically powerful idea. It would even be true in a society where people acquire paper dollars from a central distributor without having done anything to create the stock of wealth for which those paper dollars are supposed to be a receipt. But now contrast this zero-sum picture with a generally more realistic picture of market society. If I acquire more dollars by contributing more goods and services to the economy, then my participation in the economy is not inflationary. On the contrary, insofar as people give me paper dollars in exchange for goods and services I bring to market, the process by which I acquire dollars has a deflationary impact, for the result of my contribution is that there now are more goods and services in circulation with no corresponding increase in the number of paper dollars in circulation. The net impact of the process by which I amass paper dollars is that *prices fall*, unless the money supply is increased to keep pace with the increased volume of goods and services in circulation.

Many people, though, continue to be swayed (if not downright blinded) by arguments premised on the assumption that for some to have more, others must have less. For some reason, this assumption is unshaken by everyday observation of people acquiring wealth not by subtracting it from a fixed stock, but by adding goods and services to the economy.

C. Sexism

Goodin's odd picture of what it is like to participate in an economy is implicit in arguments of theorists who occasionally propose, as a way of redressing our society's sexist bias, that mothers be paid a wage simply for being mothers. This too begins with an interesting and rhetorically powerful idea: When men go to the factory and women stay home to manage the household, they both work really hard. The men get paid. Why don't the women?

Here is one answer. The problem is not that the market does not recognize *women*, but that it does not recognize what is *not brought to market*. Suppose a farmer raises a crop while his wife raises children. Is it sexist that only the man's labor earns money? To test the hypothesis, imagine a farmer saying to prospective customers, "My wife and I have two things for sale: first, the fact that we are growing a crop, and second, the fact that we are raising six kids." Would prospective customers volunteer to pay the farmer for raising crops, but not for raising children?

If they would, that might suggest a sexist bias. But they would not. Their response would be, "Just show us what you have for sale. If your crop or your day-care services are for sale, we're interested. When your kids have goods of their own for sale, we'll be interested. But if what you want is to be paid to consume your own crop and raise your own kids, then in all seriousness, we have children of our own to feed. By the way, would you be better off if the king took your money to feed our kids and took our money to feed yours? Would your daughters be better off if women were expected to maximize their family's slice of the redistributive pie by having more babies than they otherwise would want? Would that end sexism?"

When people say women should be paid to raise their own children, it is as if a farmer demanded to be paid for raising a crop without actually having brought anything to market. It is to fail to grasp what is involved in exchanging value for value. It is a mistake to criticize markets for failing to commodify children. Commodifying children would be catastrophic for everyone, but especially for women. If we want to keep making progress toward the kind of society in which men and women can flourish as political equals, we need to find another way.

VI. About Empirical Studies

I close with observations about the other major source of provocation mentioned at the outset—namely, empirical studies of income inequality.[39] Although I am a professor of economics by joint appointment, I am at heart a philosopher. I trust conceptual arguments. I do not want to win arguments I do not deserve to win, and when the terrain is conceptual, I trust myself to know where I stand. I do not feel this way about statistics. This section's main purpose is not to settle some empirical issue, but simply to show how easily numbers create false impressions.

[39] See Tyler Cowen, "Does the Welfare State Help the Poor?" in this volume for a discussion of the relatively more accurate picture painted when we measure inequality of consumption rather than income.

For example, studies of income distribution typically separate populations into quintiles according to household income. While each quintile for household income contains 20 percent of all households by definition, as of 1997 the United States's bottom quintile contained only 14.8 percent of individual persons, whereas the top quintile contained 24.3 percent. Households in the bottom quintile averaged 1.9 persons and 0.6 workers, compared to 3.1 persons and 2.1 workers in the top.[40] So, one major source of income inequality among households is that some contain more wage-earners than others. If we look at raw data comparing household incomes in the top and bottom quintiles, we will not see this, and will be misled.

We can be misled in another way when studying changes in household income in a society where the number of wage-earners per household is falling. When the number of wage-earners per household falls, average *household* income can fall even as *individual* incomes rise. If two people live in a typical college-student household today versus three in a household a generation ago, this will show up in our statistics as a fall in the bottom quintile's average income. Yet in such cases, household income falls because the individuals are more wealthy, not less, which is why they now can afford to split the rent with fewer people.[41]

It is easy to dig up a study showing that average wages fell by, say, 9 percent between 1975 and 1997, if that is what we want to hear. If not, it is equally easy to verify that such studies are based upon a discredited way of correcting for inflation (in addition, these studies ignore factors such as the burgeoning of fringe benefits) and that when we use more currently accepted ways of correcting for inflation, the corrected numbers show average wages rising 35 percent between 1975 and 1997.[42] In 1996, a panel of five economists, commissioned by the Senate Finance Committee and chaired by Michael Boskin, concluded that the consumer price

[40] Robert Rector and Rea S. Hederman, *Income Inequality: How Census Data Misrepresent Income Distribution* (Washington, DC: Heritage Foundation, 1999).

[41] Edward Wolff notes that it is easy to contrive size-adjusted family-income equivalents. But my point is that Census Bureau data—the standard source for almost any study you will read on U.S. income inequality—is not in fact corrected in this way.

[42] Both figures are in Floyd Norris, "Sorry, Wrong Numbers: So Maybe It Wasn't the Economy," *New York Times*, December 1, 1996, sec. 4, p. 1. The first number is based on the standard consumer price index at the time. The second number was supplied by Leonard Nakamura, an economist with the Federal Reserve Bank of Philadelphia. Recent reports from the U.S. Census Bureau and the Bureau of Labor Statistics contain punishingly technical discussions of alternative ways of calculating inflation.

Edward Wolff provides the first, negative number in Edward Wolff, "The Stagnating Fortunes of the Middle Class," in this volume. In a conversation in September 2000 regarding a draft of that essay, Wolff admitted that his numbers were based upon a discredited method of adjusting for inflation. He rejected the idea that he should adjust his numbers, though, because, as he put it, "we can debate endlessly about the exact nature of the required adjustment, but it wouldn't be productive." When I noted that all he needed to do was correct his data by whatever measure he considered reasonable, and that his own best judgment would thereby be shown to be incompatible with his thesis that the middle class is stagnating, Wolff appeared indifferent.

index overstates inflation by about 1.1 percent per year (perhaps as little as 0.8 percent; perhaps as much as 1.6 percent).[43] If the figure of 1.1 percent is correct, then "instead of the stagnation recorded in official statistics, a lower inflation measure would mean that *real* median family income grew from 1973 to 1995 by 36 percent."[44]

If there is one thing I would like readers to take away as the message of this section, it would not be a number. It would be the following picture. An income distribution is a bunch of people occupying steps on a staircase.[45] Pessimists use numbers to show that the bottom step is where it always has been. Even worse, they claim, the staircase has begun to stretch. The top now climbs higher than it once did, thereby increasing the gap between the top and bottom steps, that is, between the rich and poor. Optimists use the same numbers to show that people who once stood on the lower steps have moved up. While there are still people at the bottom, many belong to a younger generation whose time to move up is still coming. From a "snapshot" perspective, the picture is one of stagnation, but to people actually living these lives, the staircase is a moving escalator, lifting people to heights that did not exist when their grandparents were children. This perspective—which treats life in the way people actually live it—is a picture of incremental improvement.

I am not asking you to be an optimist. The message, instead, is that the pessimistic perspective is, at very best, only one way of being realistic. At bottom, the profound truth of the matter may be, as philosopher Richard Miller once remarked to me, that there is a place for a Democratic sort of emphasis on complaining about where some of us had to start, and also a place for a Republican sort of emphasis on accepting our starting point as a starting point and making the best of it.

A. Inequality and age in the United States

Statistics seem to indicate that the rich are getting richer. The income gap between the top quintile and other quintiles has, by some measures, been growing. What does this mean? For the sake of reference, when we divide households into income quintiles, the income cutoffs as of 1999 are as follows:

Lowest quintile: Zero to $17,262

Second quintile: $17,263 to $32,034

[43] "Statistical Guessing Game," *Economist*, December 7, 1996, 25.

[44] David Gergen, "Flying in an Economic Fog," *U.S. News and World Report*, September 8, 1997, 104 (emphasis added). See also Michael Boskin et al., *Toward a More Accurate Measure of the Cost of Living: Final Report to the Senate Finance Committee*, available on-line at *http://www.ssa.gov/history/reports/boskinrpt.html*.

[45] I borrow this metaphor from Stephen Rose, "Is Mobility in the United States Still Alive?" *International Review of Applied Economics* 13, no. 3 (1999): 417–36.

Third quintile: $32,035 to $50,851

Fourth quintile: $50,852 to $79,454

Top quintile: $79,455 and up[46]

Household income at the 80th percentile is thus 4.6 times household income at the 20th percentile. Compare this to the median household incomes of different age groups, as of 1999:

$24,031 when the head of the household is under 25

$43,309 when the head of the household is between ages 25 and 34

$54,993 when the head of the household is between ages 35 and 44

$65,303 when the head of the household is between ages 45 and 54

$54,249 when the head of the household is between ages 55 and 64[47]

Like the gaps between the quintiles, gaps between age groups appear to be increasing. Where earnings had once begun to trail off as workers entered their forties, earnings now continue to rise as workers reach their fifties, only then beginning to drop as early retirements start to cut into average earnings. Economist Michael Cox and journalist Robert Alm report that "[i]n 1951, individuals aged 35 to 44 earned 1.6 times as much as those aged 20 to 24, on average. By 1993, the highest paid age group had shifted to the 45 to 54-year-olds, who earned nearly 3.1 times as much as the 20 to 24-year-olds."[48]

The numbers seem to say that the top quintile cannot be characterized as a separate caste of aristocrats. To some extent, the quintiles appear to be constituted by ordinary median people at different ages.[49] So, when we read that median income at the 80th percentile has jumped by 46 percent in real dollar terms between 1967 and 1999,[50] we should entertain the likelihood that for many people living at the 20th percentile, that jump represents increasing opportunity for them, not just for some separate

[46] This data is from U.S. Census Bureau, *Money Income in the United States: 1999* (Washington, DC: U.S. Government Printing Office, 2000), table 13.

[47] This data is from ibid., table 4.

[48] Michael Cox and Robert Alm, "By Our Own Bootstraps" (annual report of the Federal Reserve Bank of Dallas, published in 1995).

[49] Richard Miller has referred me to a study estimating that the proportion of income inequality that is due to age inequality is 28 percent for men and 14 percent for women. See Gary Burtless, *A Future of Lousy Jobs? The Changing Structure of U.S. Wages* (Washington, DC: Brookings Institution, 1990). That is a substantial proportion, although I am a bit surprised, given the income statistics for 1999 just cited in the text. Given that average income for household heads aged 45 to 54 is now 2.7 times that for household heads under 25, I might guess the proportion of income inequality due to age inequality in 1999 was higher than the numbers cited by Burtless.

[50] U.S. Census Bureau, *Money Income in the United States: 1999*, table C.

elite. It represents what many reasonably hope to earn as they reach the age when people like them take their turn composing the top quintile. Again, the fact that 45- to 54-year-olds are doing much better today, thereby widening the gaps between income quintiles, appears to be good news for a lot of people, not only for people currently in that age group.[51]

Even if the lowest quintile has not been getting richer over time, this does not mean that the group of people flipping burgers a generation ago is still today stuck flipping burgers. Rather, the implication is that when this year's crop of high school graduates flips burgers for a year, they will get paid roughly what their parents were paid when they were the same age, doing the same things. (What else would we expect?) Again, if today's bottom 20 percent is no richer than the bottom 20 percent was a generation ago, the upshot is that the lowest-paying *jobs* do not pay much more than they ever did, not that the people who once held those jobs still hold them today.

Although the lowest-paying jobs may not pay much more now than they ever did, we know many low-pay workers did not remain low-pay workers. "Individuals in the lowest income quintile in 1975 saw, on average, a $25,322 rise in their real income over the sixteen years from 1975 to 1991. Those in the highest income quintile had a $3,974 increase in real income, on average."[52] How could people who had been in the bottom quintile gain over six times as much as people who had been in the top one? Assuming the numbers indicate something real, my conjecture would be that, again, what we call income quintiles are, to some extent, different age groups. Over sixteen years, people who had in 1975 made up a large part of the top quintile edged into retirement while younger people who had made up a large part of the bottom quintile in 1975 hit their peak earning years. This is only a conjecture, but it would explain why those who had composed the bottom quintile gained substantially more over sixteen years than those who had composed the top did.

B. While the rich get richer

Ideally, we want to know two things. First, are people doing better than their parents were doing at the same age? Second, do people do better as

[51] Martin Feldstein lists several reasons for rapid rises in income at the top of the distribution: there are more people with advanced educations; there has been an increase in entrepreneurial activity, with many new businesses being created; highly paid professionals are working longer hours; and the cost of capital is declining, reducing perceived risks of investment and entrepreneurial activity. See Martin Feldstein, "Overview" (comments delivered at symposium on income inequality hosted by the Federal Reserve Bank of Kansas City, Jackson Hole, WY, August 1998), available on-line at http://www.kc.frb.org/PUBLICAT/SYMPOS/1998/S98feldstein.pdf.

[52] Cox and Alm, "By Our Own Bootstraps," 8, citing Institute for Social Research, *A Panel Study of Income Dynamics* (Ann Arbor, MI: Institute for Social Research, 1989). The numbers are in 1993 dollars.

they get older? The answer to each of these crucial questions appears to be yes in general, although obviously I do not mean to suggest everyone is doing well. Still, in general, the numbers seem to say that it is not only the already rich who are getting richer. There are many more people *getting* rich. In 1967, only 3.2 percent of U.S. households were making the equivalent of $100,000 in 1999 dollars. By 1999, the number had risen to 12.3 percent. For whites, the increase was from 3.4 to 12.9 percent; for blacks, the increase was from 1.0 to 6.1 percent.[53] So, if we ask why the top quintile made further gains between 1967 and 1999, it apparently would be incorrect to explain the change by saying that a small cadre of people had a lot of money in 1967 and that by 1999 that same cadre had pulled even farther ahead. On the contrary, what seems to explain the burgeoning wealth of the top quintile is that millions upon millions of people joined the ranks of the rich. These people were not rich when they were younger. Their parents were not rich. But they are rich today.

In "America's Rags-to-Riches Myth," journalist Michael M. Weinstein says Americans "cling to the conceit that they have unrivaled opportunity to move up."[54] But the conceit, Weinstein says, is merely that. Yet Weinstein is aware that the U.S. Treasury Department's Office of Tax Analysis found that of people in the bottom income quintile in 1979, 65 percent moved up two or more quintiles by 1988. Eighty-six percent jumped at least one quintile.[55] Are these findings unique? There is room for skepticism, here as elsewhere. But no, the finding is not unique. Using independent data from the Michigan Panel Study of Income Dynamics, Cox and Alm's study tracked a different group occupying the lowest quintile in 1975, and saw 80.3 percent of the group move up two or more quintiles by 1991. Ninety-five percent moved up at least one quintile. Furthermore, 29 percent moved from the bottom quintile to the top quintile between 1975 and 1991.[56] In absolute terms (that is, in terms of income gains in real dollar terms), the improvement is even larger. In absolute terms, 39.2 percent of those in the bottom quintile in 1975 had, by 1991, moved to where the top quintile *had been* in 1975. Only 2.3 percent remained at a living standard equal to that of 1975's lowest quintile.[57]

These studies do *not* show us to be a nation of people lifting ourselves out of poverty "by our own bootstraps," though, because not everyone with a low income is from a poor background. Many low-income people are students who receive substantial family support. We should not infer

[53] This data is from U.S. Census Bureau, *Money Income in the United States: 1999*, table B-2.

[54] Michael M. Weinstein, "America's Rags-to-Riches Myth," *New York Times*, February 18, 2000, A28.

[55] U.S. Department of the Treasury, Office of Tax Analysis, "Household Income Changes over Time: Some Basic Questions and Facts," *Tax Notes*, August 24, 1992.

[56] Cox and Alm, "By Our Own Bootstraps," 8, citing Institute for Social Research, *A Panel Study of Income Dynamics.*

[57] Cox and Alm, "By Our Own Bootstraps," 8, citing Institute for Social Research, *A Panel Study of Income Dynamics.*

from Cox and Alm's study that family background does not matter.[58] Researchers Daniel McMurrer, Mark Condon, and Isabell Sawhill say:

> Overall, the evidence suggests that the playing field is becoming more level in the United States. Socioeconomic origins today are less important than they used to be. Further, such origins have little or no impact for individuals with a college degree, and the ranks of such individuals continue to increase. This growth in access to higher education represents an important vehicle for expanding opportunity. Still, family background continues to matter. While the playing field may be becoming more level, family factors still significantly shape the economic outcomes of children.[59]

A related issue: we have looked at the upward mobility of individuals, but we find less mobility in studies tracking households. Researchers Greg Duncan, Johànne Boisjoly, and Timothy Smeeding estimate that if we were to look at household rather than individual mobility, we would see that 47 percent of those in the bottom quintile in 1975 were still there in 1991. (Actually, they refer to the bottom quintile as "the poor," which is an increasingly untenable equation as the percentage of households officially in poverty continues to drop.) Twenty percent moved to the distribution's top half, and 6 percent moved to the top quintile.[60]

These numbers suggest household mobility is quite substantial; nevertheless, there apparently is a big difference between individual upward mobility and household upward mobility. Why would that be? Imagine a household with two teenagers, circa 1975. Two studies track this household. One study tracks household members as individuals, and finds that sixteen years later the teenagers' incomes have risen several quintiles. A

[58] I thank Richard Miller for a helpful discussion and references, including Thomas L. Hungerford, "U.S. Income Mobility in the Seventies and Eighties," *Review of Income and Wealth* 39, no. 4 (1993): 403–17. As we would expect, Hungerford finds less movement in his seven-year studies than we see in the nine-year and sixteen-year studies by the U.S. Treasury Department and U.S. Federal Reserve Bank. Hungerford also finds that between his 1969–76 and 1979–86 studies, upward mobility decreased somewhat for the bottom five deciles, while increasing somewhat for the sixth, seventh, and eighth (ibid., 407). Isabel V. Sawhill and Daniel P. McMurrer compare several studies on income mobility and find a rough consensus that about 40 percent of those in the bottom quintile at a given point in time move up in ten years; after twenty years, about 50 percent have moved up. Isabell V. Sawhill and Daniel P. McMurrer, "Economic Mobility in the United States" (report published by the Urban Institute, December 1996), available on-line at http://www.urban.org/oppor/opp_031b.html.

[59] Daniel P. McMurrer, Mark Condon, and Isabel V. Sawhill, "Intergenerational Mobility in the United States" (report published by the Urban Institute, May 1997), available on-line at http://www.urban.org/oppor/opp_4b.htm.

[60] Greg Duncan, Johanne Boisjoly, and Timothy Smeeding, "How Long Does It Take for a Young Worker to Support a Family?" *NU Policy Research* 1, no. 1 (1996). *NU Policy Research* is an on-line journal; the essay is available at http://www.northwestern.edu/IPR/publications/nupr/nuprv01n1/duncan.html.

second study tracking the original household as a household finds that the household lost the summer wages the now-departed teenagers earned while living at home and attending college. When the teenagers left home, they disappeared from the second study because the households they went on to form did not exist when the study began in 1975. That is, a longitudinal study tracking 1975 households ignores individuals who grow up, move out, form new households, and move up after 1975. Given the same data, a longitudinal study of circa-1975 households paints a picture of modest progress while a longitudinal study of circa-1975 individuals suggests volcanic upward mobility. Which picture is more realistic?

Duncan et al. do not reveal the basis of their estimates. I have no reason to doubt them, but it is interesting that Duncan et al. mention later in their article that their data set, drawn from the Michigan Panel Study, "is designed to be continuously representative of the nonimmigrant population as a whole."[61] I presume they have reasons for excluding immigrants, yet I would wager that immigrant households are more upwardly mobile than nonimmigrant households. Immigrant and nonimmigrant individuals may not differ much, relatively speaking, since they all start with teenage incomes and then move up. Households, though, are another matter, since if we exclude immigrant households, we are excluding households that are not established but are instead in a position like that of individual teenagers: they have little wealth and little income, for now, but they came here to work and make a major move up as a household. A focus on households already lends itself to an understatement of income mobility, compared to studies that focus on tracking individuals. Excluding immigrant households presumably increases the magnitude of that relative understatement.

Again, I do not mean to say that the study by Duncan et al. is especially flawed. On the contrary, it is not. Like any other study, it is potentially informative, and potentially misleading. It offers not simply numbers, but interpretations of numbers. Any study of income mobility begins with key decisions about what the researchers are looking for. Different studies measure different things, and no one is to blame for that.

Weinstein simply dismisses Cox and Alm's study of individuals on the ground that many people who moved up were people who were students when the study began. Of course students make up a big part of the bottom quintile, and of course they move up, Weinstein says, but so what? "This upward mobility of students hardly answers the enduring question: How many grown-ups are trapped in low-paying jobs?" Weinstein answers his own question by saying, "The answer is, a lot."[62] Oddly, though, the only evidence he offers that "a lot" of grown-ups are trapped is a study of poverty among children. To that study we now turn.

[61] Ibid.
[62] Weinstein, "America's Rags-to-Riches Myth."

C. Children

In their study, economists Peter Gottschalk and Sheldon Danziger separated children into quintiles according to family income.[63] Their data, Weinstein reports, shows that "[a]bout 6 in 10 of the children in the lowest group—the poorest 20 percent—in the early 1970's were still in the bottom group 10 years later. . . . No conceit about mobility, real or imagined, can excuse that unconscionable fact."[64]

Since Weinstein relies solely on Gottschalk and Danziger, I checked the original study. Gottschalk and Danziger were studying American children that were 5 years old or younger when their ten-year studies began—ten years later, the children were still children.[65] What we appear to have, then, is a cohort of mostly young couples with babies, about 40 percent of whom had moved into higher quintiles ten years later. Is this percentage bad? Out of context, it looks neither bad nor good. Has any society ever done better?

Yes. It turns out at least one society has done better: the United States itself. The figure cited by Weinstein is the result from the first decade of a two-decade study. Weinstein presents the figure from the 1970s (only 43 percent moving up) as an indictment of America today, neglecting to mention that the study's corresponding figure from the 1980s was 51 percent. Although the two figures come from the same table in Gottschalk and Danziger's paper, Weinstein evidently felt the more up-to-date number and the upward trend were not worth mentioning.

A further thought: At the end of the Gottschalk-Danziger studies, the parents of the studied children are (generally) in their early thirties, still ten years away from the time when they become most upwardly mobile. And of course, the kids are still thirty years away from the time when they become most upwardly mobile. So, the Gottschalk-Danziger studies end at a point where I would have predicted it would be too soon for there to be much evidence of upward mobility.

I myself would have been one of those kids they are talking about. I grew up on a farm in Saskatchewan. We sold the farm when I was 11 and moved to the city, where Dad became a janitor and Mom became a cashier in a fabric shop. Even before we left the farm, we had already moved up in absolute terms—we got indoor plumbing when I was about 3 years old—but we would still have been in the bottom quintile. Even after we got a flush toilet, water had to be delivered by truck, and it was so

[63] Peter Gottschalk and Sheldon Danziger, "Income Mobility and Exits from Poverty of American Children, 1970–1992" (study prepared for UNICEF's International Child Development Centre, 1999), available on-line at http://ideas.uqam.ca/ideas/data/Papers/bocbocoec430.html. The paper is also in Bruce Bradbury, Stephen P. Jenkins, and John Micklewright, eds., *The Dynamics of Child Poverty in Industrialized Nations* (Cambridge: Cambridge University Press, 2001).

[64] Weinstein, "America's Rags-to-Riches Myth."

[65] Gottschalk and Danziger, "Income Mobility and Exits from Poverty," 4.

expensive that we flushed the toilet only once a day—and it served a family of eight. Thirty-five years later, my household income is in the top 5 percent of the overall distribution. Had I been part of Gottschalk and Danziger's study, though, Weinstein would have been professing to be outraged by the "unconscionable" fact that when I was 10 years old, I had not yet made my move.

In my case, the problem with childhood poverty was not lack of money. Money was never a problem. Even the toilet was not really a problem. Lack of knowledge was a problem. Lack of educated role models was a problem. (My parents received sixth-grade educations. I did not know what a university was until we moved to the city.) I suspect that the Internet notwithstanding, the big obstacles I faced continue to be big obstacles for poor kids today.

Let us return to the study. As I said, I would have predicted that we would see precious little evidence of upward mobility in a study that ends before subjects reach their mid-teens. But let us take a look. According to Gottschalk and Danziger, among children in bottom-quintile families that received welfare payments in the early 1970s, 2.3 percent were in households that rose beyond the second quintile by the early 1980s. Bottom-quintile children living in single-parent families had a 6.4 percent chance of being in a household that moved beyond the second quintile.[66] Unsurprisingly, one-adult households brought in less income than two-adult households at both points in time, and therefore we find them in the bottom two quintiles. How bad is that? The poverty rate in the United States continues to fall and was most recently measured at 11.8 percent,[67] which means that being in the bottom two quintiles—the bottom 40 percent—is not the synonym for "being poor" that it once was.[68]

If there is a problem here, it appears to have less to do with differences in income and wealth per se and more to do with single parenthood (and

[66] Ibid., 8.

[67] U.S. Census Bureau, *Poverty in the United States: 1999* (Washington, DC: U.S. Government Printing Office, 2000), table A. The poverty threshold varies with the size of the household (and, less intuitively, with the age of the household's members). For 1999, the official poverty threshold for a household consisting of two adults under age 65 was $11,214. U.S. Census Bureau, "Poverty Thresholds: 1999," in U.S. Census Bureau, *March Current Population Survey: 1999* (Washington, DC: U.S. Government Printing Office, 2000).

[68] Furthermore, being officially below the poverty threshold does not entail material hardship. There are truly suffering people out there, but in the United States they are a small percentage of the total population. According to a U.S. Department of Agriculture survey, only one-third of 1 percent of U.S. households reported a child skipping a meal due to lack of food in 1994–95. Of households *below the poverty level*, only 3.5 percent reported having a child who needed medical care or surgery but did not get it. The original sources of this data are U.S. Department of Agriculture, *Household Food Security in the United States in 1995: Summary Report of the Food Security Measurement Project* (Washington, DC: U.S. Department of Agriculture, 1997); and Centers for Disease Control, National Center for Health Statistics, *Access to Health Care* (Washington, DC: U.S. Government Printing Office, 1997). See also Robert E. Rector, Kirk A. Johnson, and Sarah E. Youssef, "The Extent of Material Hardship and Poverty in the United States," *Review of Social Economy* 57, no. 3 (1999): 351–87.

I do not pretend to know how to solve that problem). Economist Robert Lerman estimates that half the increase in income inequality observed in the late 1980s and early 1990s was due to an increase in the number of single-parent households.[69] According to Gottschalk and Danziger, there is a big difference between being poor and white and being poor and black: blacks are more likely to stay in the bottom quintile. I am reluctant to quarrel with Gottschalk and Danziger here, and yet, according to their own numbers, the result of their ten-year study begun in 1971 is that "black children had a *higher* chance than white children of escaping poverty if they made the transition from a single-parent family to a 2-parent family by the end of the decade (67.9 versus 42.6 percent)."[70] Looking at results of the second study, begun in 1981, we find the chance of a child escaping poverty (actually, the bottom quintile) upon moving from a single-parent to a two-parent family improving to 87.8 percent for blacks and 57.6 percent for whites.[71]

The numbers seem to say that race is not the problem; again, coming from a single-parent family is the problem. However, in the 1980s, whites were nearly three times as likely as blacks to make that move from single-parent to two-parent families (which represents a closing of what had been a fourfold gap in the 1970s).[72] Furthermore, black children are more likely to be in a single-parent setting in the first place. As of 1998, the percentage of out-of-wedlock births was 21.9 percent for non-Hispanic whites and 69.3 percent for blacks.[73] I trust even hardcore egalitarians will agree that what is bad about these numbers is how high they are, not how unequal they are.

In the 1980s, Gottschalk and Danziger say, the overall probability that a child would escape poverty was higher than it was in the 1970s, although the improvement was not significant.[74] For the record—using their numbers—the chance of escaping poverty improved from 43.2 percent to 51.2 percent.[75] Oddly, when Gottschalk and Danziger say that an eight-point swing is not significant, they do not hasten to clarify what this means. What they do not say is that although the change appears huge, they did not collect enough data to be able to call the improvement *statistically* significant.[76] Uncritical readers such as Weinstein are left to infer that there was no improvement.

[69] Robert I. Lerman, "The Impact of the Changing U.S. Family Structure on Child Poverty and Income Inequality," *Economica* 63, no. 250 (1996): 119–39.

[70] Gottschalk and Danziger, "Income Mobility and Exits from Poverty," 11.

[71] Ibid., table 6.

[72] Ibid., table 7.

[73] National Center for Health Statistics, "Births: Final Data for 1998," available on-line at http://www.cdc.gov/nchs/data/nvsr/nvsr48/nvs48_3.pdf.

[74] Gottschalk and Danziger, "Income Mobility and Exits from Poverty," 9.

[75] Ibid., table 4.

[76] For the classic warning against equating statistical significance with significance in the ordinary sense of the term, see Deirdre N. McCloskey, *The Rhetoric of Economics*, 2d ed. (Madison: University of Wisconsin Press, 1998).

Gottschalk and Danziger say that "only one demographic group (children in two parent families) shows a significant decline in the probability of remaining poor."[77] (What a discouraging thought—that we have reached a point where children in two-parent families are "only one demographic group.") Within that group, the chance of escaping poverty improved from 47 percent in the 1970s to 65 percent in the 1980s. Again, there is something so odd here that I am left not knowing what to think: the authors acknowledge the massively improved prospects of "children of two parent families" parenthetically, as if that class were a small anomaly that does not bear on their contention that the probability of escaping poverty has not significantly improved.

Finally, recall that we are talking about the chance of escaping poverty (more accurately, the bottom quintile) before leaving the 10-15 age bracket. If we sought deliberately to design an experiment guaranteed to show no evidence of vertical mobility, we could hardly do better. Yet what Gottschalk and Danziger's numbers say is that nearly two-thirds of poor kids in unbroken homes escape poverty before earning their first paycheck. If Gottschalk and Danziger's numbers are right, then it is fact, not myth: these kids live in a land of opportunity.

Are growing differences in wealth and income a problem? Maybe so, in some respects. Nothing said here proves otherwise. The truly obvious problem, though, is more specific. In general, in the United States, poor people not only can but typically do move up—it is kids from broken homes who have a problem.

D. The political problem

One might argue that the problem of inequality is fundamentally caused by a lack of political will to "soak" the rich. We can imagine asking young poor people whether it is to their advantage for us to raise marginal rates on the tax brackets they are hoping to move into. It is possible they will say yes, but it is equally possible that the tax hike would take a bigger bite out of their ambitions than out of rich people's wallets. (This last claim may be very hard to imagine for people who grew up in middle-class homes and never saw working-class life as an option, but a "What's the point?" sentiment was common among people with whom I grew up at a time when marginal tax rates were higher.)

Would "soaking the rich" lead to greater equality? The answer, obviously, is that it depends on how the tax revenues would be distributed. The current U.S. federal budget is 1.7 trillion dollars. If we were to distribute that kind of money among the 14.8 percent of people who make up the poorest 20 percent of American households—roughly forty million people—we would already have enough to give a little over $40,000 to

[77] Ibid., 10.

each person. A family of four would receive over $160,000. Of course, nothing remotely like that is happening. Why not? At least a part of the story is that the federal government has other priorities, and always will. We might suspect the problem cannot be solved by giving the government more money. After all, gaps between rich and poor apparently widened in tandem with rising federal budgets.

We can hope that as the rich get richer, more money will trickle down to the poor. We can also hope that as federal budgets grow, money will trickle down to the poor. But the rich have been getting richer, and federal budgets have grown. So, if the trickle down is not working now, perhaps it never will. In particular, as federal budgets grow, we would expect to reach a point (if we have not already done so) where the trickle down would come to a halt, or even reverse itself. The reason is that as budgets grow, it becomes increasingly worthwhile for special interest groups to fight for control of those budgets at the expense of the politically disenfranchised. If unequal concentrations of political power can be thought of as a beast, then government budgets are part of what feeds that beast and gives it reason to live. Although it is beyond the scope of this essay, my guess is that an effective coalescing of will and ability to help people avoid or at least cope with single parenthood and other pressing problems is more likely to occur in those local nongovernmental organizations whose budgets are small enough and whose governance is transparent enough to be less inviting to political opportunists.[78]

VII. Summary

As economist Amartya Sen says, "[E]very normative theory or social arrangement that has at all stood the test of time seems to demand equality of *something*."[79] It is worth adding, though, that by the same token every theory, including egalitarian theories, countenances inequality as well. An egalitarian is a person who embraces one kind of unequal treatment as the price of securing equality of (what he or she considers) a more important kind.

There is a place for equal shares. Paradigmatically, there is a place for the principle of equal shares when we arrive simultaneously at the bargaining table to distribute goods to which no one has any prior claim. It would be a thankless task to try to construct a complete catalog of cases where equal shares is most salient. Suffice it to say that we can ask what the virtues of equal shares would be in a given context, were we to assess the principle without begging the question; that is, were we to assess the

[78] But see the chapter on mutual aid in Schmidtz and Goodin, *Social Welfare and Individual Responsibility*.

[79] Amartya Sen, *Inequality Reexamined* (Cambridge, MA: Harvard University Press, 1992), 12–13.

principle by reference to moral considerations that do not presuppose the principle. This is how we can try to make room for any given principle of justice within a pluralist theory.[80]

Equal respect is among the most basic of moral desiderata. Equal respect or equal treatment may be analytically built into the concept of justice even if equal shares is not. The idea of giving people their due is the basic concept of justice, not merely a contested conception. And the idea of giving people their due is hard to separate (at least at the most abstract level) from an ideal of equal treatment.

However, it would be a mistake to think that a commitment to treat people with equal respect entails a *general* commitment to make sure they have equal shares. In the marketplace, at least, meritocracy can embody one way of implementing a conception of equal treatment. Historically, "equal pay for equal work" has been seen this way within the liberal tradition.

First possession arguably is not a principle of justice at all, yet it plays a central role in any viable society. It is one of the signposts by which we navigate in a social world. We can question the principle in theory (and in theory it probably is easier to attack than to defend), but we do not and cannot question the principle in our daily practice. We would be lost without it.

Empirically, it can be hard to know what to make of recent income trends. We are barraged by numbers, or by interpretations thereof, and people skilled at gathering numbers are not always so skilled at interpreting them. If I were to do serious empirical work, I would ask why people today generally look forward to standards of living almost beyond the imagination of their ancestors from a century ago. (Life expectancy, for example, has nearly doubled.) I would ask who has been left behind by this burgeoning of real prosperity and why, and what can be done about it. I would not assume that all problems have solutions, nor that all solutions are worth their costs. Optimist that I am, I assume we can do better. Realist that I am, I know we could do worse.

Philosophy and Economics, University of Arizona

[80] Or so I argue in the larger work (David Schmidtz, *The Elements of Justice*) of which this essay will be a part.

TOO MUCH INEQUALITY*

By Richard W. Miller

I. Introduction

It used to seem so simple. In the old days (the seventies and eighties of the last century), most political philosophers who were inclined to call themselves "egalitarian" thought that one or another version of this argument established at least the approximate truth about economic justice:

I. (Basic Equality) To avoid wrongdoing, one must choose in a way that could express appreciation of the equal worth of all persons.

II. (Economic Equality) For one's political choices to express appreciation of the equal worth of all, one must support economic arrangements that provide all of one's fellow citizens with equal means, of an appropriate kind, to pursue well-being, unless there is a legitimate excuse not to do so based on one of these considerations:
   a. The need to respect the equal civil and political liberties of all, even if this entails economic inequality; or
   b. The fact that an economic inequality is an unavoidable side effect of an arrangement that is best for the worst off

III. (Neutrality) Political choices expressing appreciation of the equal worth of all must not discriminate among ways of life as more or less worth pursuing, except on the independent and prior ground that they are more or less compatible with a political outlook of appreciation of everyone's equal worth.

In order to respect Neutrality, the argument continued, the relevant measure of equality of economic means must be equality of all-purpose means, useful in pursuing all personal goals that depend on economic success. In a modern economy, such equality will consist of equal access to income and wealth.

* I am extremely indebted to David Schmidtz, Ellen Frankel Paul, Richard Arneson, Eric Mack, and other contributors to this volume for their very helpful comments on an earlier version of this essay.

Conclusion: it is wrong to support arrangements that do not provide equal access to income and wealth unless they are justified by at least one of the two excuses for inequality, IIa and IIb.

There were many variants of this argument, including diverse interpretations and modifications of the conclusion. Above all, there were heated disagreements within the egalitarian family over what type of equality to invest with ultimate authority in light of the need to respect Neutrality. Still, under the influence of some version of this argument, most egalitarians shared the practical political conclusion of John Rawls, the great pioneer of modern liberal egalitarianism: given "the constraints of simplicity and availability of information to which any practicable political conception . . . is subject,"[1] citizens should condemn large differences in income and wealth among typical occupants of different social positions as unjust, unless they are justified by IIa or IIb. The goal of economic justice asserted in this claim is what I will mean by "equality of income and wealth," making it a label for what has united self-described egalitarians and provoked their opponents.

After briefly sketching some reasons to abandon the old argument, because of weaknesses in the premises of Economic Equality and Neutrality, I will assess the moral importance of equality of income and wealth in the more complex reasoning that is the natural successor to the old argument if those challenges succeed. In working out the economic implications of Basic Equality, the surviving premise, this fragmented successor responds to diverse specific features of modern social relationships, rather than relying on the generic stance of Economic Equality, and evaluates different kinds of lives in ways that Neutrality prohibited.

II. The Fragmentation of Equality

In controversies over the old argument, the first premise, Basic Equality, which identifies moral duty with choosing so as to express appreciation of the equal worth of all, has certainly retained its force. My statement, in terms of equal worth, is just one of a variety of equivalent formulations that are now confidently deployed. Rather than signaling troubling ambiguities, this diversity adds to the power of this moral egalitarianism. In a particular context, one formulation's dictates may be clearer than others', so the relationship between alternative formulations is one of mutual aid. Some useful alternatives to my formulation in terms of equal worth speak of respect for persons, self-respect, or mutual justifiability. More

[1] John Rawls, *Political Liberalism* (New York: Columbia University Press, 1993), 182 (clarifying the egalitarianism of his seminal book, John Rawls, *A Theory of Justice* [Cambridge, MA: Harvard University Press, 1971]).

specifically, the commitment to choose in a way that expresses appreciation of the equal worth of all persons is, equivalently, the commitment:

- —to choose in ways that express full and equal respect for all persons;
- —to govern oneself by rules that everyone could self-respectfully embrace as a shared moral code;
- —to govern oneself on terms that everyone could share without anyone's having reasons to prefer general regulation by a different moral code that are more serious than anyone's reasons to object to the replacement.[2]

The single outlook that is expressed in these different dicta is often summed up as being a perspective of equal respect. In insisting on this perspective, the old argument that justice demands equality of income and wealth (with provisos IIa and IIb) was off to a good start. But confidence in the argument as a whole has dramatically weakened, for the bright endurance of Basic Equality has been shadowed by grave doubts about the other premises, Economic Equality and Neutrality.

The claim that in all relationships, appreciation of the equal worth of all must be expressed by promoting an equal distribution of the means to pursue well-being would be farfetched even if provisos about basic liberties and about the worst off analogous to IIa and IIb were imposed. Surely, I can regard the girl across the street as worth no less than my daughter without doing at all as much to advance that girl's economic future, even if her own parents can do very little. I must have equal respect for her, but I need not (indeed, I should not) have equal concern for her. I have no less respect for my fellow humans in Mali than for my fellow citizens of the United States, but my political choices need not express as much concern for the poor of Mali as they must for the poor of the South Bronx. But if equal respect does not in general require the promotion of equal means to well-being, it is hard to see what special feature of fellow-citizenship supports the demand of Economic Equality, that is, the commitment to favor laws forcing fellow citizens to provide one another with equal economic means. There is a growing fear among us egalitarians that no feature of fellow-citizenship is strong and broad enough to bear this weight.

[2] This last formulation summarizes Thomas Scanlon's current explication of his proposal that acts are wrong if they violate any system of rules that no one could reasonably reject as a basis for general agreement. See T. M. Scanlon, *What We Owe to Each Other* (Cambridge, MA: Harvard University Press, 1998), chap. 5. Scanlon emphasizes the diversity of the connections between his underlying moral perspective and the condemnation of economic inequality in his Lindley Lecture, published as T. M. Scanlon, *The Diversity of Objections to Inequality* (Lawrence: University of Kansas, 1996). Most of the concerns about excessive inequality that I will defend fall within the categories of his insightful taxonomy of these objections.

The further premise, Neutrality, promised to simplify the egalitarian project, unifying the currency of economic equality into . . . currency. But the simplicity gained by associating economic equality with equal access to income and wealth seems to be accompanied by terrible costs of neutrality for the project as a whole. A central philosophical task of egalitarianism is to justify taxing some to help others. Given their interpretations of the dictates of equal respect, which assign overriding importance to civil liberties, egalitarians must sharply distinguish the anguished protests of a billionaire who cannot afford a fourth summerhouse because of taxes for public education from the protests of someone forced to donate a kidney to save a victim of renal failure or forced to conceal the practice of a religion that disturbs others' sensibilities. How can this be done without insisting on the special role, in a good life, of control over one's body and unconstrained expression of one's religion or irreligion, and on the greater importance of education than summerhouse collecting? No doubt, the billionaire's protest, while self-assertive, is not an expression of self-respect. Indeed, it is self-degrading. But this judgment indicates an evaluative aspect of Basic Equality itself, a rating of life goals that partly determines what counts as respect for persons. No "thin theory of the good" attending to income and wealth because they are all-purpose resources would emerge from this perspective of equal respect.[3]

There are important current attempts to meet all of these challenges. The old argument is wounded, not dead. Still, its prospects are sufficiently troubled that egalitarians would do well to investigate the fate of the old conclusions in the fragmented view of economic justice that would replace it. If our political duties of concern for the economic situations of our fellow citizens respond piecemeal to the variety of relationships that bind us, and are not molded by the generic demand of Economic Equality, what duties to promote economic equality survive? If Neutrality is abandoned, so that money, the all-purpose resource in modern economic life, has no special standing among politically relevant features of economic well-being, what role should equality of income or wealth play in implementing the surviving duties to promote economic equality?

My argument will be that the fragmented view justifies broadly egalitarian concerns: the appropriate response to the various relationships that bind fellow citizens in a modern society includes a commitment to support the use of laws to reduce certain economic inequalities on the

[3] Of course, rankings of ways of life can be relevant to just political choice in some ways and irrelevant in others. Even if respect for persons requires discounting the complaints of the selfish billionaire when choosing how much to tax him to help others, the judgment that his attitude is self-degrading need not justify government efforts to improve it. Normally, an attempt to use force to change someone's self-degradation both fails to express respect and fails to make his life better. In Richard W. Miller, "Liberalism and Equality" (forthcoming), I argue, on these and other grounds, that a non-Neutralist understanding of respect for persons is the best basis for civil liberties and civic tolerance as well as for greater economic equality.

ground that the differences are too great and not just on the ground that noncomparative deprivations, such as hunger, sickness, or fatigue, ought to be relieved, the more urgently the greater the deprivation. More specifically, the fragmented view provides a basis on which we should sometimes condemn as too great at least three kinds of economic inequalities: inequalities in economic opportunities, in the economic benefits and burdens of government activity, and in the economic bases of social recognition (for example, routine recognition as a reliable participant in shared social activities).

However, other, stronger forms of egalitarianism are not justifiable in this framework. There is no duty, not even a prima facie duty, to promote an equal division of economic goods or opportunities among one's fellow citizens regardless of what social processes have caused the current differences. Moreover, although specific social processes that are an inevitable feature of modern fellow-citizenship do generate reasons to be concerned about specific kinds of consequent inequalities, they also generate serious reasons to be concerned about the costs to the better off of governmental efforts to provide more for those who have less. There is no basis in the structure of modern societies for a provisional assumption that a gain for the economically worst off is more important than its cost to others; hence, there is no basis for a prima facie duty to reduce the scale of the relevant inequality so long as this benefits the worst off.

None of the broadly egalitarian concerns that fellow citizens owe to one another is primarily a concern to avoid differences in income or wealth. So the question of the importance of these differences has to be faced once Neutrality is abandoned. Here, I will argue that attention to inequalities of income and wealth is centrally important as a device by which morally responsible citizens can monitor commitments to eliminate excessive inequalities that are not, in themselves, matters of income or wealth. It is morally misguided and politically self-defeating to insist that justice requires arrangements in which the income and wealth (or opportunities for, or lifetime expectations of, income and wealth) of those with the least should be as great as possible. But sharp increases in inequality of income or wealth are a sign of danger that the primary inequalities have become excessive, and a political community embarked on a project of eliminating these excessive inequalities ought to treat the reduction of income and wealth inequalities as the feasible and timely indicators of progress. As a case study of deliberations based on the more fragmented view of equality, I will sketch reasons to condemn current inequalities in the United States on all the primary dimensions as too great, and reasons to monitor progress in curing these moral diseases by looking at success in reversing recent increases in inequality of income and wealth.[4]

[4] For reasons of space, I will confine my discussion of broad egalitarianism to mutual political obligations among fellow citizens. But I do not mean to suggest that political duties

III. Equal Opportunity

The most popular political goal intrinsically concerned with equality is equality of opportunity. The complexity of determining when opportunities are too unequal is a useful paradigm of the complexity of reasoning about economic justice in the more fragmented view. It provides striking illustrations of how the force of egalitarian considerations depends on specific aspects of the interactions among those who are unequal, of the pervasiveness of countervailing reasons not to equalize too much, and of the diverse but limited roles of income and wealth in implementing political choices that justly respond to the reasons for and against greater equality.

A. Unequal life prospects and civic respect

In defending broad egalitarianism concerning opportunity, I will identify people's opportunities with their life prospects, that is, their chances of success in attaining economic bases for well-being in their lives as a whole, given their willingness to strive. Conditionality on willingness to strive is crucial, since if a lack of success is entirely due to the subject's choices, there is no denial of opportunity, indeed, no complaint against fellow citizens—although they might have compelling reasons to help on other grounds. No doubt, this conception of opportunity might be refined—for example, by counting it as a loss of opportunity when distorting psychological effects of unchosen circumstances make someone unwilling to make efforts that would in fact be a rational means of striving for a better life. Still, the reduction of excessive inequalities of life prospects captures a great deal of what self-described partisans of equal opportunity pursue.

Concern for burdensome inferiorities in life prospects need not be egalitarian; it can be concern for the burdens, but not for the inferiority in prospects as such. For example, people with severe ill health find economic self-advancement hard where others find it easy, and we should be concerned to help them in their difficulties, but this is typically a concern

to reduce economic inequality extend only to fellow citizens. My rationales for these duties would, in the main, support similar concern for long-term, committed residents of one's country who are not citizens. They will *not* entail the same obligations to the foreign poor, even those living in countries much poorer than one's own, since one does not impose laws on them, rely on their civic loyalty, or share their civic life. Analogous rationales could support duties of political concern for the economic inferiority of the foreign poor, but these duties would be of lesser degree and would be largely overridden by the primary concerns of domestic equality. I try to show that a perspective of equal respect for everyone everywhere requires this priority for compatriots in Richard W. Miller, "Cosmopolitan Respect and Patriotic Concern," *Philosophy and Public Affairs* 27, no. 3 (1998): 202–24; and describe the analogous though less demanding reasons for concern for foreign needs in Richard W. Miller, "Moral Closeness and World Community," in Deen Chatterjee, ed., *The Ethics of Assistance* (forthcoming).

about their afflictions, not about the gap between their prospects and those of the unafflicted. However, from the perspective of Basic Equality in its various formulations, matters are very different for those engaged in the creation of coercively enforced rules that generate differences in life prospects.

It is hard to show respect for others while taking part in a coercive project in which rules are imposed on them. Yet in their political choices, citizens of a democracy do just that. Majority rule is not enough to justify coercive imposition, as witness the injustice of religious persecution supported by a majority. Rather, a just citizen must make political choices that express an appreciation of the equal worth of all. And someone with this attitude must take it as a reason to change a set of laws that those laws give rise to unequal prospects of well-being through circumstances beyond the control of those affected. After all, self-respecting disadvantaged citizens who are aware that their fellow citizens do not regard the production of their (the disadvantaged citizens') inferior circumstances as a reason for change cannot fully commit themselves actively to uphold the laws that have burdened them—and a respectful citizen must strive in her political choices to provide a basis for such self-respectful loyalty. In contrast, it is self-respectful to uphold political arrangements that are not responsive to all brute differences in luck, so long as these arrangements include feasible aid when one has fallen below an appropriate threshold of adequacy and lacks self-reliant means to rise above it. If one's brute bad luck is not due to the dominant laws and policies, loyal support for the laws that dominate one's life does not mean support of what has *made* one's life worse than others'. Of course, people will still regard their brute bad luck as unfair, but this is a complaint against their luck, not a complaint against their fellow citizens.

The coercive enforcement of capitalist rules of self-advancement does inevitably give rise to inequalities in life prospects. Inevitably, some get further ahead than others; because of the consequent inequalities in resources for getting ahead, descendants of those who fall behind have a smaller chance of achieving a fulfilling life. So, in capitalist societies (and other sorts of societies, too, for analogous reasons), differences in life prospects can have the social basis that generates morally and politically relevant complaints.[5]

Of course, if those who complain of disadvantage were thwarted in aspirations that no morally responsible person should have in the first

[5] I will restrict my investigations of broad egalitarianism to capitalist economies, on the assumption that in the setting of modern technology some form of capitalism is morally desirable in light of the failings of the best noncapitalist alternatives. Still, the arguments for broad egalitarianism could be extended, in more or less obvious ways, to any economy in which most economic relationships are based on politically enforced entitlements, family life transfers economic advantages from one generation to the next, and governmental activity plays an indispensable role in economic prosperity.

place (say, aspirations to raid and pillage), or were asking for a political remedy that is by its nature illegitimate, they would lack a politically relevant reason to object to their situation. But the relevant complaints of unequal opportunity are complaints about having fewer resources for getting ahead by perfectly legitimate means. And the relevant political remedy is a less disadvantageous arrangement, with increased taxes for some and increased help for others, based on laws that are democratically arrived at in deliberations meant to take account of everyone's interests, deliberations giving special weight to the secure enjoyment of fruits of past legal self-advancement. The only basis for peremptorily dismissing such a political remedy would be the familiar libertarian view that all interference with the full benefits of unrestricted capitalist self-advancement is wrong. And such rigid and comprehensive opposition to coercive intrusion on laissez-faire entitlements is not the proper outcome of the perspective of equal respect that I have described. Suppose that I see someone drowning and spot a nearby life preserver ornamenting the flagpole in front of a seaside mansion. If, as I am about to throw the life preserver to the person sinking beneath the waves, its silly, selfish owner rushes out of the mansion and snatches his property away, I do not fail to show appreciation of the equal worth of all if I gently wrest back the life preserver to save the person who is drowning. If someone complains of socially created inferiority in means to legitimate self-advancement and looks to a democratic government for remedies compatible with the rule of law, his complaint deserves standing in further deliberations.

I have not claimed that the engendering of unequal life prospects by capitalist economic activity is a conclusive reason for changing laws, or that it is a conclusive reason so long as the change improves the life prospects of those whose prospects are worst. As we shall see, the circumstances of self-advancement under capitalism also generate reasons *not* to engage in political projects reducing inequalities in life prospects. When the reasons not to reduce an inequality are no less serious than the reasons to reduce it, the inequality is not excessive: one has no duty to promote greater equality even if this would benefit the worst off. Moreover, the morally serious reasons to protest the burdens of policies that reduce inequalities of life prospects reflect enduring, pervasive features of capitalist self-advancement, not just occasional social circumstances or especially costly egalitarian projects. So it would be morally misguided to approach political choice with a standing disposition to use state power to reduce these inequalities, tempered by alertness to signs that this norm is not appropriate due to special circumstances. Even if there is a prima facie political duty of compassion to relieve grave deprivations among fellow citizens who would otherwise suffer greatly, there is no prima facie duty of justice to reduce inequalities in life prospects.

What broad egalitarianism concerning life prospects *does* entail is that the effectiveness of a policy in reducing inequality of life prospects sometimes functions as an independent ingredient in a case for the policy, which would not be justified in the absence of this reason. A consideration that should not be elevated to a prima facie duty can still be a reason that lends some support to the judgment that one ought to engage in a certain course of conduct, support that is sometimes decisive.

That inequality in life prospects as such can play a decisive role is especially clear when someone's life is not bad, even though it reflects life prospects that are worse than others'. When someone recently repaired my telephone, I felt less uncomfortable than usual when he asked me what I do, and I told him, straightforwardly. "That's just what I wanted to do," he said. "But people in my part of Brooklyn didn't go on to college." The life of a telephone repairman is not severely deprived—in general, or, so far as I could tell, in his case. In asking people in better-off school districts to support aid for poor school districts that will cost them higher taxes and afford their own children more intense competition, it would be far-fetched to urge that they should do this to save other people's children from repairing telephones when another job would be more fulfilling. Unlike the situation of schoolchildren who are apt, because of virtual illiteracy, to endure a life of drudgery interspersed with long spells of unemployment, the situation of children whose prospect is work that is only mildly interesting and fairly independent does not, in itself, merit remedy through compulsory sacrifices of fellow citizens. In contrast, those who seek shifts in public resources toward worse-off school districts can plausibly appeal to a goal of reducing the extent to which differences in social advantages make a fulfilling work life less likely for some than for others. The broad egalitarian thinks that such appeals are sometimes an essential part of an adequate justification of a social policy with significant costs, even though she takes these costs to be relevant and, sometimes, prohibitive.

This willingness to impose costs in order to reduce inferiority is essential to an egalitarianism worthy of the name. Mere support for costless benefits to the worst off is quite inadequate. Anyone but a misanthrope supports costless improvements in people's lives—in the lives of the disadvantaged, and in the lives of the privileged as well.

B. Excessive equalizing

I have been arguing that equal respect for all makes socially created unequal opportunities among one's fellow citizens a cause for concern, while warning that equal respect does not entail a political commitment to minimize the burdens of those inequalities. Now it is time to survey the antiegalitarian considerations standing behind the warning—the diverse and pervasive costs of political projects aimed at reducing inequality of opportunity, costs that can constitute compelling reasons why it would be wrong to support feasible means of further improvement in the life prospects of the worst off.

One danger of going too far in reducing inequality of opportunity is that of excessive interference with legitimate plans. Usually, people make sacrifices and foreclose options in order to achieve long-term goals. If the goals are worthwhile and the past choices were legitimate, then people have a reason—which is not to say a conclusive reason—to complain of an imposed change that deprives past choices of some of their point and motivating value. After all, life would dissolve into anxious reactivity if one's projects could always be rendered pointless, retroactively, in order to relieve the burdens of those who are less advantaged. The motivating goals of those who benefit from or create unequal opportunity are, most centrally, stable achievements pursued for long-term effects: for example, they strive for a large, attractive house in a pretty neighborhood that they can live in until retirement, not just a nice current experience of housing, and for the means to help their children to prosper, not just a good current family experience. So higher taxes providing others' children with more equal life prospects can become a cause for serious complaint if those taxes significantly interfere with legitimate projects in which the better off invested their hopes and energies.

Other constraints on the reduction of inequality in life prospects involve burdens of disadvantage that egalitarians sometimes neglect, at great political peril, through single-minded attention to the worst off. For one thing, society is not divided into one group, the most disadvantaged, and another, the homogeneously advantaged better off. Plenty of people have life prospects that are lower than some fellow citizens', higher than others'. Even if those who are better off than the median have no reason to complain that their need for better prospects is being neglected, there are plenty of relevantly inferior situations in the first fifty percentiles. These situations are not all tightly "chain-connected," in Rawls's evocative phrase, rising or falling together. What helps the children of parents who have great difficulty finding and keeping even unskilled jobs may not help the children of semiskilled blue-collar workers or stably employed unskilled workers—these workers, for instance, may face wage cuts and increased unemployment under otherwise attractive proposals to help the worst off.

Even though the worst off suffer the most serious deprivations, many others have serious unmet needs affecting their whole lives. Policies of aid do not express an equal valuing of everyone's life and cannot be accepted self-respectfully by all if these policies totally neglect the less serious needs of some, which are serious nonetheless, whenever this is necessary to improve the prospects of the neediest. Such a bias is as one-sided as the policy of a hospital emergency room in which nothing is done to save anyone from blindness or the loss of limbs so long as effort can be diverted to a project of saving someone from death.

In addition, there is no way in which the costs of improving the prospects of those whose prospects are worse can be confined to those whose *prospects* are better. Governments tax incomes and purchases, which are outcomes. They must ask people who have already achieved various degrees of success to bear sacrifices, through taxes and in other ways, in order to equalize opportunities. In imposing these sacrifices, governments ought to be sensitive to current differences in resources, but they should not grade people for sacrifice-worthiness on the basis of inquiries into whether their current resources reflect past advantages, as against the overcoming of past disadvantages. Inevitably, such inquiries would be demeaningly intrusive and arrogantly speculative. Yet clearly, in any capitalist society, many of those who are well-enough off to be called on to make sacrifices in any extensive effort to reduce inequalities in life prospects *were* burdened by these inequalities and overcame the burdens. If we all were fully aware of the facts of inequality, these overcomers would have reason to complain that their burden of inferior opportunity has been made more severe in order to reduce the burdensomeness of inferior opportunity for others, including others whose life prospects are no worse than the ones the overcomers faced. So the reduction of unequal opportunity by political means ought to be inhibited by awareness that it will impose further costs on some of the victims of unequal opportunity. Of course, in reality, few have adequate self-knowledge in these matters, and many deceive themselves as to barriers overcome. But the same can be said of those who think that their failure to succeed is due to their inferior life prospects.

Another cluster of antiegalitarian considerations involves valuable aspirations, affecting the quality of a person's life, that generate or sustain inequality in life prospects. It is a testimony to the power of these considerations that they can serve as reasons why the most disadvantaged themselves might reject projects maximizing their own income or other material resources. However, these quality-of-life considerations are genuinely antiegalitarian, since they could also exclude equalizing projects that the worst off might prefer on account of extreme material deprivation.

One such quality-of-life consideration concerns the start of life. An appropriate valuing of parental nurturance entails respect for the privacy of home-life and enduring family ties, which together insure the transmission of skills and attitudes within families, even when family differences reflect past differences in success and tend to create differences in life prospects. Given the premise of Neutrality, respect for the family seemed to be a mere means to enhance the provision of all-purpose goods. Freed from this premise, morally responsible citizens can acknowledge that the inhibition of parental nurturance is itself a reason that can count against a policy. Even if the Indian Schools of the U.S. Bureau of Indian Affairs had done their job, affording children taken from their parents a better prospect of economic success, the students and their parents would still have had reason to complain of the disruption of their lives together. Where there is a national health service, there is often a plausible case for requiring doctors and hospitals to provide their care as part of it so that the service can play its proper role in reducing inequalities in life prospects. But there is no plausible justification for requiring children to be brought up in state nurseries in order to reduce inequalities in life prospects.

Other aspirations whose value constrains equalization affect later stages in life, when people are expected to be self-reliant. In interactions among interdependent adult nonintimates, life goes better if one receives benefits from others for providing what they want, so that one interacts on a basis of voluntary reciprocity. In addition, most people (including most of the worst off) want to use what resources they have actively, to get ahead on their own steam, and this reflects a proper valuing of human capacities. This preference for self-reliant reciprocity is a desperate and touching concern of the women in Kathryn Edin and Laura Lein's powerful sociological study *Making Ends Meet*,[6] who went off welfare once their children passed infancy, even though their wages did not cover their increased expenses. "The worst part [of working]," one of them succinctly notes, "is that you are no better off as far as your financial situation. . . . The good part about working is that it makes you feel good to have a job. You don't get much, but then, I have a job."[7]

The valuing of self-reliant reciprocity sets limits to the rectification of unequal life prospects through transfers from the better off to the worst-off adults who are capable of self-reliance. In a capitalist economy, getting ahead by offering nonintimates what they want usually means getting wages and working conditions in response to one's actual skills. So transfers that compensate for the absence of well-rewarded skills due to inferior life prospects risk infantilization, unless they save people from severe deprivation—for example, from a life in which the cost of self-reliance is domination by a struggle merely to survive with minimal dignity and to fulfill basic responsibilities to dependents. By the same token, someone has reason to complain if subsidies to others to compensate for inferior life prospects make it harder for him to get ahead self-reliantly (perhaps because of effects of taxation, or perhaps because the subsidies to those whose prospects are worse make them more effective competitors for scarce jobs). Such a complaint of inhibition is not a conclusive reason, but it is a serious reason that is not answered simply by noting the improved prospects of the worst off, or by providing supports and safety nets to those whose self-reliance is undercut, even if these measures make their lifetime incomes as high as they would have been had the original subsidy never been established.

[6] Kathryn Edin and Laura Lein, *Making Ends Meet* (New York: Russell Sage Foundation, 1997).

[7] Ibid., 140.

This is not to say that the value of getting ahead through self-reliant reciprocity is always at odds with demands for greater equality. The differences in economic rewards that lead parents to hope for a white-collar rather than a blue-collar fate for their children, and best of all a professional or managerial fate, are due in part to advantages in bargaining power of those farther up the hierarchy of jobs, not just to the greater value of what they do for the firms that employ them. In addition, returns to wealth need not be proportionate to prior entrepreneurial contribution. Real capitalism, as opposed to the ideal model of the "perfect competitive market" that economic theorists sometimes explore, spontaneously gives rise to situations in which many of the worse off can complain that they are not compensated in proportion to what they self-reliantly contribute while others, who are better off, receive benefits quite out of proportion to their contributions. Still, the proper valuing of self-reliant reciprocity can rule out measures that would provide the most income for the least advantaged. Freed from Neutrality, we need not regard a disinclination to take handouts, even handouts based on legal entitlement, as, at best, a source of useful incentives, at worst, a stultifying inhibition.

Politicians and political philosophers tend to specialize in one or another of the diverse reasons I have mentioned in this survey of reasons relevant to the judgment of unequal life prospects. Each is apt to claim that the most important economic institutions ought, in all important respects, to be molded by his or her favorite consideration—say, by noninterference with benefits of legitimate acts of self-advancement, or by the commitment to remove burdens of inferior life prospects. But why suppose that this sort of simplicity, which would be wildly inappropriate in moral deliberations among family members, friends, or departmental colleagues, should characterize well-conducted deliberations among fellow citizens? In every other situation of ongoing collective deliberation, morally responsible participants give a hearing to highly diverse claims, complaints, and aspirations and try to reach their ultimate conclusions from an authoritative, higher-order perspective of appropriate sensitivity to the seriousness of these diverse competing reasons. This is how they display respect for one another in their deliberations. Even if the deliberative outcome is some relatively simple norm ("Graduate students serve on search committees on these terms," "These parents divide up child care in this way"), it is properly arrived at through informed assessment of the seriousness of many competing considerations, and through ingenuity in mitigating the diverse kinds of losses that accompany the pursuit of legitimate goals.

C. *Unequal opportunity in the United States*

How might such respectful deliberations proceed among fellow citizens determining whether inequality of life prospects is currently excessive? In the fragmented view of equality, different situations dictate different deliberative agendas and justify different conclusions. So, here and elsewhere in this essay, I will offer as a case study arguments suggesting that relevant inequalities in the United States today are excessive.

The importance of reasons for changing rules of self-advancement that generate differences in life prospects is proportionate to the importance of those differences for people's lives. For most of us, the most important economic concern is getting and keeping a good job. In ranking jobs, most of us are guided both by monetary considerations and by nonmonetary ones, such as the desire for interesting, independent, clean, and secure work.[8] Monetary and nonmonetary rankings of jobs are well correlated.[9] These rankings create a pecking order of job clusters in which professionals, managers, officials, and nonretail sales workers—"upper white-collar occupations," in the jargon of mobility studies—rank on top, while "lower manual occupations" such as service workers, operatives, and nonfarm laborers, rank together with farmworkers at the bottom. Analyzing U.S. data from 1982–90 concerning men aged 25–64, sociologist Robert Hauser found that 60 percent of upper white-collar fathers had upper white-collar sons, as compared with 27 percent of lower manual fathers. Fourteen percent of upper white-collar fathers had lower manual sons, as compared with 37 percent of lower manual fathers.[10] In an earlier sociological study, Christopher Jencks and his colleagues reported:

> Those who do well economically typically owe almost half of their economic advantage to family background. . . . If . . . an omniscient scientist were to predict the economic standing of sons from different families, he would find sons from the most favored fifth of all families had predicted Duncan scores [a widely used measure of the status of occupations on a scale from 0 to 96] of about 64, while sons of the least favored fifth of all families have predicted scores of about

[8] See Christopher Jencks, Lauri Perman, and Lee Rainwater, "What Is a Good Job?" *American Journal of Sociology* 93, no. 6 (1988): 1322–57. They note, "While earnings are the most important single determinant of a job's desirability, the 13 nonmonetary characteristics [in terms of which desirability was assessed] are twice as important as earnings" (ibid., 1322).

[9] Because of this correlation, the inequality in overall desirability among jobs is much greater than the inequality in earnings. Jencks, Perman, and Rainwater found that inequality in monetary plus nonmonetary characteristics (assessed using the standard deviation when characteristics are measured on logged ratio scales) was 2.8 times greater than inequality in pay alone. See ibid., 1353. This is the opposite of the effect entailed by the familiar neoclassical explanation of wage differences, according to which greater monetary rewards compensate for the greater repulsiveness of the associated work ("Investment banking is ghastly, but someone has to do it").

[10] Table credited to Robert Hauser, in Dennis Gilbert, *The American Class Structure in an Age of Growing Inequality* (Belmont, CA: Wadsworth, 1998), 144. Tracing other rates of transition to upper white-collar occupations, Hauser found that 39 percent of lower white-collar fathers (e.g., clerical workers) had upper white-collar sons; for upper manual fathers (e.g., craftsmen and foremen) and fathers who were farmers or farmworkers, the percentages were 32 percent and 19 percent, respectively.

16. This is the difference between a social worker or the manager of a hardware store (both 64) and a construction painter (16), a farmer (14) or an auto mechanic (9).[11]

The evidence of large differences in life prospects for well-paying work is also striking. Comparing ten-year averages of parents' income and of children's earnings, economists Jere Behrman and Paul Taubman found that after they controlled for age, gender, and race, a 10 percent increase in parental income was associated with a 6 percent increase in children's earnings. (The associated increase without these controls was 8 percent.)[12]

Although these figures imply substantial differences in life prospects, they do not entirely reflect differences generated by the rules for self-advancement that citizens have chosen to impose on one another. To some extent, they reflect traits that the more successful parents developed for reasons independent of their own social advantages, traits that would be as valuable under any rules for getting ahead compatible with civil and political liberty, which contribute to parental success, and also, independently of parental success, make people apt to have successful children. The prime example of such morally neutral generation of unequal life prospects would be genetically based and transmitted superiority in the general cognitive abilities that are useful in getting ahead under any defensible rules for self-advancement. Studies of IQ differences are sometimes advanced as supporting the claim that genetically based differences in general cognitive ability have a powerful and pervasive influence on differences in life prospects.[13] But even if interpretations of differences in childhood IQ as measures of genetically based differences in general intelligence were correct, this factor would not dominate the production of unequal life prospects. In their study of economic prospects in the United States, economists Samuel Bowles and Herbert Gintis examined the likelihood that white males of average childhood IQ from families in various socioeconomic deciles would eventually enter the top income quintile; 5.5 percent of men from families in the lowest decile rose to the top income quintile, and this percentage rose steadily through the decile ranks, up to 40.8 percent for men from families in the highest decile.[14]

[11] Christopher Jencks et al., *Who Gets Ahead?* (New York: Basic Books, 1979), 81 f. In "What Is a Good Job?" 1349, Jencks, Perman, and Rainwater note that the impact of family background on overall job desirability is much greater than its impact on Duncan scores.

[12] Jere R. Behrman and Paul Taubman, "The Intergenerational Correlation between Children's Adult Earnings and their Parents' Income," *Review of Income and Wealth* 36, no. 2 (1990): 115–27.

[13] See, for example, Richard J. Herrnstein and Charles Murray, *The Bell Curve* (New York: Free Press, 1993).

[14] See Samuel Bowles and Herbert Gintis, *Schooling in Capitalist America* (New York: Basic Books, 1976), 121. The analogous probabilities among all white males are 4.2 percent for those from the lowest decile and 43.9 percent for those from the highest, with the same steady rise in between. In this study, the index of socioeconomic background is based on parents' income, father's years of schooling, and father's occupational status (rated by the

In any case, there is powerful evidence that IQ differences between people in different social milieus are not, typically, genetically determined or differences in general intelligence. For example, stable gene pools, throughout the world, have sustained large upward changes in IQ scores, such as the steady twenty-one-point increase in average Dutch IQ scores between 1952 and 1982.[15] Ninety percent of Britons born in 1877 would have had scores at or under the fifth percentile of the scores of those born in 1967: by the IQ standards applied to the later generation, the earlier group would have been, at best, at the border of mental retardation.[16] If IQ scores do not remotely reflect differences in general intelligence between people in historically different situations, why suppose they accurately measure such differences between people in socioeconomically different situations?

In addition to their contribution to children's cognitive ability, parents' roles in the development of character traits and styles of conduct also, obviously, have an important bearing on children's ultimate success. Yet the different life prospects that result do not simply reflect differences in parental commitment and nurturant skill that are independent of parents' social situations and that would affect life-starts in any society properly respectful of family life. Lives at different levels of the modern capitalist occupational hierarchy encourage the formation and transmission of different attitudes toward initiative, obedience, predictability, independent judgment, conformity, and empathic understanding.[17] The upper-echelon traits (for example, a relatively self-directed work-style) are, in turn, competitive assets for children to whom they are transmitted, since supervisors and others with an influence on their success take these traits as especially suitable for the best job ladders.[18]

In sum, there is significant evidence that the distribution and importance of every parental trait strongly associated with children's success

---

standard Duncan scores). These and other aspects of the study's methodology are described in Samuel Bowles and Valerie Nelson, "The 'Inheritance of IQ' and the Intergenerational Transmission of Economic Inequality," *Review of Economics and Statistics* 56, no. 1 (1974): 39–51. For an analysis of more recent data in which social background similarly dominates IQ in the explanation of poverty and household-income inequality, see Claude S. Fischer et al., *Inequality by Design: Cracking the Bell Curve Myth* (Princeton, NJ: Princeton University Press, 1996), esp. chap. 4.

[15] See James R. Flynn, "Intelligence and Meritocracy," in Kenneth Arrow, Samuel Bowles, and Steven Durlauf, eds., *Meritocracy and Economic Inequality* (Princeton, NJ: Princeton University Press, 2000), 36.

[16] Ibid., 40 f.

[17] See Melvin Kohn, *Class and Conformity*, 2d ed. (Chicago: University of Chicago Press, 1977); and Melvin Kohn and Carmi Schooler, "Occupational Experience and Psychological Functioning," in Melvin Kohn and Carmi Schooler, eds., *Work and Personality: An Inquiry into the Impact of Social Stratification* (Norwood, NJ: Ablex, 1983).

[18] See Richard C. Edwards, "Individual Traits and Organizational Incentives: What Makes a 'Good' Worker?" *Journal of Human Resources* 11, no. 1 (1976): 51–68. For analogous observations on styles of presentation (eye contact, ways of walking, etc.), see Troy Duster, "Postindustrialization and Youth Unemployment," in Katherine McFate, Roger Lawson, and William Julius Wilson, eds., *Poverty, Inequality, and the Future of Social Policy* (New York: Russell Sage Foundation, 1995), 461–86.

are both due, to a substantial extent, to the rules of self-advancement that we impose on one another. Still, it is and will always be impossible definitively to factor out those causes of disadvantage that are legitimate sources of complaint from those that are not. The Great Longitudinal Study that would determine the extent to which unequal parental tendencies to raise successful children are due to social inequalities among parents or parents' ancestors would only be complete when those whose just complaints are vindicated are dead and those alive face structurally different economic demands that render the Great Longitudinal Study obsolete.

In this context of uncertainty, the size of the gross differences in life prospects and the significant evidence that socially enforced rules of self-advancement contribute to them provide those who respect their fellow citizens with a serious reason to reduce inequality. Greater burdens of proof should accompany greater dangers of unjust burden. More specifically, just choice in the face of empirical uncertainty must be guided by this principle: if one alternative would impose more burdensome injustice, if it turned out to be empirically misguided, than a rival alternative would, if *it* turned out to be empirically misguided, we should put a special burden of proof on those asking us to take on the greater moral risk. For example, an empirically misguided high estimate of the extent to which social factors determine skills might support excessive taxation of investment bankers, whereas a similarly misguided high estimate of the extent to which genetic factors determine skills might support deficient public provision of education for the children of telephone repairers. In this context, a substantial yet nonconclusive case that social factors determine skills can provide a serious reason to reduce disadvantage, because the worse off have more at stake.

Current inequalities in life prospects in the United States have turned out to be serious reasons to improve the life prospects of the disadvantaged. Granted, there are also many serious reasons not to engage in equalizing projects, and just political choices must be sensitive to them as well. However, there are plenty of ways in which social policies can adequately accommodate these considerations while pursuing significant reductions in the inequality of opportunity that empirical findings indicate.

One overarching antiegalitarian consideration, as we have seen, is the need to show due respect for the legitimate long-term plans of the better off. When policies are means of improving seriously inferior life prospects, this value is respected by avoiding costs that significantly worsen anyone's life through the thwarting of legitimate projects that invest her life with value. A great many people could be taxed much more without their lives being significantly worsened.

In addition, the concerns of those whose life prospects are neither among the best nor among the worst must be acknowledged. This can be done by instituting a broad array of programs, not solely concerned with the worst off, that show proportionate sensitivity to different people's different needs.

Also, the concerns of those who have overcome disadvantages must be acknowledged. This can be done by insuring that self-reliant striving is a source of substantial benefit.

Finally, the dangers of infantilization must be recognized. Many projects of heightened equality do avoid these dangers, even when the beneficiaries are not severely deprived. For example, improvement of education for disadvantaged children is central to the pursuit of equal opportunity in part because it provides means of achieving future self-reliance to those who are currently appropriately dependent on others for these means. The public provision of cultural facilities, medical care, and shared amenities such as parks and playgrounds can make differences in economic life prospects smaller by reducing the need to rely on personal funds for the relevant goals without depriving anyone of the virtues of a self-reliant life. Likewise, the strengthening of unions, far from undermining self-reliant reciprocity, can make the labor market a better vehicle for achieving it, by reducing disadvantages in bargaining power that do not reflect the value of workers' services or output.[19]

D. *The relevance of money*

What does all of this have to do with income and wealth? Differences in income and wealth can figure as evidence that inequalities in life prospects are too great; as causes to be mitigated in order to reduce excessive inequalities in life prospects; and as signs of danger and measures of success, stimulating discussion of whether to reduce inequality in life prospects and helping to monitor egalitarian projects that are adopted. However, it is only in the third context, as signs and measures guiding public deliberation over the ultimate concern for different prospects of economically based well-being, that differences in income and wealth merit central importance.

[19] Because firms in a local labor market are vastly less numerous than their potential employees and typically have substantial reserves, while their prospective blue-collar employees typically lack substantial savings, the firms are in a better position to collaborate (usually tacitly) in resisting increased wages than blue-collar workers are to collaborate in resisting wage decreases in the absence of strong unions. (Adam Smith insists on the special power of this "tacit, but constant and uniform combination [of masters against workmen], not to raise wages," noting, "It is not . . . difficult to foresee which of the two parties must, upon all ordinary occasions, have the advantage in the dispute, and force the other into a compliance with their terms." See Adam Smith, *An Inquiry into the Nature and Causes of the Wealth of Nations*, ed. Edwin Cannan [New York: Random House, 1937], 67 f.) Because of the different relationships of employment change and of investment change to personal life, "If you don't like it here, try to get a job elsewhere" threatens in a way that "If you don't like the terms on which we offer to work, invest elsewhere" does not. A worker who sincerely insists, with legitimate pride, that she does not want more than her work is worth does not mean that she wants no more than what she would be paid in a market in which employers exploit their bargaining advantages to the hilt, advantages that strong unions can reduce.

Differences in income and wealth have some evidentiary value in arguments about whether differences in life prospects are excessive. But this evidentiary importance is small. The size of interpersonal differences in income or wealth is a bad measure of the size of differences in well-being, even in well-being that depends on overall economic circumstances. After all, most full professors at leading American universities enjoy about the same level of well-being as Bill Gates, so far as their well-being and Gates's depend on their economic roles and their success in filling them. Also, differences in income and wealth are differences in outcomes, which are, notoriously, compatible with similar or even identical opportunities. Finally, we cannot rely on monetary differences to tell us to what extent differences in life prospects are due to socially imposed rules, or to identify the point at which reasons not to equalize further should take hold.

On the other hand, once we have decided that there is too much inequality in life prospects, inequalities of income and wealth become somewhat more important as causes to be mitigated in the project of reducing the excessive inequality. For example, in the United States today, the cost of college and the impact of a college degree on subsequent economic success are together an important vehicle through which differences in parental income and wealth cause differences in life prospects. In 1995–96, the average annual sum of the tuition and other expenses of a year's full-time attendance at a four-year college ranged from $9,751 at public, non-doctorate-granting institutions to $23,391 at private, doctorate-granting universities.[20] The smaller average price of attendance was 86 percent of the average family income in the lowest fifth of all U.S. families in 1996, 23 percent of the middle fifth's average income, and 8 percent of the highest fifth's average income; for the higher price, the corresponding ratios were 205 percent, 55 percent, and 19 percent.[21] While colleges and governments (federal, state, and local) respond to financial needs with grants, loans, and work-study programs preferentially directed at families with lower incomes, the resulting net price (more properly, net current price, since aid in the form of loans must be repaid) still often imposes a severe financial strain. In 1995–96, for families with income under $20,000, this net price for a child's full-time attendance averaged $4,156 at public, non-doctorate-granting four-year institutions, and $9,652 at private,

[20] See Lutz Berkner and Andrew Malizio, *Student Financing of Undergraduate Education: 1995–96* (Washington, DC: U.S. Department of Education, 1998), 66. These averages are based on the typical student budgets that the colleges use in their financial aid calculations. In addition to tuition and fees, these budget estimates take into account costs of books and supplies and "other living expenses directly related to attendance, such as room and board, transportation, and personal expenses" (ibid., 61).

[21] Data used for these calculations is from U.S. Census Bureau, "Historical Income Inequality Tables, Table IE-1, Selected Measures of Household Income Dispersion: 1967 to 1999," available on-line at http://www.census.gov/hhes/income/histinc/ie1.html.

doctorate-granting universities.[22] The lower average net price was around 36 percent of the average income among all families with income less than $20,000 in 1996, while the higher average net price was around 85 percent of their average income.[23] The respective average net prices were $6,302 and $12,245 for families with incomes between $40,000 and $59,000, the range in which median family income fell, and were $9,326 and $21,335 for families with incomes of $100,000 or more.[24] The special economic strains that families of low income and little or no wealth face in sending a child to college contribute to substantial aptitude-independent differences in enrollment rates. Among 1992 high school graduates who were qualified for college by such standard measures as SAT scores and grades assessed in light of curricular rigor, 52 percent of those from families with incomes under $25,000 had enrolled in a four-year college by 1994, as opposed to 83 percent of those from families with incomes over $75,000.[25] Such differences in prospects of a college degree are important to economic life prospects as a whole. In 1989, among older workers, women who were college graduates earned 70 percent more than women who were just high school graduates; the college premium for men was 65 percent.[26]

Because of the high cost of college as compared with most families' current incomes, access to higher education is sensitive to differences in wealth. When one adds the importance of wealth in buying a home in a good school district, the impact of differences in wealth on differences in life prospects becomes even more significant. And current differences in wealth in the United States are extremely steep. In his study of the American distribution of wealth, economist Edward Wolff reports that in 1992,

[22] See Berkner and Malizio, *Student Financing*, 147.

[23] More precisely, these are percentages of the average income of families in the lowest quintile, which happened to have an upper limit very close to $20,000 (namely, $19,680) in 1996. See U.S. Census Bureau, "Historical Income Tables—Families, Table F-1, Income Limits for Each Fifth and Top 5 Percent of Families (All Races): 1947 to 1999," available on-line at http://www.census.gov/hhes/income/histinc/f01.html; and U.S. Census Bureau, "Historical Income Tables—Families, Table F-3, Mean Income Received by Each Fifth and Top 5 Percent of Families (All Races): 1966 to 1999," available on-line at http://www.census.gov/hhes/income/histinc/f03.html.

[24] See Berkner and Malizio, *Student Financing*, 147. Median family income was $44,756 in 1996, and $44,527 for families with one or more children under 18. U.S. Census Bureau, "Historical Income Tables—Families, Table F-10A, Presence of Children under 18 Years Old by Type of Family—White Families by Median and Mean Income: 1974–1999," available on-line at http://www.census.gov/hhes/income/histinc/f10a.html.

[25] See Susan P. Choy, *College Access and Affordability* (Washington, DC: U.S. Department of Education, 1998), 9. Among 1980 high school graduates, the proportion attending college in 1982 among those in the lowest socioeconomic quartile and second-highest cognitive quartile was smaller than that among those in the highest socioeconomic quartile and lowest cognitive quartile. See Gilbert, *The American Class Structure*, 169.

[26] Sheldon Danziger and Peter Gottschalk, *America Unequal* (Cambridge, MA: Harvard University Press, 1995), 116 f. Here, "older workers" are those with thirty to thirty-nine years of experience. Among workers with under ten years of experience, the college premium is 54 percent for women and 23 percent for men.

average financial wealth in the top 1 percent of U.S. households was $7,513,000 (giving them 45.6 percent of total U.S. wealth); the next 19 percent averaged $404,500 (46.7 percent of the total), and the bottom 80 percent averaged $16,000 (7.8 percent of the total). The corresponding figures for net worth, which also includes the value, less debt, of household assets such as a house, a car, or clothes in the closets, are $7,925,000 (37.2 percent), $523,600 (46.6 percent), and $43,300 (16.3 percent).[27]

Still, it is important not to take the undoubted causal impact of wealth differences on life prospects as entailing a centrally important role for reductions in wealth differences in just social policies. Respect for long-term plans and for the achievements of those who have overcome inferior life prospects imposes strict constraints on the reduction of wealth inequalities. Thus, in the project of reducing inequalities in life prospects, the reduction of differences in wealth should observe serious moral limits.

Even apart from their effect on major investments in children's futures—the special province of family wealth—income differences play a causal role in the differentiation of life prospects by giving parents greater resources for helping their children to get ahead once the parents have satisfied more urgent needs and desires. However, because of both causal uncertainty and moral constraints, the reduction of income differences will only play a limited role as an instrument of change in just social policies. The correlation of parental-income differences with other relevant factors (for example, differences in parents' education) makes the independent causal role of income and the causal efficacy of income transfers hard to assess. In any case, the need to avoid both infantilization and imposing excessive costs on those with higher incomes sets limits on the use of direct transfers of income as a cure for excessive inequality in life prospects.

While policies that reduce unequal opportunity should only rely to a small degree on income and wealth differences in their underlying justification, and should only equalize opportunities by reducing income and wealth differences to a limited extent, inequalities of income and wealth come into their own in the *monitoring* of the effort to avoid excessive inequalities of life prospects. They are centrally important as danger signs and as timely indicators of progress.

Increases in inequality of income and wealth are signs of moral danger that properly stimulate public discussion of the need for policies reducing inequality in life prospects. While a substantial increase in inequality of income and wealth is bound to increase inequalities in life prospects, standard antiegalitarian arguments do not apply with their usual force to the extra gains to the better off. Substantial increases in income and wealth inequality mainly derive from extra payoffs for choices made by

[27] Edward N. Wolff, *Top Heavy* (New York: New Press, 1996), 67 f.

the better off that they would have made, just as rationally, in any case. After all, the better off are not that much better than the rest of us (or the eminent economists among us) at economic fortune-telling. (Characteristic windfalls include stock market booms that increase returns to wealth, greater rewards to careers that the better off are already pursuing, and greater returns to higher education that better-off children would, in any case, acquire.) As a result, standard considerations of respect for planning do not supply reasons for protecting the additional inequalities that are as serious as the reasons not to eliminate inequalities that such considerations otherwise provide. Moreover, it takes a while for the beneficiaries of heightened inequality to make more expensive projects so central to their lives that their frustration would genuinely worsen their lives. (Not being able to maintain a recent increase in one's monthly consumption of luxury items is one thing, not being able to keep up the increased mortgage on a new, nicer house is quite another, even if the differences are the same in monetary terms.) So, for some time after increases in income and wealth inequality, the moral significance of marginal financial costs to the better off is not as great as usual. But there is a corresponding danger that unnecessary moral barriers may eventually arise to responding to others' legitimate interests in improved opportunities.

As usual, the United States currently provides a vivid illustration of morally troubling inequality, for the frequent increases in inequality of income and wealth in the United States in recent decades create a pressing need for timely response. With small fluctuations around a regular trend, the ratio of household income at the 95th percentile to household income at the 20th percentile has risen from 6.31 in 1974 to 8.26 in 1999.[28] From 1979 to 1992, the proportion of total marketable wealth owned by the richest 1 percent of families increased from 22 percent to 42 percent.[29]

[28] See U.S. Census Bureau, "Historical Income Inequality Tables, Table IE-1." In this period, there was also a steady increase in inequality of individual earnings among those who work full-time and year-round. For example, the ratio of earnings between the 90th and 10th percentiles increased from 3.84 to 5.33 among men, and from 3.01 to 4.50 among women (U.S. Census Bureau, "Historical Income Inequality Tables, Table IE-2, Measures of Individual Earnings Inequality for Full-Time, Year-Round Workers by Sex: 1967 to 1999," available on-line at http://www.census.gov/hhes/income/histinc/ie2.html). So changes in household composition, which in any case reflect such economic factors as long-term unemployment among local men, were far from the whole story of the increase in income inequality among households. Economist Paul Ryscavage and his colleagues estimate that changes in household composition were responsible for 47 percent of the increase in household-income inequality from 1969 to 1989, and for 20 percent of the increase from 1979 to 1989; see Paul Ryscavage et al., *Studies in the Distribution of Income* (Washington, DC: U.S. Census Bureau, 1992), 17–25. These estimates probably overrate the relative impact of changes in household composition, since they depend on Census Bureau tabulations that do not record the very highest incomes, the locus of the greatest individual-income gains.

[29] See Edward N. Wolff, "How the Pie Is Sliced," *American Prospect*, June 23, 1995, available on-line at http://www.americanprospect.com/print/V6/22/wolff-e.html. Marketable wealth consists of net assets minus consumer durables, pensions, and the value of future Social Security benefits. When these assets are included, there was still a substantial increase in the top 1 percent's share; it went from 13 percent in 1976 to 22 percent in 1989 (ibid.).

Even though the prior inequalities, which had persisted for many years, were already great, these more recent increases have deserved attention as important signs of danger.

The reduction of inequality of income and wealth is also centrally important in monitoring the implementation of broadly egalitarian projects. Suppose that we have decided that life prospects are too unequal, and have implemented our first best guesses as to legitimate, effective means of ending the excess. How can we monitor our success or failure? Our aim is to reduce serious inequalities in lifetime probabilities of success that are due to socially imposed rules and not due to differences in willingness to work. But if we wait for an informed analysis of lifetime consequences, any victims of injustice will be dead by the time we get the results. We need reasonably prompt, roughly accurate measures of progress and failure in lifting burdens of excessively unequal life prospects, so that we can take due care to avoid injustice. It is hard to see how we can avoid attending to substantial changes in the distribution of income and wealth, taking greater equality there as a sign of success in our different, ultimate, broadly egalitarian goals.[30]

IV. Impartial Provision

In the hope that the complexities of broadly egalitarian concern for life prospects have illuminated the overall pattern of deliberations in the fragmented view of equality, I will survey the other major aspects of broad egalitarianism more briskly. Each is important, responsive to distinct, complex social processes, and distinctively related to income and wealth.

[30] The distributions of income that can be promptly ascertained are distributions in a given year. So it is important to see whether income mobility makes these time-slices bad indicators of lifetime economic difference and whether upward trends in annual income inequality are mitigated by increases in income mobility. Although in the United States, as in all modern economies, income mobility is significant, it does not make annual income distributions an inappropriate monitor of income inequality in either of these two ways. In the largest, most representative U.S. longitudinal study, the Panel Study of Income Dynamics (PSID), the ratio of the Gini inequality coefficient for total incomes earned by male heads of household from 1967 to 1975 to the average annual Gini coefficient for income inequality during that time period was .84 for those who were 20 or older in 1967, and rose steadily through age brackets, reaching .97 for those 50 and older. Thus, inequalities of income within year-long periods tended to be a good measure of inequality in long-term income. (See A. B. Atkinson, F. Bourguignon, and C. Morrisson, *Empirical Studies of Earnings Mobility* [Chur, Switzerland: Harwood, 1992], 140. For an explanation of the Gini coefficient, see note 32 below.) In a later analysis of PSID data, it was found that seven-tenths of individuals in 1986 had moved no more than two deciles from their income-decile rank in 1979. In terms of five-year averages centered on those two years, nine-tenths of individuals moved no more than two deciles. In the course of the dramatic increase in income inequality between 1969 and 1986, there was no overall increase in income mobility—that is, none when 1969–76 mobility and 1979–86 mobility are compared. (See Thomas L. Hungerford, "U.S. Income Mobility in the Seventies and Eighties," *Review of Income and Wealth* 39, no. 4 [1993]: 406 f., 409.)

In addition to attending to inequalities in life prospects, one should condemn economic inequalities when they reflect government policies that do not display equal concern for all citizens. This condemnation is entailed by the requirement of Basic Equality among fellow citizens. I can hardly respect myself if I willingly commit myself to uphold the outcome of political deliberations whose norms do not dictate as much concern for me as for others. And one cannot respect another while coercively imposing a regime on him that he could not self-respectfully uphold.

To strengthen this conclusion, consider some rivals to the precept that equal concern should govern political deliberations among fellow citizens. A politics of equal concern is certainly more respectful of fellow citizens than a political process in which citizens see politics solely as a means of advancing their own interests. After all, a goal appropriate to this civic attitude of self-interest would be participation in an enduring coalition that dominates others' lives, paralyzing opposition through despair or fear.

A more attractive alternative, from the standpoint of equal respect, is commitment to the provision of *equal net benefit* from government policies as a whole. This is a genuine rival to equal concern. For political deliberations seeking laws that are of equal net benefit to all might provide relatively little to the neediest because their abysmal baseline of neediness makes improvement so much easier, or because others gain little on balance from projects helping the neediest, who may on average be less productive than others. Why not let this familiar standard of fairness determine the requirements of equal respect in political choice?

Equal concern is the more appropriate standard because it better reflects the moral significance of democratic citizenship. For equal concern, not concern for equal benefit, expresses the proper valuing of the institutional loyalties on which a well-ordered democracy depends. Morally responsible citizens of a just polity want its functioning to depend on willing civic commitments—for example, a preference for principled persuasion and empathic consideration of others' conflicting interests even when one could be part of a dominant coalition; a willingness to conform to laws with which one disagrees, even if they are somewhat unjust or quite foolish; and, if need be, a willingness to risk one's life for one's country. A proper appreciation of these shared institutional loyalties is displayed in equal concern for one's loyal coparticipants. Someone who properly values friendship does not abandon a friend when it turns out that the friend cannot match her benefit for benefit because of circumstances beyond his control. Similarly, the appreciation of another's loyal fellow-citizenship ought to be expressed in concern for her, not just for the fair exchange of the payoffs of association with her.

The civic duty that I have tried to establish, the duty to seek government policies displaying equal concern, creates pressure to reduce economic inequality, because there is a special connection between equal concern and attention to relative need. At the same time, other aspects of the precept of equal concern, limiting the scope of such concern and requiring attention to the weight of numbers, can impose moral limits on projects of equalization, limits to which a broad egalitarianism also attends.

Equal concern requires proportionate responsiveness to interpersonal differences in needs of relevant kinds. Equal concern for one's children provides familiar examples. A parent who has equal concern for both his young children will do more to obtain health care for the one with more serious health problems, and will provide more nurturance for the one who needs more in order to become a secure, self-confident, self-reliant person. Despite all of the differences between parenthood and fellow-citizenship, equal concern among fellow citizens should also be guided by proportionate responsiveness to relevant needs. For example, once the U.S. government embarked on the interstate highway program, the equal concern entailed by equal respect among fellow citizens required special sensitivity to the needs of areas that would otherwise have been isolated. Perhaps the interstate highway system has done more to benefit people in the Southwest than it has for those in the Northeast, whose transportation needs were reasonably well served to begin with. This is no criticism of the system, which ought to have been especially sensitive to access-deprivation.

Because concern for someone requires sensitivity to her needs, it might seem that the requirement of equal concern will rule out large inequalities in well-being. But this quick inference would neglect the connection of equal political concern with the specific topic of a political choice, as well as the appropriate role of numbers.

That we should display equal concern in providing a good politically does not entail that we should be concerned to use government to satisfy every need that would otherwise go unmet. The proper scope of political concern has to be established. No doubt, everyone's having virtually anything depends on the existence of government. But this does not entail that virtually everything must be treated as a good that government provides. If otherwise independent Celtic tribes on the ancient North Sea coast discovered that they could only save their fields by collectively constructing and manning dikes, they would be obliged not to discriminate in the provision of flood-protection, but they would hardly have to convert their fields into a collective asset for all. By the same token, to display equal concern when providing a good by governmental means requires appropriate sensitivity to the need that is served by that project, not to citizens' neediness in general. The better off should not receive less police protection because a few robberies will still leave them better off than poor people.

The quick inference from equal political concern to the exclusion of large inequalities in well-being also neglects the role of numbers in equal concern, which can diminish pressure to put those who need most first when there are many more with significant, less serious, competing needs. To adapt the sort of example that leads even Thomas Scanlon, one of the foremost contemporary critics of utilitarianism, to concede that numbers seem to matter in the final analysis: A lifeguard must show equal concern for everyone in danger when choosing whom to save. So, if she must choose between saving someone from being blinded for life by a school of jellyfish and saving someone from drowning, she must favor the one whose very life is in peril, the individual with the more serious need. But suppose that the lifeguard must choose between saving one person from drowning and rushing to a public-address system to warn people at a crowded beach to avoid an approaching school of jellyfish that will otherwise blind thousands. In this case, equal concern for all hardly prohibits the lifeguard from saving the greater number from the lesser danger, which is still relevantly serious.[31] Crass as politicians' appeals to the Great Middle Class can be, this vast majority can have the moral standing of the large crowd imperiled by the jellyfish as compared to a small minority in even more serious peril.

Because of these complications, there seems to be no general rule connecting the precept of equal political concern with overall equality of economic well-being. Still, specific, legitimate activities of modern governments make political equality of concern an important source of reasons to regard economic inequalities as excessive, reasons that add to the case for reducing inequalities of income and wealth in the United States.

For one thing, the display of equal concern in governmental activities requires sensitivity to needs in the course of fundraising. Apart from the exceptional cases in which taxes are connected with special, optional activities, such as smoking cigarettes or (in the United States) duck-hunting, taxes should constitute an equal sacrifice for all unless unequal sacrifice will be to the absolute advantage of the less-than-equal. (Presumably, this absolute advantage would involve benefits depending on stronger incentives to invest, work, or deploy special skills than equal sacrifice would allow.) For familiar reasons involving diminishing marginal returns, equal sacrifice will require taxing the substantially better off at a higher rate than that faced by the less well off. If inequality of income net of taxes is not substantially lower than pretax income inequality, then the equalizing effect is too small, unless it is justifiable from the standpoint of those with lower pretax income. In the United States, taxes create only a small reduction in income inequality: in 1989, for example, they only led to a .041 reduction in the Gini coefficient, the most widely used measure of overall inequality.[32] This does not seem to reflect the equal sacrifice that political equality of concern, prima facie, requires.

[31] See Scanlon, *What We Owe to Each Other*, 239.

[32] See Frank Levy, *The New Dollars and Dreams* (New York: Russell Sage Foundation, 1998), 207. Although federal income taxes are mildly progressive, federal payroll taxes and state and local sales taxes are regressive. Altogether, taxes *and* government benefits only reduce the Gini coefficient by .071 (ibid., 206 f.). However, I shall argue in what follows that the reduction of poverty is a mandatory political goal. If so, then the provision of benefits to the

The sphere of government activity at the other extreme from taking money—namely, help in making money—can also generate moral pressure to reduce inequality because of the imperative of equal concern. To overcome problems of instability and stagnation and to provide an adequate infrastructure for economic growth, citizens of every modern democracy support their government's engagement in the large-scale management of economic life in the interest of prosperity, through such interventions as macroeconomic steering, the crafting of taxes to encourage efficient investment, the adjustment of the framework of tariffs and loans channeling international commerce, and the development of public facilities to serve commercial needs. If fellow citizens respect one another, they must, then, seek prosperity-enhancing policies that display no less concern for the prosperity of those who are lathe operators and maids than for those who are executives and corporate lawyers.

Of course, even if government policies display equal concern, such policies may help some more than others in any given year, just as the transportation projects of a just government may, in a given year, provide more transportation aid for some regions than for others. But the generation of substantial inequalities in people's prosperity in their lives as a whole is another matter. Suppose that over the course of many years, some benefit from government policies much more than others do, and the benefits in prosperity tend to be in inverse proportion to economic need. In this situation, unless compensatory attention is paid to the prosperity of those left behind, some people's lives as a whole will be im-

---

poor is part of what should be done politically, not a means of insuring equity in sacrifices imposed in pursuit of political goals.

As noted in the text, the Gini coefficient is the most common measure of overall income inequality; it characterizes graphic representations of income distribution known as "Lorenz curves." Suppose a statistician, seeking the sum of all income in a population, first recorded the income of the poorest person, then recorded the sum of the incomes of the two poorest persons, the three poorest persons, and so on until the total was reached. A Lorenz curve represents the growth of the sums as more and more of the units in question (here, people), from poorest to richest, are included. Suppose that the x-axis of a graph corresponds to the proportion of the population that has been counted, while the y-axis corresponds to the proportion of the ultimate total that has been reached by the sum so far. Then the forty-five-degree diagonal from the origin to the (1, 1) point ("all people counted, all income accounted for") might be thought of as the diagonal of equality: on this line, every additional unit counted adds the same amount to the income sum, so the line represents a perfectly equal distribution. By the same token, a Lorenz curve that coincides with the x-axis up until a full count is achieved, at which point it shoots up to the (1,1) point, is the right angle of perfect inequality, in which nothing is added until the richest unit is counted. In any population in the real world, the actual Lorenz curve will be inside the triangle described by these two extremes. The Gini coefficient is twice the area between the diagonal of equality and the actual Lorenz curve in this representation of a distribution. Because of the doubling, a value of 1 corresponds to perfect inequality, and the actual Gini coefficient equals the ratio of (1) the area between the actual Lorenz curve and the diagonal of perfect equality to (2) the area of the triangle described by the diagonal of perfect equality and the right angle of perfect inequality. Since this ratio grows as the Lorenz curve bulges from perfect equality toward perfect inequality, the Gini coefficient can be seen as measuring where an actual distribution is located between the two extremes.

proved much more than others' through the activities of a government that all are expected loyally to support; this will be a difference in benefit that cannot be justified in terms of differences in need. In response to such a situation, a government displaying equal concern in its project of enhancing people's prosperity will seek means of reducing the gap, to help those left behind.

The consequent just transfers to those left behind in the project of prosperity are genuinely egalitarian, not mere responses to absolute neediness. Perhaps if the government had not engaged in the project of enhancing economic prosperity, the neediness of the worse off who were left behind would not be great enough to justify transfers on grounds of compassion. Still, transfers to these people are justified as part of a broadly egalitarian effort to maintain appropriate impartiality. Moreover, the duty to help those left behind in the project of prosperity is a prime example of a duty of justice requiring attention to inequalities in income and wealth. Even more than in the case of unequal opportunity, growing inequalities of income and wealth are the timely and revealing signs of danger that the morally prohibited inequality of concern has emerged, while decreases in these gaps, favoring those who are worse off, are the timely and revealing signs of success in eliminating the morally excessive inequality. Finally, unequal gains from the project of prosperity, inversely proportional to financial need, produce an especially strong case for helping those left behind, because standard antiegalitarian considerations have less force here than usual. The additional gains here are not primarily due to additional self-reliant striving, and their sources are outside of family life and similarly protected private spheres.

Recently, the connections between prosperity and government policy in the United States have created mounting moral pressure to reduce such inequalities in benefit. In recent decades, the task of promoting prosperity has gone well, if we assess it by looking at overall measures. For example, per capita gross domestic product increased 38 percent between 1980 and 1998.[33] However, in promoting prosperity, governments ought to show equal concern for the economic flourishing of all citizens, not an ultimate concern for aggregates and averages. And between 1980 and 1998, gains in people's prosperity were typically in inverse proportion to their economic need. The economist Stephen Rose, tracking the fortunes of individuals in the largest and most representative database available for the United States, the Panel Study of Income Dynamics, found that in the course of the 1980s, individuals whose family income was in the lowest quintile lost 4 percent on average, while individuals in the highest quin-

[33] See U.S. Census Bureau, *Statistical Abstract of the United States, 1999* (Washington, DC: U.S. Census Bureau, 1999), 464. The change is in inflation-adjusted dollars, like all dollar-based measurements of change that I will cite in what follows. The appropriate means of discounting for inflation are currently much disputed, but that dispute does not affect the broad trends on which I will rely, especially trends in inequality.

tile gained 63 percent. Moreover, the distribution of gains favored a best-off minority over the vast majority, not just over the worst off: average gains regularly and sharply decreased at each step from the highest quintile to the lowest. (For example, the average gains of those in the second-highest quintile were less than half of those of people in the highest one.)[34] In 1995, as compared with 1975, the average inflation-adjusted earnings of machine operators were 16 percent lower among men and 9 percent lower among women, while the average earnings of professionals were 6 percent higher among men and 18 percent higher among women.[35] In 1980, the ratio of the average pay of chief executive officers of large corporations (including exercised stock options) to the average pay among factory workers was 42. By 1993, it had become 157; by 1999, 475.[36]

Economists strenuously disagree about the relative importance of the various factors contributing to the pattern of unequal gains seen in the United States over the last quarter-century. However, these controversies need not be resolved to vindicate worries that unequal benefit from government policies has substantially contributed to the pattern. Causal factors that are uncontroversially important—and collectively of overriding importance, in the view of a large majority of economists—have served as bases for unequal benefit from government policies, policies especially beneficial to those already best off. Macroeconomic and tax policies have quickened the pace of technological change. New technology is much more apt to make the skills of middle-aged, experienced blue-collar workers obsolete than to undermine the more generic and flexible skills of managers and professionals, who, in any case, can rely on substantial personal savings to finance their own retraining. Trade policies have facilitated globalization. Greater speed and flexibility in firms' worldwide pursuit of advantageous production sites and productive inputs threatens the work lives of blue-collar workers far more than it threatens the work lives of those engaged in the coordinative and administrative tasks of U.S.-based firms. Increased immigration has contributed to the productivity of an aging U.S.-born population (and serves international egalitarian interests as well), but at the same time, the inflow, mostly from

[34] These figures are from Stephen Rose, "Is Mobility in the United States Still Alive?" *International Review of Applied Economics* 13, no. 3 (1999): 423. Rose is concerned with family income adjusted for differences in family size, since pooling of resources within families typically determines how well the members fare. Since yearly fluctuations in income are a routine feature of economic life, the family incomes he associates with the start and finish are three-year averages spanning 1980 and 1989. Individuals are arranged in quintiles according to their average family income throughout the ten-year span.

[35] Richard Freeman, *When Earnings Diverge* (Washington, DC: National Policy Association, 1997), 11.

[36] See "Executive Pay: The Party Ain't Over Yet," *BusinessWeek*, April 26, 1993, 56; and Jennifer Reingold, "Executive Pay," *BusinessWeek*, April 17, 2000, 110. The figures on executive pay are based on *BusinessWeek*'s annual survey of such pay, which in 1993 examined executive compensation (i.e., salary, bonuses, and exercised stock options) at 365 of the largest U.S. corporations, as ranked by market value.

poorer countries, tends to increase competitive pressure at the low end of the wage scale.[37] Monetary and fiscal policies contributing to overall growth have also contributed to a vast long-term expansion in stock values—registered, for example, in a Dow Jones Industrial Average at the end of 1999 that was 3.2 times its value at the start of 1990, and 12.7 times its value at the start of 1980.[38] Since the top 20 percent of American households own 92 percent of U.S. financial wealth,[39] this side effect is bound to produce unequal benefits, in inverse proportion to need. In contrast, no currently favored means of enhancing overall prosperity facilitates gains that are in proportion to need.

No doubt, some well-intentioned policies specially directed at enhancing the prosperity of those left behind would defeat themselves, through inadequate attention to incentives and market-based efficiencies. But given the resources available and the scale of the gap between those left behind by government policy and those most helped, there is a heavy burden of proof on anyone who claims that all significant further efforts to reduce the gap, in recent years or in the immediate future, would have been or will be doomed. A project of collective advancement that all are expected to support has advanced people in an unequal way that is hard to justify on a basis of equal concern.

V. A Quasi-Egalitarian Concern

A political commitment to relieve poverty on humanitarian grounds, out of compassion for those who have sunk below an absolute level of destitution, is not, as such, a concern for inequality. However, when this project is regulated by equal political concern, the combination creates considerable pressure to reduce inequalities of income.[40] Among the poor, some are poorer than others, and equal concern dictates sensitivity to greater need (admittedly, moderated at times by attention to numbers). Among the nonpoor, equality of concern will favor using progressive taxation to raise funds for poverty relief, so that citizens who ought to fund this project do so on the basis of equal sacrifice. Thus, the use of government to relieve poverty implies reductions in income gaps among

[37] At a 1995 New York Federal Reserve colloquium on rising wage inequality, participating economists attributed, on average, 58 percent of the increase in wage inequality to the three factors of technological innovation, trade, and immigration. See Freeman, *When Earnings Diverge*, 40.

[38] The data on the Dow Jones Industrial Average is from http://www.djindexes.com.

[39] See Wolff, *Top Heavy*, 67 f.

[40] More precisely, inequalities of income or wealth. I will concentrate on effects on income, because poverty programs significantly reducing wealth inequality are so far from the political agenda: the poor would not be poor if they had significant wealth; wealth distribution among the nonpoor is much more severely skewed than income distribution; and taxes on wealth provide less than 1 percent of total tax revenues in all advanced economies. But see ibid. for powerful arguments that the bias against taxing wealth is misguided.

all fellow citizens. But is there a duty to support the use of government to help the poor?

Suppose that someone is not in a position to live a life worthy of enjoyment, a life in which her choices have point and value because of their role in realizing worthwhile goals with which she can identify, thereby enjoyably expressing a wide range of human capacities and a well-developed human personality. Perhaps she lacks the means to have a home where she can enjoyably exercise her capacity for sociality and nurturance. Perhaps she has a physical condition that interferes with the enjoyable exercise of a suitably wide range of capacities, a condition that is curable for a price that she cannot afford. Because the adequate expression of human personality is blocked, anyone who appreciates the equal value of all will regard this situation as a reason to help. But it certainly will not be a conclusive reason. Indeed, every morally responsible person is aware that the world is full of hundreds of millions of such reasons which she ignores. If we were to govern ourselves by a requirement of alleviating serious deprivation whenever we could without creating similar deprivation in ourselves, we would be constantly threatened with distraction from our own self-expressive goals by neediness in others that we did not create and cannot control. So each of us may ration his humane concern by following standing policies of aid. What one must not do, if one appreciates the equal worth of all, is to reject standing policies of aid that are the best ways of expressing humane concern and that do not pose unacceptable risks of worsening one's own life. Since worthwhile life goals are flexible enough to leave a wide margin within which most of us could have less without leading a worse life, these rules can be materially demanding.

Whether this general perspective on humane concern requires extensive use of the state as a vehicle for helping needy compatriots depends on whether there are compelling reasons, in many circumstances, for preferring this vehicle of aid to the needy and for using it to help needy compatriots even if there are needier people outside the state's borders. There are such reasons.

1. *Governmental management of help for needy compatriots, on the basis of equal concern, increases the amount that can be given without unacceptable risk that this aid to others will worsen the giver's life.* Part of the value of income and wealth for advantaged households is competitive: usefulness in outbidding others, at least as well endowed, in competition for scarce resources. If I give too much to charity, I may be unable to afford a comfortable house in a quiet, pretty neighborhood, not because such houses are hard to build, but because I will be outbid by others who are not so charitable. So compulsory, tax-financed giving reduces risks of excessive charity. Since the government programs it sustains can be especially widely and reliably available, this vehicle of aid can also reduce the riskiness of giving by raising a safety net that may one day cushion the giver's fall.

2. *Imposed giving can help the needy to avoid especially oppressive forms of dependency.* Public aid can be provided as a prerogative of citizenship, reliably available so long as the recipient fulfills requirements that he himself helps to formulate in the course of democratic deliberations. If the process of applying for aid inevitably results in demeaning interactions, aid without a means test is sometimes, to some extent, a feasible alternative. Best of all, government policies can sometimes express the proper valuing of self-reliance in a context of humane concern by emphasizing the expansion of access to jobs that are escape routes from poverty. In contrast, private charity makes people depend on the benevolent will of others, who are now concerned to alleviate a burden of poverty, but could change their concern without any joint deliberation.

3. *There is a special duty to support tax-financed aid to needy fellow citizens, a duty that does not entail a similar commitment to aid the needy everywhere by every available means.* One's fellow citizens have special standing because one relies on their loyalty to shared, life-determining institutions. This creates a duty of loyal concern for them, which does not extend to the needy worldwide. This special duty responds to an expectation of institutional loyalty, and need only be implemented through support for appropriate institutional measures—that is, through political support for laws rather than through private donations.

Thus, in addition to the general duty of compassion, there is a political duty to support government policies that would help poor fellow citizens, if the costs to nonpoor fellow citizens would not be so great as to impose worse lives on them. In the United States in recent decades, many of the nonpoor seem to have had resources to spare for such projects of aid. In 1999, the percentage of families below the official poverty line was the same as it had been in 1979, while average family income was 42 percent higher in the top quintile and 66 percent higher among the top 5 percent.[41] So, assuming that government policies could help the poor, there has been an unmet duty to embark on a political project of a pervasively income-equalizing kind, whose success would be properly monitored by determining whether income inequality, net of taxes and transfers, is declining.

VI. Improving the Milieu

The last broadly egalitarian concern that I will consider is the concern to reduce economic inequalities because of the effects of a milieu of in-

[41] See U.S. Census Bureau, "Historical Income Tables—Families, Table F-3"; and U.S. Census Bureau, "Historical Poverty Tables—Table 2, Poverty Status of People by Family Relationship, Race, and Hispanic Origin: 1959 to 1999," available on-line at http://www.census.gov/hhes/poverty/histpov/hstpov2.html. Although the validity of the official poverty line is much debated, alternative definitions have little impact on the trend in the proportions of people below the line. See Danziger and Gottschalk, *America Unequal*, 62–65.

equality on one's social and political relationships. Although these effects are the object of much current distress over increased inequality, tapping into this source of broad egalitarianism is tricky business, in part because of dangers of utopianism and unjustified manipulation (which I will consider in the next several paragraphs), and in part because of dangers of resentment (which I will examine at the end of this section).

By "utopianism," I mean naive expectations concerning the economic equalization that would be achieved by the pursuit of an improved social milieu. A prime example is the view sometimes held by American political philosophers that the elimination of excessive inequality in political influence would justify great reductions in inequality of income and wealth, a view encouraged by John Rawls's current belief that his stringent egalitarianism can be based on purely political values.[42]

Suppose that the current American system of campaign funding were replaced by a European-style system of public funding, and that everyone had the leisure, literacy, and basic information needed to form political judgments on the basis of the best nonspecialized news sources. The public funding would slightly reduce the value of having more income and wealth, and the increase in minimal civic capacity would require some improvement of the worst jobs and schools. But much economic inequality would remain, as would considerable inequality of political influence. However, the residual political inequality could not be eliminated without destroying economic efficiency on which the well-being of the worst off depends. For reasonable efficiency in a capitalist economy depends on a process of production and investment that inevitably gives rise to unequal political influence.

In the capitalist division of economic labor, some people occupy managerial and professional positions giving them knowledge, skills, and networks of acquaintance (and reflecting and reinforcing interests and temperaments) that make them especially likely to be recruited to positions of political power or to offer influential advice. An investment process driven by self-interested investors' lust for returns has turned out to be by far the most efficient means of resource-allocation; in this setting, governments must take care to avoid measures creating anxiety in investors about their returns. This side of utopia, the project of eliminating the severe residual inequalities of political influence that are based on these fundamental economic processes would be so destructive of the economic well-being of the worst off that the worst off would be reasonable to reject them.

My second warning about misguided efforts to change milieus concerned "manipulation," by which I mean a project of changing people's

[42] See Rawls, *Political Liberalism*, where the connection between purely political values and the stringent egalitarianism of *A Theory of Justice* is affirmed, for example, at xlviii f. and 228 f. At Rawls, *Political Liberalism*, 328, Rawls argues that a political duty to avoid excessive inequalities of political influence creates especially strong pressure to reduce economic inequality.

dispositions to choose that employs nonrational means to which they could not rationally consent. A prime example of unjustified manipulation would be the reduction of differences in income and wealth in order to increase receptiveness to egalitarian proposals. It is eminently plausible that people who do not share similar economic fates, are not affected in similar ways by government policies, and do not have to rely on one another for security and enjoyable joint activities will be less committed to avoiding the inequalities that egalitarians find excessive. However, many of those who do not recognize the excessiveness of these inequalities are well above the threshold that Rawls now labels "reasonableness": they are willing to engage in the principled and tolerant compromise that is characteristic of well-ordered democracy. It is a central goal of respectful politics to base choices on arguments that could be offered as justifications to fellow citizens above this threshold, who are themselves concerned to seek common ground on the basis of mutual respect. Changing the social milieu in order to change the political sentiments of others would constitute a political project based on a rationale that could not be offered as a justification to those others. So pursuing greater equality in order to promote egalitarian political sentiments departs from the deliberative mutuality of mutually respectful citizenship.

Still, these dangers can be avoided through certain arguments from community that do add to the justification and the breadth of condemnations of economic inequality. These sources of egalitarian concern, at once communitarian, individualist, and liberal, include such goals of mutuality as the encouragement of political reasonableness; the provision of facilities for the routine, active expression of equal respect; and the avoidance of excessive inequalities of social recognition.

Respect for fellow citizens does not always preclude favoring milieus because of their effects on political sentiments. That the political shaping of social environments, within the limits of civil liberties, will contribute to a public culture in which fellow citizens take one another's interests and convictions seriously is a very good reason for so shaping them. For example, the fact that the racial integration of a public school system would tend to reduce bigotry is a valid political reason in favor of the integration. The process involves the manipulation of sentiments, but the bigotry that would be modified by this milieu-therapy is below the threshold of "reasonableness."

If people do not share their fates and do not intermingle on terms of social equality, they are less apt to take one another's interests and convictions seriously. For example, they are less apt to attend to others, in the course of controversy, as people with something to say, as opposed to threats or mere consumers of public time. Because of the role of superior income and wealth in avoiding the need to rely on others, in creating especially affluent neighborhoods and gaining access to them, and in producing emblems of success, sharing of fates and intermingling on a basis of social equality become less common as inequality grows. So economic inequality can put people in a worse frame of mind to listen and learn from each other. This is a threat to deliberative mutuality, not just to the distinctive goals of economic egalitarianism, and it furnishes a politically legitimate reason to reduce the underlying economic inequalities.[43]

In addition to the sharing of fates, I have appealed to mere respectful intermingling as a social process that ought to be facilitated. Even apart from the goal of political reasonableness, this aspect of community provides a further reason to limit inequality. When economic inequality reduces such intermingling, it reduces the prevalence of ongoing interactions through which people can more adequately express their appreciation of everyone's equal worth.

Our attitudes toward others are expressed in the nature of our ongoing interactions with them, not just in our deliberations about them. If my fundamental attitude is appreciation of the equal worth of all, I will prefer ongoing interactions in which I encounter people from other walks of life on a footing of equality in polite and friendly ways; in which I learn what is on their minds in a spirit of mutual learning rather than as the target of complaining, requesting, or begging; and in which I send my children to schools where they learn along with, and from, these others. In short, I will, all else being equal, prefer an integrated life to a segregated one. But some social environments make it hard to live such a life. If integrated neighborhoods are rare or run down, local schools and parks are de facto segregated, and malls and shopping districts serve customers from only one walk of life, respectful intermingling is difficult. So the widening of access to respectful intermingling is a politically relevant goal.

Of course, even those who recognize the virtues of an intermingled life may have convictions, goals, or tastes that make a more segregated life rational and legitimate on balance. (Religious convictions attaching people to an encompassing faith community are perhaps the starkest example.) Still, there is nothing objectionably manipulative in the goal of making contexts for social intermingling widely available, though avoidable. Those who recognize the virtues of an intermingled life but have their special reasons to avoid it can. Those who do not see the special objective value

[43] Claims about the atomizing tendencies of inequality are hardly susceptible to neat statistical tests. But the results of empirical inquiries lend support to these egalitarian concerns. Ichiro Kawachi et al. determined the correlations, among states in the United States, between the degree of local income inequality and the degree of social distrust as reflected in local responses to such statements as "Most people would try to take advantage of you if they got a chance." The correlations are quite strong. For example, there is a correlation coefficient of $r = .73$ ($P < .0001$) associating local income inequality (by the researchers' favored measure) with the percentage agreeing that most people would try to take advantage. See Ichiro Kawachi et al., "Social Capital, Income Inequality, and Mortality," in Ichiro Kawachi, Bruce P. Kennedy, and Richard G. Wilkinson, eds., *The Society and Population Health Reader* (New York: New Press, 1999), 2:226 f. In this essay, Kawachi et al. seek to explain the powerful association, independent of absolute income, in social environments throughout the world, between income inequality and bad health, bad health on average as well as among the worst off. If anyone could establish the mechanism underlying this association, she might provide the most powerful of all sources of broadly egalitarian concern.

of intermingling will be treated as making a mistake if equality is promoted on these grounds, but integrated environments are not promoted in order to change their outlooks. They are promoted in order to facilitate interactions, rightly sought by others, that depend on the public environment. Policies meant to preserve or restore environments facilitating the routine, active expression of mutual respect are as appropriate to just government as policies of preserving or restoring places of natural beauty.

One further milieu-centered concern about inequality (the last that I will try to establish) is an aspect of the widely noted tendency for growing inequality to make the material attainments of the worst off no longer good enough, even if they are no less than they were before. Through its effects on credence, welcome, and the sharing of concerns, greater inequality can worsen the less successful, even when they have the same as they did before, by worsening their terms of social recognition—that is, the extent to which they are appreciated as valued partners in social life.

We need to be credited by others as reliable people capable of making our way by offering what is of value and valued by others. But those whose approval we need rarely have direct knowledge of our lives. So it is important that we establish our credibility as co-participants in social life by displaying signs of sufficient success in social activity—dressing well enough, having a nice-enough home, being fluent enough in mainstream culture, and so forth. Here, what is good enough to meet most others' expectations (or, more properly, not to excite their doubts) inevitably rises as the general level of attainment grows.

In addition to economic losses and political neglect due to lack of such credibility, those who are much less successful than most cannot expect a broad welcome when they seek to interact with most others in a nonsubordinate way. Large differences in economic resources threaten to make interaction on terms of equality a source of mutual discomfort due to fears of condescension and resentment, lack of fluent grasp of local etiquette, misunderstandings of one another's capacities and aspirations, and the absence of shared pursuits that provide the routine currency of social exchange. Many people will be nervous if their children play with the children of those who are by far the worst off, however well off the worst off are.

Finally, those who are much less successful than most can expect that their characteristic life-problems will only be a focus of public attention when the attention is tinged with pity. In one of his deep inquiries into the burdens of being African-American, W. E. B. Du Bois writes, "Between me and the other world there is ever an unasked question . . . How does it feel to be a problem?"[44] This experience of being a problem is very different from the experience of having problems that are the normal challenges of life in one's society, and any self-respecting person will strongly prefer the latter.

[44] W. E. B. Du Bois, *The Souls of Black Folk* [1903], in Du Bois, *Writings* (New York: Library of America, 1996), 363.

Unequal social recognition is objectionable independently of its non-comparative costs to the worst off. A society in which people are generally unfriendly to one another, paying attention to strangers' problems only when the duty of compassion demands this, is, no doubt, a bad society. But a society in which some people have less access than others to valued partnership in social life is vulnerable to an additional charge of unfairness.

What is the relationship between inequality of wealth or income and the goal of promoting mutuality—the political openness, ease of democratic intermingling, and broad social recognition that characterize appropriately egalitarian milieus? Large inequalities in wealth will be especially important threats to mutuality because of the role of wealth in determining where people buy houses. Thus, the vast and increasing inequality in wealth in the United States in recent decades is a serious concern. The income inequality that matters for mutuality, as opposed to income inequalities that can matter as causes of unequal opportunity or as instances of unequal provision, is primarily the inequality of those far below the median; their incomes being so much less than most people's in their society contributes to their marginalization. It is a serious concern, then, that one in five U.S. households in 1992 had an income over the previous five years that was less than half of the median five-year household income, and that one in six was in this situation even when the cash equivalent of government benefits was included.[45]

Still, when a factor contributes to a morally troubling inequality, it can be misguided, nonetheless, to weaken that factor in order to cope with the problem. When we shift our focus from the causal role of income and wealth inequality in weakening mutuality to the policy question of whether income and wealth inequality ought to be reduced in order to promote mutuality, costs in terms of resentment loom large, so large that they might seem to make the defense of egalitarian milieus a politically irrelevant goal.

Suppose egalitarians argue that the mutuality imperiled by increased inequality in income or wealth ought to be strengthened by policies raising the worst off closer to others in terms of income or wealth, policies that involve redistributive taxation or programs meant to increase, preferentially, the income or wealth of those who have the least. The mutual attention that such a remedy seeks to promote is positive and empathic. But the greater the costs imposed on some in pursuit of greater equality overall, the more likely it is that resentment, not empathy, will be the outcome. Short of manipulative secrecy about their underlying justifications, how can milieu-oriented egalitarians hope to contain this psycho-

[45] Robert E. Goodin et al., *The Real Worlds of Welfare Capitalism* (Cambridge: Cambridge University Press, 1999), 276. More precisely, these proportions are 20.6 percent and 16.3 percent, and both are adjusted for differences in family size. In the most nearly comparable period that Goodin et al. could assess (1990–94), the Netherlands, whose economy is at least as dynamic overall as the United States', reduced the after-benefits proportion to 1.4 percent.

logical cost? If they cannot, then the cultivation of civic mutuality, like the cultivation of friendships, should, for all its importance, be a purely personal task.

In containing costs of resentment, piling redistributive burdens on the rich has legitimate uses, so long as the rich do not have valid reasons to complain that are more serious than the reasons to object to the constraints on mutuality that are overcome. If resources deriving from taxation of those on top are used to help the worst off, improvements in the relationship of the worst off to the vast majority between the best and worst off might, on balance, enhance mutuality. However, increasing reliance on this strategy is limited not just by effects on incentives and by the increasing moral seriousness of higher levels of imposed costs, but also by the fact that as the imposed costs rise, there will be growing resentment among the many who hope to become rich (even if these hopes are often highly overoptimistic).

Apart from concentrating tax burdens on the rich, resentment can be reduced by combining the appeal to threatened ties of community with appeals to other goals of equality: appeals to the need to make life prospects more equal or to compensate for inequalities of provision. Benefits of advantages unearned by one's own efforts are easier to give up ungrudgingly, and these other goals of equality have such gains as their sole intended target. Inevitably, attempts to implement the other goals overshoot their intended target, but intentions make a difference with respect to resentment. When costs in resentment are contained through this combination of rationales, the need to strengthen special ties of community becomes, in effect, a supplement to arguments from equality of opportunity and equality of provision, adding to the joint force of reasons to reduce inequalities of income and wealth.

In any case, the reduction of gaps in income and wealth is hardly the only project of those who seek to reduce troubling fissures in mutuality, based on economic circumstances, by political means. In particular, the public provision of facilities that enhance mutuality and are open to all is less apt to prompt resentment than the use of some people's taxes in order to increase other people's income or wealth. Indeed, in the United States today, efforts to save downtown shopping districts and emphasis on public education rather than voucher schemes as a means of improving education seem the chief expressions of the goal of egalitarian community.

Perhaps this is as it should be, given the special dangers of resentment, and the promotion of mutuality should rarely be the main justification for policies reducing gaps in income and wealth. Still, a moral interest in egalitarian milieus will add to the importance of paying attention to inequality of income and wealth when monitoring social justice. Income and wealth distributions in which many make much less than the median serve as important warnings that mutuality may be in peril. Moreover, because it strengthens the case for reducing inequality in life prospects and the case for helping those left behind by the project of prosperity, concern for reduced mutuality increases the importance of gains in equality of income and wealth as indicators of progress in social justice. For gains in income and wealth equality are the central means of monitoring the joint pursuit of all three broadly egalitarian goals.

VII. Conclusion

Is a concern that inequalities of income and wealth not become too great, as opposed to a concern for the suffering of those who suffer absolutely, an expression of equal respect, or is it simply an endorsement of envy? Egalitarians who have lost faith in the old, simplifying premises—that is, the generic connection between equal respect and equal shares and the requirement of attention to all-purpose means—lack a simple rebuttal to the charge of envy. However, if this discussion has been on the right track, they should not be embarrassed by this lack. There are several different reasons to be concerned about various economic inequalities. None of these inequalities is mainly a matter of income or wealth, and each must be judged in light of reasons not to do too much to reduce inequality. Still, there is a powerful case that capitalism as it would be without political intervention and capitalism as it is in the United States and elsewhere give rise to economic inequalities that are excessive unless they are a by-product of measures helping the worst off, an excuse that is highly unlikely to be valid in every case.[46] Moreover, the reduction of gaps in income and wealth sometimes has a role to play in reducing these ultimately troubling inequalities, and attention to inequalities of income and wealth is centrally important in monitoring the proper political response to excessive inequality.

In the fragmented view of equality I have been presenting in this essay, there is no general societal ideal of providing maximum access to income and wealth for those in the social position in which access is least. But at present, in the United States and many other countries, justice demands more movement in the direction of this ideal than any proposal on the current electoral agenda would produce. The old egalitarianism had its heart in the right place.

Philosophy, Cornell University

[46] That inequalities in Great Britain are at least as excessive as inequalities in the United States is suggested by the studies described in Ivan Reid, *Class in Britain* (London: Polity, 1998); and Gordon Marshall and Adam Swift, "Social Class and Social Justice," *British Journal of Sociology* 44, no. 2 (1993): 187–211. For studies suggesting that the same kinds of inequalities are excessive, though in varying degrees, in other relatively advanced economies, see Gordon Marshall, Adam Swift, and Stephen Roberts, *Against the Odds?* (Oxford: Oxford University Press, 1997).

EQUALITY, BENEVOLENCE, AND RESPONSIVENESS TO AGENT-RELATIVE VALUE*

BY ERIC MACK

I. IN SEARCH OF ARGUMENTS FOR EGALITARIANISM

Do differences in income or wealth matter, morally speaking? This essay addresses a broader issue than this question *seems* to pose. But this broader issue is, I believe, the salient philosophical issue which this question *actually* poses. Let me explain. Narrowly read, the question at hand is concerned only with inequality of income or wealth. It asks us to consider whether inequality of income or wealth *as such* is morally problematic. On this construal, the question invites us to consider whether the bare fact that Joshua has a greater income or net worth than Rebekah is a morally defective social state of affairs. Is there at least a significant moral presumption on behalf of equality of income or wealth such that, if an inequality of income or wealth obtains vis-à-vis Joshua and Rebekah, that inequality ought to be nullified unless some impressive positive justification for the inequality can be provided? On this narrow reading, the salient issue is whether there exists *in particular* an egalitarian presumption with respect to income or wealth. But I believe that the genuinely salient issue here is whether there exists *in general* an egalitarian presumption with respect to *whatever* factual condition of individuals one is supposed to attend to when assessing social states of affairs.[1] The crucial question is not whether income or wealth or utility or well-being is the condition the unequal distribution of which is as such morally problematic. Rather, the crucial question is whether it is true of *some* factual condition C—presumably the factual condition which most merits our attention in the course of our assessing social states of affairs—that its unequal distribution is as such morally problematic. Is the bare fact that

* A good deal of the initial work for Sections IV and V of this essay was done during my tenure as a Visiting Scholar at the Social Philosophy and Policy Center in the spring of 1997. I am very grateful for the opportunity which the Center afforded me, and especially for the encouragement I received from Fred Miller. Conversations with Loren Lomasky have, unintentionally, convinced me of the need to provide an agent-relativist account which does justice to other-regarding benevolent conduct. I want to thank Ellen Paul, Fred Miller, and the other contributors to this volume for their very helpful suggestions.

[1] I say "factual" condition so as not to be including within the egalitarian camp anyone who holds to a doctrine of equal *rights*. The idea (no doubt too crude) is that attending to rights and to their being equally accorded to each is not a matter of identifying some factual condition (e.g., the possession of income or utility) which is supposed to be equally dispersed among individuals.

Joshua possesses or attains or enjoys C to a greater extent than Rebekah possesses or attains or enjoys C a morally defective social state of affairs? That is, is there at least a significant moral presumption on behalf of equality such that, if there is an inequality vis-à-vis Joshua and Rebekah with regard to C, then that inequality ought to be nullified unless some impressive positive justification for that inequality can be provided? In short, does morality include a significant presumption on behalf of equality with regard to C, whatever C happens to be?[2]

The proposition that morality does include a significant presumption on behalf of equality with regard to C is the major premise of those who answer our initial question in the affirmative. This in itself, I believe, warrants my focus on this proposition. There is a further warrant for not focusing on the minor premise that income or wealth is that condition C which ought, ceteris paribus, to be equally distributed. This further reason is that many, if not most, people who are intuitively disposed to answer our initial question in the affirmative do not really subscribe to the minor premise that it is income or wealth which really matters. What many, if not most, of these people do believe is that, within the sort of social orders they are contemplating, an individual's possession of income or wealth is the crucial source of that individual's having or attaining or enjoying what really matters—utility or welfare or happiness or well-being, for example. Inequality of income or wealth is *seen* as problematic *as such* because it is perceived as the essential, constant, and unremitting ground of inequality in the distribution of what ultimately matters. The moral stain that, strictly speaking, discolors the latter inequality is perceived as spreading back to and discoloring the former inequality.[3] I believe that many, if not most, of those who are initially disposed to say that inequality of income or wealth as such is morally problematic will on reflection acknowledge that what is really morally problematic as such is some *other* inequality—the inequality of condition C—that is *generated by* an unequal division of income or wealth. So we are led back again to the conclusion that the crucial issue posed by the question "Do differences in income or wealth matter, morally speaking?" is whether morality includes a significant presumption on behalf of the equal distribution of some condition C.

This essay is directed against the major premise of those who are disposed to say that differences in income and wealth matter, that is, the

[2] Note that the mirror image of the egalitarian is the person who holds that differences in the distribution of C matter, morally speaking, because there is a moral presumption on behalf of *inequality*. For this inegalitarian, equality would be morally problematic in the way that inequality is problematic for the egalitarian. The nonegalitarian position I subscribe to rejects both this inegalitarianism and the aforementioned egalitarianism.

[3] Cf. the labored discussion, at G. A. Cohen, *Self-Ownership, Freedom, and Equality* (Cambridge: Cambridge University Press, 1995), 197–203, of the disposition to see as intrinsically unjust the sort of circumstances that one believes necessarily produce interactions that one takes to be intrinsically unjust.

proposition that the factual condition C—the possession or attainment or enjoyment of which really matters in the lives of individuals—ought, ceteris paribus, to be equally distributed among individuals. Of course, the plausible candidates for C are utility, welfare, happiness, and well-being. For this reason, in the course of this essay, I shall take friends of egalitarianism to be maintaining that it is inequality of utility or welfare or happiness or well-being among individuals which is as such morally problematic. Indeed, to simplify matters, I shall speak solely in terms of well-being and arguments for a moral presumption on behalf of equality of well-being.

As Robert Nozick has noted, however, it is much easier to find assertions of this sort of moral presumption on behalf of equality than it is to find arguments for it.[4] Often the most one can find are arguments that purport to move from the *absence* of any sound primordial claim or right to an *unequal* distribution of some valued condition to the *presence* of a sound claim or right to an *equal* distribution of that condition. An example that is literally at hand as I write is supplied by G. A. Cohen, who allows the inference from "no one has more right to [worldly resources] than anyone else" to "equal rights in [worldly resources] should therefore be instituted."[5]

How might friends of egalitarianism better argue for a moral presumption on behalf of the equal distribution of what ultimately matters in life? In asking myself this question, I found myself recalling a particular argument for utilitarianism that is suggested by J. J. C. Smart. This argument, in effect, starts with the intuitive idea that benevolence is a good and reasonable thing; surely we all take benevolent people to be good and sensible people. But what general normative stance stands behind and explains our positive assessment of benevolence? Smart's suggestion is that this general normative stance is utilitarianism, that is, the impartial endorsement of the overall good of others as our ultimate aim. Since utilitarianism is the general normative stance that best comports with and explains our positive assessment of benevolence, our positive assessment of benevolence should extend back from it to an endorsement of utilitarianism.[6] As I recalled this argument, it occurred to me that a better version of it would be an argument that moves from the intuitive goodness and reasonableness of benevolence to the endorsement of egalitarianism as the best explanation for the

[4] Robert Nozick, *Anarchy, State, and Utopia* (New York: Basic Books, 1974), 233.

[5] Cohen, *Self-Ownership, Freedom, and Equality*, 110. I say that Cohen "allows" this inference because he does not offer it on his own behalf, but on behalf of a position ("the starting gate theory") that he himself does not endorse. Cohen seems to find the inference itself unobjectionable.

[6] J. J. C. Smart and Bernard Williams, *Utilitarianism For and Against* (Cambridge: Cambridge University Press, 1973), 30–33. My depiction of Smart's argument gives it a much more cognitivist cast than Smart himself would recognize.

intuitive goodness and reasonableness of benevolence. For the benevolent agent does not so much focus on the overall good of others as on the separate well-being of each possible recipient of his benevolence and, especially, on the well-being of the possible recipients who are most in need of his sympathy and care. Given this understanding of benevolence, egalitarianism seems to have a stronger claim than does utilitarianism on being the general normative stance that best comports with and explains our positive assessment of benevolence.

So the question that seems to me worth exploring in the search for some argument on behalf of egalitarianism is whether the intuitive goodness and reasonableness of benevolence can be enlisted as a premise in a best-explanation argument for the endorsement of egalitarianism. This search, which is carried on in earnest in the next two sections of this essay, turns up two arguments. The first of these is the "impersonalist argument." In its first phase, this argument maintains that if one is to best explain the intuitive goodness and reasonableness of benevolence, one must invoke the impersonal value of every individual's well-being. In its second phase, the impersonalist argument maintains that the most reasonable form of subscription to this invocation of impersonal value is egalitarianism. The second argument I will consider is the "pretheoretical argument"; it is the egalitarian analogue of Smart's argument for utilitarianism. In this essay, I reject both of these attempts to enlist benevolence on behalf of egalitarianism. I seek to rescue benevolence from the grasp of the friends of impersonal value and equality. To carry out this act of Good Samaritanism I have to spell out and point to problems within these arguments (Sections II and III) and offer a competing explanation for the goodness and reasonableness of benevolence (Sections IV and V). The gravamen of my alternative account is that the goodness and reasonableness of benevolence is a matter of the *personal* value of an agent's benevolence for the agent and the subjects of his conduct. As we shall see, the arguments that move from benevolence to egalitarianism turn on the other-regarding character of benevolence. The chief difficulty for an alternative, personalist account of benevolence is to accommodate this other-regarding character of benevolence.

II. Benevolence, Impersonal Value, and Equality

Benevolence, we are almost all prepared to say, is a good and reasonable thing. It is such a good and reasonable thing that one can give a nice boost to key propositions within one's favorite moral theory if one can show that these propositions explain benevolence's being a good and reasonable thing. These propositions will explain the goodness and reasonableness of benevolence by explaining why people have reason to be benevolent. If one takes the goodness and reasonableness of benevolence to be a highly salient truth about the moral realm, one will take the propositions that (one believes) explain the goodness and reasonableness of benevolence to be highly salient within sound moral theory. Friends of impersonal value and equality often seek to support their commitments within moral theory in this way. Impersonal value and the value or propriety of equality in the distribution of valuable conditions among individuals are said to explain (or otherwise be implicated in) the goodness of benevolence, and the salience of benevolence within the moral realm vindicates assigning prominent positions to impersonal value and egalitarianism within moral theorizing. As announced in Section I, my intention is to reject explanations of the reasonableness of benevolence that appeal to impersonal value and egalitarianism and provide instead an account of the reasonableness of benevolence in terms of personal (agent-relative) value.

Given this intention, a word or two is necessary to clarify my use of the terms "agent-relative," "personal," "agent-neutral," and "impersonal." The value of some condition is "personal" or "agent-relative" if and only if that value is *value for* some particular individual who stands in some special relation to that condition. For instance, the value of a particular agent's sensorial pleasure is personal or agent-relative if and only if that value is *value for* the agent whose pleasure it is. The value of some condition is "impersonal" or "agent-neutral" if and only if that value is *not simply value for* a particular individual. If the value of an agent's sensorial pleasure is impersonal or agent-neutral, that pleasure is not merely valuable in relationship to that agent—even though that pleasure obtains only in relationship to that agent. If a condition has personal or agent-relative value for agent A, that value (directly) provides only agent A with reason to promote that condition. If a condition has impersonal or agent-neutral value, that value (directly) provides all agents with reason to promote it.[7]

The recalcitrant fact about benevolence that an agent-relativist account of benevolence has to accommodate is that benevolence is essentially *other-regarding*; interest in the well-being of another is an essential element in a benevolent agent's motivation. Moreover, because benevolence is essentially other-regarding, any explanation of an agent's conduct being reasonable must indicate how the value of the (intended) outcome for the other party ("the recipient") contributes to the agent's having reason to

[7] The distinction between agent-relative and agent-neutral value is concerned with the question of *for whom* the value of a given condition has directive force. This is quite different from the question of whether the value of a given condition is subjective or objective, that is, whether the value conferred upon it is a matter of its being desired or preferred or not. Unfortunately, these two issues are often conflated. This conflation often takes the form of use of the term "personal" to refer both to the agent-relativity and the subjectivity of value and use of the term "impersonal" to refer to both the agent-neutrality and the objectivity of value. In the present essay, "personal" simply means "agent-relative" and "impersonal" simply means "agent-neutral."

promote that outcome for the recipient.[8] This is easily enough done if the value of the well-being of the recipient is impersonal. For impersonal value, by definition, provides everyone—including the agent in question—with reason to promote it. By contrast, the explanation of the reasonableness of benevolence is not so easily accomplished if the only type of value available to justify an agent's action is personal (agent-relative) value. On the one hand, if the only value that gives an agent reason to act in a way that promotes another's well-being is personal value *for the agent*, that agent's motivation and conduct will not be other-regarding, and hence will not be genuinely benevolent. On the other hand, it is difficult to see how the personal value *for the recipient* of the conduct's outcome can provide the *agent* with agent-relative reason to act on the recipient's behalf. Eventually, I do hope to describe how the personal (agent-relative) value for the recipient of the conduct's prospective outcome contributes to there being personal (agent-relative) value for the agent in promoting the recipient's good.

One way of proceeding against the view that neither impersonal value nor egalitarian strictures can explain the reasonableness of benevolence would be to argue that neither impersonal value nor egalitarian strictures can explain anything because neither obtains as part of sound moral theory. In this essay I do not proceed in this way. I do not advance *independent* arguments against impersonal value and egalitarianism. Rather, I am concerned solely with the relative plausibility of accounts of the value of benevolence that implicate impersonal value and/or some deep egalitarian norm in morality and the sort of account that I shall sketch, which proceeds entirely in terms of personal (agent-relative) value. I hope to weaken the case for an ethic of impartial service to impersonal value and/or equality and to enhance the case for an ethic of personal value by showing that the latter better accounts for the goodness and reasonableness of benevolence.

I have a second motivation that is related to the first but not identical. I wish to avoid the common picture of a deep conflict between an individual's devotion to his own personal values and commitments—that is, to the constituents of *his* well-being—and that individual's benevolence. The explanation of benevolence offered by the friends of impersonal value and equality represents benevolence as being essentially a matter of impartial devotion to the well-being of individuals at large. Benevolence as

[8] Throughout this essay, I inquire about whether the value of outcome O explains A's having reason to promote O, and I have in mind A's having reason to promote O both in the sense that there is a reason for A to promote O (whether or not A is aware of that reason) and in the sense that A is aware of that reason (i.e., he *has* that reason). Hence, a more precise statement of the inquiry would be that it concerns whether the value of O *plus* A's awareness of this value explains A's having reason to promote O. To simplify matters, however, I assume that if O has value, A is aware of this value. Thus I speak only of the value of O and not (also) of A's awareness of this value.

such becomes "pure impartial benevolence."[9] To be benevolent on this construal is to be equally devoted to impersonal value wherever it may be located. An agent's benevolence and his special attachment to his own values and commitments are then seen as fundamentally antithetical motivations at war within a radically divided self. As this conflict is depicted by Thomas Nagel, one important representative of those from whose grasp I hope to wrest benevolence, there is

> a division in each individual between two standpoints [that represent the two sides of our "naturally divided selves"], the personal and the impersonal. The latter represents the claims of the collectivity and gives them their force for each individual. If it did not exist, there would be no morality, only the clash, compromise, and occasional convergence of individual perspectives.
>
> It is clear that in most people, the coexistence of the personal standpoint with the values deriving from the initial judgment of the impersonal standpoint produces a division of the self. From his own point of view within the world each person . . . is extremely important to himself. . . . But from the impersonal standpoint which he can also occupy, so is everyone else: *Everyone's* life matters as much as his does, and his matters no more than anyone else's.[10]

So profound is this division within the self that we must, according to Nagel, address the question, "How can we put ourselves back together again?"[11]

The conflict that Nagel depicts *within* the self reflects a pervasive clash *among* selves. The portion of one's self that is concerned about one's own projects and commitments is in conflict with the portion of one's self that is (supposed to be) responsive to the potentially overwhelming "claims of the collectivity." The general theme here is of course the familiar one about the demandingness of impartiality. My somewhat more specific point is that when benevolence is cast as such impartiality, benevolence itself becomes the enemy of any self that has its own particular interests and allegiances. It becomes something that such a "subjective" self can only embrace grudgingly as the price of its reunion with its "objective" companion.[12] I hope to suggest a less conflictual view of intrapersonal and interpersonal relations—one in which benevolence, albeit essentially

[9] Thomas Nagel, *Equality and Partiality* (New York: Oxford University Press, 1991), 16; cf. ibid., 15, 31.

[10] Ibid., 3–4, 14.

[11] Ibid., 16.

[12] And this assumes that a reunion with the so-called "objective" self is something worth paying for.

other-regarding, is a boon to the personal life of the benevolent agent.[13] Let us consider two lines of thought that move from the goodness and reasonableness of benevolence to the affirmation of egalitarianism, understood in somewhat Orwellian fashion as the belief that each person's well-being or happiness equally summons everyone to its service, but that the well-being or happiness of the worse off equally summons everyone more.

Since the first line of thought turns on claims about impersonal value, I refer to it as the impersonalist argument. As mentioned above, there are two phases within this argument. The first phase moves from the reasonableness of benevolence toward every individual to the impersonal value of every individual's well-being. The second phase moves from the impersonal value of everyone's well-being to the egalitarian conclusion that preferential treatment is to be accorded to the well-being of the worse off. I take the move represented by the first phase to reflect one of the arguments Nagel offers for the existence of impersonal value in *The View from Nowhere*.[14] Here is how this argument goes. Nagel imagines himself to be a patient in the burn ward of a hospital. He further envisions a fellow patient who "professes to hope that we both will be given morphine." Nagel maintains that insofar as he himself is thinking in terms of "personal values that others cannot be expected to share," he cannot understand the *reasonableness* of the profession of his fellow patient. "I understand why he has reason to want morphine for himself, but what reason does he have to want *me* to get some? Does my groaning bother him?"[15] What is the intended force of Nagel's concluding rhetorical question? Surely, if Nagel's groaning is bothering the other patient, that patient *does* have (some) reason to favor Nagel's receiving some painkiller. So why wouldn't the fact that the fellow patient is bothered by Nagel's groaning reveal to Nagel a reason that this patient has to want Nagel to get some morphine? The answer has to be that Nagel wants to understand how the fellow patient has a reason to be concerned about Nagel's pain—in contrast to being concerned about his own bothered state of mind. Nagel wants to understand the reasonableness of the fellow patient's *other-regarding* concern, not that patient's self-regarding concern. If the other patient's sole purpose is to quiet Nagel down so that he (the other patient) can better

[13] By insisting that genuinely benevolent conduct is other-regarding, I do not intend to disparage conduct by agents who benefit others *without* intending to do so. Also, it is perhaps needless to point out that much actual human conduct proceeds from a complex intertwining of significantly other-regarding motivations with predominantly self-regarding motivations.

[14] Thomas Nagel, *The View from Nowhere* (New York: Oxford University Press, 1986). Subsequent to his early work, Thomas Nagel, *The Possibility of Altruism* (Oxford: Oxford University Press, 1970), Nagel has acknowledged the existence of personal value in addition to impersonal value. My focus within the text of this essay on Nagel as a representative friend of impersonal value and equality does not gainsay his acknowledgment of personal value.

[15] Nagel, *The View from Nowhere*, 160.

follow some game show on TV, then this patient's profession can be comprehended by Nagel as reasonable vis-à-vis that patient's personal values, but cannot be comprehended as reasonably benevolent. The fellow patient's *benevolent* desire that Nagel also receive some painkiller cannot be comprehended as reasonable if one thinks only in terms of "personal values that others cannot be expected to share." Hence, according to Nagel, the other patient's benevolent desire that Nagel receive some analgesic can only (or at least best) be understood as reasonable by representing that patient as being responsive to the *impersonal* value of a mitigation in Nagel's pain. If desires (or actions or dispositions, all of which I shall tend to refer to as "conduct") are to be understood as reasonably benevolent, impersonal value must obtain. If benevolence is central to the moral life, then the affirmation of impersonal value must be prominent within sound moral theory.

The second phase within the impersonalist argument is the claim that giving preference to the promotion of impersonal value in the lives of the worse off is a more reasonable form of responsiveness to impersonal value than is maximizing net value across individuals. In contrast to those who take impartial devotion to impersonal value as pointing to a utilitarian ethic, Nagel takes such regard for impersonal value to point to an egalitarian ethic. Why? Nagel cites "the problem for the impersonal standpoint" of determining how to combine the "enormous multitude of things that matter impersonally, values positive and negative pointing in every conceivable direction." This leads to Nagel's declaration that

> my belief is that the right form of impersonal regard for everyone is an impartiality among individuals that is egalitarian not merely in the sense that it counts them all the same as inputs to some combinatorial function, but in the sense that the function itself gives preferential weight to improvements in the lives of those who are worse off as against adding to the advantages of those better off.[16]

Nagel's overall conclusion by way of the impersonalist argument is that insofar as one lives as an agent "under the direction of an impartial benevolent spectator of the world," insofar as one is moved by "pure impartial benevolence,"[17] one will focus on and promote everyone's equally impersonally valuable well-being, and this will take the form of giving preference to improvements in the lives of the worse off.

The second line of thought, the pretheoretical argument, also begins with benevolence and ends with egalitarianism. It simply appeals to our pretheoretical sense of benevolence—specifically, to an intuitive sense of benevolence that is *not* informed by an account of benevolence as responsiveness to impersonal value. According to the pretheoretical argument, if

[16] Nagel, *Equality and Partiality*, 12.
[17] Ibid., 15, 16.

we simply begin with an intuitive understanding of benevolence, we see that a benevolent agent will, ceteris paribus, give preference to improvements in the lives of the worse off. If a benevolent agent is faced with the choice between adding five units of happiness to the life of someone who otherwise will have zero net happiness and adding five units of happiness to the life of someone who otherwise will have ten, the benevolent agent will, ceteris paribus, add five units of happiness to the life of the first individual. Indeed, the benevolent agent will choose to add five units of happiness to the life of the first individual even if he has the alternative of adding six units of happiness to the life of the party who otherwise will enjoy ten.

Let us suppose that a benevolent patient in a burn ward will favor sharing the available analgesic with other patients rather than receiving it all himself.[18] What sharing will such a benevolent agent favor? Will he propose that the shared analgesic be redirected so as to minimize net pain among the patients at large? Or will he propose that it be redirected to the patient (or patients) who otherwise will be in the worst pain? Suppose that some portion of the painkiller could be used to move patient B from twenty units of pain to ten or to move patient C from thirty units of pain to twenty-three. Is it not plausible that our benevolent patient will favor the redirection of the painkiller to patient C rather than B? If so, it again seems that benevolence manifests the propriety of giving special weight to the condition of the worse off. It seems that those who hold that the centrality of benevolence within any sound moral perspective points to a salient egalitarian strand within sound morality occupy a more reasonable position than those who, like Smart, hold that the centrality of benevolence within any sound moral perspective points to a salient utilitarian strand within sound morality.[19]

It is worth noting that there is a tension between the impersonalist argument and the pretheoretical argument. The conclusion of the pretheoretical argument, namely, that equality has a better claim on being the underlying root of benevolence than does value-maximization, depends upon *not* construing benevolence as responsiveness to impersonal value. For suppose that we do construe benevolence as responsiveness to impersonal value. That is, suppose we accept, as the first phase of the

[18] This patient is markedly more benevolent than the fellow patient in Nagel's own example, who, while favoring Nagel's receipt of painkiller, gives no indication of being willing to supply that painkiller out of a supply he would otherwise have exclusively.

[19] It is commonly held that egalitarianism is a demand of justice while benevolence is not. This may lead to the thought that it would be odd for anyone to attempt to build arguments for egalitarianism upon an endorsement of benevolence. As a result, it might further be thought that in ascribing any such argument to an aspiring egalitarian, I am foisting an argument upon him that he himself would eschew. But this line of thought ignores Nagel's advocacy of the impersonalist argument. More generally, this line of thought cannot be pursued on behalf of any reasonably ambitious egalitarian. For such an egalitarian (like his similarly ambitious utilitarian counterpart) *does* tend to conclude that benevolence (also) is a demand of justice. The idea that benevolence is clearly not a demand of justice is readily held only if one rejects all ambitious forms of egalitarianism and utilitarianism.

impersonalist argument proposes, that benevolence is a matter of the promotion of impersonal value (and the mitigation of impersonal disvalue). It will then be hard to resist the conclusion that value-maximization among individuals is the underlying root of benevolence. If benevolence is a matter of being responsive to the equal impersonal value of each unit of well-being, a purely benevolent agent will be indifferent between adding five units of well-being to the life of the worse-off individual and adding five units of well-being to the life of the better-off individual. A purely benevolent agent, so understood, will favor adding six units of well-being to the life of the better-off individual over adding five units to the life of the worse-off individual, and will decide who should receive the reallocated painkiller on the basis of which administration of the analgesic will minimize the amount of pain among the patients.

My contention here runs contrary to the second phase within the impersonalist argument, namely, Nagel's claim that responsiveness to impersonal value appropriately takes the form of giving preference to the promotion of impersonal value in the lives of the worse off. Thus, if Nagel provides significant support for this second phase, my contention will be in trouble and the tension between the impersonalist and pretheoretical arguments will be relieved. However, it is noteworthy that Nagel provides no such support. As we have seen, what Nagel does say is that there are deep problems in combining the impersonal value and disvalue of different sorts of states of affairs. Nagel's reasonable point is that in theory and/or in practice this incommensurability of values and disvalues undermines any program for the maximization of value across individuals.[20] Yet this hardly provides positive support for the alternative egalitarian program; the undermining of the maximizing response hardly constitutes an argument on behalf of the egalitarian response.[21] Worse yet, the incommensurability to which Nagel appeals also undermines the egalitarian program. This is because such incommensurability, at the very least, vastly complicates judgments about who is worse off, who is better off, and who among the better off will remain in that category after costs are imposed upon them to make the originally worse off better off.[22]

I conclude that if one construes benevolence as Nagel does, that is, as impartial responsiveness to impersonal value, one needs to come up with some independent argument to press this responsiveness into an egali-

[20] If the incommensurability is between the value of qualitatively different states of affairs, then measuring two batches of qualitatively identical pains against one another will not be precluded by incommensurability.

[21] Perhaps the conclusion that should be drawn from this incommensurability is that any choice of a valuable alternative is reasonable—except, perhaps, choices that involve the direct destruction of impersonal value. Or perhaps the conclusion that should be drawn is that no choice among valuable alternatives is reasonable.

[22] It seems that the only form of egalitarianism that can escape this problem posed by the incommensurability of basic goods (and evils) is an egalitarianism of resources. An egalitarianism of resources escapes this problem *if and only if* such an egalitarianism is not itself advanced as the most feasible institutional realization of an equal distribution of ultimate goods.

tarian mold.[23] Egalitarianism, it seems, will have to be introduced as an independently potent constraint against maximizing net impersonal value. I, however, shall concentrate on contesting the first phase within the impersonalist argument for egalitarianism, namely, the claim that reasonable benevolence is a matter of responsiveness to impersonal value. In the course of doing so, I shall sketch an account of benevolence that accommodates the egalitarian tilt on which the pretheoretical argument focuses, but which does not take that tilt to be indicative of any deep or robust egalitarian truth.

III. Reasonable Benevolence and Value for the Recipient

At the outset of Section II, I asserted that because benevolence is essentially other-regarding, any explanation of its being reasonable must indicate how the value of the (intended) outcome for the recipient contributes to the agent's having reason to promote that outcome. This "responsiveness premise" is crucial to the first phase of Nagel's impersonalist argument. A more structured statement of that phase is as follows.

(a) Some conduct on the part of agent A toward recipient R that is productive of beneficial outcome O is benevolent and reasonable.
(b) A's benevolent conduct toward R will be explained as reasonable if and only if the value of O contributes to A's having reason to engage in that conduct. (This is the responsiveness premise.)
(c) The value of O will not contribute to A's having reason to engage in the benevolent conduct if the value of O is personal value for R.
(d) Hence, the value of O will contribute to A's having reason to engage in the benevolent conduct only if that value is impersonal.
(e) Therefore, A's benevolent conduct toward R will be explained as reasonable only if the value of O is impersonal value.
(f) Therefore, impersonal value should be affirmed as essential to the best explanation of conduct that is benevolent and reasonable.

One way of challenging Nagel's impersonalist argument would be to deny the responsiveness premise, that is, to maintain that one can explain the reasonableness of A's benevolent conduct without citing the value of the (intended) outcome for R. My project, however, is to show how one

[23] And it is hard to imagine what this argument for egalitarianism *as a basic moral principle* would be. See Harry Frankfurt, "The Moral Irrelevance of Equality," *Public Affairs Quarterly* 14, no. 2 (2000): 87–103.

can *accept* this premise without being driven to an impersonalist explanation of the reasonableness of benevolence. Indeed, in this section, I want to refine the responsiveness premise to make it consistent with the fact that the reasonableness of some benevolent conduct may not be a matter of the reasonableness of that conduct's benevolence.

Suppose A conducts himself in a way which in fact advances the well-being of R. Certain explanations for such conduct will undermine its classification as benevolent. For instance, if it is shown that A has acted solely for monetary payment, the beneficial action will be revealed to be nonbenevolent. Advocates of psychological egoism attempt to offer such self-regarding explanations for all actions by A that benefit R—even those actions that seem to be performed on behalf of R's well-being. Thus, Thomas Hobbes seeks to explain (apparently) compassionate action in terms of the agent's interest in minimizing his own discomfort. The agent acts so as "to deliver his mind from the pain of compassion."[24] This motivational explanation for the action in question explains *away* its benevolence. In contrast, we may take compassion or benevolence more seriously. Perhaps as the result of some evolutionary process, (many) individuals are hardwired to be moved to some degree to promote those conditions in other persons that they perceive to be beneficial to those persons. Given such a disposition in individual A, pointing to A's perception that outcome O is beneficial to R provides a motivational explanation for A's benevolent conduct; A's conduct is accounted for *as* benevolent conduct.

Of course, neither of these citations of motives shows the conduct in question to be *reasonable*. We will see the Hobbesian explanation as disclosing the reasonableness of A's action only if we implicitly rely upon the additional premise that a diminution of A's discomfort is valuable for A. Similarly, we will see the benevolent-disposition explanation as disclosing the reasonableness of A's conduct only if we implicitly rely upon the additional premise that A has reason to engage in this conduct. But on what grounds might we say that the agent who is moved by a benevolent disposition (and the perception that the action in question will have a beneficial outcome) has reason to engage in this conduct?[25]

One possibility is that it is pleasing to A to act in accord with his benevolent orientation—or displeasing to him not to act in accord with it—*and* that this pleasure (displeasure) is valuable (disvaluable) *for A*. That is, it is valuable for A to indulge the benevolent sentiments that are wired into his motivational structure. Insofar as we accept at face value

[24] Thomas Hobbes, *Leviathan*, ed. C. B. Macpherson (New York: Penguin, 1985), 193. The obvious question to be raised here is, *Why* does the prospect of another's pain cause pain to the agent?

[25] Within this discussion, I limit my attention to *value-based* reasons for an agent's conduct. I am setting aside all consideration of deontic reasons for an agent's acting on behalf of another, such as A's having promised R that he will perform the action that is beneficial to R. I believe that the domain of practical rationality includes such deontic considerations and that these constitute *additional* other-regarding reasons for action (or omission).

the picture of A's being subject to an ingrained benevolent disposition the indulgence of which is pleasing to him, it is perfectly plausible to hold that the value of that pleasure provides A with reason to indulge that sentiment and thereby engage in this benevolent conduct. This justification of A's benevolent action is a matter of indicating that A has a self-regarding reason to engage in this other-regarding conduct. The fact that the indicated reason for A's action is self-regarding does not negate the action's being other-regarding; it remains other-regarding in virtue of its being the product of A's benevolent sentiment and his perception that the action in question will benefit its recipient. A is really *moved* by the prospect of promoting a certain benefit in R, but what gives him *reason* not to extirpate this orientation (if he could) is that it provides him with opportunities to attain the pleasures of satisfying this drive. So here we have one way in which genuinely benevolent action can apparently be shown to be reasonable *without* appealing to the value of the outcome engendered in the recipient.[26] Contrary to my initial formulation of the responsiveness premise, A's benevolent conduct toward R can be reasonable without that conduct being responsive to the value of the (intended) outcome for R. Conduct that is benevolent under one description, namely, being motivated by the prospect of promoting a beneficial condition in another, can be reasonable for the agent under another description: providing that agent with valuable satisfaction.

This does not so much confute the responsiveness premise as call for its more refined articulation. The fact that A's conduct can be benevolent under one description and reasonable under another reveals that friends of the responsiveness premise do not intend to make the broad claim that conduct that is benevolent can only be reasonable if the value of the outcome engendered in the recipient contributes to the agent's having reason to engage in the conduct. Rather, they intend the narrower claim that conduct can only be *reasonable in its benevolence* (i.e., reasonable in its other-regardingness) if the value of the outcome engendered in the recipient contributes to the agent's having reason to engage in the conduct. For A's benevolence to be reasonable in the intended sense, it is not enough that the conduct be triggered by the prospect of a benefit for R and that there be some adventitious reason for A's engaging in that conduct—some reason that is incidental to the conduct's being other-regarding. Rather, the conduct has to be reasonable (at least in part) in virtue of the value of the outcome for R. Just as the benefit for R of the conduct has to appear within the motivational explanation of A's conduct for that conduct to be benevolent, the value of that outcome has to appear

[26] Recall that we have gone out of our way to picture A as being hardwired to be moved by the prospect of benefiting R. The idea is to exclude from the present picture A's being disposed to benefit R on the basis of A's recognition of the *value* of benefits within the lives of others. If the explanation of A's disposition itself turns on A's recognition of the value of such occurrences, then a justifying explanation for A's benevolent action would be implicit within the citation of that disposition.

within the justificatory explanation for A's conduct if that conduct is to be shown to be reasonable qua benevolent conduct. The justificatory explanation for the benevolent conduct has to be transparent; it has to cite the value of that which, by motivating the conduct, makes the conduct benevolent.

The impersonalist argument is, therefore, a best-explanation argument that proceeds from the existence of conduct that is *reasonable in its benevolence* to the existence of impersonal value. So the refined version of the whole argument—including the more careful articulation of the responsiveness premise (b′)—is as follows.

(a′) Some conduct on the part of A toward R that is productive of beneficial outcome O is reasonably benevolent (i.e., is reasonable in its benevolence).
(b′) A's reasonably benevolent conduct toward R will be explained as reasonable if and only if the value of O contributes to A's having reason to engage in that conduct. (This is the refined responsiveness premise.)
(c) The value of O will not contribute to A's having reason to engage in the benevolent conduct if the value of O is personal value for R.
(d) Hence, the value of O will contribute to A's having reason to engage in the benevolent conduct only if that value is impersonal.
(e′) Therefore, A's reasonably benevolent conduct toward R will be explained as reasonable only if the value of O is impersonal value.
(f′) Therefore, impersonal value should be affirmed as essential to the best explanation of conduct that is reasonably benevolent.

I think it is clear that Nagel himself understands his impersonalist argument as starting with the idea that he ought to be able to understand the *reasonableness of the benevolence* of the fellow patient in the burn ward. It is this reasonableness that Nagel holds cannot be understood if one thinks in terms of personal value. Hence, the first premise of the refined argument is a bit more contentious than the first premise of the initial formulation, but not much more contentious. The refined premise (a′) is equivalent to (a) plus the proposition that the reasonableness of some benevolent conduct is not merely incidental to its being benevolent. I join Nagel in the affirmation of both (b′) and (a′). As a result, my challenge to the first phase of the impersonalist argument for egalitarianism *must* focus on (c).

Whatever plausibility (c) has, it has because of the implicit supposition that if the value of O plays any essential role in explaining A's having reason to promote O, that value *fully explains* A's having that reason. In other words, if the value of O contributes to A's having reason to promote O, it does so by supplying that reason all by itself. This, I believe, is Nagel's own supposition. The awfulness of Nagel's pain is supposed to explain *by itself* the reasonableness of the other patient's desire that Nagel receive the analgesic. This notion of full explanation is present in a remarkably Nagelian passage offered by Loren Lomasky.

> [I]f you asked me why I provided the suffering individual with a dose of morphine, and I told you that it was because he was in excruciating pain, it would be remarkably obtuse of you not to understand me as having provided a *full* explanation of my action. . . . [W]e recognize that the sufferer's pain is a misfortune for him, and in virtue of our correctly apprehending its badness for him we thereby understand that we have (some) reason to disvalue the occurrence of the pain, and thus (some) reason to take action to alleviate it.[27]

Lomasky seems at first to be talking about a motivational explanation for his providing the painkiller. But it becomes clear that he is actually concerned about justificatory explanation. The badness of the sufferer's pain fully explains Lomasky's having reason to promote its alleviation. It would be "obtuse" to think that any value beyond the badness of the sufferer's pain need be cited in order to understand Lomasky's having this reason.

This, I think, must also be Nagel's view; the reasonableness in benevolent conduct must entirely be a matter of the value of the (intended) outcome engendered in its recipient. Since benevolence is other-regarding, it must be *exclusively* other-regarding, and the value that explains the reasonableness of benevolence must entirely be the value of outcomes engendered in persons other than the agent. If this is so, then the badness of the sufferer's pain cannot be agent-relative. For, by definition, the agent-relative goodness or badness of some condition of another cannot *as such* provide one with reason to promote or eliminate that condition. If the badness of the sufferer's pain (or the goodness of a beneficiary's gain) fully explains the agent's having reason to alleviate that pain (or promote that gain), then that badness (or goodness) must be agent-neutral, and the explanation of reasonable benevolence requires the existence of agent-neutral value.[28]

It is, however, far from obvious that the value of the outcome sought by the benevolent agent must *fully* explain his having reason to promote that

[27] Loren Lomasky, "Response to Four Critics," *Reason Papers* 14 (1989): 118.

[28] Lomasky (in personal conversation) denies that his remarks amount to a case for the agent-neutral badness of the sufferer's pain. He would rather simply be taken as saying that as a basic datum, we should notice that if R has reason to get rid of the pain, there will be a "transmission" of a reason (the very reason that R has?) to A to get rid of R's pain. But any explanation of this transmission that cites only the disvalue of R's pain seems to require the agent-neutral disvalue of that pain. The language of "transmission" here is from Lomasky's earlier formulation of this argument in Loren Lomasky, *Persons, Rights, and the Moral Community* (Oxford: Oxford University Press, 1988), 63–65.

outcome. In the next two sections, I will sketch an account of reasonable benevolence that accords with the insight that the value of the outcome for the recipient must contribute to the benevolent agent's having reason to promote that outcome, but sees the reasonableness of the agent's conduct as a type of joint product of the personal value of the outcome for the recipient and the personal value for the agent of being responsive to such value.

IV. Benevolence as Responsiveness to Agent-Relative Value

From the most passing exchanges of courtesies (with a cashier in the airport parking lot), to minor moments of mutually acknowledged coordination (with other cooperative merging motorists), to amiable acquaintanceship (with neighbors over the backyard fence), to friendship (with long-term intellectual and spiritual comrades), to life-defining love (for spouse and children), there is immense personal value for us in connections of mutual apprehension, regard, and concern. Participation in relations and networks of reciprocal apprehension, regard, and concern is conspicuously among the things that make one's life worth living. Such participation has lots of extrinsic rewards, but it is also valuable in itself. Connection through mutual apprehension, regard, and concern is a fundamental human good; one might even say that it is the realization of our selves as social beings. It needs to be emphasized that what we value is not merely its *seeming to us* that we are connected to others through mutual apprehension, regard, and concern. We value and seek this connection itself. We take pleasure in our experience of such connection with others precisely because we take that experience to mark our achievement of that connection.

Moreover, this mode of connection with other persons seems to be an objective good in the sense that it is not one's desire for participation in relations and networks of reciprocal apprehension, regard, and concern that confers value upon such participation. Rather, such a desire is rational for an agent because of the value to which it makes that agent receptive. Persons who are bereft of a desire for participation in the relevant sorts of relations and networks are defective. They lack the capacity to realize an important dimension of the human good. All of this, of course, is consistent with the value of connectedness being agent-relative, that is, with the connectedness that is ultimately valuable for agent A being *A's connectedness* to others. The connectedness with others that A, in the first instance, has reason to promote is *his* connectedness—although, by its very nature, this must involve the promotion of others' connectedness as well.[29]

[29] Hence, although I maintain that the value of A's connectedness to others is agent-relative (the connectedness is *valuable for* A), I also maintain that the value of that connectedness is objective in two senses. First, the value attaches primarily to A's connectedness to others, not to A's experience of that connectedness. Second, the value for A of that connectedness is not conferred upon it by A's having a desire for that connectedness.

The value of participation in interpersonal relations and networks is available only to those who are responsive to the good of others, that is, only to those who are disposed to apprehend, manifest their apprehension of, welcome, and even promote others' particular and separate goods. Hence, this responsiveness *to the good of others* is itself of immense value to each individual who has it; this responsiveness is something that each agent has reason to welcome in herself, to foster, and to indulge. It is crucial here to see the several facets of this valuable responsiveness. Such responsiveness is valuable for A because it is crucial to A's achieving a connectedness with others that is partially constitutive of his objective well-being. The value of this responsiveness and of the connectedness for which it is essential is its agent-relative value for A. But this responsiveness consists in a disposition to apprehend, manifest apprehension of, welcome, and even promote *others'* particular and personal goods. The connectedness that an agent's responsiveness facilitates is that agent's connectedness *to others*. The responsive agent is, therefore, disposed to respond to the good of others; the good of others is an essential part of his motivational structure. And yet, this responsiveness and the connectedness it yields is *personally* valuable for the agent.

A further crucial fact is that an agent's valuable responsiveness is not uniform responsiveness to all and sundry. Uniform responsiveness to all would *not* be valuable for the responsive individual. Rather, valuable responsiveness is limited, complexly discriminating, and highly individualized—indeed, highly individualizing. It is substantially through the selectivity of our responsiveness to the good of others that we become the particular individuals who we are. Indeed, part of the value of valuable responsiveness is this individualizing function. Arguably, the agent who is uniformly responsive to all is as defective in his affective nature as the agent who is simply unresponsive.

Each agent's personal responsiveness is a matter of which specific types of human good she apprehends, the particular sorts of instantiations in which she apprehends them, whose lives she apprehends them in, when she apprehends them, and how she associates them with other apprehended types of human good. The responsiveness that is valuable for any particular agent will depend heavily upon the given particularities of that agent and her circumstances. Agents are more likely to apprehend and be responsive to instantiations of ends that are similar to ends they themselves pursue, that they can readily imagine themselves pursuing, or that are pursued by other individuals they already are highly responsive to. A responsive agent may become more focused on the good of other particular individuals because she is more responsive to the types of instantiations of human goods that are actually or potentially present in their lives. Or she may become more responsive to those types of instantiations because she is more focused upon those particular individuals on the basis of physical proximity, cultural or ethnic identification or other forms of shared self-understanding, or even on the basis of a perceived need to develop responsiveness for the sake of interaction that could potentially be intrinsically valuable or extrinsically rewarding.

Since we vary from one another in which particular ends we treasure and apprehend well, in which neighborhoods we live, and in what dimensions of responsiveness promise us valuable connectedness or extrinsic rewards, the content and shape of valuable responsiveness will vary greatly among us. Over time, specific dimensions of responsiveness will make their appearance within or depart from one's responsive personality, or become more or less prominent within it. And different individuals will come within range or pass out of range of the stratified ken of one's responsive personality as it is constituted at this or that phase of one's life. Each agent's valuable responsiveness will range from being highly intense and energizing with regard to those persons (and causes and institutions) closest to her along one or more of the dimensions that comprise her responsive personality to being highly diffuse and motivationally negligible with regard to persons (and causes and institutions) who are furthest from her along all those dimensions. Presumably for all or almost all of us who possess valuable responsiveness, there is some (defeasible) goodwill that extends to those at the edge of the range of our responsiveness and that would dispose us to move a finger rather than have others die. Or perhaps it is not that even this level of goodwill extends to all, but rather that one's happening to become aware that specific others could be saved by one's moving one's finger *brings* those others within the range of one's responsiveness.

In addition to the complexly discriminating structure of valuable responsiveness, at least for almost all of us, there is an upper limit on how much personal responsiveness is valuable. There is a point—or set of points along various responsiveness dimensions—beyond which the costs of further connectedness and responsiveness, in terms of distraction from the realization of other human goods in our lives and even in terms of threats to integrity, exceed the benefits of additional connectedness and responsiveness (and of the other benefits for the agent, discussed below, in promoting others' attainment of their good).

Among all the different forms and concatenations any given person's responsiveness could take, reason is relatively silent. Reason commends to the individual a structure of responsiveness that will facilitate her achieving an array of relations of mutual apprehension, regard, and concern that is cohesive with and supplementary to her attainment of the other goods of human life. But reason will not adjudicate among different structures of responsiveness that would comparably satisfy this condition. This is partially because we cannot describe in advance what it would be like to have each of these different comparably satisfying structures, and, as a result, we cannot lay the alternatives out before us and make a rational deliberate choice among them. It may also be that the quality of some modes of valuable responsiveness are simply not commensurable with the quality of other modes of valuable responsiveness.

There may, for example, be no way of weighing the units of connectedness available to members of a traditional religious community against the units of connectedness available to a crusader for free thought. So even if we can lay alternative structures of responsiveness before us, there may be no rational way to rank them. For these reasons, we should recognize that to affirm the value to an individual of possession of such a structure of responsiveness is not to recommend to her the project of identifying in advance a desirable structure and setting out to construct it. One may do best by relying upon processes through which highly individualized structures of responsiveness emerge unplanned. This could happen, for instance, in reaction to particular individuals' diverse capacities for responsiveness across its many possible dimensions, or in response to the particular opportunities for responsiveness and role models for responsiveness that these diverse individuals encounter.

Relations of mutual apprehension, regard, and concern are extremely valuable for individuals. As a condition of partaking in such relations, being responsive (within reason) to the good of others is extremely valuable for A. A therefore has reason to be responsive to the particular goods of others that fall within the range of the responsiveness that is valuable to him. If the value for recipient R of outcome O falls within this range, then it is valuable for A to be disposed to welcome or promote O. Being so disposed makes A capable of entering into valuable relations of mutual apprehension, regard, and concern. By acting in accord with such a disposition, A realizes this connectedness and affirms and reinforces his valuable responsive disposition. Because A has reason to be responsive and his being responsive is a matter of taking another's personal good as a reason for welcoming or even promoting that good, the personal good of another triggers or activates A's having reason to welcome or even promote the good of that other. However, the value of the outcome engendered in R does not *fully explain* A's having reason to promote O. Rather, the explanation requires both the value of O for R and the occurrence of this value within the range of responsiveness to values that is valuable for A. The valuableness for A of participation in relations of mutual apprehension, regard, and concern and of being (within reason) responsive to the good of others provides a medium through which the personal value of O for R gives rise to A's having personal reason to promote O. That the value of O enters into A's rational motivation by triggering or activating A's having personal reason to welcome or promote O does not, of course, prove that the value of O *cannot* be impersonal value. It only shows that one *need not* take the value of O to be impersonal value in order to account for the reasonableness of A's benevolence. That is, it only rebuts premise (c) of the impersonalist argument. Something else counts more directly against construing as impersonal the value of the benefits, for recipients, that prompt benevolent conduct. This is the radical variation that exists with respect to how much reason—from very strong reason to no reason at all—the value of diverse outcomes for possible recipients activates in one benevolent agent versus another.

Since A's rational responsiveness is not directed uniformly at all and sundry, there can readily be outcomes that are of equally extensive agent-relative value to the individuals they directly affect, but which differ from each other in their capacity to give rise to A's having reason to promote them. Consider, for instance, an outcome O_1 that is as personally valuable for recipient R_1 as outcome O_2 is for recipient R_2. A may have reason to welcome or even promote O_1, but not have reason to promote or even welcome equally valuable O_2. This may be because the range of A's rational responsiveness extends to R_1, but not to R_2. Or it may be because that range extends more intensely to the former individual than to the latter. For example, A may welcome the relief from (undeserved) pain of anybody in the world but only have reason to risk ending up with insufficient analgesics for himself if taking this risk will relieve the (undeserved) pain of someone relatively near to him on some dimension that defines the structure of A's responsiveness.

A's response may also be discriminating because his rational responsiveness extends (with the necessary degree of intensity) to the type of end instantiated by O_1, but not to the type of end instantiated by O_2. If A is a soccer player, for instance, his rational responsiveness might extend to donating money to send an impoverished child to a soccer tournament, but might not extend to helping send him to a basketball tournament—even though the value for the child of each tournament is the same. At the same time, the structure and content of agent A_1's rational responsiveness may give rise to her having reason to promote O_2 but not O_1. This differentiation of the normative effects on A and A_1 of the value of others' ends obtains only because the value of those ends does not fully explain the agents' reasons for promoting those ends. Rather, the personal value of those ends for the recipients gives rise to reasons for the agents through the medium of their rational responsiveness. Different reasons arise for different agents because they differ with respect to the structure and shape of their rational responsiveness. If the value of the recipients' ends were the full explanation for the reasons possessed by A and A_1, the reasons of those agents would not be differentiated as they are.

I take this differentiation from one agent to another in what is reasonable benevolent conduct to be important evidence against any impersonalist account of the reasonableness of benevolence. I should note, therefore, one way in which a friend of the impersonalist full-explanation account of the reasonableness of benevolence might seek to accommodate the fact that in the face of the same prospective positive outcomes for others, different conduct will be reasonable for different agents. What may be proposed is that benevolence is an imperfect duty. According to this proposal, whatever the details of the foundation of this duty, it is not plausible to hold that each agent has a duty to act benevolently to each and every other individual toward whom he could be benevolent.[30] Each agent's duty of benevolence merely requires that he act beneficently toward *some* of those who might be the object of his good offices. Since no agent's imperfect duty of benevolence requires that he choose any particular one of his prospective recipients, each agent has discretion within this choice. In the exercise of this discretion, each agent may break the tie between prospective recipients of his beneficence by giving some weight to his own preferences among these prospective beneficiaries. In effect, one may fulfill one's quota of benevolence in many different ways, and one has discretion between any two courses of benevolent conduct that would equally fulfill one's quota.

I do not think that this imperfect-duty account of benevolence captures the way in which reasonable benevolence is individuated across agents. On the imperfect-duty account, whenever there are two courses of action available to A such that the benefit for R_1 of one action is as extensive as the benefit for R_2 of the other action, rational benevolence will equally recommend the two actions to A. A will be like Buridan's ass between two equally large piles of hay. Any special resonance between A and one or another of the particular ends at stake or between A and one or another of the particular recipients whose ends are at stake is taken to be irrelevant to the primary judgment about what reasonable benevolence commends to A. Any special resonance, any differential concern by A for one of the particular ends at stake or one of the particular prospective recipients, is allowed in only as a method of arbitrarily breaking ties between different courses of action that would equally extensively and disinterestedly promote valuable outcomes in others. And, it seems, whenever one course of action by A would more extensively benefit one of the possible recipients—that is, whenever one course of action would better fulfill A's benevolence quota—A's differential appreciation or concern for a particular sort of outcome or for a particular recipient will not even play a tiebreaking role. In effect, the imperfect-duty understanding of the directive force of benevolence still construes genuine benevolence as "pure impartial benevolence."[31]

Against this impersonalist reading of benevolence, I submit that the course of conduct commended to a particular agent by rational benevolence more centrally depends upon the particularities of the structure and content of that agent's rational responsiveness. Even if the aforementioned soccer and basketball tournaments are equally valuable for the child and the cost to A of sending the child is the same for each tourna-

[30] Cf. the nice discussion in Thomas Hill, "Beneficence and Self-Love: A Kantian Perspective," *Social Philosophy and Policy* 10, no. 1 (1993): 1–23.

[31] I admit to being uncertain as to whether I have produced an argument here that specifically strikes against the imperfect-duty account, as opposed to merely producing a restatement of my opposition to impersonalism.

The quoted phrase is from Nagel, *Equality and Partiality*, 16.

ment, the fact that soccer is within the range of *A's* rational responsiveness explains why, in this case, reasonable benevolence takes the form of A's sending the child to the soccer tournament. It is *not* that sending the child to the soccer tournament and sending him to the basketball tournament tie with respect to reasonable benevolence, and then A's preference for soccer breaks the tie. If concern and appreciation for basketball plays the role within A_1's rational responsiveness that soccer plays within A's, then in A_1's case, reasonable benevolence takes the form of A_1's sending the child to the basketball tournament. The values that attach to the child's going to the tournaments do not fully explain the reasons that benevolence provides for A and A_1, because those values give rise to reasons for A and A_1 through the media of the different and differently intense modalities of responsiveness that are respectively valuable for them.

A has personal reason to be responsive to the good of others *to the extent* that the connectedness attained through his responsiveness to the good of others and through the maintenance of this degree and type of responsiveness is valuable for him. (Here it must be recalled that connectedness *with others* is itself among the constituents of A's well-being, as is A's experience of this connectedness. An appropriate degree of responsiveness to others is personally valuable for A primarily because it is essential to this valuable connectedness.) Although this valuable responsiveness may be quite considerable, it is nevertheless highly discriminating and limited. It operates only upon a certain range of valuable ends and only (or only with gusto) upon those prospective instantiations of these encompassed ends that are close enough to A. A's valuable responsiveness is not equally susceptible to the value of each *successive* instantiation of some human good—even if they are instantiations of goods responsiveness to which is encompassed within the structure of A's valuable responsiveness. Although the value for R of O may give rise to its being of considerable value for A to promote O, the equal value, for R_N (the nth and last member of a series of possible recipients), of the realization of the qualitatively identical and comparably extensive outcome O_N may give rise to no value at all (or no significant value) for A in the promotion of O_N. A's need for connectedness and his value-promoting capacity for responsiveness can become sated and, hence, less capable of channeling reasons from others to A. For this reason, the prospect of successive instantiations of such goods in the lives of others does not impart to A an accumulation of reasons that overrides or even threatens to override A's devotion to his own (other) life-defining projects and commitments. Reasonable benevolence does not call upon one to sacrifice these core ends and allegiances.

I take this limitation upon what reasonable benevolence demands of any agent to be further evidence against any impersonalist account of the reasonableness of benevolence. I should note, therefore, one way in which a friend of the impersonalist full-explanation view of the reasonableness of benevolence might seek to account for the fact that successive opportunities to promote the good of others will have decreasing directive force for a reasonably benevolent agent. On the impersonalist full-explanation view, each successive opportunity to promote an equally valuable outcome O_N for a recipient R_N provides A with *as much* reason to promote *that* outcome as is provided to A by the first opportunity to promote an outcome of that value for another. Each successive reason that is beamed at A is received with the same reason-generating power as previously transmitted reasons—because there is no medium that selects and filters those transmissions. The cumulative weight of those reasons, it seems, will readily overbalance agent-relative reasons that are reflective of A's own core projects and commitments. Against this tide of demands from impersonalist benevolence, the advocate of a full-explanation account has every right to point to two facts. The first is that the costs to A of acting upon reasons that are transmitted to him are to be included in any determination of whether, all things considered, A has reason to promote the ends of others. The second is that the cost to A of the promotion of each successive unit of other agents' good will typically be greater than the cost to him of promoting the previous unit.[32] It is possible, then, that even though A has all-things-considered reason to promote $O\text{-}O_{N-1}$ *and* the reason he has to promote O_N is as full powered as the reason beamed to him by each of the outcomes $O\text{-}O_{N-1}$, A will not have all-things-considered reason to promote O_N. The increased marginal cost to A of promoting O_N may defeat the reason beamed to A by the value of O_N. Hence, the friend of impersonalist benevolence can point out, there *may* be some point at which it is no longer rational for A to promote valuable outcomes in others. But of course, there may *not* be any such point. The (alleged) impersonal value of O_N may continue to overbalance the impersonal (and personal) costs of A's promoting O_N. To note this is, of course, merely to point again to the extremely demanding character of any impersonalist ethic, even ones that try to provide some sort of cushion for personal projects and commitments by (somehow) allowing agents to double- or triple-count the value of their own ends and allegiances. A more targeted point is that even if the impersonalist can maintain that the cost to A limits the extent to which, all things considered, A should sacrificially devote himself to valuable outcomes in others, the impersonalist view of benevolence must depict this limitation as an instance of the general clash between an agent's concern for value in his own life and his being reasonably benevolent. On this depiction, reasonable benevolence usually wins out against an agent's concern for value in his own life, but in the

[32] For instance, even if the financial costs to A of promoting each successive unit of benefit for others remains the same, the utility cost to A of doing so will increase with each successive unit. The utility cost to A of funding each successive unit of benefit for others will not increase if (because of the efficiencies of larger-scale production?) the financial costs of promoting successive units of benefit drop low enough.

case of O_N, the agent's concern for value in his own life wins out over the call of reasonable benevolence.

Against this conflictual view of the relationship between an agent's concern for value in his own life and his reasonable benevolence, I maintain that although reasonable benevolence must proceed from an appreciation of the good of others, its reasonableness also depends upon the value for the agent of being responsive (in the relevant way) to the good of others. Admittedly, it is an implication of this position that if it were not for the fact that relations of mutual apprehension, regard, and concern are valuable for A, the (personal) valuableness for others of their various ends would be "motivationally inert" with respect to A.[33] This is because the (personal) valuableness of various outcomes for others would not have any medium through which to generate reasons for A to promote them. This will sound worrisome if, but only if, one forgets how deep a fact it is that relations of mutual apprehension, regard, and concern *are* (objectively) valuable for us, and therefore forgets how different a world would be in which this deep fact did not obtain. Imagine such a world—that is, a world in which there is no value for one in participating in such relations, a world in which connectedness with others is not a component of human well-being. To recall a previous example, is it at all clear that in such a distant world A would have reason, at some discernible cost to himself, to give R some of his analgesics?[34]

V. The Agent-Relative Value of Responsiveness

I want to continue my venture into speculative moral psychology in ways that may further explain why responsiveness to others' agent-relative values is valuable for the respondent. Part of the value for A of participation in relations of mutual apprehension, regard, and concern is the value for him of having the value of his projects and commitments appreciated by others. Or, more precisely, it is the value for A of seeing his values being apprehended by others. A_1's apprehension of the components of A's own good provides an external mark of—a mirroring of—A's good as well as a type of confirmation for A of his assessment of these states as valuable for himself. Were we unable to elicit this apprehension from others, our confidence in the worth of our accomplishments and goals would be diminished. We do not at all like others' failing to apprehend the value for us of what we treasure—at least if those others are the

[33] Lomasky, "Response to Four Critics," 117. Lomasky means inert with respect to *rational* motivation.

[34] Recall Lomasky's claim that it would be obtuse to think that any value beyond the badness of the sufferer's pain need be cited in order to understand Lomasky's having reason to relieve the sufferer's condition. Actually, what would be obtuse is failing to realize that any agent who points to the disvalue of the sufferer's pain to explain his (the agent's) alleviating it is also indicating that the alleviation of this pain (at the costs actually involved) falls within the ambit of his (the agent's) rational responsiveness.

people from whom we expect such apprehension. In cyclical fashion, A's appreciation of A_1's apprehension of his (A's) good will be valuable for A_1 because it will confirm in A_1's eyes that she is attuned to the good things of life and on target in her assessment of her own accomplishments and goals.

What emerges is a type of intersubjective validation of the value of realizing the ends that are being promoted. We each recognize one another as agents who have reasons to attain certain ends that "can be understood and affirmed from outside the viewpoint of the individual who has them."[35] The key factor underlying this validation is that it is valuable for an agent to see his values apprehended by others.[36] This valuable (for A) visibility to others of A and his values is not so much the product of A's declarations; it is to a considerable degree the product of A's responsiveness to the values of those to whom A wishes to be visible. For it is through A's responsiveness to their values that these other persons attain insight into A and his values.

It is likewise valuable for A that the types of conditions he values as being instantiated in his life (or which he would have valued as being instantiated in his life had he composed his life somewhat differently) also obtain as valuable instantiations in the lives of others. Not only are there circumstances in which A_1's apprehension and concern for A's good offers A valuable confirmation of that good, there are also circumstances in which A sees the good of A_1 as mirroring or reflecting his own actual (or possible) valued ends. In these instances, realizations of A_1's good offer A examples of the attainment of the values he seeks or might seek.

The value for A_1 of the realization of some fundamental human good in her life reaffirms A's sense of the value for him of its realization (or the realization of kindred human goods) in his life. The realization of these goods in the life of A_1 testifies to the fact that these and kindred realizations, and the virtues required for them, can be achieved. Furthermore, the instantiation of these goods *as goods for others* marks A's membership with others in a community of beings for whom realizations of these goods are valuable. It shows that A is not alone in his reasonable pursuit of value; these realizations of value for others show that A inhabits a "world of reasons, including [A's] reasons, [that] does not exist only from [A's] own point of view."[37] All this helps explain how the value of connectedness is possible.

[35] Nagel, *The View from Nowhere*, 153.

[36] See Nathaniel Branden, *The Psychology of Self-Esteem* (New York: Bantam, 1969), chap. 11. In David Kelley, *Rugged Individualism: The Selfish Basis of Benevolence* (Poughkeepsie, NY: Institute for Objectivist Studies, 1996), Kelley uses the value to one of one's "visibility" to others and related phenomena to develop an account of benevolence. Kelley is continually tempted by the idea that sometimes it is rational to promote another's good (in part) because it is her good. However, he always manages to resist this temptation, and therefore attempts to provide an entirely self-regarding justification for other-regarding behavior.

[37] Nagel, *The View from Nowhere*, 140.

Others' successes at achieving their own good are, then, of value to A as external presentations of what is valuable for himself, as evidence that the world is hospitable to A's achievement of value, and as companions to the realizations of value within A's own life. Just as it is valuable to A that *value for A* be apprehended, it is valuable for A to see *value for others* attained. Consider, for example, the value for any of us of seeing a dedicated athlete overcome adversities to win an Olympic medal or of hearing of a kidnapped child being rescued and returned to her parents. Note that a limited number of exemplary realizations of agent-relative value in the lives of others will provide A with most, if not all, of the good that can accrue to him through others' attainment of their good. Additional realizations will have decreasing marginal value for A, so promoting these further realizations will not, all things considered, be valuable for A if promoting them involves increasing (or even constant) opportunity costs to A.

Still, everything else being equal, a responsive agent will favor the realization of larger numbers of valuable outcomes for strangers over the realization of smaller numbers. She will favor five drowning strangers being saved rather than one, and if she were steering a lifeboat, she would steer toward the five rather than toward the one. Each of the strangers is (equally) within the range of her rational responsiveness, so she acts more in accord with that motivational structure if she saves the five rather than the one. This endorsement of the rationality of saving the five is entirely consistent with denying that the survival of the five is impersonally better than the survival of the one. That is, it is entirely consistent with denying that there is some agent-neutral metric of value according to which there is more overall value in the survival of the five than in the survival of the one. On the other hand, if the one—as a friend or loved one of the agent, or as an exemplar of some trait the agent prizes—occupies a salient position on the map of the agent's rational responsiveness, she will have strong reason to save the one rather than the five.[38]

What about the choice between distributing analgesic to alleviate the condition of the most-pained stranger and distributing it to alleviate the most net pain among strangers? I have argued that a reasonable benevolence will (at least sometimes) opt for alleviating the most-pained stranger rather than alleviating the most pain among strangers. I indicated that it does not look as though an impersonalist ethic can accommodate this feature within its account of reasonable benevolence.[39] Why might a reasonably benevolent patient P with some analgesic to spare (at some cost or risk to himself) favor its allocation to the fellow patient in the most pain, even if another patient's pain would be reduced more were she to

[38] Cf. John Taurek, "Should the Numbers Count?" *Philosophy and Public Affairs* 6, no. 4 (1977): 293-316. Taurek only goes wrong in maintaining that if the *numbers* do not explain why the rescuer has reason to save five strangers rather than one stranger, then in no way is it more reasonable to do so.

[39] This was the difficulty noted in the second phase of Nagel's impersonalist argument.

receive the drug? My intuition is that the benevolent P surveys his fellow patients with an eye toward taking a stand against the suffering that he disvalues in others. The fellow patient in the most pain is or becomes the natural focal point of this stand. P is most responsive to disvalued suffering in others when he acts to diminish *this* patient's suffering, even though this response does not most reduce disvalued suffering. It is because P's responsiveness is valuable for P, and because his responsiveness may readily focus upon the patient in the most pain, that the reasonably benevolent P may act to help the most-pained fellow patient rather than to alleviate the most net pain among all of his fellow patients.

VI. Conclusion

It remains true, however, that the amount of painkiller that reasonably benevolent P will convey to *any* other patient will depend upon the degree and shape of responsiveness that is personally valuable for P. Since personally valuable responsiveness does not involve an open-ended disposition to assist all and sundry (at least when this is personally costly), and since it does involve a disposition to assist most those who are closest to one, reasonable benevolence will not be generally egalitarian. So, contrary to the pretheoretical argument, the reasonableness of benevolence is not indicative of a strong egalitarian strand within rational ethics. And, as we have seen, contrary to the first phase of the impersonalist argument for egalitarianism, one can account for the reasonableness of benevolence without positing the impersonal value of the objects of benevolent conduct. As against the impersonalist understanding of benevolence, the reasonableness of an agent's benevolence is best explained in terms of the personal value, for the agent, of his being responsive to the agent-relative good of others.

Both the pretheoretical argument and the impersonalist argument maintain that providing the best explanation for the goodness and reasonableness of benevolence requires that we endorse at least a strong presumption on behalf of equality of well-being as a component of sound morality. But both of these arguments fail. Neither provides a basis for thinking that differences in utility or well-being as such are morally problematic. And unless we believe that differences in utility or well-being as such are morally problematic, it is hard to see how one can reasonably believe that differences in income or wealth are morally problematic. It seems, then, that in the relevant sense, differences in income and wealth do not matter.

Philosophy, Tulane University

HOW EQUALITY MATTERS*

BY HILLEL STEINER

I. INTRODUCTION

"Should differences in income and wealth matter?" is a paralyzingly big question. Does it refer to some differences? All differences? Daily differences, periodic ones, initial ones? Do they matter regardless of how income and wealth are acquired? Regardless of what can be done with them? Regardless, indeed, of what 'mattering' means?

To escape the paralysis, we evidently have to constrain our attempts to answer the original question; we do this by making various simplifying assumptions. More specifically, what we do is to get hold of some roadworthy moral intuition—in this case, one that I will call *sibling parity*—and then see how the aforementioned battery of assumptions steers this intuition in the direction of an answer. Doubtless, whatever gets filtered out by those assumptions inevitably makes a heavy contribution to counterarguments aimed at circumventing the given answer. So, on that cautionary note, let us begin with the assumptions.

II. ASSUMPTIONS

Mattering, I will suppose, can have a general sense and at least one more specific sense. For something to matter in the general sense, it looks like its presence or occurrence must have positive (or negative) moral value, and its absence or nonoccurrence must accordingly be an object of moral concern (or approbation). It matters that my young children go for a regular dental checkup, but it does not matter whether they go on Tuesday or Wednesday. Of course, it could come to matter on which of these days they go: Wednesday might turn out to be the only day that they can have their after-school music lessons. But if it does not, and if no other such constraining consideration arises, then the choice of day for going to the dentist does not matter.

A more specific sense of mattering is motivated by the fact that, typically, more than one thing matters in the general sense of mattering. My childrens' attending their music lessons matters, as does their having their dental checkup. If two or more things matter positively, and if the

* This essay has benefited considerably from comments supplied by Jerry Cohen, Peter Vallentyne, Andrew Williams, the editors of *Social Philosophy and Policy,* and the other contributors to this volume.

disjunctively performable actions respectively required to achieve them are—as is so often the case—*jointly unperformable,* we find ourselves uncomfortably having to determine which one matters more. Philosophers offer various different accounts of how these determinations can be made. One method is to find some single common underlying value that itself explains why both of these jointly unachievable things matter, and then to ascertain which of them would realize that value to a greater extent. Often enough, the different things that matter to us are readily subjected to this sort of commensurating calculus.

But some appear not to be. Where a single underlying common value is not to be found, we are perforce compelled to consider which *kinds* of mattering thing matter more, and which matter less, than others. That is, we are compelled to *rank* these independently valuable kinds of thing.[1] Just how these rankings can be determined is a subject of profound complexity, and one into which I shall not enter here.[2] But however uncertain this manner of determination may be, there is one thing we can know for sure: one of these ranked kinds of mattering thing will be found to matter *most.* It will enjoy lexical primacy over the rest, and any demand instantiating it will thus be more important—will matter more—than any other kind of demand with which it is jointly unsatisfiable.[3] In the context of political philosophy—that is, in the context of what makes its concerns a distinct subset of those of moral philosophy—the demands of this lexically prime value will have a claim to *legal enforcement* that is denied to others. This is the more specific sense of mattering that I have in mind.

That is one simplifying assumption. Here is another, or rather, two more. Should differences in income and wealth matter, regardless of what

[1] Or we can, alternatively, *weight* them (i.e., numerically). I will here confine my remarks, on the additional complications raised by this possibility, to footnoted asides, since they do not centrally affect the main thrust of this essay. Ranking reflects an incommensurability, a discontinuity, between different kinds of mattering thing. Weighting reflects an exogenous continuity between them: lacking any *shared* empirical (i.e., measurable) property that is valued, their relative scaling is determined by reference to numbers assigned to them as a matter of logically unconstrained moral choice. This is importantly distinct from the endogenous continuity implied by a single common underlying value; where such a value is present, all mattering things are presumed to share a particular measurable empirical property that is valued (such as being productive of happiness), and their relative scaling is deducible solely from the magnitude of that property. Those kinds of mattering thing that are ranked or weighted are, so to speak, values in their own right. But whereas the 'better than' relation—mattering more—is represented *ordinally* in a ranked set of values, in a weighted set of values it is expressed *cardinally.*

[2] Cf. Hillel Steiner, *An Essay on Rights* (Oxford: Blackwell, 1994), chap. 4, where I argue that *some* of these rankings can be deduced from others, while those others are themselves not deducible. The same is not true of weightings.

[3] This is not true in a set of *weighted* independent values. There, questions of which of two competing demands of different kinds matters more are answered not only by reference to the weights of the independent values respectively underpinning them, but also by reference to the extent to which satisfying either demand would realize its underpinning value. If family loyalty and patriotism are two such independent underpinning values, then even if the former is the more heavily weighted, it is nonetheless possible that a major act of patriotism matters more than does a minor act of family loyalty.

can be done with them? I am going to assume that one thing that can be done with income and wealth is mutual conversion: that (contractually unencumbered) income and wealth can be readily substituted for each other by those who have them—loans can convert income into wealth, annuities do the reverse, and so on. That is, I am not going to devote separate discussion to income and wealth when considering whether differential holdings of them should matter: hereafter, I will just refer to them jointly as *wealth*. There are undoubtedly many interesting issues that could be raised by such separate treatment. And, in many legal and political contexts, glossing over this distinction, as I propose to do, would be a surefire recipe for irrelevance.

My excuse for avoiding that distinction here is prompted by a further assumption: namely, that the legal and political context I shall take as the background for what follows—as what matters in the more specific sense—is a classical liberal or libertarian one: one in which all or most property titles are held by private individuals or groups, in which the prevailing legal regime is relatively permissive on what are loosely called "social issues," in which the state exercises little or no regulatory power over the economy, and in which everyone is possessed of all the standard personal rights and civil liberties comprising what many of us think of as self-ownership.[4] What can be done with income and wealth in such a society is immensely variable and certainly includes mutual conversion.

One final simplifying assumption is needed to provide the argument that follows with its desired focus. Wealth matters,[5] I take it, for the well-being it delivers. By "well-being" I here mean nothing more than preference-satisfaction. I shall not suppose that this instrumental relation between wealth and well-being is an isomorphic one: the much-discussed

[4] I take *libertarianism* and *classical liberalism* to refer to any political theory or doctrine that exhibits the following three properties: (a) the content of all the particular moral rights it underwrites is constrained by the requirements of self-ownership; (b) the duties correlative to those rights enjoy lexical priority over—are side constraints on the pursuit of—all other moral duties; and (c) those rights are construed along the lines of the will or choice theory of rights (rather than the rival interest or benefit theory), whereby right-holders are vested with the Hohfeldian powers to waive and, alternatively, demand/enforce compliance with the duties correlative to their rights (i.e., right-holders *control* the duties owed to them). These three properties are jointly necessary and sufficient to entail a *historical entitlement* conception of distributive justice. An explication and defense of the will theory is to be found in Steiner, *An Essay on Rights*, chap. 3, sec. A, and in Hillel Steiner, "Working Rights," in Matthew H. Kramer, N. E. Simmonds, and Hillel Steiner, *A Debate over Rights* (Oxford: Clarendon Press, 1998), 233–301. An argument for the aforesaid lexical priority is offered in Steiner, *An Essay on Rights*, chap. 6, secs. A and B. The particular version of libertarianism advanced in this essay has been called *left-libertarianism*. Embracing the above properties, left-libertarianism further maintains that natural resources are justly owned in some egalitarian manner. For an indication of the variety of positions derived from all of these premises, see Peter Vallentyne and Hillel Steiner, eds., *The Origins of Left-Libertarianism: An Anthology of Historical Writings* (Basingstoke, UK: Palgrave, 2000); and Peter Vallentyne and Hillel Steiner, eds., *Left-Libertarianism and Its Critics: The Contemporary Debate* (Basingstoke, UK: Palgrave, 2000).

[5] In the general sense of 'matters' sketched above.

existence of both ascetics and epicures proves otherwise.[6] What I shall suppose is captured in the thought that an ascetic and an epicure *both* get more preference-satisfaction if the former transfers some of his wealth to the latter than they would get if the ascetic lacked that wealth to transfer in the first place. That is, broadly speaking and within the constraints imposed by everyone's rights,[7] others' wealth, as well as our own, delivers well-being to its possessors. This fairly loose connection between wealth and well-being seems to me sufficiently plausible as not to require much defense. So if well-being matters, wealth matters—even to an ascetic.

Let us suppose that well-being does indeed matter. Although this, too, is an assumption, I am disinclined to regard it as a simplifying one. We could, it is true, *try* to imagine a world consisting *solely* of really stringent ascetics. But a moment's reflection suggests that even with its unrealism aside, this is no easy thought experiment. What would a world of universal and pervasive self-denial look like? I frankly have no idea, and I find quite obscure those religious and other moral doctrines that seem to celebrate such a world as an ideal. And as soon as we reduce, even only slightly, the imagined scale of this comprehensive self-denial—either in some or all of such a world's inhabitants—then, on the previously introduced assumption, well-being, and therefore wealth, matter.

III. Sibling Parity

Since wealth matters, should *differences* in wealth matter, at least in the general sense of 'matter'? It seems hardly open to doubt that at least some such differences should so matter, and matter profoundly. The standard case is siblings. No parent of several offspring seems to be in much doubt that, ceteris paribus, they should each enjoy equal well-being, and hence, ceteris paribus, should each possess equal wealth. And I take it that such parents can therefore have no reason for denying that, ceteris paribus again, the same parity relation should hold within each set of siblings who are the offspring of others. Of course, "ceteris" are rarely "paribus." In addition to ability-level differentials between siblings, factors as arcane as primogeniture rules and as diverse as adult offspring's self-chosen lifestyles have played significant roles in modifying this moral presumption of sibling parity.

[6] As does the existence of disabled persons. For what is relevantly true of epicures here is also true of the disabled—namely, that compared to ascetics, they are both inefficient transformers of wealth into well-being. It takes more wealth for an epicure or a disabled person to attain any given level of preference-satisfaction than it takes for an ascetic to reach the same level.

[7] I enter this additional constraint—rights—to exclude from our accounting the well-being of sadists, or at least the well-being of those sadists who do not confine their characteristic interpersonal activities to masochists.

But this is hardly an objection to the presumption as a presumption. For all these modifying factors simply reflect other independently valuable considerations that, as was previously observed, need to be incorporated into the ranking or weighting that also incorporates the value of sibling parity. (This is so, regardless of whether what matters is ranked or weighted.) The presence of these modifying or crosscutting considerations, when they are present, evidently does not imply that sibling parity does not matter. For instance, the fact that some consideration subserved by primogeniture matters does not imply that sibling parity does not matter. All that it implies is that such parity may not invariably matter *most*. Not mattering most is, certainly in principle, entirely different from not mattering at all. And it seems reasonable to expect that the world will continue to allow us the space for these two ideas to be different in practice as well.

Why, then, would not the same also be true of the comparative wealth holdings of *nonsiblings*? Here, I take myself to be pushing at an open door, for the kind of normative latitude opened up by the foregoing paragraph seems to undercut any plausible basis for dissent from the suggestion that it should matter that nonsiblings have equal amounts of wealth. So long as the demand for such parity is conceived of as constrainable by competing other values, that demand looks like an exercise of an entirely uncontroversial—because it is discountable—bearing on our moral reasoning about distributive questions.

That said, however, what the discussion of ordering independent values *does* do is give us an elementary framework for thinking more systematically about the apparently numerous kinds of considerations that would reasonably permit, and even mandate, departures from such universal parity. We need to gather these considerations into a manageable taxonomy that will more clearly illuminate the differences between those mattering things that plausibly justify or permit such departures and those that do not. In this way, we might expect to arrive at some overall view of whether there are interpersonal wealth disparities that matter sufficiently—matter in the more specific sense—to warrant elimination by law.

IV. Permissible Disparity

Let us return to the case of siblings. One reason I might well have for believing that a wealth disparity between two of my adult offspring should *not* matter negatively could arise in the event of one of them being disabled. Indeed, in such circumstances, many would concur with the view that my disabled son *should* have more wealth than his able-bodied sibling, in order that they each enjoy equal levels of well-being. Such a view is, for instance, often reflected in parental bequests.

Of course, even this view could plausibly be held to be subject to a variety of qualifications, most of them having to do with the *source* of the relevant disability. If the disability arose from an action—or, more generally, a lifestyle—that was chosen by the disabled individual and that he knew carried a risk of such disablement, then our inclination to judge the aforesaid wealth disparity as warranted might diminish, and we would tend to regard our sibling-parity commitment as overriding. But if, alternatively, the disability arose from the deliberate or negligent injurious actions of others, then we would regard that disparity as warranted. And, moreover—at least in a libertarian society—those injuring others would be legally required to supply that disparity-making increment in the form of compensation, thereby restoring sibling parity of well-being. For libertarians, it matters, in the more specific sense, that such compensation be paid and that it be paid by the injurers.

What if an individual's disability arose from neither of these two types of sources—neither self-choice nor the choices of others? What if, that is, it was the result of *brute bad luck*? Here, I think, libertarians implicitly divide. Virtually all libertarians would presumably agree that achieving the compensating wealth disparity—so as to restore sibling parity of well-being—should matter. But many of them would insist that it matters only in the general sense: it would be good if a disabled person whose disability is neither his own fault nor anyone else's were to have that compensating wealth increment. Persons who voluntarily supply it are doing a good thing, and persons who decline to supply it, for no sufficiently mattering reason, are acting wrongly.

Other libertarians implicitly take a more stringent view. For them, the supply of the compensating increment also matters in the more specific, legally enforceable sense. But the reason it matters for them in this more stringent way is not simply that without it, the disabled individual will secure less well-being than will his able-bodied sibling. If that were their sole reason, these libertarians would be logically committed to thinking that the provision of the increment would also matter, in the enforceable sense, in the case of self-incurred disability. But they do not think that.

What they believe is that a person's well-being should no more be subject to destruction by brute bad luck than by the injurious acts of others. How do they sustain such a view? On the face of it, it looks like legally enforcing a wealth transfer to a disabled individual to offset a disparity, caused by brute bad luck, between his well-being and that of his able-bodied sibling amounts to the morally unprofitable exercise of depriving one innocent person to avert another innocent person's deprivation. If sibling parity matters that much, it could be objected, why balk at taking the same redistributive measure when the disabled individual's disability is self-inflicted? In short, what's so special about brute bad luck? To answer this question and see how some libertarians have inferred that enforceable redistribution in this case is indeed warranted, we need to take a brief detour to reflect on what, in general, brute bad luck is.

V. Luck and Responsibility

Most current discussions of brute bad luck and its proper relation to distributive justice are motivated by a desire to distinguish strongly between two kinds of egalitarianism. On the one hand, we have *strict egalitarianism*, according to which all interpersonal disparities of well-being should be eliminated, by legal enforcement if necessary. This seems to me a perfectly coherent view, and few, if any, of the numerous objections leveled at it cast—or are even intended to cast—serious doubt on its intelligibility.[8] What these objections do succeed in doing is showing that such an egalitarianism simply allows no space for a range of other strongly embedded moral values, the most significant of which is captured in the notion of *personal responsibility*. An egalitarianism that is to avoid imposing compensatory liability on innocent others for my self-incurred adversities cannot be a strict egalitarianism.

Accordingly, to create some conceptual space for the distributive relevance of personal responsibility, *liberal egalitarian* theories have urged the enforceable elimination, not of interpersonal well-being disparities per se, but rather of interpersonal disparities in the necessary conditions for securing well-being. Such theories hold that equality of *resources* for well-being, or equality of *opportunities* for well-being, is a necessary and sufficient condition for justice, and hence warrants legal enforcement.[9] If people are equally situated with respect to these necessary conditions, then what each person chooses to do under them is properly and solely a function of his ambitions, preferences, and other moral values, and is no concern of justice.[10] If, by virtue of his own choices or negligence, an individual in this situation incurs adversities, it is (sometimes) a good thing to help him, but a bad—indeed, unjust—thing to force other per-

[8] The objection that strict egalitarianism creates *moral hazard*, though broadly true, is essentially a moral objection and not one challenging the intelligibility, nor even the practicability, of strict egalitarianism. This objection reflects an aspect of the disvalue we usually ascribe to policies that have the effect of *leveling down*. Strict egalitarianism, in reducing incentives to behave prudently, achieves its equality at the cost of fostering absolute losses of aggregate well-being. But since its concerns are solely with comparative shares of well-being, it is not strictly inconsistent in neglecting such losses.

[9] That is, like other theories of justice, liberal egalitarian theories standardly assign lexical primacy to justice in an ordered plurality of independent moral values. I should also note that in referring jointly to equal-resource and equal-opportunity theories, I do not wish to suggest that they are alike in all respects. They are not, since they often embrace different lists of what are to count as necessary conditions of well-being.

[10] Some liberal egalitarian theories, however, seem to me less clear than others as to whether this equality with respect to necessary conditions is to be conceived as only an initial equality or a more recurrent one. Evidently, the space for personal responsibility in liberal egalitarian theories, and the corresponding distance of such theories from strict egalitarianism, are both truncated by more continuous conceptions of the required equality. This is because different resources or opportunities for well-being are standardly linked to each other in causal sequences, such that a person's neglecting or choosing not to exploit an accessible antecedent resource or opportunity is often a sufficient condition for the inaccessibility of a subsequent resource or opportunity. Sequenced educational levels are an obvious example of this.

sons to help him. Liability for the self-incurred adversities should lie with him alone. On the other hand, where those adversities are not self-incurred, liberal egalitarianism treats them *all* as brute bad luck, and the object of distributively just taxation and public-provision policies is said to be to establish the individual at the position of parity.

One failing of many such liberal egalitarian theories, it seems to me, lies in their inconsistent—because incomplete—understanding of the space needed for personal responsibility. In exhaustively dividing liability-occasioning adversities into only two categories—those that are self-incurred and those that are not—these theories neglect the fact that the latter category itself relevantly subdivides into two subcategories: my non-self-incurred adversities can be caused either by particular others or by no one. So a more consistent understanding of the shape of that required space for personal responsibility would operate with this *three-fold* division of liability-occasioning adversities.[11] And it would, as libertarians do, assign enforceable compensatory liability to only those particular others who injure me, rather than assigning it to innocent taxpayers in general. It is those particular others who bear personal responsibility for the adversities their actions inflict on me, and the public should no more be forced to indemnify me for those injurious doings than it should be forced to indemnify me for my self-incurred adversities.

Now, a striking fact, and one that brings us squarely back to the problem of brute bad luck, is that a symmetrical failing seems to beset many libertarian views. For they, too, operate with only a binary classification of liability-occasioning adversities: those that are self-incurred and those imposed by the actions of particular others.[12] That is, whereas liberal egalitarians neglect—regard as distributively irrelevant—the fact that some of the adversities that I can experience may be caused by particular others, many libertarians correspondingly neglect the fact that some of my adversities may be caused by no one. They regard this as distributively irrelevant inasmuch as they permit the liability for those adversities—like liability for my self-incurred adversities—to remain with me.

Such neglect is certainly inconsistent with the requirement that we each be held liable for all and only those adversities that we cause, whether to ourselves or others. If choice and personal responsibility are to be given their proper conceptual space in distributive matters—if the latter is to be isomorphic with the former—then our respective liabilities cannot be extended to include liabilities for those adversities that are caused neither by

[11] This, too, is a simplifying assumption, and radically so. In the real world, many adversities are multifactorial rather than unifactorial: they are the joint products of factors issuing from more than one of these three kinds of sources. Accurate assignments of liability must, therefore, take such proportional considerations into account.

[12] A clear presentation of these libertarian views can be found in Richard Epstein, "Luck," *Social Philosophy and Policy* 6, no. 1 (1988): 17–38, where Epstein demonstrates their embodiment in common law principles of redress and argues for their moral desirability. See also note 18 below.

us nor by particular others. Those adversities, and those adversities alone, it seems to me, are the ones that are properly labeled as "brute bad luck."

VI. Luck and Nature

I am going to take it as given that any scientifically respectable conception of causation must attribute brute bad luck to the *doings of nature*. If none of us did *x*, what—other than nature—could have done so? So, if nature inflicts an adversity on me, who should be liable to compensate me?

If your dog bites my leg, should you be liable? The answer obviously must depend on a number of considerations, all of which have to do with norms that bear on the *circumstances* of such an adversity and that are taken, very broadly, to signify the presence or absence of consent—yours or mine—to such an eventuality. If I were trespassing on your property and/or you had posted signs around about your dog, then we would be inclined to regard my adversity as self-incurred. If, on the other hand, the bite occurred on my property, onto which your dog had strayed, the liability should be yours. If I knew that the dog was bad-tempered and nonetheless allowed you to bring it into my house, then maybe I am liable. If you had failed to comply with some dog owners' obedience-training requirement, then maybe the liability is yours. And so forth. In all these instances, the adverse occurrence is *constructively subsumed* under the set of events for which one or the other of us can sensibly be held to be personally responsible. By virtue of such subsumption, the effects of the doings of nature are converted from instances of brute luck into instances of option luck—which, being optional, are held to fall within the domain of the personal responsibility of those who so opt.

What if, instead of being bitten by your dog, I am struck by lightning or buried by an earthquake? Again, we will probably want to know where—on whose property—this doing of nature occurred, how foreseeable it was, and whether it could have been avoided. Can we plausibly convert this sort of doing of nature into a piece of option (bad) luck? Well, maybe. We might, for instance, plausibly say that if the incident occurred on my property, then maybe it was self-incurred. Maybe the exposure of the relevant piece of land to lightning storms or earthquakes is a well-known fact, and perhaps even one that was reported in the real estate survey I commissioned before buying the property. Or maybe it was not, or maybe the property was not my land.[13] But even if the land's riskiness was not known or the property was not mine, isn't it necessarily true that, faced with a given adverse doing of nature, I could have chosen simply

[13] I leave aside the epicyclic objection that even if some specific danger was not known or knowable, it could have been generically insured against. This objection *is* epicyclic inasmuch as it simply transforms, rather than answers, the distributive question here into one of who should have to purchase such insurance—the person injured or the landowner (where they are different persons)—or, if both of them are insured, whose insurance company should be liable to pay.

to move myself out of its path or not to have put myself in it in the first place?

In general, aren't we justified in taking the view that all those natural adversities that befall me could have been avoided by my having chosen to *locate* myself elsewhere? And if so, aren't those libertarians who operate with only a binary classification of liability-occasioning adversities—self-incurred and other-imposed—correct? I think that binary view is indeed often correct in particular cases, but not in general.

For each such natural adversity, it is possible that I could have chosen to locate myself elsewhere: I might have chosen to be here, away from where the adversity would have occurred, rather than there. But what I have absolutely, and not merely probably, *no* choice about is being *somewhere*. And while this lamentable restriction is one that besets not merely me but all of us, what is also true is that it besets some of us a great deal more than it does others. Some of us are, even initially, better placed than others are to escape from the path of a lightning storm without running headlong into an earthquake zone.[14] Whether I have five other places I could *permissibly* be and you have none, or whether I can run five times as fast as you can, the adversity we would each experience from a lightning strike would be the same. However, the personal responsibility we would each have for that adversity would differ.

If we want the allocation of liability for adversities to track, rather than distort, the contours of the space for personal responsibility, it looks like we have to ensure that there is some initial parity in the extent to which the aforesaid restriction that we must be somewhere bears down upon each of us. We need, in the current phrase, to *level the playing field*, to share out equally its high and low sections, making sure that one set of goalposts is not on top of the mountain while the other is down in the valley. With that (enforceably) in place, people can justly get on with their various liability-occasioning activities—injuring themselves and others—and paying the corresponding prices.

It is, I think, precisely this parity that forms the morally significant core of Locke's "enough and as good" proviso on the interpersonal distribution of entitlements to the use of nature. That proviso famously stipulates that any person's just appropriation of unowned natural resources is constrained by a duty either to leave an equivalent amount for others or to make compensatory redress to others for an appropriation in excess of that amount.[15] Such a duty is readily motivated by the premise that in the

[14] By "initially," I mean when we first attain moral agency. Prior to that, we are in the custody of particular others who, accordingly, bear personal responsibility for what happens to us. On some of the distributive complexities introduced by this consideration, see the references listed in note 17 below.

[15] Another normative function of the proviso is to supply intergenerationally durable validity to the duties that are correlative both to the property titles created by initial appropriation and to the rights successively derived from exercise of those titles; cf. Robert Nozick, *Anarchy, State, and Utopia* (New York: Basic Books, 1974), 176; and Steiner, *An Essay on Rights*, 106–8.

absence of the appropriation, those others would possess an equal liberty to use the relevant resources: an excessive and unredressed appropriation thus violates persons' foundational rights to equal liberty. Although the appropriate basis for calculating the compensatory redress has been the subject of some scholarly dispute, the motivation for the duty to supply it has been examined less.[16] My reason for mentioning the Lockean proviso here is that brute luck's relation to justice is tightly linked to this motivation, and can therefore plausibly be brought within the purview of Lockean foundational premises.

For nature's doings are major causes of both adversities and benefits. Being the effects of no person's choices, these doings' equal allocation undercuts no one's self-ownership, while their unequal allocation distorts the shape of the space for personal responsibility—in much the same sense that runners' personal responsibility for their respective outcomes in a running race would be distorted by a failure to start them all at the same starting-line. If the sources of brute luck were pooled, this initial parity would ensure that the adversities for which persons are respectively liable would bear an isomorphic relation to their chosen (and negligent) conduct. Elsewhere I have argued that a serviceable conception of such pooling, among persons who are distributed over an indefinitely large number of overlapping generations in a fully appropriated world, broadly consists in a *global fund*: each current person has an enforceable right to an equal part of the fund's assests, and each current owner of a portion of nature enforceably owes to the fund a payment—a tax—equal to the current (rental) value of that portion.[17] One's right to a part of the fund's assets, it should be noted, cannot be assimilated to the various sorts of foundational *positive* rights that are centrally characteristic of many current redistributive regimes and that libertarians correctly reject as entailing encroachments on individuals' rights of self-ownership and,

[16] Cf. John Locke, *Second Treatise of Government*, in Locke, *Two Treatises of Government*, ed. Peter Laslett (Cambridge: Cambridge University Press, 1967), chap. v; Nozick, *Anarchy, State, and Utopia*, 174–82; Eric Mack, "Distributive Justice and the Tensions of Lockeanism," *Social Philosophy and Policy* 1, no. 1 (1983): 132–50; Hillel Steiner, "Capitalism, Justice, and Equal Starts," *Social Philosophy and Policy* 5, no. 1 (1987): 49–71; and Steiner, *An Essay on Rights*, chaps. 7, 8. Anticipations and elaborations of the Lockean proviso, as well as current debate on it, are presented in Vallentyne and Steiner, eds., *The Origins of Left-Libertarianism*; and Vallentyne and Steiner, eds., *Left-Libertarianism and Its Critics*.

[17] Cf. Steiner, *An Essay on Rights*, chaps. 7, 8. These chapters also advance arguments, the elaboration of which here would take us too far afield, (a) against the coherence of the idea of posthumous rights, and (b) for the inclusion, in what counts as "nature" here, of germ-line genetic information. The former argument is shown to entail the justifiability of annexing the full value of dead persons' estates to the global fund, while the latter entails that appropriators of germ-line genetic information—biological parents—owe payments to the fund in the same way that other appropriators of natural resources do. This latter argument is further refined, in the light of the growing prospect of extensive genetic manipulability, in Hillel Steiner, "Silver Spoons and Golden Genes: Talent Differentials and Distributive Justice," in Justine Burley, ed., *The Genetic Revolution and Human Rights: The Oxford Amnesty Lectures, 1998* (Oxford: Oxford University Press, 1999).

more generally, on individuals' negative rights to others' forbearance. As a right to redress, it no more signifies a foundational positive right than do any standard restitutional claims against perpetrators of theft, personal injury, or contractual default—claims of a kind that libertarianism strongly underwrites. These redress rights are rights to compensation for particular persons' failures to respect individuals' foundational *negative* rights; they do this by engrossing a larger amount of natural resources than is compatible with leaving "enough and as good" for each other individual.[18] So, taking some such entitlement as given, we can now factor it into our thinking about sibling parity.

VII. Sibling Parity Again

What was previously suggested about sibling wealth parity is that it should matter, but only ceteris paribus. Because wealth matters only as a deliverer of well-being, the value of sibling wealth parity is conditional on its delivery of sibling well-being parity. But the value of sibling well-being parity, we will suppose, is itself constrained by considerations of personal responsibility. Where one of my adult children has made disabling choices that reduce either his well-being or his means to it below that of his sibling, I will place less value on the elimination of that disparity than I would if the disability had occurred as a result of others', or no one's, choices. In these latter cases, conversely, elimination of the disparity will have very great value and, in a Lockean-proviso-based libertarian society, will be legally enforceable.[19]

What if these two siblings are an ascetic and an epicure? That is, what if one of them can transform wealth into well-being much more efficiently than the other, with the consequence that wealth parity between them results in well-being disparity?[20] Since it is parity of well-being, rather than wealth, that matters, shouldn't we look favorably on the idea of the epicure getting an offsetting increment of wealth?

[18] Such failures are readily attributable to those engrossers on the basis of the conception of *strict liability* ably defended in Richard Epstein, "A Theory of Strict Liability," *Journal of Legal Studies* 2, no. 1 (1973): 151–205; and many other writings. However, in Epstein, "Luck," 26–28, Epstein's argument *for* the legitimacy of unencumbered natural resource titles derived from first possession—and thereby *against* the aforesaid redress for persons deprived by others' natural resource acquisitions—turns on the claim that the informational requirements and transaction costs of such apportionment exceed any identifiable social gains that would make it worthwhile. This claim, if true, obviously does warrant weighty consideration. But Epstein is mistaken if he is suggesting that, weighty or not, the claim can count as a reason for *libertarians* to deny the validity of the redress right. (It can, of course, count as such a reason for *utilitarians*.) For libertarians, it can count only as a reason why the holders of those redress rights should themselves each choose to waive them.

[19] It will be enforceable ex ante (through the global fund mechanism) in the case of disabilities that are not caused by particular others, and ex post (through civil/private lawsuits) in the case of those that are.

[20] That is, the epicure just cannot get through a day without consuming several Havana cigars and a generous helping of caviar.

The answer, I think, depends on whether the epicure's inability to transform wealth more efficiently should be regarded as a disability and, if so, what caused it. The case for regarding it as a disability seems clear: described at this level of abstraction, the inability generates the same preference-stultifying effects as most conditions conventionally regarded as disabling. Hence, what needs consideration is whether this disability, like any other, is self-incurred or externally imposed, either by others or by nature. If it is self-incurred—if the epicure, having arrived at the threshold of moral agency unencumbered by it, proceeded to cultivate expensive tastes—then believers in personal responsibility as well as sibling parity would be disinclined to regard the resultant sibling well-being disparity as warranting an offsetting departure from wealth parity. If, however, the disability is nature-imposed (i.e., genetically driven), then the global fund mechanism for nature-pooling that I just discussed seems to apply, and some offsetting wealth disparity is warranted.[21]

Could the epicure's disability be one imposed by particular others? I have no definite views on this. But what does seem clear is that the answer depends, inter alia, both on the details of our understanding of *moral agency* and on what the point is of the various norms relating to the conduct of minors' custodians. The problem is this. On the one hand, it is probably part of our very concept of moral agents that they can revise their pre-agency commitments and preferences. At the same time, many of our custodial norms—let alone our willingness to expend enormous resources on entrenching them—are predicated on the belief that what we experience, as minors, strongly shapes not only what we choose, but also what we *can* choose, in later life. There is obviously some considerable tension between these two thoughts, and identifying the point (if there is one) where they are in equilibrium seems to be a necessary condition for supplying a plausible answer to this paragraph's opening question. So the most that can be said here is a reiteration that *if* the epicure's disability can meaningfully and accurately be described as imposed by particular others, and *if* sibling well-being parity *and* personal responsibility matter, then it matters that there be some offsetting wealth disparity between the epicure and the ascetic. And moreover, it matters in the specific, enforceable, sense that the offsetting increment be supplied by those others.

VIII. Conclusion

Where we have gotten to so far is a moral position in which the value of sibling wealth parity is constrained by that of personal responsibility, with all its attendant complexities. What happens, then, when we try to extend this normative structure in the direction of *nonsibling* parity? Is

[21] Again, the details of how this mechanism might be applied to genetic differentials are discussed in the work mentioned in note 17 above.

this a bridge too far? What values might intervene to block this extension? More precisely, what values *that do not intervene* in—outrank or override—the pursuit of sibling parity might nonetheless plausibly do so with respect to its nonsibling counterpart?

Am I being pathetically blinkered or unimaginative in finding that there are few of these values to be discovered? On the face of it, we might be inclined to suppose that quite a few independent values could intervene in this way. The fact that I think there ought to be wealth parity between my sons Josh, Sam, and Jacob seems, at first sight, to go nowhere in the direction of extending the desirability of that parity to their friend Ben. But once we have allowed that the desirability of sibling wealth parity is conditional on its realization of sibling well-being parity, and that the latter is in turn desirably constrained by considerations of personal responsibility, what reasons could I have for not including Ben's wealth in this same complex distributive nexus?

One reason I *cannot* have is that Ben's lifestyle yields him less wealth—or more—than my sons' lifestyles do, since that is already covered by our personal responsibility caveat: a caveat that, as we have seen, may equally apply to disparities between Josh, Sam, and Jacob. I could perhaps say, "Look, Ben, unlike the others, is not my son, and that is a good enough reason." But this depends on how much magic we are prepared to find in the adjective "my." Can the bare fact that something is mine make it matter more than an identical thing that is yours? This looks to be implausible.

We might try conjoining such bare proprietorial facts with some moral premise to the effect that each of us should enjoy a protected liberty to do what he wishes with what is his. But this premise, utterly indisputable in my view—and fully enforceable in a libertarian society—just will not do the job here. For no one is disputing that it would be wrong to *force* me, or anyone, to establish parity between Ben's wealth and that of my sons. (Here it is important to recall that I have advanced no argument to suggest that even *sibling* parity, of either wealth or well-being—even when constrained by personal responsibility—should matter in the more specific, enforceable, sense.) What is in question is *not* whether Ben has a right to such parity, but whether I and/or others *exercise our rightful liberties wrongly* in withholding it from him. We know that people *can* exercise their rightful liberties wrongly: I can, with rightful impunity, refuse to hold the door open for a colleague who is heavily laden with books and papers. Why wouldn't our failing to bring about Ben's parity count as just such a wrong exercise?

One kind of answer could go like this:

> Yes, Ben's parity—nonsibling parity, in general—matters. But other things matter, too. And some of these other things matter more, perhaps much more, than nonsibling parity. So where its demands get in the way of the demands of these other things, it is the demands

> of nonsibling parity that must be overridden. Failing to bring about that parity is, under these conditions, regrettable but not wrong. Indeed, it would be wrong to do otherwise.

This answer makes sense. Perhaps there are seventeen other kinds of thing that matter more than nonsibling parity.[22] And the world being as it is, there is no doubt that the demands of these things frequently conflict with the demands of nonsibling parity, as well as with each other. The problem, as I see it, is to find a compelling reason why the demands of these other things do not equally override those of *sibling* parity. "They just don't" does not seem to be that reason.

Philosophy, University of Manchester

[22] *Not* includable among these, however, is the loving conduct that parents unquestionably have a duty to bestow upon their own young children. A lucidly persuasive essay, Jennifer Roback Morse, "No Families, No Freedom," *Social Philosophy and Policy* 16, no. 1 (1999): 290–314, argues (a) that such conduct is a necessary condition for the childhood development of durable trusting and, therefore, trustworthy dispositions in adults; (b) that such dispositions are necessary to sustain the framework of free societies; and (c) that such loving conduct is considerably less likely to deliver the development of trusting when it is bestowed by commercial or state agencies. Nothing in this argument, however, suggests that the capacity of parents to discharge this duty is diminished by the redistributive demands of nonsibling parity.

INDEX

For EU product safety concerns, contact us at Calle de José Abascal, 56–1°, 28003 Madrid, Spain or eugpsr@cambridge.org.

www.ingramcontent.com/pod-product-compliance
Ingram Content Group UK Ltd.
Pitfield, Milton Keynes, MK11 3LW, UK
UKHW042142130625
459647UK00011B/1147

* 9 7 8 0 5 2 1 0 0 5 3 5 7 *